ELDORADO

ELDORADO

THE CALIFORNIA GOLD RUSH

Dale L. Walker

A Tom Doherty Associates Book
New York

ELDORADO: THE CALIFORNIA GOLD RUSH

Book design by Michael Collica

A Forge Book
Published by Tom Doherty Associates, LLC
175 Fifth Avenue
New York, NY 10010

www.tor.com

Forge® is a registered trademark of Tom Doherty Associates, LLC.

ISBN 0-312-87833-8

First Edition: January 2003

Printed in the United States of America

0 9 8 7 6 5 4 3 2 1

To Richard Shaw Wheeler

CONTENTS

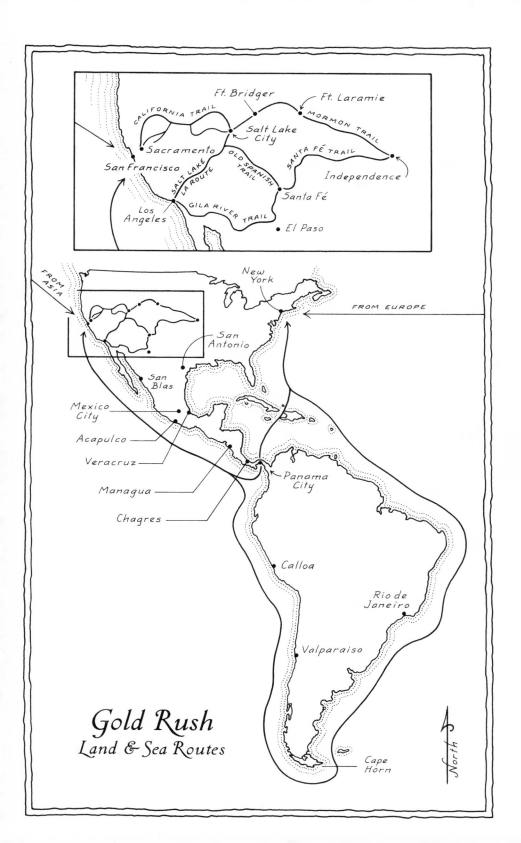

Gold Rush
Land & Sea Routes

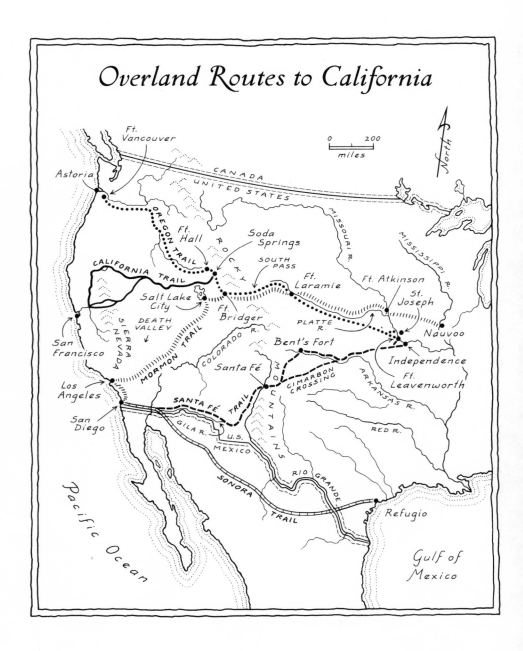

Overland Routes to California

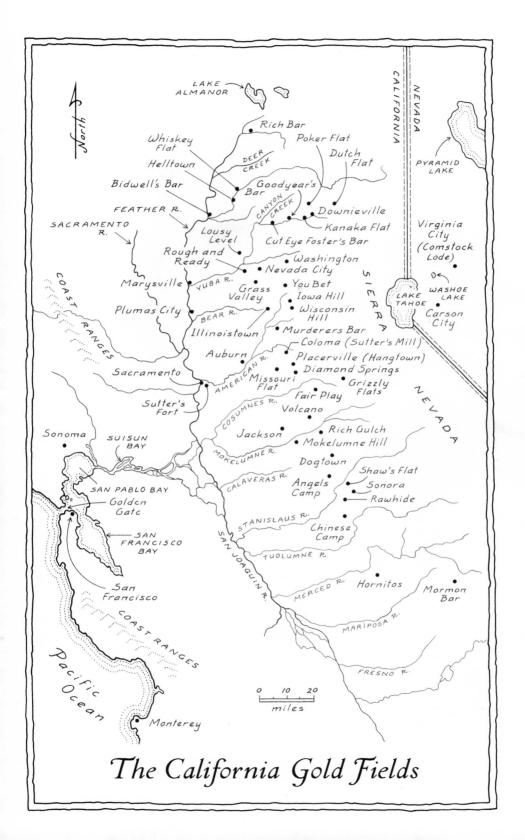

The California Gold Fields

ELDORADO

GOLD

From the Old English gelos, "yellow."
The most precious metallic element.
Chemical symbol, Au, from the Latin aurora, "shining dawn."

PREHISTORIC HUMANS FOUND rocks streaked with it and gazed on it in puzzled enchantment.

It was prized by all the earliest of civilizations—Egyptian, Minoan, Assyrian, Etruscan—and crafted by them into wondrous shapes that survived the millennia.

On the monuments of the Fourth Dynasty of Egypt, erected nearly three thousand years before the birth of Christ, are depictions of people kneeling like supplicants, washing gold from the banks of the Nile. From such labors the inestimable treasures of the tomb of Tutankhamen were fashioned.

In about 1200 B.C., some rapacious Mediterranean state sent an expedition to Armenia to seize the gold being sieved from river sands by the use of sheepskins, and from this mission derived one of the immortal romantic epics. In his *Argonautica*, the Greek poet Apollonius of Rhodes told the story of Jason's voyage on the *Argo* with a crew of fifty heroes in quest of the Golden Fleece, suspended from a sacred oak in the barbarous land of Colchis. With the help of the sorceress Medea, Jason was able to complete the labors required to find the fabled sheepskin and return with it to his homeland.

The Greeks also told the story of Midas, king of Phrygia in Asia Minor, who earned the gratitude of Dionysus, god of the potency and fertility of nature, and was granted a wish. Midas desired that everything he touched would turn to gold, but when even his food was thus transformed, he begged that the "golden touch" be removed. Dionysus had Midas bathe in the river Pactolus, and the curse ended. Ever after, it was said, the sands of the Pactolus were threaded with gold.

Gold is mentioned so often in the Bible that a separate concordance would be required to list the references to it. In Genesis 2, the land of Havilah, near the Garden of Eden, is recorded to be a place of gold, and "good" gold at that; and in Revelations 21, the holy city of Jerusalem and its streets are constituted of pure gold. In Exodus, God orders a sanctuary to be built where the Jews may worship Him and specifies: "Thou shalt overlay it with pure gold, within and without. . . ."

The Arabian city of Ophir, which served as a way station for Phoenician ships sailing westward from India, is often mentioned in the Bible as celebrated for its fine gold. In Kings I, Solomon's Tyrian sailors fetched four hundred and twenty talents of gold from Ophir (as well as silver, ivory, apes, and peacocks) for the king; and in the Book of Job, wisdom is said to be more precious than the gold of Ophir.

The Romans used jets of water to expose gold-bearing ore in the hills of Spain, a process called "hydraulicking."

Alchemy, which may have originated with the Greeks of Alexandria, and which became the chemistry of the Middle Ages, was concerned with transmuting base metals to gold by use of an elixir called the Philosopher's Stone, made of earth, sulphur, mercury, and other more cryptic ingredients. The experiments were never successful but the idea was so compelling that alchemists kept at the task for fourteen centuries.

Every civilization of recorded history had its gold lust and sent its explorers to the edges of the earth to sate it.

In August, 1492, upon reaching San Salvador, Columbus saw natives wearing gold plugs in their noses and had his crewmen trade beads for them. The Admiral of the Ocean Sea was certain his vessels were near Cipangu, as Spaniards called Japan, and was anxious to see the Japanese palaces which Marco Polo said were roofed with gold.

Gold was necessarily on the navigator's mind. King Ferdinand of Spain had commanded him, "Get gold, humanely if possible, but at all hazards, get gold."

In Mexico, every step northward taken by *conquistadores* was taken in the belief that golden lands lay just ahead.

DECADES BEFORE THE first Europeans spied its foggy coastal islands from the starboard rail of their tiny *caravel*, California had been named and portentously described as a land of gold.

The name and description originated in an early sixteenth-century literary work, *Las sergas de Espandián* ("The Deeds of Espandián"), a sort of Spanish *Odyssey*. The author of this splendid fantasy, Garcí Rodríguez Ordóñez de Montalvo, told of an island called California that lay "on the right hand of the Indies" and "very near the Terrestrial Paradise," inhabited by a tribe of black women "without a single man among them and living in the manner of Amazons." These women, led by the Queen Calafía, were "robust of body, strong and passionate in heart, and of great valor," and bore "arms all of gold, as is the harness of the wild beasts which, after taming, they ride."

Ordóñez de Montalvo was quite specific about the gold: "The island everywhere abounded with gold and precious stones and upon it no other metal was found."

Such gilded fables inspired Hernán Cortés in 1533 to send ships north along the Pacific coast of Mexico. The expedition discovered Baja California and its scribes, mindful of the description of Queen Califía's domain, wrote of it as an island. But the explorers found neither Amazons with arms of gold, the Seven Cities of Gold of Indian legendry, nor the king, El Dorado, whose subjects, it was told, dusted him with gold each morning and washed it off each night.

In Peru, also in 1533, Francisco Pizarro imprisoned the Inca king Atahualpa, ordered a 22 × 17-foot room be filled with gold as ransom, then, when the gold was gathered and the room filled, had the king strangled to death in a public square.

Sir Francis Drake, too, had gold on his mind when he brought his crew of freebooters to California. After a terrible seventeen days threading the Strait of Magellan, his *Golden Hind* crawled northward along the South American coast, sacking settlements, capturing Spanish vessels, and making off with a shipload of gold and silver bullion, precious gemstones, and other plunder. These corsairs spent a summer month in 1579 careening and provisioning their ship, trading with Miwok Indians above San Francisco Bay, and claiming the land which they had named Nova Albion.

Drake's chaplain, Francis Fletcher, described California in his diary as a country seeming "to promise rich veins of gold and silver," but the expedition found none.

The Spaniards brought the Christian cross to California in 1769 and over the next fifty years Franciscan missionaries established twenty outposts from San Diego in the south to Solano de Sonoma

on the north, connected by a mule-cart path called El Camino Real.
The missions flourished; great parcels of land were claimed by the
Catholic fathers; Indians were given some instruction in Christianity,
taught a few farming skills, and indentured as virtual slaves to work
the grain fields, fruit orchards, and cattle herds.

Occasionally a native would come forth and timidly show a mission priest an acorn cup or goose quill filled with gold dust. But the
fathers discouraged their converts from such secular pasttimes as gold
hunting.

In 1821, with Mexico's independence, nearly three centuries of
Spanish rule of the Californias ended. The Spaniards, the most insa-
tiable argonauts the world had ever known, discovered no gold in
California, and in the twenty-five years Mexico governed the
province what gold was found lay in profits from trade with the outside world. Among its many treasures, California had an abundance of
wild cattle, wide-horned, lean and long-legged beasts, and when the
territory was opened to foreign commerce in 1822, a hide-and-
tallow business drew ships from Mexico, Europe, and Russia, and
principally from the eastern seaboard of the United States. San Diego
and Monterey became bustling trade anchorages, and later, San Luís
Obispo, Santa Bárbara, and Yerba Buena, the tiny enclave inside San
Francisco Bay. At these places, cowhides, called "California bank-
notes" by American merchantmen, were salted, staked out to dry,
folded and bundled, and the tallow packed in rawhide bags. Both
commodities were borne to market in the holds of the trade ships.

The cowhides were traded at a value of two to four dollars each;
the tallow at two American dollars per *arroba* (a Spanish measure
equaling about twenty-five pounds).

Since California manufactured little, the American trade goods
(everything from brooms to millstones, bolts of cloth, glass for windows, arms and gunpowder, hardware, billiard tables and pianos) often
included shoes, boots and saddles, candles and soap—manufactured
from California hides and tallow.

Suet, pickled beef, timber, wheat, beaver and otter skins, and *aguardiente*, a raw, fiery brandy, were eventually added to the trade.

The ubiquitous Yankees, called "Bostons" by the Californians
since most of them sailed out of Massachusetts ports, commonly realized a three hundred percent profit from a trade voyage to the Pacific
Rim.

As the years of Mexican rule of California, so brief in the scheme of its history, rolled on toward the American conquest, gold—real gold, raw or in coin—had no significant place in the province.

In those languorous pre-conquest times, California's *gente de razón*, its landed gentry, were a generous, carefree people, the majority illiterate (there were no schools in Mexican California) and as ignorant of the outside world as that world was of theirs. The women tended their homes and children, supervised their servants, prepared weddings and funerals. The men, all supreme *caballeros*, minded their land and stock, spending their waking hours riding their smallish, wiry horses so effortlessly they seemed virtual centaurs to outlanders.

The rancho of this "don," this gentleman of California, lay among piney, summer-scorched hills and gentle valleys where a creek watered his animals, served his adobe hacienda with its red-tiled roof and cool verandas, fed his shade trees, orchards, grape arbors, and produce fields.

He had his horses, cows, and *vaqueros* to occupy him, and Indians to serve him. He had his children, gambling, bull baiting, cock fighting, grizzly hunting, *bailes* and *fandangos* to amuse him. He had the church to forgive his sins, little governance to pester him, traders to buy his goods and supply what needs and luxuries he desired. He had the freedom of a vast, apathetic, *laissez-faire* land to give joy to the days of his life.

Gold? What did he need of it?

CALIFORNIA WAS COVETED by all who saw it: The British, from 1778, when the greatest of English navigators, Captain James Cook, found the north Pacific rich in gray whales and sea otters; the Russians, from 1805, when they ran south from Sitka to trade in Monterey for supplies and food for their starving, scurvy-plagued colonists in Alaska; the Americans, from the first sighting of its wild coast by Nantucket whalers.

Richard Henry Dana, scion of a wealthy Cambridge, Massachusetts, family who spent two years before the mast on the trader *Pilgrim* in California waters in 1834–1836, wrote in his celebrated book, "In the hands of an enterprising people, what a country this might be!" And the chief prophet of American expansionism, Senator Thomas Hart Benton of Missouri, envisioned California (without ever actually seeing it) as "the road to India," and "the garden of the world." He believed the province was "ripe for colonization," and warned that if the United States did not act to claim it, England was poised to annex it.

By 1841, Americans in swelling numbers were laboring toward the Rockies on faint trapper's trails. These emigrants were mostly midwestern farm folk swept west in the wake of a financial panic and the rumor of great tracts of fertile land for the taking out beyond the Snowy Mountains. Many of the pioneers drifted to the Oregon country where the Americans had a foothold while British control was weakening; others seeped across the Sierra Nevada and shouldered their way into the wilderness of California to build their cabins on Mexican lands.

These American squatters—some honest, hardworking, and wellmeaning folk, and a good many from a bad lot—made up the trespassing cadre which, given any incitement, was prepared to fight to stay where they were unbidden and unwelcome.

THE AMERICAN "CONQUEST" of California took six months, from the seizure of the customs house at Yerba Buena by the crew of the sloop-of-war *Portsmouth* on July 9, 1846, to the Treaty of Cahuenga, signed near Pueblo de Los Ángeles on January 13, 1847. The Californians fought two small but lethal cavalry battles with the interlopers, brave and well-trained Mexican lancers against brave and well-trained United States Army dragoons, but the Americans could not be prevented from entering San Diego, joining forces with naval battalions and volunteers commanded by John C. Frémont, and marching wherever they pleased.

The nation's larger war with Mexico lasted seventeen months, cost a hundred million dollars and 13,000 American lives. The cost to Mexico was uncountable in casualties and nearly as much so in lost territory: The Treaty of Guadalupe Hidalgo, signed on February 2, 1848, on the outskirts of Mexico City, divested Mexico of 40 percent of its territory at a pen scratch—530,000 square miles of lands ceded to the United States, including all of the future states of New Mexico, Arizona, and California, and parts of Colorado, Wyoming and Utah.

Alta California alone extended over ten degrees of latitude with a coastline of 1,264 miles, a land surface of 159,000 square miles, and altitudes ranging from 14,495 feet at the top of its highest mountain to -282 feet in its lowest desert.

For all these lands, the greatest acquisition since the Louisiana Purchase, and one which changed the course of American history and the configuration of the continent, President James K. Polk paid Mexico fifteen and a quarter million dollars.

News of the treaty reached California on August 6, 1848, and was announced the next day by the military governor at Monterey, Colonel Richard Barnes Mason. "From this new order of things there will result in California a new destiny," he said.

At the time he received the news, Colonel Mason had another matter on his hands, something of an unexpected bonus for the American conquerors of California. On August 19, he reported to Washington: "I do not anticipate any rebellion or revolution on the part of the Californians . . . in fact, the minds of all men are so intently engaged upon getting gold, that for the present they have not time to think of mischief."

Gold in California? Certainly there had been rumors of it for decades, rumors that the Indians and mission padres knew of it, that the Russians at Bodega Bay had reported as early as 1815 that there was gold in the Yuba River area. In 1840, the American consul at Monterey had sent a quantity of gold dust and nuggets to Boston, gold he had received as payment for goods sold in his general store. A few years later, a French-Canadian found traces of gold in rocks near Pueblo de Los Ángeles, and a Mexican laborer discovered some in a stream off the Sacramento River.

Nothing derived from these sightings; gold, after all, was ubiquitous in small deposits the world over and if there were real quantities of gold in California, the Spaniards would have found them long ago.

But gold was there, more of it than the Spaniards ever dreamed might pave the Seven Cities—a tract of gold and gold-bearing minerals seventy miles wide in some places and running the length of California, from the Klamath Mountains in the north to the Mojave Desert in the south. The richest portion of this fabulous zone lay in the wilderness of the western foothills of the Sierra Nevada where gold lay hidden in streams cold and pure and shaded by live oaks, pines, and redwoods; where it lurked in the wildflower-covered hills themselves, places grazed by deer and grizzly bears; where it was cached by nature in a 120-mile-long string of gold-bearing quartz pockets that came to be called the *Veta Madre*, the Mother Lode.

THIS CALIFORNIA OPHIR had been 150 million years in the making, beginning when colossal plates of the earth's crust shifted, pressing against the ancient floor of the Pacific. This stressed mass thrust up as a vast tilted block—the granitic Sierra Nevada range—and liquids and gases rose, carrying with them minerals that penetrated fractures in the granite, forming veins of ores, gold among them.

Volcanic water, wind erosion, the abrading of rocks on rocks, the pounding of Sierra rains, the riving frosts of the mountains, the swelling of tree roots that split cliffs into talus slopes, the simple impact of gravity—all these natural processes broke gold-bearing boulders into smaller and smaller pieces. Some of these were dumped into streams where the rushing waters of the passing millennia and the crushing impact of streambed cobbles reduced them to sands and silts and fashioned the soft gold into a myriad of shapes or ground it to dust. The rivers and streams carried the mountain debris along, but the gold, about eight times heavier than sand, dropped to the bottom whenever the flowing water detoured behind a rock outcrop or reached an impediment. This stranded gold, in the beds of waterways, in bedrock, and in surface rocks and streamside deposits, was called "placer" gold (a Spanish word for a gravel bank) by miners. Specimens from a placer were described variously as dust, pellets, grains, threads, scales, seeds, sparks, specks, and streaks.

NEITHER THE SPANIARDS nor the Mexicans discovered California gold, but a true irony lay in who *did* discover it: an American working in lands that had been granted by Mexico to a German who named his domain New Switzerland.

I
EMPRESARIO

Gold will be slave or master.
—Horace, *Epistles*

ONE

A WANDERING LORD
OF JEOPARDY

ON A GUSTY August day in 1839, a dozen or so American and European residents of the windblown village of Yerba Buena rowed out and boarded the *Monsoon*, a Boston trade ship and the sole vessel then anchored in San Francisco Bay. The occasion was a banquet celebrating a man preparing to plunge into California's northern wilderness on a quest none of his gathered friends could quite comprehend. In fact, for all the wit and wassail, toasts and tales of the occasion, the honoree himself remained as much a mystery as his mission.

John Augustus Sutter had that effect on people. He always learned more of others than he permitted them to learn of him. A Bostonian named William H. Thomes, who as a teenager sailed to Alta California on the brigantine *Admittance* in 1844, attested to this. While his ship swung at anchor off Yerba Buena, Thomes said, "Captain" Sutter came aboard with a gang of laborers to deliver a lot of two hundred cowhides and some bundles of beaver furs. Shipboard scuttlebutt preceding the visit described Sutter as liege lord of a domain "way off, up the Sacramento River somewhere," where he had a strong fort and ten thousand savage Indians under his command. The young seaman described this fantastic personage as "a short, stout man, with broad shoulders, large, full face, short, stubby mustache, a quiet, reserved manner, and a cold blue eye, that seemed to look you through and through, and to read your thoughts, no matter how much you tried to conceal them. . . ."

In Thomes's time and for many years following, rumors about Sutter were so commonplace that the most scandalous of them scarcely raised an eyebrow: He had deserted his wife and children, leaving them penniless somewhere in Europe; he was rich as a maharajah and ruled like one over so much territory he had himself not seen the outer boundaries of it; he had Indian slaves and many Indian mistresses, and an army of cutthroats manning the battlements of his fort;

he was friendly, gregarious, and generous, but such a dangerous man to cross that even the Mexican authorities who had bestowed upon him an immense grant of land gave him no orders, levied no taxes on him, and left him alone.

And even in 1839, on the eve of his departure into the northern hinterlands of Alta California, those who raised their glasses to celebrate their friend knew little about him except that he seemed to be a man of several nations who was not really allied with any of them.

JOHANN AUGUSTUS SUTTER, born in 1803 in Kandern, Grand Duchy of Baden, Germany, a few miles north of Basel, Switzerland, came from Swiss forebears. His father, a paper maker, moved the family to the Jura Mountain town of Neuchâtel in 1819 and there Johann apprenticed with a bookbinder and received some education in a military academy. While he later claimed to have served as a captain of artillery in the Royal Swiss Guard of King Charles X of France, in fact he served in the Swiss army reserve corps in Bern with the undistinguished, bottom-rung rank of under-lieutenant.

In about 1826 Sutter found work as a bookbinder in Leipzig and began a descent into debt that dogged him to the end of his days. By now he had married Anna Dübeld, and by 1834, while he was working as a draper's clerk in Burgdorf, Switzerland, had Anna, her mother, and four children under his rented roof, was threatened by an arrest warrant for nonpayment of loans and obligations, and was planning an escape from all of it.

America appears to have been on his mind as the perfect place to flee. While there is no record of what inspired his choice, he must have conceived of the United States, particularly its unsettled western frontier, as a place where he could be swallowed up and start over with a new identity and an erased slate thousands of miles from his old burdens. At age thirty-one, like so many of his contemporary hearthside dreamers, he had certain Rousseauesque notions of pristine Arcadias far from the ancient, stultifying social mores, traditions, and laws—particularly laws—of Europe. He had read assiduously, sponging up every droplet of news from America. He may have had American friends and business acquaintances in Germany, France, and Switzerland, who fired his appreciation of the opportunities across the Atlantic. He had even picked up a workable knowledge of English in his scurryings around the continent, a step or two ahead of the bill collectors.

For all his poverty of property and means—and conscience, for he did abandon his wife and children, condemning them to sixteen years of penury—Sutter possessed certain traits that were to serve him well in America and its Pacific outstations in the years ahead. He had a natural amiability and charm, and a quick, inventive, and eager mind. He had no grand schemes, nor even small ones, but was willing instead to be tugged along by chance and circumstance, letting opportunity happen without banging on its door. And he had a species of courage, a confident daring, seated in the enormity of his self-confidence. His biographer, Julian Dana, viewed him as "a wandering lord of jeopardy," a man who believed he could free himself from any snare and survive any vicissitude by the sheer force of his personality and will. Such a vanity would often require employing desperate measures, such as the one he contrived to outlive the distresses of his life in Europe—running away.

That he did in the spring of 1834. He borrowed funds for the passage to New York and wrapped up his affairs by asking his brother Friedrich to look after Anna and the children, promising to send money as soon as he got some to send.

He sailed from Le Havre in July and among shipboard acquaintances learned of the riches to be made in the great blank places on the charts of the trans-Mississippi west. Mexico, so the steerage chatter had it, had opened to outside trade and all manner of goods could be bought cheaply in Missouri and transported to the fabled trade emporium of Santa Fé where they earned huge profits, paid in silver and gold.

(In fact, with the first American trade wagons reaching the old town in 1821, the year of Mexico's independence and Missouri's statehood, the Santa Fé trade flourished and its trails from the Missouri frontier were well trodden by the time Sutter heard of them.)

A few days after debarking in New York, Sutter hurried on to St. Louis and there sought out the German colony in the bustling city, presenting his bogus Swiss Guard history and convincing the burghers to advance him funds for a plunge into the Santa Fé trade. He had nebulous plans but he was presentable, affable, a soldier, and a German—all trustworthy characteristics to his backers.

In 1834, he reached Independence, on a bluff above the Missouri

River and a few miles inside the western boundary of the United States. In this noisy hamlet, the main frontier depot for the mule- and ox-drawn trade caravans heading southwest on the eight-hundred–mile trek to Santa Fé, Sutter launched his chaotic, adventurous American career.

The four years separating his advent in New York and his arrival in California are nebulous—he kept no records and wrote no journal. He did become a Santa Fé trader, for a time in partnership with a similarly impecunious German gentleman he met either on the Atlantic passage or in St. Louis. The two managed to outfit themselves, on credit advanced by the St. Louis merchants, with goods, wagons, draft animals, and horses, and joined the commercial caravans on the rutted trails between Independence, Bent's Fort on the Arkansas River, and Santa Fé.

Sutter profited little from these excursions, or from horse-trading among the Apaches, Shawnees, and Delawares he encountered in his travels in Missouri and New Mexico. According to some of his friendlier contemporaries, he managed to send small sums of money home to Anna together with pleas for her patience, but this is probably a story of his own invention. If he felt any pangs of regret about leaving Anna and their children to an uncertain fate in Switzerland, he did not talk about it, write about it, or brood about it.

Less friendly speculation relating to his first years in American and Mexican territory circulated many years later. He was said to have bilked his German financiers in St. Louis, in effect running west with their money and making no attempt to pay it back from his trade profits. There was even a story that he killed one man sent to collect a debt. California historian H. H. Bancroft dismissed this as a canard but did say that some of Sutter's activities in Missouri were "not favorable" to his reputation.

The Swiss managed to bank some nonpecuniary profits from these opening years in the West. He came to know, either in Santa Fé or at Bent's Fort, such influential traders as Ceran St. Vrain and Charles Beaubien, both of whom had acquired land grants from Mexico, and Charles Bent who, with St. Vrain had constructed the great fort on the north bank of the Arkansas which flourished as a center of the Indian trade, collecting furs and buffalo robes and outfitting Santa Fé Trail merchants.

The French-Canadian Beaubien, *alcalde* (a magistrate or mayor) of

Taos, seems to have befriended Sutter and told the Swiss tales of trapping expeditions he had made to California.

Sutter's New Mexico experiences provided him a frontier education that would prove even more useful than his native charm and fake credentials. He learned the Spanish language, absorbed the rough niceties of frontier diplomacy—haggling with Mexican traders, bribing Mexican customs officers, and cajoling Mexican provincial army officers and bureaucrats—and absorbed the survival lore of the wilderness trail and camp.

On a trip to Taos, the trade depot fifty miles north of Santa Fé, he encountered another French-Canadian trapper recently returned from the beaver streams of California. This unidentified man, Sutter later recalled, spoke dreamily of the golden warmth of the place, its fur riches, and the fortunes being made there by the "Bostons," the Americans bringing their merchant vessels around Cape Horn to San Diego, Monterey and points north. Foreigners, the trapper said, were welcomed. There were flags from many nations in the anchorages serving the hide and tallow trade. Governance was lax, laws almost nonexistent, Mexican port officials pliable, opportunities limitless and far less competitive than those along the Santa Fé Trail.

Somewhere between Taos and the Missouri settlements, Sutter acquainted himself with the Perthshire nobleman William Drummond Stewart, a wealthy sportsman who roamed the Rocky Mountains, usually with an entourage of gentlemen hunters, servants and gun-bearers, as if on safari. Seventh baronet of Murthly Castle, late of the Fifteenth King's Hussars, and a veteran of the Peninsular War in Spain and of Waterloo, Sir William had hunted in the Oregon country and may have influenced the Swiss's forthcoming impromptu visit to the Pacific Northwest.

Stewart invited Sutter to a hunt he was planning that summer of 1838. The Scotsman, who wisely traveled into the mountains with veteran mountain men as guides, was heading for the Wind River Range of the Rockies. He had attached his party to a caravan taking trade goods and supplies to the "rendezvous," the trappers' annual trade fair, to be held that year on the Popo Agie River in central Wyoming.

Sutter tagged along, riding with Stewart and his retinue ahead of a wagon and pack mule train. Guide for the party was Irish-born Andrew Drips, a fabulous figure from the earliest days of the fur trade who had dealt with most of the native tribes along the upper Missouri, and whose knowledge of the trails and beaver streams of the Rockies was matchless.

The route, over the still dimly etched Oregon Trail, followed the Platte River 650 miles from western Missouri to Fort Laramie, a whitewashed adobe fort in prime buffalo lands, then plodded on northwest into the Wind River Mountains.

Sutter later claimed to have met Kit Carson at the 1838 rendezvous and it is likely that he did. The little gray-eyed Kentuckian had been working traps in the Yellowstone country with another of the West's storied mountaineers, Jim Bridger, the year before, and with Bridger and several other American Fur Company trappers rode to the Popo Agie gathering that summer.

(Sutter would get to know Carson better seven years hence, in far touchier circumstances, when Kit marched into California with John C. Frémont's expedition.)

There were missionaries accompanying Andrew Drips's caravan to the rendezvous, among them William H. Gray, a Utica, New York, cabinetmaker, heading to Oregon's Willamette Valley as "secular agent" to the Congregationalist missions there, as well as Elkanah Walker and Cushing Eels and their wives, destined to minister to the Spokane Indians. They were to be guided west by Francis Ermatinger, a Canadian of Swiss heritage working for the Hudson's Bay Company. Sutter naturally sought out his countryman and once the rendezvous ended, joined Ermatinger's party as they resumed travel on the Oregon Trail.

It is likely that Sutter met one of the most celebrated of mountain men during the Oregon Trail journey. This was Joseph Reddeford Walker, a giant Tennessean who had trapped the western mountains since 1819 and now, in 1838, was returning from California with a horse herd to sell among the trading posts of the Rockies. From him Sutter learned much about Alta California: In 1833 Walker had led fifty men from the Green River in Wyoming to the Mary's (later the Humboldt) River in northern Nevada, made a three-week crossing of the Sierra Nevada, and discovered the primeval Yosemite Valley. Afterward he and his company spent the winter in the Sacramento and San Joaquín River valleys.

Ten years after their meeting somewhere near the South Pass of the Rockies, Sutter must have remembered the giant Tennessean who blazed the trail in 1833 that thousands of gold hunters were following into California.

THE ERMATINGER PARTY crossed the Rockies at South Pass, reached Fort Hall, a Hudson's Bay Company post on the Portneuf River of Idaho, and some weeks later Fort Walla Walla, the timber-walled Hudson's Bay trade center on the east bank of the Columbia River. Sutter seems to have visited the missions of the Walla Walla and Willamette Valleys before arriving at Fort Vancouver in October.

He tarried there three weeks, touring the immense rectangular fort that had been built in 1825 on the north bank of the Columbia near the mouth of the Willamette. He admired its stout log palisades, its great gate with the Union Jack flying over it, its cannon-mounted bastions, and the scurrying of the workers, trades-, and craftsmen inside its ramparts. Here were shops for bakers, mechanics, smiths, coopers, tanners, wheelwrights, saddle and harness makers; and store-houses, worker quarters, kitchens, and a huge dining hall for the *voyageurs* returning from their trapping expeditions. He saw Indian trading posts, offices, chapels, a jail, a schoolhouse, a powder magazine, and houses for the chief factor and other fort officers. Surrounding the fort were gristmills, sawmills, orchards, and cultivated fields that were cleared and plowed by idle Hudson's Bay trappers in summer months. The company grew wheat, barley, corn, potatoes, and produce; had coops of chickens, a few head of cattle, many horses and hogs, and an international crew of tradesmen, laborers, and field and kitchen work-ers. French-Canadians were predominant but there were also employ-ees from Scotland, England, Ireland, Wales, and Russia, and Kanakas—natives of the Sandwich Islands—as well as many Indian workers, some Iroquois, but more local tribesmen, Chinooks in partic-ular.

Fort Vancouver's chief factor, John McLoughlin, a Québec-born physician, seems to have been away at the time of Sutter's visit but James Douglas, the fort's second-in-command, an urbane Scotsman married (as was McLoughlin) to a Cree Indian woman, served as the Swiss's guide. Douglas must have been impressed by the letters of rec-ommendation from Sir William Drummond Stewart and other nota-bles whose paths Sutter had crossed, and probably endured a barrage of questions about his thriving fort-in-the-forest.

The Scotsman was instrumental in Sutter's decision to try to locate in the north of Alta California, somewhere along the Sacramento River. Douglas had been there on Hudson's Bay business in 1837 and again the following year, exploring beaver streams with the approval of Mexican authorities.

While he enjoyed the hospitality and comforts of the fort's guest quarters, Sutter decided not to spend the winter there and sought the factor's advice on a passage to California. He told Douglas of a plan he had devised to drive a herd of Mexican cattle north to the beef-starved Willamette Valley.

The Company had no vessels routed to California but the Hudson's Bay brigantine *Columbia* was soon scheduled to take a cargo of lumber to the Sandwich Islands and Douglas offered Sutter a berth on the ship, advising him that at Honolulu he could eventually find a trader bound for San Diego or Monterey.

The factor had been impressed by the Swiss, as indeed were most who met him. Sutter had a polite, even courtly manner, a soldier's bearing—he played well the part of a former officer of the Royal Swiss Guard—and a disarming ingenuousness. He listened intently, blotting up news and knowledge, asked intelligent questions in good Germanic-English, and was a deft raconteur, full of tales of his peripatetic life in Europe. There was something about this short, moon-faced, blue-eyed, affable man with his curly blond hair and groomed moustache and side whiskers that elicited trust. He seemed ambitious, but not so overtly as to cause suspicion; he was energetic, restless, willing to take chances, and these were admirable traits in a world as full of jeopardy as the untamed lands of the Pacific coast.

James Douglas wrote letters for the newcomer, one of them to the Hudson's Bay agent in the islands, another to the American consul in Honolulu, and a third to an eminent American merchant there. Like the others he carried, these epistles he treated as *bona fides*, useful in his travels and enterprises, and with them in his valise, and after great expressions of gratitude to his host, Sutter paid the Company £15 for cabin accommodations and sailed from Fort Vancouver on October 23, 1838.

ONE DISAPPOINTMENT AWAITED him after the twenty-eight–day voyage to Honolulu: After the port quarantine cleared the vessel and he stepped ashore from the *Columbia*'s lighter, he learned that an American vessel had departed for California only six hours before and that three or four months might pass before the next California-bound trader might offer him passage.

Still, Sutter had much to do and see, and so made quick contact with the Hudson's Bay agent, George Pelly, who read the letters Sutter presented, taking particular note of the one from Factor Douglas at Fort Vancouver. Much impressed by Sutter's credentials, Pelly introduced the impatient visitor to a number of other island notables, among them the wealthy American merchant and sugar mill owner, William French, and the American consul at Honolulu, John Coffin Jones. Sutter may even have had an audience with King Kamehameha III during his stay in Hawaii, and certainly met the king's emissary, Oahu Governor Mataio Kekuanoa.

How much time he spent contemplating the lush paradise his detour had presented him, or how widely he traveled in the islands, is unknown. Nor do we know, as one of his early biographers asserted, that Sutter's mind seethed with plans for his California venture. He probably did not, at first, have any definite plans beyond examining the Sacramento country as Joseph Walker and James Douglas had advised him. He was certainly not thinking of "empire-building"— he was by nature spontaneous, lurching forward in accidental momentum—but he did have five months to think of his next step before the opportunity arose for him to take it. And by then, he had learned a great deal about California from islanders who had been there.

William French took an interest in Sutter, was perhaps even enthralled by this former soldier, Santa Fé trader, Rocky Mountain trapper, friend of a British baronet and a Hudson's Bay officer who had glowing letters from them and others in his portfolio. French was a shrewd businessman, the "Merchant Prince of the Islands," and not easily guiled. He had sailed to the Pacific in 1819 representing a Boston commercial firm and had spent seven years in the turbulent trade marts of Canton, China, before headquartering in Honolulu. There he was such a familiar figure that his advertisements in the town's newspaper did not even carry the address of his office and headquarters.

He listened to Sutter's vague ideas of settling in Alta California's northern wilderness and perhaps building a fort and trade center along the lines of those he had seen—Fort Laramie, Bent's, Fort Vancouver. This greatly interested the Merchant Prince. He could use such a commercial connection to Mexican California. He had things to sell there, and there were things to buy.

He proposed a profitable way for his new friend to get to California—a scheme that involved another detour, maybe three thousand miles or so, round-trip.

At anchor off the long, scimitar-shaped beach of Waikiki, at the foot of the extinct volcano called Diamond Head, lay a brig of eighty-eight tons, the *Clementine*, owned by Jules Dudoit, France's consul to the islands. The ship was idle and William French proposed chartering it, hiring a crew of sixteen men, loading it with a cargo of fruit, produce, salt, sugar, and miscellaneous other goods, and dispatching it to Sitka, capital of Russian America. Sutter could serve as unsalaried supercargo, handle the trade with the Russians and on the return voyage, disembark at San Francisco Bay with a share of the profits, start-up money for his Sacramento River exploration.

Sutter needed no coaxing. He had learned from Hudson's Bay agents in Fort Vancouver, and from Pelly, French, Jones, and others in Oahu, of the ripe opportunities for trade at Sitka. Too few supply ships were stopping at New Archangel and the Russians there hungered for fresh fruit and vegetables to ward off the scourge of scurvy. The Russians, he had learned, needed everything and bought nearly anything offered to them.

In April, with contracts signed, the ship chartered and manned, the $8,000 in goods purchased and stowed, the *Clementine*, commanded by a Cockney salt named John Blinn, was ready to sail.

Sutter took aboard a big bulldog he had somehow acquired, and new letters from Pelly, French, and Consul Jones. The latter, in a letter recommending him to the eminent military chief of Alta California, Mariano Guadalupe Vallejo, described Sutter as "a Swiss gentleman, and a man of the first class, honored with talent and esteem."

In a last-minute development, Governor Kekuanoa of Oahu offered Sutter nine male islanders, two with wives, who would work for him in California. The natives were each to be paid ten dollars a month. They were strong and dependable laborers and the Swiss was delighted to have them.

At the end of April, the *Clementine* reached New Archangel and warped under the cannon guarding Baranov Castle to anchor in Sitka Sound. The governor of the Russian-American Fur Company, Ivan Kuprianov, was so thrilled with the cargo he arranged to purchase all the perishables and most of the other goods as well, then gave Sutter, French, and Captain Blinn a tour of the town and its fur storage sheds and warehouses. (The Russians were formidable animal slaughterers on land and sea and had tons of walrus ivory, and hundreds of bales of furs—sea otter, sable, martin, fox, mink, muskrat, beaver, bear, and wolf—much of it destined for the vastly profitable trade at Canton.)

In his talks with Kuprianov, Sutter learned that his hosts were interested in selling their California fur trading posts, built in 1812 by eighty fur hunters and fifty conscripted Aleut Indians as products of the Russian dream of a trans-Pacific empire. Called Fort Ross by Americans, *Rossiya* (an obsolete, poetical word meaning "Russians") lay fifty miles north of San Francisco Bay and consisted of fifty buildings, most clustered around a central, log-palisaded fort. A smaller station was located eighteen miles south of Ross above Bodega Bay at the mouth of the Russian River.

The forts were no longer profitable, Kuprianov said, and were to be abandoned.

This intelligence Sutter filed away as perhaps eventually useful, as would be the letter he collected from Kuprianov to add to his cache.

With three-quarters of its cargo off-loaded at Sitka and sold at a fine profit in Russian gold, the *Clementine* sailed in June and after weathering heavy gales en route entered San Francisco Bay "in distress," Sutter said, on July 2, 1839, dropping her hook close to a dismal string of tents, shanties, and adobe huts scattered among the sandhills and beach of Yerba Buena Cove.

FRANCISCAN MONKS AND their Indian converts built a mission three miles southwest of the cove in 1776 and in the 1820s, the new Mexican government erected a makeshift presidio on the site, but not until four years before Sutter saw it were there any permanent dwellings there. Among the first of these were a poopdeck cabin, serving as somebody's residence, that had been removed from a wrecked hulk in the bay; and a tarpaulin tent supported by four redwood posts and roofed with a ship's sail, erected by W. A. Richardson, an English merchant captain appointed harbor master by the Mexican governor of Alta California.

The place had been named Yerba Buena ("good herb") for a native mint plant from which a fragrant tea was brewed.

Isolated from the commerce and administration centers at San Diego, Pueblo de Los Ángeles, and Monterey, Yerba Buena, except for its ill-equipped and undermanned presidio, was more foreign than Mexican. Yankee whalers and merchantmen from England and Russia made it a regular port of call, and there were several British and American skippers in and near the village who had been sanctioned by the Mexican government to deal in the hide and tallow and sea otter trades.

The great bay that sheltered the settlement, first seen from the high hills of San Mateo in 1769 by an overland party of Spaniards, had been coveted by every nation whose ships visited it. Prevailing winds put the bay on sea lanes that linked ports in India, China, and Manila, and Bahía de San Francisco came to be regarded as the key to commerce in the trans-Pacific Orient. Nor was its strategic value underestimated. The American explorer Charles Wilkes of the sloop-of-war *Vincennes* anchored at Yerba Buena in 1841, and said the bay was spacious enough to shelter all the world's navies.

Mexico exerted only nominal control over its greatest possession in the northern province but did require that foreign vessels, especially trade ships, have permits and pay cargo duties for use of their commercial ports. Thus, as soon as the *Clementine* anchored in the bay a boat was rowed out from the presidio landing and a Mexican officer and his escort climbed the jack ladder to the quarterdeck. There Captain Blinn was informed that he must move on to the capital at Monterey to obtain papers before he or any of his passengers could come ashore.

Sutter's luck held. He had letters to show, including the one from Consul John Jones to General Mariano Vallejo, and through the intervention of some prominent merchants ashore who prevailed upon the presidio commander, the *Clementine* was granted a forty-eight-hour visit to provision, fill water casks, and make some repairs.

SUTTER REACHED MONTEREY on July 4, 1839, with fortuitous timing. The best-known American in the capital, Thomas Oliver Larkin, was giving an Independence Day party at his home and the Swiss was able to present his letters there to some of the most influential men in Alta California.

Larkin was a genial, thirty-seven-year-old New Englander who had reached California in 1832 and had risen to prominence as a merchant and agent for American shipping firms in Monterey. He traded with Mexico and the Sandwich Islands in furs, horses, lumber, and flour, had a store in Monterey, a mastery of the Spanish language, and the trust of provincial authorities despite the fact that he had neither applied for nor shown any interest in Mexican citizenship. He was known as "Don Tomás" and "El Yánqui de Bostoño" and ran his businesses shrewdly and with what a contemporary said was "no particular veneration for revenue laws."

En route to Monterey from Honolulu in 1832, Larkin met on shipboard Mrs. Rachel Holmes and a year later, married the widow at Santa Bárbara. Their lovely two-storied home of adobe bricks, hand-hewn redwood roof shakes, and windows of imported glass, became a social center of Monterey with "Don Tomás" and "Doña Raquela" entertaining visitors from many nations with *bailes*, fine food, and a buzz of talk about trade and politics and the limitless opportunities in the golden land of California.

At the Larkin celebration Sutter had talks with William A. Leidesdorff, a prominent Yerba Buena businessman of Danish-African descent who had left the West Indies as a young man, became a merchant captain in New York and New Orleans, and settled in California, like Larkin, as a trader-merchant.

Most important, for his immediate purposes was Sutter's introduction to Juan Bautista Alvarado, the thirty-year-old former customs inspector and first native-born governor (born in Monterey, in fact) of Alta California. Alvarado read with interest the letters from James Douglas, Governor Kuprianov, William French, and Consul Jones, the latter recommending Sutter as "a Swiss gentleman who goes to California with the intention of settling there if the country meets his expectations."

Sutter and the governor must have had several meetings in the days that followed in which the Swiss presented further credentials, his life story (excepting, of course the unfortunate business of abandoning Anna and the children), and his ambitions. He told Alvarado, no doubt in his most diplomatic guttural Spanish, that he wished to settle in the northern province, that he had four white men and nine Kanaka workmen to help him clear land, build an outpost, and plant crops. He said he was interested particularly in exploring a site somewhere along the Sacramento River.

Alvarado seemed interested in the idea and the two talked of Sutter's proposed rancho serving as a buffer against the Indians in that area, these natives notorious as ruffians and horse thieves, harrassing the inhabitants around the village of San José and the sprinkling of settlers to the east and north of Yerba Buena and Sonoma. The latter was a small presidio where Alvarado's uncle, General Mariano Vallejo, lived, and Sutter carried a letter recommending him to that gentleman.

During the course of their meetings, Alvarado suggested and queried and Sutter explained and embroidered. From the word "settlement" grew the idea of building a "rancho"; the rancho evolved into a "fort" to protect the northern limits of Mexican California; the nebulous notion of locating somewhere along the Sacramento River transformed into building on the American River near its confluence with the Sacramento, putting the rancho-fort in command of a waterway running 320 miles from the Sierra Nevada to the Pacific.

By the end of the meetings, Sutter, in effect, had agreed to be an agent of Mother Mexico, or at least of its untended stepchild called Alta California, protecting its interests in the north. He even proposed to develop a fur trade up there that would force out such competitors as the Hudson's Bay Company and the Russians, both recent but now apparently erstwhile friends. Sutter's opportunistic abandonment of them occurred after Alvarado said he "suspected" them of trapping illegally in Mexican lands.

All he needed to put these plans into action, Sutter said, was a grant of land and the government's official sanction for him to begin working on its behalf. Alvarado assured that this posed no problem. Sutter would need only to sign a paper confirming his intention of becoming a citizen of Mexico, go north and mark off a tract of land that suited him, and return to Monterey in a year for his naturalization and grant documents.

Sutter signed the letter of intent, gathered his papers from Alvarado, including another introduction to Vallejo in Sonoma, and set out again on the *Clementine* for Yerba Buena.

★   ★   ★

WITH THE REMAINDER of its cargo sold off in Monterey, the *Clementine* returned to Honolulu while Sutter, set ashore at Yerba Buena with his Kanakas, baggage and bulldog, and paid calls on some local merchants—Jacob Leese, married to one of Vallejo's sisters; Nathan Spear and William S. Hinkley, who owned a general store in the village—and the harbor master, Captain Richardson.

With Richardson he rowed across the bay to the Sonoma *embarcadero* to pay a courtesy call on *Commandante General* Vallejo and rode with the general's *vaqueros* to his headquarters opposite the Sonoma mission. The high-born Californio, keenly intelligent, striking in appearance with his wavy black hair, muttonchop whiskers, and dark, penetrating eyes, greeted the Swiss warily. He asked many questions about Sutter's plans and at a dinner that evening in his home, continued to talk, warning Sutter of the untamed Indians, dangers, and disease awaiting him in the wilderness and suggesting that he locate closer to Sonoma where rich pasturage was available. Sutter politely countered that he wished to settle and build along a navigable river in order to have a commercial avenue to San Francisco Bay.

After a tour of the Sonoma presidio—consisting of fifteen soldiers in a motley of hand-me-down uniforms, and a few rusted field guns—Sutter borrowed horses and departed Vallejo's domain for a visit to the Russian outposts at Bodega Bay and Fort Ross. As Alvarado's northern agent, he needed to see what the Russians were up to.

To the governor of Rossiya, Baron Alexander Rotchev, Sutter presented a letter from Ivan Kuprianov, governor of the Russian-American Fur Company, and other credentials, and was allowed to inspect the redwood-palisaded fort and its fifty-odd outbuildings. He found it much better equipped than Vallejo's sad presidio at Sonoma; in fact, he believed Ross comparable to the American Fort Laramie and a miniature version of Fort Vancouver. Especially impressive were the fields of wheat and barley, the gardens and orchards outside the fort proper, and the outpost's equipage, furniture, and arsenal.

Upon his return to San Francisco Bay, Sutter hurried to put his inland expedition in order. From Nathan Spear and William Hinkley he worked out a credit agreement whereby he was supplied with seed and farm implements, carpenter and blacksmith tools, muskets, rifles, powder and ball, three small cannons, and provisions for his party. The merchants also let Sutter charter their two small schooners, the *Nicholas* and *Isabel*, to convey his men and supplies upriver. Captain John Wilson, another Vallejo brother-in-law, sold the Swiss a four-oared pinnace for use in making runs down the Sacramento to the bay.

Now, with a half-dozen recruits gathered from among the shipless seamen and unemployed lingerers on the Yerba Buena waterfront, he was eager to find his place in the wilds and build on it.

HIS FAREWELL PARTY aboard the *Monsoon* lasted till sunrise and while Sutter was always a man of the moment, not much given to contemplation of the past, he must have allowed some time to consider the five years that had passed since he sailed for America. In Europe he had been a debt-ridden clerk with a hungry family, no future, and warrant servers baying at his heels. Now he was a debt-ridden entrepreneur with a bulldog, a malacca cane, eleven Sandwich Island natives, a fourteen-year-old Indian boy he had "purchased" (from Kit Carson, some said) at the Popo Agie rendezvous, a German cabinet-maker named Wetler, some flotsam from the beaches of San Francisco Bay to work for him, and a brain swirling with chancy ideas. He had been a Santa Fé trader and an Oregon Trail pioneer, had a long list of influential friends from outposts as far-flung as St. Louis, Taos, Fort Vancouver, Honolulu, Sitka, and Monterey, and letters from them giving him credit and attesting to his sterling character.

He had accomplished more in the past half-decade than in the first thirty-one years of his life and as he stepped down the ladder from the *Monsoon* to the pinnace and its Kanaka oarsmen awaiting alongside on that morning of August 9, 1839, he may have given some thought to even grander achievements in the days to come.

More than likely, however, being a man of the moment, he thought more of destination than destiny.

TWO

THE POTENTATE OF THE SACRAMENTO

THE PINNACE SLID silently up the bay past Angel Island and the southern tip of Mare Island, around Point Pinole, through Carquinez Strait, and toward a rancho on the starboard shore owned by Don Ignacio Martínez, a former commander of the Yerba Buena garrison.

Sutter had his oarsmen pull to the beach fronting the pastures of Rancho Pinole and paid a call on Martínez. The Swiss, who lacked everything but confidence, spoke to the bemused Don Ignacio about a future trade, offering beaver furs, wheat, and produce for horses, sheep, and cattle, and promising to return once established on his land.

The profitable visit ended, Sutter directed his Kanakas northeast to Suisun Bay and on August 10 they found the boggy deltas of the Sacramento and San Joaquín Rivers, a sweltering place of tule marshes, humming clouds of mosquitos and black flies below hills blanketed in wild oats.

Although Suisun Bay was discovered by Spaniards in 1775 and the Sacramento River in 1808, there were no dependable maps of either so inevitably the entrance randomly chosen from the maze of swampy inlets proved to be the wrong one, that of the San Joaquín. The mistake cost the expedition two days of ascending the river, shoring the boats at night, reconnoitering, and making campsites, before Sutter decided to turn back to the delta to start over.

After searching the entire northern shore of Suisun Bay, penetrating every slough, bayou, and marshy pocket, the true inlet to the Sacramento was found at last and the pinnace led the way into the reeds with the schooners lagging a considerable distance behind.

The boat labored up the broadening river in breezeless summer heat past old sycamores, cottonwoods, and elms lining the banks, the Kanakas suspecting they were being watched from copses of trees and the thick brush along their route. Sutter had seen bundles of white feathers, prayer offerings to river gods, tied to branches canopying the waterway and had been warned that the Indians of the area were numerous and unpredictable. He had lain in a supply of gifts for the likely encounter with them.

He met the first delegation of them on the day he found the mouth of the Sacramento, close to two hundred Walagumne people, and they appeared suddenly on the banks of the river and approached the pinnace in reed canoes, bodies and faces garishly painted, all armed with bows, arrows, and spears. "They seemed to be very keen for a fight," Sutter later remembered.

He ordered his men not to fire the muskets they had loaded, impulsively ordered the boat ashore, and approached a clot of natives, yelling at them "A Diós, amigos!"—hoping that among them might be a former mission Indian who understood a smattering of Spanish. It happened that there were several who grasped his shouted message that he had come to farm and live among them as a friend so he sent a courier downstream to tell the schooners to hurry forward, then distributed trade beads, blankets, shirts, and bandannas to the tribesmen, and watched them disperse.

After moving his command to the *Isabel*, the boats continued upstream to the American River fork where camp was pitched and where Sutter discovered what he called his "perfect place." It bordered the American near its confluence with the Sacramento, a fertile valley thick with grass and stands of pines, redwoods, cottonwoods, sycamores, live oaks, and elms. The land was flat, the soil ripe and ready for plowing, and below, the wide river teeming with fish and wildfowl. He saw elk and deer skittering, alarmed at the noise he and his crew made; there were wolves, coyotes, and grizzlies in the woods, and wildflowers and lush greenery at every point of the compass.

Sutter had a name for his perfect place, and may have invented it before he ever found it: In honor of his ancestral homeland he called it New Helvetia.

He organized the unloading of the schooners and sent them back down to Yerba Buena for more supplies. And, since six of the drifters he had "signed up" just before departure were no longer interested in pioneering after learning there were painted and armed Indians in the area, Sutter obliged them by sending them back on the *Isabel* and *Nicholas*. A nine-round cannon salute was fired upon the boats' departure, something he was sure would impress any lurking hostiles.

Left with his Hawaiians, the German woodworker, two other men who had come along as laborers, and the Indian boy, Sutter put them all to work. Tents were pitched and hunters sent into the woods to bag game. The Kanakas built some grass huts. Trees were cut and whipsawed. Mud and straw were mixed for bricks, and ground marked off for an adobe structure, roofed with tules, that would eventually serve as a blacksmith shop, kitchen, and Sutter's quarters.

After only a month ashore, he wrote a letter to Martínez and sent it in the pinnace to Rancho Pinole, sixty miles downriver. He apparently told Don Ignacio that he was now settled and ready to close the bargain they had made in July. He asked for draft oxen to transport his supplies and equipment from the riverbank to high ground, asked for beef steers, beans, wheat, jerky, corn, lard, saddles, rope, and candles. What thought process prompted this amazing shopping list from a man who as yet had nothing to trade and which seemed to assume Martínez was proprietor of a trading post rather than a *ranchero*, is not known, but not surprisingly, Martínez did not hurry to respond. When in October, out of his natural Californio generosity he sent a cow, a heifer, a couple of horses, and a few *fanegas* of wheat to New Helvetia, Sutter complained that the cows were scrawny, the mares unbroken, the wheat maggoty. For a man with a tin cup, the Swiss was very picky.

He had better luck with his creditors at Yerba Buena and as time passed made regular schooner runs down to San Francisco Bay and returned with the provisions and supplies he needed. Eventually he would even take things to trade.

Sutter's islanders were his best and most faithful workers and he came to love them for their tirelessness and good cheer. According to one of his later ill-chosen associates, a German named Heinrich Leinhard, Sutter came to love one of them literally, a girl named Manuiki. Leinhard said she bore "the Captain" several children.

IN AUGUST 1840, Sutter returned to Monterey, riding with four armed men as escorts, to fulfill his promise to take the oath as a naturalized citizen of Mexico. He was able to make an astonishing progress report to Governor Alvarado. In the year past New Helvetia had taken shape and was functioning as a farm. Indeed, by the end of 1839, several adobe buildings were standing and in use, fields had been broken and wheat planted, *embarcaderos* had been constructed on the banks of both the American and Sacramento rivers with rough cart paths cleared to each. He was now employing Indian laborers, paying them in trade goods and promises, and had a few new recruits up from Yerba Buena including a cook, a smith, a French sailor who served as "right hand man," and a couple of *vaqueros* to take care of his small cattle herd.

His *pièce de résistance* for his report to the governor was to announce that his Indians, faithful Kanakas, beached sailors and other vagabonds, had cut pine beams from trees twenty miles up the American, hauled them downstream, made thousands of adobe bricks, and were constructing a fort under his supervision. It would consist of an eighteen-foot-high adobe wall, two-and-a-half-feet thick, enclosing a space 320 feet long by 160 wide, with bastions at the corners housing the brass cannons he had brought up on the schooners.

Sutter's Fort, he said, would be larger than three of its models, Bent's on the Arkansas, the trapper's post on the Laramie River, and the Russians' Fort Ross.

Alvarado, much impressed, promised Sutter that his land grant would be officially conferred in a few months, after his citizenship declaration and other papers were approved by the provincial government. "He has sufficiently demonstrated his industry, good conduct, and other qualifications required in such cases," the governor wrote, "and he has already advanced, manifested by his great efforts and constant firmness, a truly patriotic zeal for our institutions, civilizing a large number of savage Indians. . . ."

Sutter returned home with judicial powers but not the military title he coveted. For the time he had to be content with his self-bestowed captaincy and General Vallejo would remain the only genuine military officer in the northern province.

While his fort was under construction, the Swiss faced some Indian problems and dealt with them severely in his newly awarded capacity as magistrate and the only law in New Helvetia.

"The Indians were sometimes troublesome," he would recall, "but on the whole I got along very nicely with them." On the whole he did, but he also told of a night when several Indians managed to get inside the fort and made "an attempt to assassinate me." Sutter's Hawaiian bulldog clamped his jaws on one of the assassins and brought him down, then ran to another and held on to him until he was subdued. The captives said they were only after plunder and had nothing against the captain.

Sutter said, "I sewed up the wounds of the savages and told them I would forgive them this time but that any further attempts in the same direction would be met with swift punishment."

He kept his word: In October, 1840, after some wives and children of his field hands were kidnapped by an Indian raiding party, he mounted a punitive expedition of forty men, half of them natives. He found the raiders and captives in a village on the Sacramento thirty miles above the fort, captured nearly forty of them, and had fourteen executed by firing squad.

"The distant tribes," he said, "continued to look upon my establishment as an object for pillaging, and I had to undertake several campaigns against these Indians, in most cases as punishment for stealing cattle. But finally I had subjugated all the Indians of the Sacramento Valley. . . ."

Governor Alvarado appreciated "Don Juan Agosto's" severe work as well as that which went into raising and improving the fort and farming the land. In mid-1841, when Sutter received his land grant papers, the governor said the Swiss had "sufficiently proved his assiduity, good behavior, and all other qualities."

The grant was magnanimous, the largest allowed by the Mexican government: eleven square leagues—just under 49,000 acres—between the Sacramento and its hundred-mile-long tributary, the Feather River.

SUTTER WAS OCCUPIED four years in building and refining his fort, but it seemed to rise so quickly that General Vallejo, dubious of the Swiss's intentions from the outset, grew alarmed. He was particularly bothered by Sutter's expeditions against the Indians and the usurpation of powers that were not assigned to him. He wrote his brother, "This establishment, with its treacherously venomous exudations, is extremely dangerous."

If Sutter knew of such ill will exuding from Sonoma, he gave it no heed. His days were filled with work; his land and his fort preoccupied him to the exclusion of everything else, including his mounting debt and what others were saying about him.

His successes were phenomenal. He organized Indians to hunt and

trap for him, and to serve as fort guards and his personal escort. He
enlisted wandering French-Canadian and American trappers, Yerba
Buena beachcomers, merchant ship jumpers and miscellaneous other
human driftwood, to work for him. They hunted, fished, tended the
fort's cattle, sheep, and horse herds, sowed wheat and reaped it with
sickles, butcher knives, and hoop iron. These itinerants planted fruit
orchards and vineyards and irrigated in drought times by fashioning
wooden pipes and troughs to carry water from the river. They
manned his tannery, grain mill, boathouse, workshops, and a distillery
which made a tolerable brandy (to which Sutter developed a notice-
able affinity) from local wild grapes.

Outside the fort walls were the tannery and several dwellings for
workers and guests; fenced areas for cattle, sheep, horses, and chickens;
plowed fields for wheat and vegetables; orchards of apple, peach, pear,
fig, and olive trees; and two acres of Castilian roses, the cuttings given
him by mission priests. Inside were worker barracks, a bakery, gra-
nary, blanket factory, blacksmith, gunsmith, wheelwright, and carpenter shops, and a flour mill run by four mules, the team changed every
four hours. Sutter's own headquarters, a rough-raftered three-room
adobe with unpaneled walls, evolved into spacious offices, audience
rooms, and private apartments with redwood benches and tables made
by his own woodworkers, fireplaces, candelabra, and Indian rugs
woven on the fort's looms.

Some of the furnishings were acquired after Sutter, in one of his
many audacious, foolhardy moves, purchased Fort Ross from the Russians.

Originally, in the sumer of 1841, he offered to buy the cattle herd
at Ross but the Russians were not interested in selling the fort piece-
meal. A year later, Sutter was invited by Rossiya governor Rotchev on
board his schooner *Constantine*, to tour the fort and the outpost at
Bodega Bay. The result of this excursion was an agreement by which
the Swiss agreed to pay thirty thousand dollars for Ross and the
smaller post, their buildings, furnishings, equipage, and stock. (The
land itself belonged to Mexico and was thus not part of the arrange-
ment.) Sutter made a down payment of two thousand dollars in cash
and signed promissory notes to pay the Russians five thousand dollars
in wheat for the first two years, ten thousand in wheat in the third
year, and make a final cash payment to close the contract. On paper, he
agreed to mortgage New Helvetia, if necessary, to make all obligations.

The agreement made, he had his *vaqueros* and laborers begin the operation of bringing the Russians' cattle, sheep, and horses down to New Helvetia, and dismantling the wooden structures and hauling them, with the furnishings, on the *Constantine* to San Francisco Bay and upriver to Sutter's Fort.

This process occupied two years' work, since the thirty thousand dollars had purchased in stock alone 1,700 head of cattle, calves, and oxen; 940 horses and mules, and 200 sheep. In addition there were tools: forty-nine plows, ten carts, tannery and dairy equipment, a fishing boat, four other small craft plus kayaks and canoes, draperies, books, paintings, a piano, windmills, millstones, forty rusty cannons, and many muskets—most of the arms captured from the French during Napoleon's retreat from Moscow in 1812—with attendant powder and iron shot, and a staggering quantity of lumber from the fort's barracks, storehouses, outbuildings, boathouse, threshing floors, and corral fencing.

Sutter regarded the price he paid the Russians a "ridiculously low sum" but the purchase plunged him deeper in debt than he had ever been in his debt-ridden life. He owed the Russians, owed merchants Tom Larkin of Monterey, William Leidesdorff and Nathan Spear of Yerba Buena; owed Mariano Vallejo and Ignacio Martínez for cattle bought on credit; still owed William French in Honolulu for the startup money advanced him in 1839; still owed the Hudson's Bay people at Fort Vancouver for debts incurred during his brief stayover there. He owed so much to so many that in a few years he would have creditors coming to the fort to attach his schooners and other properties and demand payment for bills so long in arrears he could not remember them.

Because of his poor memory for what he owed and to whom he owed it, he remained optimistic. New Helvetia demanded all his time and attention. "I was everything," he recalled, "patriarch, priest, father, and judge." He presided at marriages and funerals, dealt with lawbreakers (the fort had a dungeon for the worst of them), set schedules for his workers, his personal guard of twelve to fifteen "mounted Indians under command of a very intelligent sergeant," and the fort sentries. He supplied those guarding the fort with a "half-hour glass" so that all night, every time the sand ran out, one of them would shout "All is well!" to assure him there were no Indians or other intruders, fires, or disturbances.

At the peak of his success, Sutter had a two-hundred-man native military guard, dazzling in blue and green Russian uniforms and armed with Napoleonic flintlocks salvaged from the Fort Ross armory. This force, he said, was necessary to defend the property and retaliate against Indian raiders.

His treatment of both the Indians he hired and those he regarded as "hostiles" was criticized in his own day, even more severely later, as at least repressive if not cruel. His punitive expeditions, by his own admission, resulted in the killing of at least thirty natives and a similar number may have been executed for various crimes including horse and cattle rustling. Sutter had seen Indian laborers treated as virtual slaves in New Mexico and in California, as they had been from the days of the Spanish *conquistadores* and the mission-founding Franciscan fathers. On occasion he acted little differently from these subjugators in that he sold, or leased, his Indian workers to other landholders in the Sacramento Valley as if they were chattels. General Vallejo, among others, found his Indian practices so onerous he referred to the Swiss as a petty despot and slave master. The eminent Californio also accused Sutter of calling himself "Governor of the Fortress of New Helvetia," thus attaching a spurious authority to his campaigns against the natives.

But for the most part Sutter treated his Indian workers well, certainly better than Mexican authorities expected him to. He depended on them—Nisenans, Miwoks, Yokuts, and other people of the river valleys—and paid them in tin scrip—homemade coins tradeable at the fort's stores—for their stoop-labor, farming, fishing, hunting, trapping, tanning, butchering, and herd-tending. He praised the Kanakas who had joined him in clearing the land for the fort in '39, but he knew who made his successes at New Helvetia possible and after the "subjugation" of the tribes in the first year or two of his building Sutter's Fort, he had few problems with them.

In those opening years of building and planting his domain, he said, "We lived very simply, roast beef and vegetables being our principal dishes. Sometimes we could not get any coffee and at times there was not a single lump of sugar in the house. We found that peas were a good substitute for coffee, but still better we liked acorns from which we made a drink which was hard to distinguish from coffee." But by 1844, five years after locating on the American River and ten years after sailing for America, life at New Helvetia had grown complex. Sutter now ruled a considerable wilderness empire. In harvest time he employed as many as five hundred field hands, most of them natives; his launches made regular passages down the Sacramento to San Francisco Bay carrying hides, tallow, furs, wheat, and produce, and returned with cargos of lumber and supplies while he stayed buried in paper—correspondence, bills of lading, duns from creditors, ledgers, rolls, schedules.

By now he had added girth and begun to look the part of the prosperous Baden burgher, his moon face beaming at the loud industry and traffic of his fiefdom. He was brimful of new ideas: experiments with cotton, improving the irrigation system, developing a fishery, finding new timber sources and the mills to handle and dress lumber. If he worried he gave little hint of it; if he thought of his wife and family in Switzerland he left no record of it.

For all his energy and accomplishment, not all his enterprises were successful, and for each admirer he had a critic. He could not resist dabbling in politics and intrigues, snapping at the hands that had welcomed and trusted him, bestowed on him the land on which New Helvetia was built, rewarded his diligence, and given him the opportunity for wealth. He connived with agents of the Hudson's Bay Company, and later with certain highly placed French visitors to his fort, on an idea of declaring his domain independent of Mexico. Nothing came of this scheme, but rumors of it reached Monterey and Los Angeles with the result that he was thereafter declared no friend of Mexico or its representatives in Alta California.

Nor did he ingratiate himself to the Hudson's Bay people, with whom he was in debt for both succor and specie, and with whom it was said he had plotted to wrest the Sacramento Valley from Mexico.

From his Santa Fé and Rocky Mountain experiences, Sutter planned to make the fur trade an important part of New Helvetian commerce. He had even suggested to Alvarado that Hudson's Bay trappers were poaching furs in the north of the province and that he might put a stop to it. "I did not think it was right that the Hudson's Bay Company was allowed to carry off large quantities of furs every year," he would explain. "I also disliked the fact that the trappers bought stolen horses from the Indians." The provincial government was for a time powerless to stop these incursions but at Sutter's suggestion, began levying a high export duty on the furs. The result, he said, was that "trapping ceased to be a profitable business for the company" and it thereafter "abandoned the valley of California" and opened a trading post at Yerba Buena.

These machinations outraged Sir George Simpson, governor of the Hudson's Bay Company. In 1841, this eminent gentleman visited the California coast and while not actually sailing up to New Helvetia, knew of and wrote a letter about the man he called "a Swiss potentate." Sutter, he believed, wanted to make his Sacramento domain "another Texas," referring to the former province of Mexico that in 1836 declared itself a republic. A year later, Simpson wrote his governing board in London about the duplicitous John A. Sutter: "Now that he has, I may say, defrauded almost every one with whom he has come into contact, he has seated himself down in a stronghold of the Sacramento . . . bidding defiance not only to creditors but even to the public authorities and laws of the country."

For all his work and chicanery, Sutter never made a significant profit from the fur trade. When he launched into it he enlisted veteran trappers, mostly French-Canadians who had wandered into California, outfitted them with horses, traps, and provisions, and sent them out to the icy steams of the Sierra Nevada and eastward. But beaver, once the prime source of fur revenue, had been trapped out by the early 1840s and so, after his efforts failed to corner the trade, he had to be satisfied in buying small numbers of pelts from roving trappers and shipping them to Yerba Buena.

IN AUGUST 1841, Sutter received a party of naval officers from the American sloop-of-war *Vincennes*, anchored off Sausalito in north San Francisco Bay. The officers represented one of the ship companies of the massive, government-sponsored Pacific Scientific and Exploratory Expedition led by Commodore Charles Wilkes. The Swiss greeted the officers at the *embarcadero* with his customary courtesy, had his cannons fire a salute, and entertained them at a dinner in the fort. "They were very much surprised to find a flourishing settlement in this wilderness," Sutter said, "and it made a very good impression upon the Indians to see so many white men visiting me."

The officer in command of the delegation, Lieutenant Commander Cadwalader Ringgold, had orders to make a survey of the Sacramento River and did so with Sutter's help. (Two of Ringgold's sailors deserted during their stay at the fort and could not be found before the delegation had to return to the *Vincennes*. "Afterwards," Sutter said with some delight, "they came out of their hiding places and I employed them in my tannery.")

Commodore Wilkes was much taken by San Francisco Bay and in his report to his superiors in Washington said, "The location of California will cause its separation from Mexico in the next few years. . . . It is evident that it will fill a large and important niche in the world's future history."

Wilkes was not implying that the "separation" of California from Mexico would be precipitated by the United States; in fact, except for the great northern bay he seemed to think California not worth the cost and consequences of an American intervention.

Others thought differently. The Hudson's Bay Company governor, Sir George Simpson, viewed Sutter's Fort as central to a future American takeover of San Francisco Bay if not all of California. He wrote in 1841, "The Americans, as soon as they become masters of the interior [of California] through Captain Sutter's establishment, will discover they have a natural right to a marine outlet. Whatever may be the fate of Monterey and the more southerly ports, San Francisco [Bay] will, to a moral certainty, sooner or later fall into the possession of the Americans—*unless the English take it.*"

Simpson had reason to worry about American aims on the Pacific coast: American missionaries and settlers had already invaded the Oregon country where Hudson's Bay's hegemony had been unassailed since the War of 1812. He also probably knew, from his political contacts in London, that England was too busy fending off American intervention in Oregon to be interested in "taking" San Francisco Bay from Mexico.

JOHN BIDWELL WAS born to pioneer.

In 1839, the year John Sutter established New Helvetia on the American River in California, Bidwell, age twenty, left the family farm in Ohio with seventy-five dollars in cash, the clothes on his back, and, he said, "nothing more formidable than a pocketknife." He got as far west as Platte County, Missouri, and taught school there for a year, spending his free time dreaming of a plunge into the western wilderness to start his life over.

Bidwell began hearing about California from trappers who had been there and learned more from a series of letters appearing in Missouri newspapers written by a man named John Marsh, a native of Danvers, Massachusetts, who claimed to have studied medicine at Harvard.

Among the ambiguous information Marsh offered those thinking of emigrating west was advising them to start out on the Oregon Trail from the Missouri border and at Fort Hall, the fur trading post in Idaho, to "cut south for California." It sounded simple and it was from such a source that John Bidwell's itchy feet took direction.

(As Bidwell learned later, Marsh was a peculiar specimen of a pioneer. In his youth he drifted into Minnesota, fought in the Blackhawk War on the Iowa frontier in 1832, became a gunrunner to the Indians, and fled to Missouri after a federal warrant was issued for his arrest. After failing as a storekeeper in Independence he wandered down the Santa Fé Trail and in 1836 made his way to California where he cadged from Mexican authorities a grant of land on the eastern slope of Mount Diablo in the San Joaquín Valley to raise cattle. In 1838 he began the series of newspaper letters Bidwell read, boosting California's climate, fertile land, and the availability of Indian labor—the natives, he said, "submit to flagellation with more humility than negroes.")

Bidwell was young, handsome, tireless, and infectiously confident. He threw himself into organizing a Western Emigration Society with such eloquence and fervor that within a month he had five hundred "pledges," mostly farm folk from Missouri, Illinois, Arkansas, and Kentucky, electrified by his eloquence and the newspaper articles written about him. All felt it was time to go. The Panic of 1837 was still suffocating them: banks had closed, prices for farm products were plummeting, foreclosures were reported everywhere, and even worse than a ruinous economy, a cholera epidemic had swept through the south, the midwest, and across the Mississippi, erasing families and decimating towns and settlements.

In signing their pledges, the emigrants agreed to buy a "suitable outfit," meaning wagons, draft animals, and provisions, and rendezvous at Sapling Grove, Kansas, just west of Independence, Missouri, the great way station for travelers on the Santa Fé and Oregon Trails. There, in May, 1841, when all were "armed and equipped to cross the Rocky Mountains to California," they would head west.

"The ignorance of the route was complete," Bidwell wrote later.

"We knew that California lay west, and that was the extent of our knowledge." This was said only slightly tongue-in-cheek. There were shallow trails to be followed, and advice from mountain men and missionaries who had made the journey and returned. Even so, there remained a significant ignorance of the route to California. Fanciful maps of the "Great American Desert," said to lay between the Rockies and the western ocean, were still being consulted, these showing a body of water representing what would later be named the Great Salt Lake, with two rivers running out of it and emptying into the Pacific. The rivers seemed wide enough to be navigable, and fireside geographers who had not been there and did not intend going suggested that maybe those managing to reach the shores of these rivers might build canoes and rafts and sail them down to California.

Bidwell's problems were more immediate than avoiding nonexistent rivers. He barely had the means to buy a small wagon, a gun and supplies, and when he finally found a partner with a horse and fifteen dollars in cash, had to persuade the man to trade these pitiful holdings for one "sorry-looking mule" to serve as a pack animal and a yoke of oxen to pull the wagon.

Then, when they reached Sapling Grove in May, Bidwell discovered that all but a few of his party had opted to stay home. Selling a farm to finance a two-thousand-mile journey across *terra incognita* occupied (as they had been warned by friends, neighbors, and St. Louis newspapers) by bloodthirsty savages, to a destination as remote as the moon from the civilization they knew, had sunk in, between the dreaming and the doing, as a fool's errand.

A few families, with their wagonloads of belongings, did show up at Sapling Grove, however, and by the time they departed in the second week of May 1841, the Bidwell emigrant train consisted of sixty-nine people, including five women and several children, a dozen wagons, many mules, horses, and yokes of oxen.

The journey took six months, following the Oregon Trail route along the South and North Platte to Fort Laramie, Wyoming; to the Sweetwater River, across South Pass of the Rockies, to Soda Springs at the northernmost bend of the Green River. There, Bidwell's party split, a few over half continuing on with a group of missionaries and their guide to Fort Hall in Idaho, thence to Oregon, Bidwell's half drifting southwest toward the Humboldt River. They toiled across the Utah and Nevada wastelands until in mid-October they reached the eastern escarpments of the 13,000-foot Sierra Nevada range. By then they were eating their oxen and mules to survive and praying there would be no early winter in the mountains.

On November 1, after struggling blindly over half a continent, Bidwell and his thirty-one pilgrims crossed the Sierra into the San Joaquín Valley and a few days later, with the last of their wagons abandoned and with miraculous luck, found John Marsh's rancho in the parched eastern foothills of the Coast Range.

They had arrived in a drought, crops had failed, cattle were starving for grass, and their welcome wore thin quickly. Bidwell said, "After our company had encamped near his [Marsh's] house for about two days and a small hog and bullock had been killed for us, he began to complain of his poverty. . . . We had already paid him five-fold in powder, lead, knives, etc."

Marsh charged Bidwell and his party three dollars each for "Mexican passports," and was delighted to see them leave.

"Marsh was a creature of undeterminable impulse and his vagaries drove the emigrants quickly on," wrote Sutter biographer Julian Dana, but Bidwell got the last word when he wrote a memoir of his California days in 1892. "Marsh," he said, "is perhaps the meanest man in California. . . . There is not a person in California who does not dislike the man."

After his party split up again, half this time heading for the San Joaquín River to spend the winter hunting, and half departing for Pueblo San José, a village about forty miles to the south, Bidwell got directions from Marsh to New Helvetia.

"We had already heard that a man by the name of Sutter was starting a colony a hundred miles away in the Sacramento Valley," Bidwell wrote, and with three others started out. Marsh told them the journey would take two days but it took eight. They were afoot, it was winter, and the dim paths were awash in a cold rain. They were three days without food; game was plentiful but the powder for their flintlocks had gone damp. They camped in sodden, makeshift arbors huddled around their fires and when they reached Sutter's headquarters cabin on November 28, 1841, they were as desperate as when they trudged into Marsh's rancho a month earlier.

"Sutter received us with open arms and in a princely fashion," Bidwell remembered, "for he was a man of the most polite address and the most courteous manners."

The two men became instant friends, then colleagues, and the relationship, which never seems to have had a serious rift, benefited both. In Bidwell, the shrewd Swiss found an educated, self-made frontiersman, pleasant, well-spoken, honest, and tireless. Bidwell's first impression of the empresario was that the man had "a fine and commanding presence," and was generous to a fault. The latter trait he found particularly touching. Sutter, he wrote, "employed men, not because he always needed and could profitably employ them, but because in the kindness of his heart it simply became a habit to employ everybody who wanted employment."

Bidwell's loyalty to his employer remained immutable in the good and hard times to come.

Sutter offered the American a clerkship at the fort and never had cause to regret the faith he placed in him nor the responsibilities he heaped upon him. He taught Bidwell a workable Spanish, turned over to him the fort's chaotic ledgers, invoices, bills, and correspondence; put him in charge of the Fort Ross operation and Hock (Hoch, or "Upper") Farm, a satellite of Sutter's Fort on the Feather River; and made him majordomo of New Helvetia.

In a short time, Bidwell learned that his employer was "immensely—almost hopelessly—involved in debt." The "ridiculously low price" of $30,000 he had paid the Russians for Fort Ross and the post at Bodega Bay, was actually nearer $100,000 with interest included, Bidwell said, and the payments in wheat were made impossible by drought and crop failure. Sutter's solution had been to plant more acreage in grain, buy more cattle and horses on credit, and the lumber and hardware for a flour mill, everything driving him deeper in the red.

The purchase of Fort Ross carried with it more than a huge mortgage. Some Mexican authorities and Californios feared that Sutter was arming his settlement with the brass cannons, muskets, and powder stores from Ross, as if preparing for a siege. Bidwell said the rumors were made worse by the growing number of foreigners, mostly American drifters with a small mix of honest settlers, who were making New Helvetia their headquarters.

In fact, Sutter had his own fears, chief among them that a new governor sent to Alta California might look enviously upon his little empire and try to dispossess him. In such a precarious time, he was comforted by the arrival of the Bidwell party, seeing it as signaling the advent of an American migration to California that might exceed that moving to the Oregon country. The Americans represented reinforcements, strength in numbers, and through the perfect circumstance of its location, Sutter's Fort stood ready to welcome these newcomers as they struggled over the Sierra.

"Everybody was welcome—one man or a hundred, it was all the same," Bidwell said.

ONE EVENT RECORDED by John Bidwell that may have escaped Sutter's notice in 1841 occurred near Pueblo de Los Ángeles when a French-Canadian trapper named Baptiste Ruelle, formerly employed by the Hudson's Bay Company, found gold in some beaver streams he was working. Bidwell said the "mines" discovered "proved too poor" and that Ruelle later came up to work at Sutter's Fort.

THREE

THE SERVANT OF THREE MASTERS

JOHN SUTTER REJOICED that the first party of Americans to cross the Sierra Nevada landed in the lap of New Helvetia. John Bidwell told him to look for more when the spring grass was ready along the Platte River. Then, he said, others will point their wagons and stock out on the Oregon Trail and many will drop south, as he had done, to cross the mountains into California by way of Sutter's Fort.

That the Yankees were coming came as no surprise to the Swiss. Nearly every Californio and foreigner in the province knew it, and many of both groups welcomed the idea as the only remedy to the malignant neglect of California by its mother country. Some of the native-born preferred independence, or a takeover by the British, but an American intervention seemed the inescapable destiny of their beloved land.

Bidwell claimed that Sutter's American leanings were never in question: "The object of his admiration was the Republic of the United States. He was always an American at heart and longed for the day when Mexico and her revolutions would, as he believed, lose California to the United States." In fact, the Missourian said, Sutter's "one glaring fault" surfaced in his pro-American candor: "Because of it, the Mexicans began to early view him with suspicion. . . . [His] attitude was so friendly and his fort so invariably the headquarters of all Americans reaching the Pacific coast, that his actions fostered jealousy and hatred among the native Californians."

But Sutter's loyalties were slippery: He was a German-Swiss with Mexican citizenship who had flirted with the British, French, and Russians, and who now professed a strong American allegiance. He had the appearance of a man shuffling through his passports to identify the one that would give him the best advantage. If Mexico had been powerful, not so divided by revolution, and more attentive to its distant province, Sutter might have made the most of his pledge of fealty to the mother country.

No opportunity arose to test this, however. Both native and adopted Californian had long ago ceased worrying about Mexico, viewing the governors it sent to the Pacific province as little more than jumped-up tax collectors, the central government and its perpetual state of revolt an embarrassment. Californians were not even interested in their own provincial politics, often as turbulent, in a miniature way, as those of the homeland. Californians, at least the *gente razón*, led a leisurely life in a bountiful land, not much concerned with such abstractions as equality or democracy, but making the most of the greatest abstraction of them all—freedom.

No gift of foresight was required to see that enterprising hands were reaching for California and that Mexico's grasp on it was fatally weakening.

In 1842, Manuel Micheltorena, a close associate of Mexico's peripatetic President Antonio López de Santa Anna, was appointed to the California governorship. The new chief executive, well-meaning and friendly, but lazy and indecisive, disembarked at San Diego with a collection of three hundred "soldiers" who were shortly to cause his undoing. These rough conscripts were called *cholos* by irate Californios after they learned that most were thugs and freed convicts from the backstreets and *calabozos* of Mexico City. Within a year of their arrival, and after the citizenry had suffered robberies, rapes, and murders by the *cholos*, former governor Juan Alvarado and General José Castro, the prefect of Monterey, engineered a revolt against Micheltorena. This insurrection culminated in a ludicrous "battle" at Cahuenga Pass near Los Angeles on February 20, 1845, with casualties including a decapitated mule, a wounded horse, and Manuel Micheltorena, who raised the white flag and agreed to take his ruffian soldiery and himself back to Mexico City.

There were other casualties as well.

John Sutter, unwounded and unrepentant, was taken to Los Angeles as a prisoner by the victors but freed soon thereafter to return to the Sacramento. He had formed a friendship with Micheltorena, had hopes the governor might increase his land holdings in the Sacramento Valley, and feared that if his erstwhile sponsor Alvarado and the anti-American José Castro rose to power they might expel him and other foreigners from California. So, when news of the brewing revolt reached New Helvetia, Sutter organized twenty-eight men into a volunteer company to support the governor and had them paraded and inspected in San José, the temporary capital. From Micheltorena he received fifty muskets, some carbines and ammunition for his men, and for himself the rank of "captain of the Sacramento Militia."

His military career at an abrupt end at Cahuenga Pass, Sutter and his men were freed from jail and decamped north while the new rulers of California installed themselves in office. The military chief Castro located in Monterey; the new governor, Pío Pico, four hundred miles south in Los Angeles, with Alvarado pledging loyalty to both. Pico, a homely, pockmarked, unassuming former ranchero and civil leader among the *abajeños* (southern residents) of Alta California, was destined to be the last Mexican governor of the province and to have a shorter reign than Micheltorena. Pico denounced all Yankee influences in the province and advocated a French or British alliance to block American colonization and save the province from the "miserable Republic of Mexico." He viewed American settlers as "lawless adventurers" and "avaricious strangers," and in a telling diatribe that says much of the indolence and lack of ambition of Californios of the time, he sought to protect the "thoughtless and merry lives" of his countrymen: "We are threatened by hordes of Yankee emigrants," he said. "Already the wagons of these perfidious people have scaled the almost inaccessible summits of the Sierra Nevadas, crossed the entire continent and penetrated the fruitful valley of the Sacramento." He continued in what appeared to be a veiled reference to John Sutter: "They are cultivating farms, establishing vineyards, erecting mills, sawing up lumber, building workshops and a thousand and one other things which seem natural to them but which Californians neglect or despise—we cannot stand alone against them."

Besides Sutter, the "they" in Pico's statement referred to men like John Marsh, Bidwell's "meanest man," whose cattle spread lay on the flanks of Mount Diablo, and Moses Bradley Carson, Kit's half-brother, who came to California in 1832, became a Mexican citizen, and established a rancho on the Russian River.

By the time of the Micheltorena affair, many of Sutter's workers and neighbors had used New Helvetia as their conduit to the Sacramento Valley and with Sutter's encourgement and advice found a watered square of land to begin a squatter's farm. Several of these men, and Sutter's aide-de-camp and closest associate, John Bidwell, were conspicuous members of Sutter's "legion" which surrendered at Cahuenga Pass. And many, including a long-faced, moody, New Jersey carpenter and wheelwright named James Marshall, would, in a year or so, be identified by Pico and Castro as *Osos*—participants in the Bear Flag Revolt.

A year after the overthrow of Micheltorena, William L. Todd, a nephew of Mary Todd Lincoln who had settled in the Sacramento Valley, wrote in a letter home, "If there are any persons in Sangamon [County, Illinois] who speak of crossing the Rocky Mountains to this country, tell them my advice is to stay at home. There you are well off. You can enjoy all the comforts of life—live under a good government and have peace and plenty around you."

Todd knew of Governor Pico's pronouncements from Los Angeles, and said of them, "The Mexicans talk every spring and fall of driving the foreigners out. . . . There will be a revolution before long. . . . If here, I will take a hand in it."

Another participant in the Micheltorena coup was a man named Pablo Gutiérrez, about whom nothing is known except that he had a

modest grant of land somewhere on the Yuba River, a branch of the
Sacramento above the fort, and that he worked for Sutter. In March
1844, about a year before the Cahuenga dust had settled, Gutiérrez
reported to John Bidwell that he had found gold on the Bear River, a
stream flowing out of the Sierra foothills northeast of the fort. This
news may have been reported to Sutter but nothing came of it.

ON MARCH 6, 1844, John Charles Frémont with his guide, Kit Carson,
and a party of twenty-four men, made a sudden appearance at Sutter's
Fort.

The son-in-law of expansionist Senator Thomas Hart Benton of
Missouri, Frémont's star was ascending as a lieutenant of the Army
Topographical Corps. Born in Savannah, Georgia, he was now thirty-
one, a celebrated explorer of the American West, a brilliant leader in
the rough company of mountain men on trail and in camp. Married
to the vivacious Jessie Benton, and comfortable in Washington social
circles, where his gracious southern charm surfaced, elsewhere Frémont was imperious and demanding, often terse and outspoken when
silence and diplomacy would have better served him.

His appearance in Sutter's midst that spring day was, so the
explorer said, a dire necessity. He and his men had crossed the plains
and central Rockies at South Pass, explored the Great Salt Lake, and
reached Fort Vancouver in the Oregon country as planned. But on
the return journey, hunger and fatigue had forced them to detour
from their intended route home to St. Louis. They had drifted south
to the Sacramento Valley, were given directions by Indians to "Captain" Sutter's Fort and now, nine months from the start of the expedition, needed horses and mules to replace the thirty lost in the
mountains before they could move on.

The expedition had far exceeded what had been expected of Fré-
mont by his superiors in the Topographical Corps, particularly in his
surveying of the Great Basin between the Rockies and the Sierra
Nevada. His work and maps preceded a notable migration on the
Oregon Trail, as many as 1,500 souls, most headed for the Willamette
Valley of Oregon, but a significant number bound for California.

Sutter was overjoyed to have the explorer and the mountain Nim-
rod, Kit Carson, as his guests and treated them royally.

The Governor of the Fortress of New Helvetia, as he sometimes styled himself, at first impressed Frémont. Sutter, now stout, with a fringe of gray-blond hair around his balding crown and a clipped salt-and-pepper moustache, had become a cherubic "margrave of the Upper Sacramento," as Frémont's biographer Allan Nevins called him. He excitedly exchanged news, conducted his guests around his domain, and treated them to a banquet of salmon, venison, fort-grown bread and vegetables, topped by toasts with a good Rhine wine he had saved for such an occasion.

In touring New Helvetia and listening to his host, Frémont made mental calculations: Sutter had thirty white men, mostly Americans, employed, and forty uniformed Indians on duty at the gate to the fort. He had twelve Russian cannons on the walls and muskets, carbines, and ammunition for eighty men in his armory. There were wheat fields and orchards all about; corralled cattle, horses, and mules; and within the fort proper a hive of shops, storehouses, and sleeping quarters. Sutter's Fort was as strategic as Bent's, and as well-provisioned and defended. Small wonder Commodore Charles Wilkes, whose officers had visited Sutter in 1841, wrote in his report that the Swiss "was using all his energies to render himself impregnable" and that the Americans in California regarded the fort as a rallying point in the event Mexico decided to eject them from the province.

To Frémont, the Swiss also had an impressive record of straddling the fence between his Mexican overlords and the foreigners, particularly the Americans, who were arriving, as yet in a thin stream, to the fort on the American River. Sutter's talent in this regard was diminishing, however, as New Helvetia stood as a 49,000-acre mote in Mexico's eye, its proprietor *persona non grata*, the more so after the botched Micheltorena affair. Governor Pico and General Castro were said to have offered Sutter $100,000 for the fort, stock, and improvements to the land, but had been turned away. He had compounded this diplomatic outrage by suggesting that the Mexican government should allot parcels of land to the Americans along the San Joaquín, Stanislaus, and Merced River valleys. Perhaps two leagues per person, he advised, and if that idea did not appeal he was prepared to offer parcels of his own holdings to the newcomers.

While arrogant toward those whose sanctions had made his little empire possible, Sutter found ways to massage the toes he trod upon: He reported Frémont's arrival at the fort to Mexican authorities, as well as to Consul Thomas O. Larkin, with the result that the government in Monterey sent a party of officials north to intercept the explorer. Upon receiving news of this, the Swiss deftly pirouetted and warned Frémont that a Mexican delegation was en route to question him. After accepting drafts for the purchase of twenty-five horses, sixty mules, thirty head of cattle, and five milch cows, on March 22 Sutter watched the explorer and his party march southward toward the San Joaquín Valley, some days ahead of the Mexican dignitaries.

Frémont did not leave in good humor. He had accused some of his own men of theft, but the Swiss, as magistrate of New Helvetia, found them innocent after hearing the evidence. After he departed the lieutenant of topographers learned to his fury that Sutter hired them to work at the fort.

The Pathfinder would return in December 1845, his exploration work ostensible, his real work that of *agent provocateur*, and in his dealing with the Swiss, his humor had not improved.

THOMAS O. LARKIN, trader and and general agent for American shipping firms at Monterey, kept an eye on events in the north and learned much from his rambling correspondence with Sutter. Larkin was an articulate observer and able administrator and businessman who managed to maintain cordial associations with Mexican authorities, Californios, and foreigners in the province, talents recognized by the State Department in Washington. In 1842, he was named United States consul to Alta California and in October 1845, became a "confidential agent"—a *sub rosa* informant—for the American government. His mission, to "conciliate" the people of California, meant he would find diplomatic ways to prepare them for an American takeover. His progress reports and observations on the state of the province were to be directed to James Buchanan, secretary of state in the new administration of President James K. Polk.

With the help of vice consul William Leidesdorff at Yerba Buena, Larkin covertly gained friends and adherents to what he called "the American Cause." He wrote copious reports to Secretary Buchanan of such matters as the presence of Hudson's Bay Company ships in Monterey Bay and the gossip that the British were encouraging Mexico City to send troops into California to hold the restless population in check. He shared the president's Anglophobia and believed England hoped to establish a foothold, a colony of some kind, in California, part of a larger scheme to threaten American interests all along the Pacific coast from Oregon southward. Occasionally he let his views be known in the eastern press, as in his writing to the *New York Herald* in 1845, "We must have it [California], others must not."

Sutter wrote Larkin regularly, buying farm implements and other goods (always on credit to be followed by apologies for late payments on his debts), commenting on newly arrived pilgrims—giving names, birthplaces, and occupations of each—and on such news as the visits of the Wilkes party, Frémont, and other important passers-through. Nor did the Swiss hesitate to boast that he had always thrown open the gates of his fort to the Americans and would continue to do so no matter the cost. He was counting on a bigger stream of Americans funneling through the fort in 1845 and said, "Nothing can stop this migration. In case of opposition, they would fight like lions."

BEGINNING IN THE spring of 1845, Sutter was to serve three masters in as many years: the first, a man he never met who lived on the opposite side of the continent; the second, a man he had met who returned to plague him; the third, the inanimate nemesis of gold, which made him rich before it ruined him.

The first of the human masters who for two years seemed to control Sutter's lot and destiny was James Knox Polk, a North Carolinian and Jacksonian Democrat who took office as the eleventh president of the United States in March 1845. This rigid, suspicious, and humorless man announced that he would serve but a single term in office, and that he had a clear and rigid agenda of what he intended to accomplish in those four years. He would revise the protective tariff of 1842, a matter few outside Washington could comprehend; he would settle the Oregon boundary dispute with England; and the United States under his leadership would acquire California and other Mexican territories above the Rio Grande and from the Rocky Mountains to the Pacific. He wished to make these acquisitions by diplomacy and America's formidable purchasing power. He said he hoped to avoid war to win these lands—530,000 square miles of Mexican territories, 258,000 of the Oregon country, increasing the area of the United States by one-third—but made no secret that he was prepared to force their attainment if necessary.

From his secluded enclave in the north, Sutter was an eager receptacle for news but knew nothing of Mr. Polk's plans. What news he received was many months old by the time it reached the fort. He had to be content listening to the tales told by the new immigrants who reached the Sacramento Valley after months on the trails from the Missouri frontier; hearing political stories from his friends in Yerba Buena who got them from the masters of trade vessels which had battled Cape Horn to reach the Pacific; and depending upon Tom Larkin in Monterey to add a few lines of national information in his letters to New Helvetia.

For Sutter, 1845 began with Cahuenga and the demise of the Micheltorena affair, and ended with the return of John C. Frémont, the second of his masters, to the fort. Between these brackets, remote from his view and knowledge, Mexico and the United States were beating a path to war.

Frémont came in with Kit Carson and a company of Indians and shag-bearded frontiersmen on December 10. Just six months earlier, accompanied by his father-in-law, Senator Benton of Missouri, he had visited President Polk in the executive mansion. "California stood out as the chief subject in the impending war," Frémont wrote later, "and with Mr. Benton and other governing men at Washington it became a firm resolve to hold it for the United States."

Frémont had mounted his third Western expedition in St. Louis in June, 1845, and by the time he reached Bent's Fort in August had Kit Carson, now thirty-two and still agile as a cat, at his side together with a front-riding guard of a dozen Delaware Indians. By the time he marched west he had added fifty other "experienced, self-reliant men," two hundred horses and pack mules, and two hundred fifty head of cattle.

The journey began as a survey of the Arkansas and Red Rivers, to find a good wagon road to California by way of the Great Salt Lake and Sierra Nevada; then the mission seemed to be to find an easier route between Oregon and the interior of northern California. But by the time the explorer reached Sutter's Fort with his small but well-armed army the prevalent suspicion held that he had been sent to California to foment rebellion.

Sutter claimed to have no idea why the explorer had returned.

"War had not yet been declared," he recalled, "and Frémont acted strangely toward me, as if he were guilty of some crime. Every few days he would move his camp further up in the valley." He said, perhaps too naïvely, "It never occurred to me that Frémont had come to the country to prepare the way for the annexation of California to the United States."

In May, a naval officer stopped at the fort, borrowed horses and Sutter's favorite mule, and with a guide found Frémont and his men at Klamath Lake above the Oregon border. There the courier delivered a packet of messages, the contents of which were never divulged but which are believed to have been written by President Polk, Secretary Benton, and perhaps the secretaries of state and war. Their effect was to turn the explorer back to California where he set up camp near the Marysville Buttes north of Sutter's domain.

For nearly a year, Frémont had control of New Helvetia, and until the explorer himself became a prisoner at Sutter's Fort, held John A. Sutter a virtual captive there.

FOUR DAYS AFTER Frémont received his secret dispatches at Klamath Lake, and unknown to him or anybody in California, the United States had declared war against Mexico and deployed an army to the Rio Grande. Before the end of May, a force of dragoons marched out of Fort Leavenworth, Kansas, headed for California. United States naval forces were already patrolling the Pacific coast, poised to come ashore as aggressors, and reinforcements were sailing toward the Horn, the Peruvian port of Callao, Honolulu, and the waters off San Pedro, Monterey, and Yerba Buena.

Sutter's Fort, meantime, became the staging area for the short-lived Bear Flag Revolt, for which Frémont gave at least tacit encouragement. It was a futile affair that culminated on June 13, 1846, when a band of about thirty American settlers in the Sacramento Valley seized the military garrison and stores of the mission town of Sonoma and took the eminent General Vallejo prisoner. The rationale behind the takeover was a widespread rumor that General José Castro, the military commander of Mexican California, had gathered a force and was marching toward the Sacramento Valley to evict the Americans from their farms and ranches.

The successful capture of Sonoma, and the now assured advance of

Castro's cavalrymen to quell the revolt, spurred Frémont to action. He ordered Sutter to raise the Stars and Stripes over the fort, dispatched a letter east resigning his army commission, and set about organizing volunteers into what he called the "California Battalion."

Sutter reacted to the turmoil by renouncing his Mexican citizenship and working to convince Frémont of his allegiance to the United States. Of the commandeering of his property, he insisted, "I remained in absolute command of the Fort; no attempt was made to supercede me." But while he maintained "I was generally regarded as an officer of the United States Government," to others he appeared to be Frémont's prisoner-of-war.

The volunteers, with the original exploration party and the Bear Flaggers as nucleus, included over two hundred other settlers and Sutter employees. By June 25, 1846, Frémont had taken command of the battalion and two weeks later learned that the United States and Mexico were officially at war. The occasion for this news was the seizure of Yerba Buena on July 9 by a naval shore party from the American sloop-of-war *Portsmouth.*

AMONG THE OTHER American ships which reached the Pacific coast that summer, two were of special significance. The frigate *Congress* anchored in Monterey Bay on July 25. This man-of-war was the flagship of Robert Field Stockton, commodore of the Pacific Squadron and designated by the War Department to command all military forces in California. Then, on July 31, the *Brooklyn*, a civilian vessel of 370 tons, entered San Francisco Bay and disembarked 270 men, women, and children, most of them Mormons led by Samuel Brannan of Maine. This disquieting church elder and fiercely ambitious businessman, before learning that Mexico and the United States were at war, had hoped to establish an independent Mormon colony in California. The dream faded when the ship reached Honolulu and vanished altogether when the passengers filed down the gangway at Yerba Buena and spied the Stars and Stripes fluttering over a low, red-tiled building fronting an open square, and marines guarding the plaza and customs house. Brannan, standing at the rail of the *Brooklyn* and seeing the evidence that the American conquest of California had begun, is said to have flung his hat to the deck and growled, "There's that damned rag again!"

He was a hat-flinging kind of man, impatient at all times and capable of explosive fury when his schemes fell apart, as they so often did in his schemer's life. The Mormon colony idea was half-baked and he knew it, but he had many other ideas in mind to make a profit.

DURING THE SIX-MONTH "conquest" of California—a word too powerful for the acts involved—Sutter was immobilized. His fort, appropriated by Frémont and his battalion, was used as headquarters and supply depot for a series of forays south to Monterey and the outskirts of Los Angeles. Finally, on January 13, 1847, at Cahuenga Pass, a place of sad memory to Sutter, the explorer forced the surrender of the Californians, nine months before the end of the fighting in Mexico.

The occupation of California had involved sharp battles in the south, Mexican lancers against American dragoons commanded by General Stephen Watts Kearny, at San Pascual, San Gabriel, and La Mesa, riverside map-specks on the route to San Diego. There had also been a particularly acrimonious battle for command of the American invasion forces between Kearny and the navy's Commodore Stockton. Frémont was eventually to be crimped in a vise between the two contenders, stripped of all authority, his brief tenure as the first military governor of American California at an end. He was placed under house arrest for insubordination and mutinous conduct.

With the California fighting over and a treaty signed, Yerba Buena was renamed San Francisco by its first American *alcalde*, an officer from the *Portsmouth*. The town now had a population of 459, three hundred of the inhabitants American or European, and 157 ramshackle homes, business places, and warehouses.

IN JUNE 1847, Frémont dawdled at Sutter's Fort, waiting for Kearny's arrival, and Stockton's. As soon as the commanders gathered, with their officers and escorting troops, the long march east would begin, past the appalling remains of the Donner party, lost in the Sierra snowdrifts the previous winter, and on to Fort Leavenworth. There the explorer would learn for the first time the details of his arrest and that he would face court-martial in Washington.

While he waited, a messenger arrived from Monterey bringing a letter and a deed from Thomas O. Larkin. Frémont had sought the consul's assistance in finding a tract of land below the southern end of San Francisco Bay and near the San José mission where he intended building a home and rancho for himself, Jessie, and their children. He gave Larkin $3,000 to purchase the property but the deed Larkin forwarded was for ten square leagues of land, over 44,000 acres, somewhere in the wilds of the San Joaquín Valley, high in the western Sierra foothills at the gateway to the Yosemite forests. This land, nearly the size of New Helvetia, was owned by former governor Juan Alvarado and called "Las Mariposas" for its profusion of butterflies. Frémont was furious: the tract was huge but inaccessible. He wrote back indignantly, telling Larkin that he didn't want it and would have the San José land or his money returned.

Sutter meantime had his fort back, and among his first business ventures was to find a place with plenty of timber and water to build a sawmill. Lumber was in demand everywhere, especially in booming San Francisco, and regular schooner runs down the Sacramento to the bay with a cargo of planking would return a handsome profit.

He had the perfect man to find the spot and build the mill. James Marshall, who had come to the fort with his box of tools in July 1845 in a party from Oregon's Willamette Valley, had been immediately hired by Sutter. Marshall was a carpenter, and when not working at the fort tended a few head of cattle at his small ranch on a creek north of New Helvetia. Lately, when not on the march with Frémont's California Battalion, the lean and distant New Jerseyan worked at the fort as a "mechanic," fixing what was broken, from wagons to spinning wheels, and hammering up new outbuildings for the fort.

On May 16, 1847, Sutter sent his skilled employee out to scout along the American River and find a site for a sawmill.

II

DISCOVERY

There is thy gold—worse poison to men's souls,
Doing more murther in this loathsome world,
Than those poor compounds that thou mayest not sell.
—Shakespeare, *Romeo and Juliet*

FOUR

A NOTIONAL KIND OF MAN

JOHN BIDWELL, OVERSEER at New Helvetia, believed the sawmill plan was James Marshall's and had no confidence in either the plan or its author. "Surely no other man than Marshall ever entertained so wild a scheme as that of rafting sawed lumber down the canyons of the American River, and no other man than Sutter would have been so confiding and credulous as to patronize him," Bidwell wrote many years afterward.

Whether or not the mill had been Marshall's idea it had Sutter's approval and financial backing—from an empty wallet, a condition that never dissuaded him from spending. By the end of the war his debts amounted to at least $80,000, a staggering sum in 1847. He was staking his future on a great American migration to California and dreamed at his desk of projects to pay off what he owed so he could borrow more. Six miles up the American River from the fort he had a flour mill under construction in which twenty *fanegas* of grain could be ground each hour. The mill employed men from the Mormon Battalion who had straggled into San Diego in January, too late to participate in the fighting. They had drifted to New Helvetia hoping to make a few grubstake dollars so they could move on to Brigham Young's settlement at Salt Lake, and Sutter, always magnanimous beyond his means, put them to work. Lumber was in short supply, the trees around the fort long ago hewn and whipsawed for buildings. He knew he could make a solid profit from planking in San Francisco, had to locate new timber sources for his own fencing and construction, and needed to devise a system to avoid the ruinous cost of sawing it by hand from the coastal redwoods and transporting it by schooner to the bay. He had explored the idea before, sending parties out in 1846 to search for a likely mill site. The nearest timberlands and water power lay in the Sierra foothills above the fort and to the east, outside the New Helvetia grant. He told Marshall to reconnoiter in that direction.

Bidwell's schoolmaster pessimism probably had to do with the expense in labor and materials a sawmill would entail, the haphazard planning behind it, and his observations that Marshall was "highly eccentric, and perhaps somewhat flighty," a kinder assessment of the man than was held by others, including Sutter.

Virtually all who knew Marshall saw something strange and off-center about him.

He came west in 1831, when he was twenty-one, from Lambert-ville, New Jersey, were he had been trained by his father as a carriage maker, wheelwright, and carpenter. He spent time wandering in Indi-ana, Illinois, and Missouri, and settled for a time near Fort Leaven-worth, working a piece of land on the west side of the Missouri River above its confluence with the Kansas. The fevers and agues common on the Western frontier in the day forced him to move on and in May 1844, with a horse, toolbox, bedroll, and a change of clothes, he attached to an Oregon-bound wagon train. After winter-ing at Fort Hall, the Hudson's Bay Company rest stop in the Oregon country, Marshall reached the Willamette Valley in the spring. What little of the farmer he had in him has been wrung out in Kansas and he did not tarry long among the nesters in Oregon, choosing to tag along with a party headed for California.

At Sutter's Fort he found immediate work. In time he took over a patch of ground near the Marysville Buttes north of the fort and cap-tured a few head of wild cattle, but lost what he had built up during his absences with the Bear Flaggers and Frémont's California Battalion.

By the time he returned to work for Sutter in July 1846, Marshall was in his thirty-sixth year, a good physical specimen, lean, broad-chested, sun-burnt, and given to wearing white linen trousers covered by buckskin leggings, a faded linsey-woolsey shirt, moccasins, a Mex-ican serape and sombrero. He was coarse-featured, with a high fore-head, brown hair and eyes, a set of scraggly whiskers around his chin and downturned mouth. H. H. Bancroft, who appears to have met Marshall after the gold rush, wrote of the man's "penetrating eyes," which the historian described as "by no means unintelligent, yet lacking intellectuality, at times gloomily bent on vacancy, at times flashing with impatience."

Opinions of him from coworkers and contemporaries varied. Henry W. Bigler, a Virginian lately discharged from the Mormon Battalion who worked for Marshall in building the sawmill, said he was "an entire stranger to us, but proved to be a gentleman." Bidwell thought him insane but in a harmless way and said "he was neither vicious nor quarrelsome." Others found the carpenter's ill temper and dark moods intolerable and shied away from him.

Bancroft said he was "taciturn, with visionary ideas, linked to spiritualism, that repelled confidence, and made him appear eccentric and morbid; he was restless, yet capable of self-denying perseverance that was frequently stamped as obstinacy."

Sutter, who probably knew his unstable mechanic better than all others, said Marshall "was like a crazy man," and provided an example of the man's "visionary ideas." He recalled a time when the two were seated in a San Francisco restaurant when Marshall said, "Are we alone?" Sutter replied that yes, they were alone. "No, we are not," Marshall said. "There is a body there which you cannot see, but which I can. I have been inspired by heaven to act as a medium, and I am to tell General Sutter what to do."

Clearly, this café babble did not impress the empresario. Sutter was no spiritualist, regarded Marshall as "a very queer person," and wouldn't have taken orders from him under any circumstances. Sutter did, however, have enough faith in his employee's skills to enter into an agreement with him, the paper prepared by the Swiss's very dubious amanuensis, John Bidwell. Sutter would supply the money and labor, Marshall would superintend construction of the mill, work there after it was completed, and would receive one-fourth the profits from the sale of the lumber.

Marshall recalled that he set out on May 15 (Sutter said the 21st), 1847, "with my rifle, blanket, and a few crackers to eat with the venison. . . . I was to build the mill, and he [Sutter] was to find provisions, teams, tools, and to pay a portion of the men's wages. I believe I was at that time the only millwright in the whole country." Typically, in this version, of the many he gave of the event to newspaper writers and others in later years, Marshall failed to mention those who accompanied him—a Indian guide named Nerio, and men named Treador, Graves, and Gingery.

They ascended the American River to a point about forty miles above the fort and, a short distance up the south fork of the river, found a valley of rolling hills covered with thick stands of pine, balsam, and oak trees. Marshall was enthusiastic about the place; he estimated the lumber would have to be hauled only eighteen miles to be rafted down the American to the fort.

Sutter later learned the place was called "Culuma," translated as "beautiful vale" by local Indians and soon Americanized to Coloma.

The first order of business was to send for more laborers, including some Mormons and Maidu Indians, to help cut trees for the construction of log shelters for the winter. These included one sizable house with a passageway to a smaller one, built a quarter-mile from the mill site. The larger building housed the workers, the smaller served as quarters for Peter L. Wimmer, supervisor of the Indian workers, and his wife Jennie, who agreed to serve as cook. Sutter sent up ox-carts filled with provisions—haunches of mutton, Graham flour, peas, wheat, coffee, brown sugar, and the like—plus mules, a flock of sheep, kegs of gunpowder, more saws, axes, picks, and spades, and nineteen more men. He inspected the work in the autumn and was satisfied with the progress, writing in September to army lieutenant Henry W. Halleck, acting secretary of state for conquered California, "One of my flour-mills, driven by water power, is now in operation; the other, and the saw-mill, are erected and will be in operation in thirty days."

The sawmill took a little longer than he guessed, but by New Year's Day, 1848, the wooden housing had been erected, the iron machinery and wheel installed, and a ditch dug to channel water from the river. This tailrace presented problems. It had to be forty to fifty rods long and required gunpowder blasting and hand digging to loosen the red soil so that large rocks and boulders could be removed. A sluice gate was then constructed and opened at night to wash away the smaller debris.

IN THE EARLY Sunday afternoon of January 23, 1848, Marshall strolled out along the tailrace of his three-week-old sawmill, inspecting the work and chatting with James Brown, one of his Mormon employees.

"It was my custom in the evening to raise the gate and let the water wash out as much sand and gravel through the night as possible," the carpenter recalled, "and in the morning . . . I would walk down and, shutting off the water, look along the race and see what was to be done, so that I might tell Mr. Weimar [Wimmer], who was in charge of the Indians, at what particular point to get them to work for the day."

At the spot where the race entered the American River, Marshall stopped to inspect the jumble of slatey rock near the tailgate, a mass six feet wide by fifteen or more long. Brown said the mass was "so soft that it might be scaled up with a pick, yet too solid to be carried away by the water."

Marshall peered down through a foot of water at the shale-like detritus and, in one of the accounts he gave of the historic moment, said, "My eye was caught with the glimpse of something shining in the bottom of the ditch. . . . I reached my hand down and picked it up; it made my heart thump, for I was certain it was gold."

In fact, he was more hopeful than certain, as his subsequent account proved. But he may have known of the earlier gold sightings by Baptiste Ruelle near Los Angeles in 1841, and Pablo Gutiérrez, on the American River in 1844. Both men eventually became employees at the fort and the carpenter had heard from them, or perhaps another worker, that the American River valley had some features ideal for gold deposits.

"The piece was about half the size and of the shape of a pea," Marshall said. "Then I saw another piece in the water. After taking it out I sat down and began to think right hard. I thought it was gold, and yet it did not seem to be of the right color: all the gold coin I had seen was of a reddish tinge; this looked more like brass." Still, he said, gold leaped to his mind and "I trembled to think of it!" He placed the shiny pea on a river stone and hammered it with another. "It was soft, and didn't break: it therefore must be gold, but largely mixed with some other metal, very likely silver; for pure gold, I thought, would certainly have a brighter color."

He told one of the workmen he believed the shale contained "minerals of some kind," and pointed out that the hills around the race contained white quartz and that this was an "indication of gold." He did not explain the source of this sudden expertise.

Brown, who thought his boss "rather a notional kid of man," was sent to the cabin he was sharing with five other Mormon workers to bring a pan or bowl to wash some of the rocks they had picked out of the race. When this experiment failed to reveal more bright specks, Marshall told the men to hoist the gate and let the water flow. When they closed the gate in the morning and checked the race again, he said, "I believe we will find gold or some kind of mineral here."

Early next day the Mormon workers heard a pounding noise—

Marshall shutting the gate of the tailrace—but went about their breakfast before reporting to the sawpit. En route they found him standing by the race, hat in hand. "Boys, I have got her now," he told them.

Brown stepped foward as Marshall opened his hat. Inside were ten or twelve small gold scales. The Mormon bit a piece, which he estimated was worth about fifty cents, held it aloft and exclaimed, "Gold, boys, gold!" Later, by his account, the men found some hot-burning manzanita firewood and ran a test on a hammered-flat yellow scale. "It was plated as thin as a sheet of notepaper," he said. "The heat did not change its appearance in the least."

Marshall's recollection differs. He said he sent an Indian to the cabin to fetch a tin plate, washed some of the tailrace dirt and separated enough grains of gold to cover a ten cent coin. During the evening he told his workers, "Boys, I believe I have found a gold mine," to which somebody replied, "I reckon not; no such luck."

More tests were run. A worker named Azariah Smith had a five dollar gold piece and the bitten and flattened specimens were compared to it. Jennie Wimmer, the only woman in camp, was making soap in a clearing by her cabin and Marshall had her boil the largest pea-shaped piece in lye. It did not discolor. Mrs. Wimmer later charmingly described the gold as resembling "a piece of spruce-gum just out of the mouth of a school-girl."

Marshall and some workmen collected about three ounces of the yellow metal in pinhead-sized, grains, flakes, and peas, and on the 25th of January the carpenter rode down to Sutter's Fort with the gold burning a hole in his pocket.

Sutter's numerous versions of how he learned of the Coloma discovery vary in detail but it appears that Marshall rode into the fort in a driving rain late in the afternoon of January 28 and entered the office as Sutter sat at his desk writing a letter. The carpenter stood dripping in the doorway and abruptly asked for a private audience with his employer and sawmill partner. Sutter led him to a private room where, according to the Swiss, this tableau took place:

"Are you alone?" Marshall unnecessarily asked.

"Yes."

"Did you lock the door?"

"No, but I will if you wish it."

"I want two bowls of water," Marshall said.

Sutter rang for a servant and two bowls of water were brought in.

"Now I want a stick of redwood, and some twine, and some sheet copper."

"What do you want of all these things, Marshall?"

"To make scales."

"But I have scales enough in the apothecary's shop," Sutter said, and had a pair brought in.

Sutter recalled that he thought "something had touched Marshall's brain, when suddenly all my misgivings were put at an end by his flinging on the table a handful of pure virgin gold. I was fairly thunderstruck. . . ."

"I believe this is gold," Marshall said, "but the people at the mill laughed at me and called me crazy."

The two ran more tests. First, aqua fortis (nitric acid) was applied to the grains and tiny nuggets; next, using Archimedes's test for relative specific gravity, silver Spanish dollars were put on the scales and balanced by the gold specimens, then both were immersed in water— down went the dust, and up the silver coins. Finally the entry on gold in a volume of the *American Encyclopedia* was consulted. "I declared this to be gold of the finest quality, of at least twenty-three carats," Sutter remembered. "After this Mr. Marshall had no more rest nor patience, and wanted me to start with him immediately for Coloma; but I told him I could not leave, as it was late in the evening and nearly supper time." Marshall then wrapped his serape around him, pulled down his sombrero and without waiting for a meal, rode off into the rain.

The Swiss got little sleep. Bancroft, who interviewed Sutter many years later, wrote, "Though he knew nothing of the magnitude of the affair, and did not fully realize the evils he had presently to face, yet he felt there would soon be enough of the fascination abroad to turn the heads of his Men, and to disarrange his plans. In a word, with prophetic eye, as he expressed himself to me, he saw that night the curse of the thing upon him."

On the morning of January 29, Sutter struck out for the sawmill on a mule, his walking stick under his arm, a gift of jackknives for his workmen, and a jug of *aguardiente* for the non-Mormons among them. About halfway to Coloma he found Marshall waiting for him on the trail.

At the mill, after Sutter was settled in a borrowed cabin, they inspected the race. "On our arrival, just before sundown," he recalled, "we poked the sand about in various places, and before long succeeded in collecting between us more than an ounce of gold, mixed up with a good deal of sand."

That night, with the gate raised, water ran through the race until morning when Sutter, Marshall, Henry Bigler (who called Sutter, then age forty-five, "Old Cap") and some other workers examined the channel on their knees, picking out specks and flakes of gold. They walked along the riverbank and found traces of gold in rivulets and ravine beds. "I myself, with nothing more than a small knife, picked out from a dry gorge . . . a solid lump of gold which weighed nearly an ounce and a half," Sutter said.

He returned to the fort the following morning. On that day, January 31, 1848, Sutter would have been fascinated, probably pleased, to learn the fate of his old nemesis John C. Frémont. After an eighty-three-day court-martial in Washington, the topographical officer was found guilty of mutiny, disobedience of a superior officer, and "Conduct to the Prejudice of Good Order and Military Discipline" for antagonizing his superiors in the late conquest of California. President Polk approved the charges but remitted the sentence of dismissal from the service and ordered Frémont released from arrest to "resume his sword, and report for duty."

The proud explorer, however, was not receptive to the presidential largesse, said he was innocent of all charges, and resigned from the army on February 19, "as a matter of honor." He announced he would soon return to California to investigate the land he owned in the Sierra foothills.

Meantime, before leaving Coloma, Sutter called his workers together. "I told them that I would consider it as a great favor if they would keep this discovery secret only for six weeks," he said, and promised to double their wages for their secrecy. But, since he had paid them nothing to date, the vow seemed empty. One of his Mormon employees wrote from Salt Lake City in 1894, "While we, the members of the Mormon Battalion, did do the hard labor that discovered the metal, it is also true that we were in Sutter's employ at that date, and that we did not get paid for our labor. . . . I worked 100 days for the firm, and never received a farthing for it."

Sutter left Coloma with little hope that his workers would keep their word and that he would have a six week hiatus after which both his flour mill and sawmill would be in full operation. In later years he lamented that on the mule ride home from Coloma, "instead of feeling happy and contented, I was very unhappy, and could not see that it [the gold discovery] would benefit me much, and I was perfectly right in thinking so." He said that as soon as the gold news passed around the fort, "my laborers began to leave me, in small parties first, but then all left, from the clerk to the cook, and I was in great distress; only a few mechanics remained to finish some very necessary work. . . ."

James Brown summed up the immediate aftermath of Marshall's "glimpse of something shining": "To Sutter's capital and Marshall's shrewd sagacity has been given the credit of the great gold discovery in California. The facts are that James W. Marshall discovered the first color, and in less than an hour six Mormons found color as well, and in less than six weeks had discovered it in hundreds of places that Mr. Marshall had never seen, the most notable of which was Mormon Island, to where the first rush was made."

AMONG THE SAWMILL laborers, Henry Bigler became the first true prospector, scarcely waiting for Sutter's downtrail dust to settle before he set out on foot with a musket and some biscuits under the pretext that he was going duck hunting. He proceeded to dig around in streamside rocks until he had accumulated nearly two ounces of gold flakes, knotted them in his shirttail and showed them to the others. On February 6, Bigler and another of the Mormon crew collected more specks from rock crevices and made a scale to weigh them, using a silver Mexican *real* as a counterweight.

Besides protecting his mill operations from shutdown, Sutter needed time to resolve a greater problem: The sawmill lay in what American authorities were calling "Indian lands" and to make a claim to it and the gold in its vicinity seemed to require some kind of official document. In the days following his first visit to the mill, Sutter called on the Culumas, Yalesumnis, and some of their Indian neighbors to parley. From them he obtained a three-year lease of a ten- or twelve-square-mile tract of land, with Coloma at the epicenter, on payment of some shirts, hats, handkerchiefs, shoes, flour, and other articles, and a promise of a cash payment of $150 a year.

On February 8, sixteen days after the gold discovery, Sutter selected one of Marshall's sawmill supervisors, a veteran of the First Dragoons named Charles Bennett, to ride down to Monterey with the Indian lease paper to appeal to Colonel Richard B. Mason, military governor of California, to pronounce it legitimate. Bennett also carried a gold sample but apparently was told to try to secure the land, mill, pasturage, and all mineral rights, with the lease paper as "proof" of the legitimacy of the claim, and to say nothing of the gold discovery unless necessary.

In Bancroft's words, Bennett "was too weak for the purpose," having six ounces of gold in a buckskin bag "which, by the time he reached Benicia, became too heavy for him."

En route to San Francisco Bay, the ex-dragoon stopped at a store run by Edward von Pfister, among the *Brooklyn* passengers who had come to California with Sam Brannan. When somebody in the store announced that a seam of coal had been discovered near Mount Diablo, Bennett blurted out: "Coal? I have something here which will beat coal, and make this the greatest country in the world." He then produced his sack of gold dust and passed it around.

When he heard the story, Robert Baylor "Long Bob" Semple, a six-foot-eight-inch-tall Kentuckian, prominent among the Bear Flaggers, said, "I would give more for a good coal mine than for all the gold mines in the universe," but he was practically alone in the opinion.

Once he reached San Francisco, Bennett appears to have shown the dust to Brannan, then to one Isaac Humphrey, who had mined gold in Georgia. Humphrey looked at the Coloma sample, pronounced it genuine, and rode down to Monterey with Bennett.

They arrived on March 4 and in an audience with Mason the gold came quickly out of the bag. The governor's aide-de-camp, the redheaded, twenty-eight-year-old Lieutenant William Tecumseh Sherman, flattened a piece with a hatchet. It was gold all right, he decided. As to Sutter's letter, Mason replied that California was yet a Mexican province★, held by the United States by right of conquest, and that no American laws yet applied to it, much less the land or preemption laws, which could only apply after a public survey.

★The Treaty of Guadalupe Hidalgo, signed outside Mexico City on February 2, 1848, would not be ratified until the end of May and would not be known in California until August.

Moreover, he said, the United States did not recognize the right of Indians to lease land.

Bennett stowed the governor's reply and his gold specimen in his saddlebag and headed back to New Helvetia. The Georgia miner Humphrey must have rode ahead, for he reached Coloma on March 7 and immediately took up prospecting.

At Sutter's Fort in the third week of February, Henry Bigler told three of his former battalionmates about the gold, pledging them to keep mum. The men turned up at the sawmill a few days later and soon made the first significant gold strike after Coloma, on the south fork of the American River halfway between the mill and the fort. They named the place Mormon Island and by April 12, when Bigler visited the makeshift camp, seven men were washing as much as $250 in dust a day from the stream using Indian blankets as sieves. Bigler himself was finding an ounce a day in the Coloma vicinity and on some good days as much two ounces, worth over $30, a month's wages for a *paid* laborer.

The secret Sutter hoped could be contained for six weeks was out, and had been from the moment James Marshall stood by the tailrace and declared, "Boys, I have got her now." Even Sutter himself, who knew he had the most to lose by leaking the news, could not restrain himself. On February 10, eleven days after he sought the six-week pledge of confidence, he wrote to General Vallejo, "I have made a discovery of a gold mine, which, according to experiments we have made, is extraordinarily rich." Vallejo's reaction was generous, considering his long-held view that the Swiss mistreated the Indians around the fort and usurped the general's authority in the area. He told Bidwell after receiving the letter, "As the water flows through Sutter's mill race, may the gold flow into Sutter's purse."

The news flowed faster than water or gold. The matter simply could not be contained, no matter the pledges and precautions. Even the forty miles that separated the fort and the Coloma mill site served as a chamber for the gold echo.

ONE OF MARSHALL'S sawyers, an Englishman named James Gregson, wrote many years after his labors at Coloma, "We had salt salmon and boiled wheat, and we, the discoverers of gold, were living on that when gold was found, and we were suffering from scurvy afterward."

To this claim, Bancroft wrote testily that Gregson was not at the mill when gold was found, and as for the scurvy claim, said that it was "an affliction this man might undergo almost anywhere, being, if like his manuscript, something of a scurvy fellow."

Even so, keeping the mill workers fed became a problem after game in the area had been thinned out by hunters, and provisions had to be transported to the mill by the wagonload. One of Sutter's trusted teamsters, Jacob Wittmer, a Swiss, hauled supplies and food-stuffs to Coloma in mid-February and proved that Sutter's faith in his countryman was unwarranted.

At the mill, as Wittmer chatted with Jennie Wimmer, camp cook, lye soap maker, and wife of the supervisor of the Indian laborers, one of her boys announced, "We have found gold up here." Wittmer scoffed at this until Mother Wimmer produced a sample and gave it to the teamster.

Upon returning to the fort, Wittmer made tracks to the outbuild-ing store rented by Sam Brannan and operated by Brannan's partner, C. C. Smith, and tried to buy a drink of *aguardiente* with the pinch of dust.

According to Sutter, this exchange ensued:

"What is that? You know very well that liquor means cash money," Smith said.

"This is money," the teamster said. "It is gold."

"Damn you, do you mean to insult me?" roared Smith.

"Go to the Fort and ask the Captain if you don't believe me."

Whereupon the proprietor took the pinch to Sutter who had to confirm that it was genuine.

"I should have sent my Indians," Sutter later lamented about Wittmer's mission to Coloma, to which Bancroft added, "It seems that the gentle Swiss always found his beloved aborigines far less treacherous than the white-skinned parasites."

In his diary that day, Sutter wrote that Wittmer "told every body of the Gold mines."

So, for that matter, did C. C. Smith, who passed the word to Sam Brannan.

John Bidwell heard so many gold reports he rode up to Coloma in March, became convinced of the authenticity of the stories, rode back and told friends at the fort. Later, while building his rancho on the Feather River he discovered a particularly rich placer that came to be known as Bidwell's Bar.

In San Francisco, Army Quartermaster Joseph Folsom learned of the discovery, saw some gold samples, and at first thought they were pieces of mica. He dismissed a story told him about a man who had dug, pried, and chipped twenty ounces of gold in eight days' work along the American River, but he felt a panic might be in the works, even if one chasing fool's gold. He wrote to Lieutenant W. T. Sherman in Monterey that he'd not be surprised if he ended up the sole resident of San Francisco, adding that "only lunatic asylums can affect a cure of the present ills of the body politic—at least until hunger drives all the visionary fools from the gold 'diggins.'"

In March, less than two months after the discovery, Edward Cleveland Kemble, the teenaged editor of Brannan's San Francisco weekly, the *California Star*, watched a launch from New Helvetia, crewed by Kanakas and "Digger Indians," make a landing off the foot of Clay Street, a short distance from the beach. He hoped to get an item of news about Sutter's wheat crop being planted that spring, and as he told the story later, he questioned several passengers as they disembarked from Sutter's boat. None seemed to know anything about wheat but one man did offer to show the editor something he had brought with him and waved Kemble into a nearby store.

"I cannot remember this man's name," Kemble wrote. "He had been in the employ of Captain Sutter, but had come down on business of his own. He was black-eyed, bushy bearded, lank and nervous, and chewed tobacco as a school girl chews gum—as though the lower jaw was run by clock-work. Standing at the counter, he took out a greasy purse, and out of it protruded a little rag, which he carefully opened, disclosing a few thin flakes of a dull yellow metal. 'That there,' said he in an undertone, 'is gold, and I know it, and know where it comes from, and there's plenty in the same place, certain and sure!'"

Kemble did not take the matter seriously, perhaps sharing Captain Folsom's belief that the purported gold was mica, perhaps iron pyrites, sulphuret of copper, or other *ignis fatuus*. The *Star* carried no mention of gold until March 18.

At the sawmill meantime, Marshall's men continued to find gold in riverside seams and crevices, devising wooden scales to balance it against a Mexican *real de plata*, worth about a quarter-dollar.

By April, Sutter's diary reflected his anxiety. The sawmill was forgotten; Coloma and its environs were the "mines" and "Mountains":

"Many men went up to the gold mines. . . ."

"More and more people flocking to the mines."

"Great hosts continue to the Mountains."

Bancroft likened the spread of the gold news to the attraction of vultures to carrion: "As when some carcass, hidden in a sequestered nook, draws from every near and distant point myriads of discordant vultures, so drew these little flakes of gold the voracious sons of men." The "little scratch upon the earth" represented by Sutter's sawmill, "touched the cerebral nerve that quickened humanity, and sent a thrill throughout the system," and, he said, "if Satan from Diablo's peak had sounded the knell of time; if a heavenly angel from the Sierra's height had heralded the millennial day; if the blessed Christ himself had risen from that ditch and proclaimed to all mankind amnesty—their greedy hearts had never half so thrilled."

FIVE

THE SORDID CRY

Gold Mine Found. *In the newly made raceway of the saw-mill recently erected by Captain Sutter on the American fork, gold has been found in considerable quantities. One person brought thirty dollars worth to New Helvetia, gathered there in a short time. California, no doubt, is rich in mineral wealth; great chances here for scientific capitalists. Gold has been found in every part of the country.*
                    —The Californian, March 15, 1848

THE EXTRAORDINARY FACT that California had two English-language newspapers in operation at the time of the gold discovery was traceable to the timely arrival of the two aforementioned ships on the Pacific coast in the summer of 1846.

On July 26, when Commodore Stockton's flagship *Congress* sailed into Monterey Bay, the war with Mexico was seventy-four days old, the Bear Flag Revolt had ended, the customs houses at Yerba Buena and Monterey were flying American colors, Frémont was moving his California Battalion down from Sutter's Fort, and a force of dragoons under General Kearny had begun a grueling march across the Southwestern deserts toward San Diego.

Among the officers of the *Congress* probably none had a busier schedule than the frigate's chaplain, Walter Colton, a fifty-one-year-old self-styled "teetotaler and sin-chaser." Added to his shipboard duties of tending to the seamen in sick bay and preparing Sunday services, Stockton selected him to serve as *alcalde* of the town, with duties as mayor, magistrate, and chief lawman, requiring much paper shuffling and report writing.

For all this activity, Colton could not resist the call of his other profession. Before he received his naval commission from President Andrew Jackson in 1830, he had been a newspaperman, writing and editing in Philadelphia and New York. In Monterey, to his delight, he learned the whereabouts of a "stiff and rheumatic" Ramage printing press manufactured in Boston, salvaged it, and with some fashioning of parts out of pieces of tin and scraping and tightening with a jack-knife, he tinkered until he fixed it. He also found a half-keg of congealed ink and a box of rusty type slugs, and was able to press some test paper under the machine's iron screw.

Robert Semple, the giant Kentuckian and vagabond dentist and printer, happened to be in Monterey at the time Colton was getting the Ramage running, and became the chaplain's partner in launching California's first newspaper.

The *Californian* debuted on August 15, 1846, an 11¾ × 10¼ sheet, a little larger than common foolscap, printed on coarse packing paper used in a cigar shipment. The two-column sheet had no rules and had to be printed without use of the letter "w"—not used in the Spanish language—substituting for it two "v's," and when these ran out, side-by-side "u's," giving flavor to an item about "a gale that struck Key Uuest."

The first edition of the *Californian* contained a long prospectus of its purpose, some three-month-old news of the war with Mexico, and a few lines on the arrival of "la frigata *Brooklyn*" at Yerba Buena. The paper was scheduled to appear every Saturday morning, the subscription rate five dollars a year.

"This is the first paper ever published in California, and though issued upon a small sheet, it shall contain matter that will be read with interest," the proprietors confidently announced.

Within five months, the *Californian* had competition.

On the last day of July 1846, just five days behind the *Congress's* advent at Monterey, the merchant vessel *Brooklyn*, six months out of New York Harbor, plowed into San Francisco Bay, rounded Telegraph Hill with its windmill-like signal house, and anchored in a cove, sharing water with an American man-of-war already berthed there. The *Brooklyn* carried the first shipload of American emigrants to reach California: 130 men, 60 women, and 40 children, most of them Mormons, the first complement of what their self-anointed leader, Samuel Brannan, had envisioned as a profitable Latter-Day Saints empire on the Pacific.

The son of an Irish emigrant whiskey distiller, Brannan was born in 1819 in the coastal village of Seco, Maine, and as a teenager apprenticed in the printing trade. His family became followers of Joseph Smith in 1832, when Smith's Church of Jesus Christ of Latter-Day Saints had but a nine-year history, and young Sam became much more a Mormon than he subsequently admitted. In his early career as a journeyman printer he served for a time as publisher of a weekly Mormon newspaper. His proselytizing speeches, writings, and general stump-and-hall commotion for the church earned him the short-lived name "Young Lion of Mormonism." He briefly toyed with "plural marriage"—the Mormon euphemism for polygamy—and fell from grace for a time as church elders determined to rid Mormonism of this ruinous practice. He even traveled to Nauvoo, in the western Illinois swamplands, and met Brigham Young and others of the Saints' hierarchy. "Brother Brannan," sometimes "Elder Brannan," was regularly mentioned in Young's correspondence, usually connected with some controversial statement or deed committed by the obstreperous printer from Maine.

Brannan's motives in taking passage to California may have been purely business, as he later insisted, but the real Mormons in his entourage were escaping the hatred and fear directed toward their sect that culminated in the June 1844, murder of Joseph Smith in a Catharge, Illinois jail. Soon after, Brigham Young, Smith's successor at the head of the church, made plans to lead the Saints out of Nauvoo in search of a homeland in the West and suggested to Brother Bran-

nan that he might lead a flock by sea to California for the same purpose.

He leapt at the idea, no doubt seeing monetary profits in the venture and himself as a sort of Mormon emperor on the Pacific.

By the first week of February 1846, the same week that Brigham
Young sent the first company of Saints and their wagons across the
Mississippi, Brannan had 230 of the faithful signed up for the voyage,
their passage fees and investment money financing most of the enterprise. He chartered the *Brooklyn*, hired a skipper, and oversaw the
cargo stowed below decks: enough farm implements for eight hundred men; a printing press and stock of paper and ink; machinery for
saw- and flour mills; carpenter and blacksmith tools and grindstones;
school books and slates; dry goods, twine, iron, brass, and copper
sheets; tinware and crockery; foodstuffs and barrels of water; two
milch cows, forty pigs, countless chickens, and hay and feed for the
animals.

The *Brooklyn* crashed its way around Cape Horn on April 10,
stopped to trade at Juan Fernández Island off the Chilean coast, and
reached Oahu in the Sandwich Islands on June 20.

Brannan's first sighting of the "damned rag" that he and his flock
were fleeing occurred in Honolulu during their stayover in the islands
to reprovision and take on water. The flag was flying from the mast
of the American naval frigate *Congress* laying at anchor in the road-
stead. The *Brooklyn*, after finding a berth nearby, was boarded by a
party of *Congress* officers, including the commander of the United
States Pacific Squadron, Robert F. Stockton. This notable informed
the ship's company and passengers that the United States was at war
with Mexico and that California was in an "unsettled state." He
warned those intending to disembark in San Francisco Bay to carry
arms.

BEFORE THE END of 1846, Brannan had supervised construction of
two flour mills at Yerba Buena, started a farm at the juncture of the
San Joaquín and Stanislaus Rivers, performed the first English-
language sermon and marriage ceremony in California, and published
the second newspaper in the province.

He had stowed in the cargo hold of the *Brooklyn* a press manufactured by Hoe & Company, a typebox, and a paper and ink supply. He

rented a gristmill on Clay Street in Yerba Buena, described as "about the largest frame structure in town," to establish "S. Brannan, Printer," in business as of September 5.

One of the non-Mormon passengers on the ship, seventeen-year-old Edward Cleveland Kemble, became Brannan's assistant, and helped worry the stout iron and wood Hoe machine up the stairs to the mill's loft. Kemble was the son of the editor of the Troy, New York, *Budget*, had worked for his father and later on the New York–based *Prophet*, a Mormon weekly. An associate who knew him in 1848 later reminisced that the teenager "was attired in a neatly fitting light-blue roundabout or jacket; his nether garment was of fine black cloth. . . . His cheeks were like a ripe peach, rosy and smooth as velvet." The colleague said "E. C." was "a gentleman of strict integrity and moral worth . . . unassuming, generous, and magnanimous; and we will venture to say that he never wrote a word that would cause a blush to tinge the cheek of the most fastidious maiden, for his writings were always couched in elegant phraseology and of high moral tone."

On October 24, S. Brannan, Printer, issued an "Extra in Advance of the *California Star*," a double-sided sheet, 13 × 18 inches in size, known in the trade as a "shinplaster," after the paper money of the era that was valued at less than a dollar. The first weekly number of the *Star* appeared on January 9, 1847, and was priced at six dollars for a year's subscription.

The paper's first editor, Elbert P. Jones, was depicted by the subsequent editor, Edward C. Kemble, as "a thin, green-spectacled, bilious-looking personage who came into the country with the Fall immigration of the year before. He emigrated, it is believed, from Tennessee, where he had practiced law. He was a man of very fair abilities, and his editorials are written with a good deal of nervous energy and a sort of uncouth felicity of thought and expression."

Jones promised that "While on the editorial tripod, all private pique and editorial feeling and jealousy will be laid aside," and Brannan promised "to support no sectarian dogmas." Yet the first issue of his paper made January 9 appear as a sort of All-Saints Day. Brannan addressed to his "Beloved Brethren" his conviction that California was the ultimate destination of Brigham Young's hegira out of Nauvoo and said, "As soon as the snow is off the mountains we shall send a couple of men to meet the emigration by land, or perhaps go

myself." He cautioned the Saints Brigham Young was leading overland to bring thick clothing, and said that he and his people were "all
busily engaged in putting in crops for them to subsist upon when
they arrive," this apparently a reference to the "settlement" he was
farming on the San Joaquín River. He also told about "twenty males
of our feeble number" who had "gone astray after strange gods,
serving their bellies and their own lusts," and of four persons excom-
municated from the church during the passage for "a list of griev-
ances . . . of the most disgusting character." Finally, he cautioned the
Saints among his readership that "Governor Boggs is in this country,
but without influence even among his own people that he emigrated
with." This was a reference to Lilburn W. Boggs, governor of Missouri in the 1836–1840 period when the Saints were driven from the
state under his anti-Mormon administration. Boggs (who was married to a granddaughter of Daniel Boone) and his family emigrated
overland to California in 1846 and later settled in the Napa Valley,
north of Yerba Buena.

For all the high-mindedness in his statement of purpose, Brannan
kicked up a miniature press war with his rival, the *Californian*, by
touting his *Star* as "the only paper of a respectable size and typo-
graphical appearance now published on the whole coast of the
Pacific. . . . We have the only office in all of California in which a
decent looking paper can be published." The *Californian* responded,
saying the *Star* was "published and owned by S. Brannan, the leader
of the Mormons, who was brought up by Joe Smith himself, and is
consequently well qualified to unfold and impress the tenets of his
sect."

A species of yellow journalism rose up a half-century before the
term was invented when editor Elbert Jones of the *Star* assailed editor Walter Colton of the *Californian* as "a lying sycophant," his assistant, Robert Semple as "an overgrown lickspittle," and their weekly,
in a superfluity of commas, as "a dim, dirty, little, paper."

But by April Jones had spent his verbal powder and ball and
"retired" from the *Star* editorship, his place taken by E. C. Kemble,
who described himself as "one of the printers in the office, a mere
lad, who came out on the *Brooklyn* with Saml. Brannan, though not
one of the Mormons." He said the exchange of editors "was not
affected without harsh words, even blows, as most revolutions are
accomplished." Jones, he said, "threw up the editorship with a

tremendous explosion of wrath and other raw materials of his editorials. . . . [He] was summarily ejected from the office. Nobody was much hurt, but the scene was highly ludicrous."

One of Jones's last acts was to help compose a special edition of the *Star* aimed at potential emigrants in Missouri and the east. The paper, dated April 1, 1848, carried a long essay by Victor Forgeaud, a native of North Carolina who emigrated overland with his family in 1847, and was now a San Francisco physician and amateur scientist who had recently assayed some gold specimens for John Sutter. Dr. Forgeaud's article, titled "The Prospects of California," stated that those sick and wounded healed faster in California, that fruits and vegetables grew with abandon in the wilds there, and that gold awaited those with the perseverance to find it. "We saw, a few days ago," he wrote, "a beautiful specimen of gold from the mine newly discovered on the American Fork, in the Sacramento Valley. From all accounts the mine is immensely rich, and already we learn that gold from it collected at random and without any trouble, has become an article of trade in the upper settlements. This precious metal abounds in this country." He predicted "a Peruvian harvest of the precious metal."

Brannan had 2,000 copies of the special edition printed up and paid to have them carried east by an express party led by Kit Carson who was taking military dispatches to Washington. The papers reached the Missouri frontier in July and Washington in August, and while Forgeaud's article was reprinted in St. Louis and in some eastern seaboard papers, his Peruvian prediction stirred little interest.

GOLD, AND NEWS of it, remained contained in California for most of 1848. Brannan's *Star* acknowledged it briefly in March, borrowing from Dr. Forgeaud—"So great is the quantity of gold taken from the mine, recently found at New Helvetia, that it has become an article of traffic in that vicinity"—but a month passed before the paper actually investigated the find.

And others remained skeptical: "I doubt, sir," one bystander wrote in the *Californian*, "if ever the sun shone upon such a farce as is now being enacted in California, though I fear it may prove a tragedy before the curtain drops. I consider it your duty, Mr. Editor, as a conservator of the public morals and welfare, to raise your voice against the thing. It is to be hoped that General Mason will despatch the volunteers to the scene of the action, and send these unfortunate people to their homes, and prevent others from going thither."

On April 15, Kemble, chief skeptic of the *Star*, announced in the paper his intention to "ruralize among the rustics of the country for a few weeks," packed his kit and rode out to New Helvetia. Sutter welcomed him and accompanied the editor on a jaunt around the fort, fields and vicinity, leading the way astride his beloved mule Lucy, pointing with his gold-headed cane, fanning himself with his wide-brimmed planter's hat.

He took Kemble to Coloma on April 19 and the two made a desultory effort to sieve gold from the riverbank using an Indian basket. The few particles they retrieved did not impress Kemble although on April 22 he reported, "We have been informed, from unquestionable authority, that another still more extensive and valuable gold mine has been discovered towards the head of American fork, in the Sacramento Valley. We have seen several specimens taken from it, to the amount of eight or ten ounces of pure virgin gold." By the time he returned to Coloma he had fallen under the gold spell, stopping at a San Francisco hardware store to buy an iron pan, already the method of choice to prospect in streambeds. But no pans were available: sly Sam Brannan had bought them all. Originally priced at twenty cents, they were selling at the Brannan and Smith store at Sutter's Fort for a half-ounce to an ounce of gold—eight to sixteen dollars, depending on the number in stock.

Still, Kemble made only a flippant reference to what his paper had been "informed," writing on May 6, "Great country, fine climate; visit this great valley, we would advise all who have not yet done so. See it now. Full-flowing streams, mighty timber, large crops, luxurient clover, fragrant flowers, gold and silver."

Bancroft could not explain Kemble's myopia toward the greatest news story of the century unfolding in his back yard, writing, "Whether he walked as one blind and void of intelligence, or saw more than his interests seemingly permitted him to tell, does not appear."

As late as mid-May, Kemble editorialized that the rush for gold was "a sham . . . got up to guzzle the gullible."

His employer disagreed.

Brannan knew of Marshall's discovery as early as February when the Coloma sawmill supervisor Charles Bennett carried some samples to Monterey, and from reports by his partner C. C. Smith at their store outside Sutter's Fort. Erwin Gudde, editor of Sutter's New Helvetia diary, states that Brannan "went to the mines" (the Coloma sawmill) on May 4, returned to San Francisco on the seventh, and "A few days later a man ran through the streets of S.F., swinging his sombrero in one hand and a bottle of gold dust in the other and shouting at the top of his voice: 'Gold! Gold! Gold from the American River!'" This man, Gudde said, was none other than Samuel Brannan, "advancing his interests by a subtle method which suspicious persons had attributed to Sutter himself. These shouts seemed at last to have made the people of California realize that digging for gold was more than just a fad. Within a few weeks the country went crazy."

The story of Brannan's theatrics had several permutations but seems to have been witnessed by Henry Bigler, the Coloma sawmill worker, who recorded the date of the hat-waving and shouting as May 12. Brannan, accompanied by his partner C. C. Smith, visited the diggings at Mormon Island in early May, and was convinced, Brannan is supposed to have said, that "there was more gold than all the people of California could take out in fifty years."

He returned by way of Benicia, the settlement on the north side of the Carquinez Strait named for the wife of Mariano Vallejo. Upon stepping from the ferry onto the Montgomery Street wharf, said Bigler, Brannan held up a quinine bottle of gold dust and swung his hat as he marched along, yelling the news of "Gold on the American River!"

The effect of Brannan's gold cry may have been only slightly exaggerated. Bancroft states that San Francisco had about 600 males in its population of 900 that day of Brannan's foray and three days later the number was 2,000, most passing through in scurrying toward Sutter's Fort and the American River. "The conversion of San Francisco was complete," he wrote. "Those who had hitherto denied a lurking faith now unblushingly proclaimed it; and others, who had refused to believe even in specimens exhibited before their eyes, hesitated no longer in accepting any reports, however exaggerated. . . ."

Sutter marked the date of the "gold rush" as May 19, a week after Brannan's shout, writing that on that date "the great rush from San Francisco arrived at the fort," and on that date his regiment of servants dwindled to a single Indian boy. "All was in confusion," he said.

Brannan displayed his bottle of gold at his two-story redwood home at Washington and Stockton Streets in San Francisco and invited several Mormon elders over to view it. The occasion was the last time he pretended to be one of the faithful. Later, when he began assessing a 10 percent fee from Mormon miners, he claimed it was not a tithe but was based on "the right of discovery"—a mysterious phrase lost on the Mormon leaders in Salt Lake City and everybody else except Brannan. A story that attached to him in those days of his apostasy is that he collected so much money in the Sacramento Valley in the early months of the gold rush Brigham Young wrote him inquiring when the funds would be forthcoming for the "Lord's Treasury." Brannan is said to have instructed Young's courier, "You tell Brigham that I'll give up the Lord's money when he sends me a receipt signed by the Lord."

Very soon, Brannan would not need his fraudulent tithe. He stocked his store at the fort with picks, shovels, pans, and other mining tools, cornering the market for such essentials, and during the last months of 1848 and the year following, the store's sales had profited him $150,000.

IRONICALLY, THE FLIGHT to the "diggings," potentially a story that would cause a newspaper circulation to skyrocket, spelled the end of California's two weeklies.

Kemble of the *Star* reported on May 20 that "Fleets of launches left this place on Sunday and Monday, closely stowed with human beings. . . . Was there ever anything so superlatively silly?" But on the 27th he began sounding the knell, reporting that "Stores are closed and places of business vacated, a large number of houses tenantless, various kinds of mechanical labor suspended or given up entirely and nowhere the pleasant hum of industry salutes the ear as of late." He said that the desertions had the appearance of a curse that "had arrested our onward course of enterprise," and that "everything wears a desolate and sombre look, everywhere all is dull, monotonous, dead."

The *Californian*, which had moved from Monterey to San Francisco some months before, closed on May 29, announcing in its last number that "The majority of our subscribers and many of our advertisers have closed their doors and places of business and left town. . . . The whole country from San Francisco to Los Angeles and from the seashore to the Sierra Nevada resounds to the sordid cry of Gold! Gold! GOLD! while the field is left half-planted, the houses half-built and everything neglected but the manufacture of shovels and pickaxes and the means of transportation to the spot where one man obtained $128 worth of the real stuff in one day's washing, and the average for all concerned is $20 per diem."

By June 1, with two thousand men (double that number by the end of July) spread out along the South Fork of the American River for thirty miles, Kemble turned about, denying he had ever been skeptical, but too late to save his reputation or the *Star* from folding. In 1858, when he wrote a history of California newspapers for the Sacramento *Union*, Kemble wrote about the young editor who did not believe his ears and who, against all evidence to the contrary, "attempted to check the rising waves with a broom."

He wrote of himself in third person: "He was probably honest, both in believing and declaring the 'reputed wealth of that section of the country, thirty miles in extent, all sham,' for the sober truth had been magnified so many hundred times, and was so much out of proportion, that it was not recognizable under any form or coloring. . . . The editor thought he was doing his duty by riding a tilt against the aggregated rumors, as Don Quixote charged the windmills."

On June 10th, eleven days after the *Star* suspended publication, Kemble wrote a "leader"—a page one story—which opened, "The excitement and enthusiasm of gold washing continues—increases." It was his, and the *Star's*, swan song.

Kemble later acquired the type, paper stock, and remnants of the *Californian*, merged these assets with the *Star's*, and in November 1848, now at age twenty, became proprietor of the *Alta California*, and while it prospered went on to launch the *Placer Times* in Sacramento.

ON MAY 25, 1848, Thomas O. Larkin, the former United States Consul in Monterey, wrote a letter while on a business trip to San José. In it he told governor Richard Mason, "I arrived here after two days' travel and . . . everyone has gold or yellow fever. Santa Cruz and

Monterey in 30 days will lose most of their American population, unless bloodshed or fever or ague stop the excitement."

On the same day Larkin wrote his letter, John Sutter quit writing in his diary. It was futile and he saw no reason to record the doleful day-by-day events of his own downfall. He was only forty-five years old, had come to California only nine years past, and now saw that "all my plans and projects came to naught."

At his tannery, a profitable business, the vats were left filled and half-finished leathers were spoiled; the shoe, saddle, hat, and black-smith shops were deserted. "While everybody else was digging and washing gold," he said, "I tried to harvest my wheat crop. With the help of the Indians, I saved at least part of it. Two-thirds of the harvest, to be sure, had to be left in the fields"—this because his Indian field hands were hired away to work for the miners.

His own attempts at mining also came to naught. He became a partner in a gold digging company at Coloma with Peter Wimmer, James Marshall, and Isaac Humphrey, the Georgia miner, but lamented, "I furnished the company with Indians, teams, and provisions, but I soon found that I was losing money and gave up the undertaking." He next set up a gold camp ten miles above Mormon Island on the south fork of the American, and had a hundred local Indians and a large number of Kanakas working in the river bottoms. In a few weeks, however, the place was crowded with other miners and Sutter abandoned it and returned to his fort, an onlooker to his ruination, watching the flood of gold hunters up from the Bay streaming toward the mines.

In May 1848, San Francisco had a population of about nine hundred, two hundred buildings, two fair-sized hotels, twelve stores, a billiard parlor, a tenpin alley, and two wharves. Those seeking the quickest route to the gold fields traveled by water up the Bay by sloop, lighter, rowboat, canoe—"every rickety cockleshell" as Bancroft put it—steering for the Carquinez Strait, thence across to Sausalito by launch and by mule, horse, or shank's mare, via San Rafael and Sonoma into the Sacramento Valley. Another route lay around the southern end of the Bay and through Livermore Pass, named for an English sailor who settled in California in the 1820s.

These early argonauts, the "forty-eighters," followed faint trails and rough roads, using the sun for a compass and mountain peaks as guideposts. Many went to the diggings without a dollar to their name, equipped only with the ubiquitous shovel (the price of which, thanks to Sam Brannan's monopoly, jumped from a dollar to ten and more), neglecting even blankets and food, believing they could simply shovel up some dirt, pick the gold out of it and go on home a rich, or at least richer, man. Since these poor dreamers could not afford the price of a horse or mule, even at fifteen or twenty dollars for a fair animal in the months before similar mounts were *renting* for $100 a week, a common sight was the bedraggled miner walking the whole distance inland and crossing a stream by hanging on to the tail of a comrade's horse.

The few gold hunters with money to spend hired laborers to do the digging, brought tents and boxes of food and clothing, wagons, horses, mules, and yokes of oxen, and suffered only the discomfort of waiting at Robert Semple's ferry at Martínez, which was often inundated with as many as two hundred customers and their wagons and animals lined up to cross San Pablo Bay.

By mid-June San Francisco looked deserted; three-fourths of the male population, in the phrase of the day, had "gone to the mines."

IN MONTEREY TOWARD the end of June, Lieutenant W. T. Sherman of the Third U.S. Artillery and acting assistant adjutant general, prepared to join his commanding officer, Colonel (soon to be Brigadier General) Richard Mason of the First Dragoon Regiment, on a trip to Sutter's Fort and the gold country beyond. Sherman had been present in February when Charles Bennett brought some papers and gold specimens down from New Helvetia and remembered the occasion vividly. Bennett placed a packet on the governor's desk containing about an ounce and a half of a yellow metallic dust and flakes.

"What is that?" Mason said. "Is it gold?"

Bennett said it was indeed gold.

Sherman, who had seen similar specimens in his native Ohio offered to test the metal. He bit one of the larger pieces, then sent for a hatchet and hammered it flat.

"Still," he recorded in his memoir of his California days, "we attached little importance to the fact, for gold was known to exist at San Fernando at the south, and it was not considered of much value."

Throughout the spring of 1848 stories of gold, increasingly fabulous, crept downcoast, talk of men taking fifty dollars, then a hundred, then a thousand, a day in gold from the American River and its byways. Soon, talk turned into deed: people in Monterey and points north toward and around San Francisco Bay were trudging off toward the mines, some well equipped, most not. Worse, for Sherman and his commander, soldiers were deserting their posts, and sailors the ships in the bay, coaxed to the gold country by tales of instant riches.

"I of course could not escape the infection," Sherman wrote, "and at last convinced Colonel Mason that it was our duty to go up and see with our own eyes, that we might report the truth to our Government."

He selected an escort of four soldiers, the governor's black servant Aaron, "a good outfit of horses and pack-mules," and set out with Mason in the last week of June, stopping in San Francisco, where Quartermaster Captain Folsom joined them. The party crossed the bay to Sausalito by launch, visited General Vallejo in Sonoma, and reached New Helvetia on July 2. They found Sutter's Fort nearly deserted. The Swiss told Mason he had only two mechanics remaining, a wagonmaker and a blacksmith, and was paying them an exorbitant ten dollars a day wage. He said he brought in some profits by renting rooms to merchants at $100 a month and had a two-story house on the grounds he was leasing as a hotel for $500 a month.

Mason noted that Sutter was in the process of trying to find the manpower to gather his wheat, an estimated yield of 40,000 bushels, and that flour was already selling at thirty-six dollars a barrel at the fort and expected to go to fifty. He also found that the principal store outside the fort, Sam Brannan's, received $36,000 in gold in payment for its goods between May 1 and July 10.

Sutter prepared a July 4 celebration at the fort for his Monterey guests and invited friends in the New Helvetia vicinity. He had a huge table set in an old armory building on the grounds and had his servants load it with beef, game, fowl, "and all the luxuries which a frontier life could offer," with bottles of sauterne and Madeira a French naval officer had brought in, and plenty of the fort's scalding *aguardiente* for those who could stomach it.

Mason, Sherman, and their escort departed the fort on July 5 and after a hot and dusty twenty-five-mile ride reached Mormon Island in the south fork of the American River. There, to their amazement they found three hundred Mormons toiling in the furnace heat with picks, shovels, buckets, and an early form of a "rocker" that washed and sifted sand and gravel. The hillsides were strewn with canvas tents and brush-and-board shanties, and even a makeshift store was in operation, selling a meager collection of tools and provisions.

"I recall the scene as perfectly to-day as though it were yesterday," Sherman wrote nearly thirty years later. "In the midst of a broken country, all parched and dried by the hot sun of July, sparsely wooded with live-oaks and straggling pines, lay the valley of the American River, with its bold mountain-stream coming out of the Snowy Mountains to the east." There, he wrote, lay a gravel bed and "On its edges men were digging, and filling buckets with the finer earth and gravel." The four men operating the "rude machine" they called a "cradle," he said, "could earn from forty to one hundred dollars a day."

Prominent among the diggers, Sherman said, was Sam Brannan, "on hand as the high-priest, collecting the tithes," and noted that when one of the miners asked Mason, "Governor, what business has Sam Brannan to collect the tithes here?" Mason answered, "Brannan has a perfect right to collect the tax if you Mormons are fools enough to pay it."

Mason also informed the miners, "This is public land, and the gold is the property of the United States; all of you are trespassers, but, as the Government is benefited by your getting out the gold, I do not intend to interfere."

The last six words were evidence of good thinking on Mason's part; he did not have the men or means to interfere and in any event it was far too late to interfere.

The governor and his entourage moved on to Coloma, saw the still-unfinished sawmill and visited with James Marshall and Jennie Wimmer, who showed the visitors a collection of coarse grains of gold, souvenirs of the discovery six months earlier.

They continued the ride up the valley of the American Fork, visiting many small camps in what were called "dry diggings," where water was carried in buckets to wash dirt from dry stream beds, "and where the gold was in every conceivable shape and size, some of the specimens weighing several ounces," Mason said.

At Weber Creek, he told of visiting Weber's store, a selection of goods and groceries laid out in a ramshackle hut, and of a man who came in and picked up a box of Seidlitz Powders (a popular anti-acid) and asked its price. German-born Charles M. Weber, who had come to California with the Bidwell-Bartleson party in 1841 and had cleared a rancho in the San Joaquín Valley, said the powders were not for sale. The customer offered an ounce of gold, then an ounce and a half—twenty-four dollars for a box that cost Weber fifty cents.

Prices were so high, Mason said, that "Indians, who hardly knew what a breechcloth was, can now afford to buy the most gaudy dresses."

The governor was staggered at what he had seen and heard. This stern, handsome, fifty-one-year-old officer of dragoons reported that there were as many as four thousand men, half of them Indians, swarming the Sierra foothills; told of a small ravine that had yielded $12,000 in gold and another spot where two men had taken out $17,000 in two days; said $30,000, perhaps as much as $50,000 in gold, from the tiniest mote to hefty nuggets, was being taken out of a scattering of crude diggings *daily*. He told of John Sinclair, a long-time friend of Sutter's, whose rancho lay three miles above the fort on the north side of the American River. The Scotsman said he employed about fifty Indians to work with close-woven willow baskets on the North Fork, close to its juncture with the main river. In three weeks' time he had profited $16,000. "He showed me the proceeds of last week's work," Mason wrote in his report to Washington, "fourteen pounds avoirdupois of clean washed gold."

By the time the party returned to Monterey, Mason had dispatches awaiting him carrying the official news that the war with Mexico was over and that American and Mexican commissioners were arranging for a peace treaty conference at Guadalupe Hidalgo.

By then, so contagious had the gold fever become, Sherman wrote, that everybody wanted to run off to make a fortune. The volunteer regiments in California, he said, would have deserted en masse had they not been assured of honorable discharges in the offing, and many regular army soldiers did desert, including most of those who had accompanied Mason and Sherman to the gold fields. Only Aaron, among the governor's servants, remained loyal.

One of the deserting soldiers even had the temerity to steal Lieutenant Sherman's prized double-barreled shotgun.

SIX

NED BEALE'S RIDE

IN HIS MONTEREY office, Mason prepared a voluminous report on his gold district expedition and findings, addressed to Roger Jones, adjutant general of the army, in Washington.

"I have no hesitation now in saying that there is more gold in the country drained by the Sacramento and San Joaquín rivers than will pay the cost of the war with Mexico a hundred times over," he stated in transcribing the testimony of John Sutter, John Sinclair, and others at the fort, at Coloma, Mormon Island, Weber Creek, and the miscellaneous camps and diggings, wet and dry, he had visited. He reported the story he obtained upon returning to the military capital, of a Mr. Dye, "a worthy gentleman residing in Monterey," who had himself just returned to the town from the Feather River, a tributary of the Sacramento. This man, Mason said, had joined a company of gold seekers which had worked the river bottoms, creeks, and ravines off the Feather for seven weeks and two days with fifty Indians as "washers." Dye told Mason that that the company's "gross product was 273 pounds of gold," and that his one-seventh share, after expenses, amounted to about 37 pounds, which, Mason said, "he exhibited in Monterey."

The specter of mass desertions from the army preoccupied his professional soldier's mind. Victorious in the war with Mexico, the army in California, few of its soldiery having seen any fighting, was caught up in the tedium of garrison duty while all about it civilians were marching off to the mines and returning with saddlebags, pokes, and bottles filled with gold. Moreover, by mid-1848 prices for everything from a drink of whiskey to a trinket for a wife or sweetheart had shot skyward. Nothing was in the reach of an enlisted dragoon or foot soldier or, for that matter, their officers.

"At no time in the history of our country has there been presented such temptations to desert," Mason told his War Department superiors. "The struggle between *right* and six dollars a month and *wrong* at $75 a day is rather a severe one."

According to Walter Colton, Mason's own staff had thinned to such a degree he was reduced to cooking his own dinner, spending time in the kitchen in his headquarters "grinding coffee, toasting a herring, and peeling onions."

Mason warned that deserters faced little risk of apprehension in the gold country wilderness, that bounties and rewards were trifles "as laboring men at the mines can now earn in one day more than double a soldier's pay and allowances for a month; and even the pay of a lieutenant or captain cannot hire a servant. . . . Could any combination of affairs try a man's fidelity more than this?"*

At the end of July, the governor called upon the people of California to apprehend deserters. He talked about leading a column of dragoons into the mines to search for the miscreants, but too many of his men had obtained furloughs to hunt gold.

The navy's desertion problems were even worse. Commodore Thomas ap Catesby Jones of the Pacific Fleet reported to the secretary of the navy on July 28, "I have no fear of not being able to suppress desertion within ordinary bounds, but to accomplish that end some severe examples may be necessary. Prevention is always better than cure. I shall therefore by much cruising afford as little opportunity as possible for desertion."

But three months later he wrote the secretary from his flagship *Ohio*, "Nothing, sir, can exceed the deplorable state of things in all Upper California at this time, growing out of the maddening effects of the gold mania. I am sorry to say that even in this squadron some of the officers are a little tainted and have manifested restlessness under moderate restrictions imperiously demanded by the exigencies of the times."

Then, on November 2: "For the present, and I fear for years to come, it will be impossible for the United States to maintain any naval or military establishment in California; as at the present no hope of reward nor fear of punishment is sufficient to make binding any contract between man and man upon the soil of California. To send troops out here would be needless, for they would immediately desert. . . . Among the deserters from the squadron are some of the best petty officers and seamen, having but few months to serve, and large balances due them, amounting in the aggregate to over $10,000."

---

*Mason's concerns were not overstated. From July 1, 1848, through the end of 1849, the Army of Northern California lost 716 men to desertion out of a force of 1,290.

With this communiqué the commodore enclosed an advertisement "widely circulated for a fortnight, but without bringing in a single deserter," which announced: "$40,000. A New Gold Discovery. Forty thousand dollars will be paid for the apprehension and delivery to me of deserters from this squadron." The flyer offered sums of from $500 to $2,000 for the apprehension of deserters, the rewards to be "paid in silver dollars immediately on the delivery of any deserter as aforesaid on board other of the ships of the squadron."

Toward the end of his report, dated August 17, 1848, Mason addressed the ticklish matter of levying a governmental "rent" or fee "for the privilege of procuring this gold." He wrote that, due to "the large extent of the country, the character of the people engaged, and the small scattered force at my command," he had resolved "not to interfere but to permit all to work freely, unless broils and crime should call for interference."

Finally, underscoring the magnitude of the gold discovery, Mason recommended that a mint be established somewhere within San Francisco Bay; otherwise, he said, "gold to the amount of many millions of dollars, will pass yearly to other countries to enrich their merchants and capitalists."

Sherman apparently suggested to the governor that his report be dispatched to Washington by special courier, together with other official papers, and advised Mason to send along some gold samples as well. Captain Folsom in San Francisco made the arrangements, purchasing nearly $4,000 in raw gold—230 ounces, fifteen pennyweights, and nine grains, as it subsequently weighed out*—and had it packed in either an oyster can, as Sherman claimed, or a box described as a "tea caddy," according to others.

Folsom also chartered a barkentine, the *Lambayecana*, to convey the courier as far as Payta, on the Peruvian coast.

The officer selected for the mission, Lieutenant Lucien Loeser, a Pennsylvanian in Sherman's Third Artillery regiment, was given a plotted route. He would sail from Monterey to Payta and there board a British coastal steamer bound for Panama. He would cross the Isth-

---

*The gold was measured in avoirdupois ounces (sixteen to the pound), rather than troy ounces (twelve to the pound). When raw gold first appeared in payment for merchandise in California, storekeepers took it at $10 a "common" ounce; by the spring of 1849 the price had increased to $14 and soon after settled at $16 per common ounce.

mus as best he could, and with as much alacrity as possible, to the Atlantic side, find passage to Kingston, Jamaica, and New Orleans, thence to New York and Washington. The journey was reckoned to take three months.

Three weeks before Loeser's sailing from Monterey on August 30, official news reached Monterey of the peace treaty signed the previous May at Guadalupe Hidalgo. California was officially United States territory and among the first effects of the new status was to reduce the military forces there. After the regiment of New York volunteers mustered out, a single company of dragoons remained stationed at Los Angeles, and one company of artillery at Monterey.

"None remain behind but we poor devils of officers who are restrained by honor," Sherman wrote.

For extra money he worked briefly as a surveyor, then, in September, he, Mason, now a brigadier general, and a Captain Warner made a trip up to Sutter's Fort, then to some newly discovered gold deposits on the Stanislaus River, southeast of the fort. While Mason had to return to Monterey on government business, Sherman stayed on at the fort. "In order to share somewhat in the riches of the land," he wrote later, "we formed a partnership in a store at Coloma." The three officers put up $500 each and took on a fourth partner to run the store. In two months each man had trebled his investment.

ELEVEN DAYS BEFORE Lucien Loeser's courier mission began and just two days after Governor Mason completed his report to Washington, the first news of the gold discovery in California appeared in an eastern newspaper. On August 19, the *New York Herald* carried an item dated April 1, 1848, allegedly written from San Francisco by a hospital steward of the First Regiment of New York Volunteers. The anonymous informant said that "Several mines have lately been discovered in this country. . . . I am credibly informed that a quantity of gold in value $30, was picked up lately in the bed of a stream of the Sacramento. . . ." The writer went on to say, with peculiar geological detail, that "The gold mine discovered in December last [sic] on the south branch of the American Fork, in a range of low hills forming the base of the Sierra Nevada, distant thirty miles from New Helvetia, is only three feet below the surface, in a strata of soft sand rock. From explorations south twelve miles and north five miles the continuance of this strata is reported, and the mineral said to be equally abundant and from twelve to eighteen feet in thickness; so that, without allowing any golden hope to puzzle my prophetic vision of the future, I would predict for California a Peruvian harvest of the precious metals as soon as a sufficiency of miners, etc., can be obtained."

The erudite hospital steward did not exist; the story was a clever rewrite of "The Prospects of California" article by Dr. Victor Forgeaud that had appeared in the April 1 special edition of Sam Brannan's now-defunct *California Star*, carried east by Kit Carson's express party.

The item was not reprinted by other eastern papers, but news of the gold discovery was headed east by other means than Lieutenant Loeser.

Thomas O. Larkin began writing gold letters in June 1848, to his former chief in Washington. With the war over, Larkin was no longer consul, but ever the keen and articulate observer, he wrote Secretary of State James Buchanan, "You certainly will suppose from my two letters that I am, like others, led away by the excitement of the day. I think I am not. . . . I have the pleasure of enclosing a paper of this sand and gold, which, from a bucket of dirt and stones, I washed out myself in half hour, standing at the edge of the water. The value of it may be $2 or $3."

The letter, written on June 28, would not be delivered until the end of August.

Also in June, Larkin began writing a series of letters under the name "Paisano" for the *New York Herald*, the first of which, published in September, said, "We are in danger of having more gold than food; for he that can wield a spade and shake a dish, can fill his pockets *a su gusto*." He wrote, "A six-year-old child can gather $2 or $3 a day; a man $20 to $30; old and young ladies in proportion, according to how they admire to stand two feet deep in water, or can dig with shovels. . . . I saw on the ground a lawyer who was last year attorney general for the king of the Sandwich Islands, digging and washing out his ounce and a half per day. Near him can be found all his brethren of the long robe, working in the same occupation."

In a letter dated Monterey, July 1, 1848, "Paisano" referred to the *Herald*'s publisher James Gordon Bennett: "Were I a New Yorker instead of a Californian, I would throw aside your paper and exclaim, 'Bennett had better fill his paper with, at least, probable tales and stories, and not such outrageous fictions of rivers flowing with gold.' . . . Oh this California, to what will it come at last!"

While these letters would not appear in the *Herald* until September, in the meantime Larkin directed his excited correspondence to his old friend from conquest days, Commodore Jones, commander of American naval forces in the Pacific: "This part of California is at present in a state of great excitement from the late discovery of an extensive gold region on the branches of the Sacramento River. All our towns are becoming vacated," he wrote, adding much of the detail in his "Paisano" compositions.

How much influence Larkin's communications to Jones had on the events to follow is unknown, but the commodore drafted some letters of his own, to the Navy Department in Washington, included another message from Larkin, and found an officer willing to cross Mexico on horseback to get them to Washington.

The story of how the news of the gold discovery in California reached the United States was to have a peculiar twist. Lieutenant Lucien Loeser of the army carried the information by sea; Lieutenant Ned Beale of the navy carried the information by land.

HISTORIAN BERNARD DEVOTO's blunt characterization of Edward Fitzgerald Beale as "a first-rate man" would have been endorsed by such contemporaries as Kit Carson, a close friend of Beale's to the end of Kit's life; Bayard Taylor, the "Poet Laureate of the Gilded Age" who met Beale when both were en route to California in 1849 and remained a lifelong friend; Ulysses S. Grant, whose presidential candidacy Beale supported and with whom he often dined and drank; and even John Charles Frémont, a man notoriously hard to befriend, whom Beale admired, rode with, and defended from the witness chair during the explorer's court-martial.

For a man who loved the Western wilderness and felt at home in it as much as Carson or Frémont, and for one who would make six journeys across the continent in two years, Beale's choice of a career in the navy could only have been a family tradition. He was the son of a naval officer who had served with distinction at the Battle of Lake Champlain in 1812, and his mother's father had fought the French in the West Indies and retired from the navy as a commodore.

Born in 1822 on his father's estate in Washington, a mile from the

White House, Beale, called "Ned" from his childhood, attended Georgetown College for a time, receiving, when not truant, the rudiments of a classical education. When his father died, his mother visited President Jackson to appeal for a midshipman's warrant for the son of a valorous veteran and won the day. Beale entered the navy in 1837 in a homemade uniform, a stocky, wide-eyed, handsome teenager with curly collar-length hair and a fringe of beard on his chin and jaw. He was ready to see the world, ready to quote Cicero, Horace, Virgil, Ovid, and Sappho to his shipmates, and ready to scrap with them when his volatile temper boiled over.

In the early years of his service he sailed to Kronstadt, the Russian port on the Gulf of Finland; to Brazil, where at age eighteen he developed a taste for liquor, especially brandy, which never dulled in his life; to the West Indies, and the Mediterranean. After eight years in the navy he progressed to "passed midshipman," the limbo before a lieutenancy, fell in love with the romantic poets and tried his own hand at verses emulating Keats and Shelley, and in 1845 had the good fortune to be assigned to the warship *Porpoise* in Commodore Robert Stockton's squadron on the Texas coast. During this duty, Beale received the first of what was to be a long string of courier assignments: Stockton selected him to carry dispatches to Washington containing the news that the Texas Congress had accepted the offer of annexation by the United States.

He stayed with Stockton's command and sailed in October 1845, aboard the squadron flagship *Congress*, bound for Cape Horn, Callao, Peru, the Sandwich Islands, and California.

When the man-of-war reached Monterey on July 20, Beale, now twenty-four and as yet only an acting lieutenant, was detached from shipboard duties to serve with General Kearny's land forces. He fought and was wounded in the battle at San Pascual, east of San Diego, in December, and with Kit Carson made a daring night penetration through enemy lines to take news of Kearny's desperate holding action to Stockton in San Diego. The mission, a "forlorn hope," as Carson characterized it, called for the men to split up and move thirty miles over rocky, waterless terrain. Beale, suffering from exposure, for a time became "mentally deranged," an official report said, and his health was impaired for two years afterward. Carson too was temporarily crippled and incapacitated from the ordeal.

With the fighting in California over in January 1847, Beale and

Carson had recovered enough to take dispatches overland to Washington. For Beale it was the first of six such missions, the second of which was to carry news of the gold strike.

HE RETURNED TO the Pacific after testifying at the Frémont court-martial in Washington and had a temporary assignment in La Paz, Baja California, when news reached him in July 1848, of the gold discovery in the Sacramento Valley.

He had arrived at a difficult career crossroads. Still an "acting" lieutenant after a decade in the navy, he was drinking heavily, succumbing to the periodic melancholia that plagued him throughout his adult life, and contemplating what future he could have in the service in peacetime.

BEALE HAD A rough relationship with Thomas ap Catesby Jones, Stockton's replacement in command of the Pacific Squadron. The problem, it was rumored, had to do with a caricature Beale had drawn of the lordly commodore. Even so, when the acting lieutenant learned that Jones was preparing reports on the gold rush for Washington, he volunteered to serve as courier and take the papers overland, across Mexico to Vera Cruz and on to Washington. So anxious was he to have this important assignment (and to be able to visit family and friends in the capital), he said he would make the trip at his own expense. Among his qualifications were his excellent naval record, his experience as a courier, and his good conversational Spanish.

Jones took him up on the proposition and on July 29 Beale embarked on the *Congress* from La Paz and crossed the Gulf of California to Mazatlán, the chief west coast Mexican port. There he boarded a small Mexican schooner and arrived in the first week of August at San Blas, three hundred miles south of Mazatlán.

In the week he spent in the old town, set among mangroves, banana, and avocado plantations alive with insects and snakes, he explored its chapel, built of lava rocks, and its customs house and fort overlooking the Pacific. These were relics of distant times when Spanish galleons from Manila sailed to the bustling port with their cargos of silks, damasks, spices, chinaware, and beeswax, trade commodities gathered in the Far East. In his wanderings, and after buying a horse and hiring a guide, Beale found the governor of San Blas and told the man of his intent to travel on to Tepic, the mountain town fifty miles to the east, thence to Mexico City. The governor listened politely to the bulky, brown-haired naval officer with the admirably bushy mustache and informed him, "Señor, an American like yourself could not travel a dozen miles in Mexico without being robbed and murdered."

Such warnings Beale had heard in Mazatlán and elsewhere—that the roads and trails into the interior had been swarming with *ladrones* and assassins since the end of the war. But he had been in hostile Mexican country before, admittedly with Kit Carson at his side, crossing the Southwestern desert with dispatches. Now, tanned, armed with four revolvers and a Bowie knife, dressed in leather breeches, a red flannel shirt, and a big sombrero, he looked like a bandit himself and liked his chances.

He got underway on August 12 and in Tepic took the precaution of making copies of all of the commodore's dispatches and letters, sending them ahead by mail, said to be dependable since Tepic had a busy shipping office, to Nathan Clifford, the American minister in Mexico City.

Beale's guide led him out of the town through swamplands and mangrove banks loud with squawking parrots and nameless tropical birds and the buzzing and whining of mosquitos and insects beyond number. They crossed an estuary on a raft-ferry, poled past spear fishermen in canoes on shallow rivers with water snakes slithering alongside them and alligators dozing on the banks. They reached a road built by Spaniards in 1768, rode past salt beds, banana, fig, and palm groves. They rode night and day, bought fresh horses at wayside inns, rode east on the waist of Mexico to the town of Tequila, its jungly hillsides covered with the bayonet-leaved *maguey* plants. There, as they turned south toward Guadalajara, 350 miles from the capital, they had a scary brush with *bandidos* when a gang of them boiled out of the roadside brush behind them and gave chase. Beale said he sent a fast message of rifle shots in their vicinity and they fled.

At one inn on their route to Guadalajara, where they traded their lathered horses for fresh mounts, the proprietor told Beale he might join a party of eleven Mexican travelers, a short distance ahead, who were also traveling to the capital. He found them, all eleven dead, apparently ambushed and murdered by another party of brigands, and decided not to bury the corpses since the killers might be lurking nearby. Beale and his guide rode on east to León, an iron manufacturing town, and after again exchanging horses, and enjoying their first full meal since starting out, rode on, to the southeast and a ridge of mountains that signaled the ancient capital.

In Mexico City, Beale turned over dispatches to Minister Clifford and received others to deliver to Secretary of State Buchanan in Washington. Before moving on, he visited the heights of Chapultepec Castle where the great battle of the war had taken place less than a year before as General Winfield Scott led 14,000 men from Vera Cruz through the mountain passes and stormed the gates of Mexico City. At the army's headquarters in the capital, Beale met Ulysses S. Grant, also age twenty-six, who had been brevetted a first lieutenant for his gallant service. "Sam" Grant was an encyclopedia of the war with Mexico since he had participated in nearly all of it. He had served with Zachary Taylor in Texas, fought at Palo Alto and Resaca de la Palma, battles waged before war was declared, and in Mexico at Monterrey; transferred to General Scott's command and saw action at Vera Cruz, Cerro Gordo, Churubusco, Molina del Rey, and the storming of Chapultepec. He and Beale became instant and enduring friends.

The 280-mile ride from the capital to Vera Cruz exhausted Beale's guide, who collapsed at the end of the grueling pace his employer had set and had to be sent back to Mexico City in a *diligencia*. Beale himself seems not to have suffered, enjoying the pine forests, the views of Mounts Popocatépetl and Ixtaccíhuatl; the mountain summits at the Continental Divide, 10,500 feet above sea level; the villages of Río Frío, San Martín Texmelucán, and Huejotzingo; the Toltec pyramid at Cholula; and the towns of Puebla and Cerro Gordo, where cannon shot still littered their battlefields.

He waited four days at Vera Cruz before finding passage on the American sloop-of-war *Germantown* to Mobile, landing there in early September and arriving in Washington by stagecoach on September 14, 1848, covering four thousand miles by ship, horse, foot, and stage, forty-seven days after departing La Paz.

NED BEALE'S NAME had celebrity status even before he reached Washington. On September 12, 1848, the New Orleans *Picayune* carried the first United States news of his mission in a column filled with speculative detail.

The story, datelined Mexico City, August 20, announced, "Lieutenant Beale, United States Navy, bearer of dispatches from Commodore Jones, commander of the squadron in the Pacific, arrived here today on his way to Washington." The unnamed correspondent wrote, "Lieutenant Beale carries with him highly interesting information in regard to the discovery of gold mines in Upper California. . . . From the meager information which has so far been had of these mines, there remains very little if any doubt that California is destined to become probably the richest and most important country on the continent of North America."

Beale's trans-Mexico adventures, and his delivery of the California dispatches to President Polk and Secretary Buchanan, were written up fulsomely in the eastern, midwestern, and Missouri press and captured the national public imagination. A *New York Herald* reporter wrote on September 21, "All Washington is in a ferment with the news of the immense bed of gold, which, it is said, has been discovered in California. Nothing else is talked about. Democrats, Whigs, free soil men, hunkers, barnburners [factions of the New York Democratic party], abolitionists—all, are engrossed by the wonderful intelligence. The real El Dorado has at length been discovered." The *St. Louis Daily Union* carried an editorial noting the arrival in Washington of "Midshipman Beale" bringing dispatches from Commodore Jones that confirmed what Thomas O. Larkin had written about the "new El Dorado." The writer, one of the few dubious ones, said "The account is evidently exaggerated," while the *St. Louis Weekly Reveille*, on September 24 said, "If Lieut. Beale's account of the discovery of gold in California is half correct, there will soon be an increased tide of emigration flowing into that territory."

When the *Washington Intelligencer* published "A Ride Across Mexico," written by William Carey Jones (Frémont's brother-in-law), Beale's heroism at San Pascual and his mission through enemy lines with Kit Carson were added to the colorful details of his Mexican journey and made Beale a national sensation. Thomas Hart Benton introduced him in the Senate, where the lieutenant warned the lawmakers that California faced starvation because the farmers there had deserted their fields for the mines, and P. T. Barnum wrote inquiring about an "eight pound lump of California gold" he had been told was in Beale's possession, offering to buy it "for public gratification."

Beale, in fact, had only a few ounces of coarse gold, most of which he turned over to the government, keeping enough to have a jeweler design an engagement ring from it for Mary Edwards, his childhood sweetheart whom he would marry the next year.

He was given little time to enjoy the limelight. In early October he had dispatches to deliver to military authorities in California. This time there was no hurry and he would travel from St. Louis as far as Fort Leavenworth with a cavalry escort of seventeen men.

He crossed Ratón Pass in ten-foot snowdrifts and reached Santa Fé on Christmas Day, 1848, rode out with a small army detail on January 11 to the Gila River and picked up Kearny's old route to California via the Colorado River and Mojave Desert.

WHILE NED BEALE'S swift passage across Mexico stole the headlines and held the public in thrall, Lucien Loeser's tea caddy filled with 230 ounces of California gold revived the story that faltered after Beale's departure from Washington.

Lieutenant Loeser, the artilleryman selected by California's military governor to convey dispatches and gold specimens to the United States, completed his assignment at a seagoing amble compared to Beale's landlocked horse race. The Pennsylvanian, a six-year army veteran, sailed from Monterey to the Peruvian port of Payta on the chartered trader *Lambayecana* on August 30, ten days after Beale reached Mexico City. Loeser next took passage on a British steamer to the Pacific side of Panama, and crossed the isthmus in October, proceeding to Kingston, Jamaica, thence, on the schooner *Desdemona* to New Orleans where he telegraphed the War Department of his arrival there.

The *New Orleans Mercury* sent a reporter to interview him and on November 28 the paper declared, "He fully confirms the most glowing accounts heretofore received in the States, of the richness and extent of the gold region. He says the whole truth cannot be told with any prospect of being believed—that the gold is found from the tops of the highest mountains to the bottoms of rivers."

On December 5, within days of Loeser's arrival in the capital, James K. Polk inserted in his annual address to Congress some words on the gold discovery that erased all doubt as to the substance of the fabulous reports from California.

"The accounts of the abundance of gold in that territory [California] are of such extraordinary character," he said, "as would scarcely command belief were they not corroborated by the authentic reports of officers in the public service who have visited the mineral district and derived the facts which they detail from personal observation. . . . This abundance of gold, and the all-engrossing pursuit of it, have already caused in California an unprecedented rise in the price of all the necessaries of life."

The day after the presidential address, the *Hartford Courant* took a disdainful approach to the gold story, editorializing, "The California gold fever is approaching its crisis. We are told that the new region that has just become a part of our possessions, is El Dorado after all. Thither is now setting a tide that will not cease its flow until either untold wealth is amassed, or extended beggary is secured."

California, the *Courant* writer said, was, "In a moment, as it were, a desert country, that never deserved much notice from the world," but now "all creation is going out there to fill their pockets with the great condiment of their diseased minds."

When the tea caddy and its contents were exhibited in the War Department library on December 13, they produced the kind of sensation P. T. Barnum envied. Horace Greeley's reporter visited the display and wrote in the *New York Tribune*, "Any goose who could talk of 'mica' after seeing these specimens would not be worth noticing; it is no more like mica than it is like cheese."

In his *Tribune* on December 9, Greeley wrote, "It is coming—nay, at hand, there is no doubt of it. We are on the brink of the Age of Gold! We look for an addition, within the next four years, equal to at least one thousand millions of dollars to the general aggregate of gold in circulation and use throughout the world."

Before being displayed, most of the gold Loeser delivered had been sent by War Secretary William Marcy to the United States Mint in Philadelphia for assaying. On December 11 the director of the mint reported, "The gold was of two sorts in external character, though apparently not different as to quality. The first, from the dry diggings was in grains, which averaged from one to two pennyweights; the other variety, from the swamps or margins of the streams, being in small flat spangles, of which, on an average, it would take six or seven to weigh one grain." The director said assays of the melted gold were made with great care and the results showed "a variation in fineness from 892 to 897 thousandths, the average of the whole being 894. This is slightly below the standard fineness [for gold coinage], which is 900." He valued the gold which Quartermaster James Folsom had purchased in San Francisco at "$18.05-⅓ per [troy] ounce."

Such was the minutiae that had to satisfy the eastern press and public in the waning days of 1848, together with exciting but stale dispatches from "Paisano"—Thomas Larkin—in the *New York Herald* and occasonal repetitive testimony from others who claimed to have worked, or at least seen, the "diggings." But it was enough for the thousands making plans and organizing groups and "companies" of like-minded, gold-minded friends.

On the Atlantic there was much consulting of globes and charts, calculating distances, making inquiries to shipping companies, much talk of "Panama" and "Cape Horn." Farther west, fingers traced overland routes on undependable maps, Rocky Mountain trappers were sought out as guides, wagons and draft animals were purchased, and questions asked about the Oregon Trail, "cutoffs" and detours, to hurry the way to California.

"Hitherto small though sure profits dwindled into insignificance under the new aspect," Hubert Bancroft wrote, "and the trader closed his ledger to depart; and so the toiling farmer, whose mortgage loomed above the growing family, the briefless lawyer, the starving student, the quack, the idler, the harlot, the gambler, the henpecked husband, the disgraced; with many earnest, enterprising, honest men and devoted women."

These turned their faces westward, he said, and "Stories exaggerated by inflamed imaginations broke the calm of a million hearts, and tore families asunder, leaving sorrowing mothers, pining wives, neglected children, with poverty and sorrow to swell their anguish; the departed meanwhile bent on the struggle with fortune, faithful or faithless; a few to be successful, but a far greater number to sink disappointed into nameless graves."

SEVEN

THE '48ERS

THAT FALL OF 1848 no army of gold dreamers was as yet laying siege to the foothills and waterways of the Sierra Nevada, but the troops were massing and California lay waiting for them.

Until the end of 1848, when President Polk's address to Congress gave the gold stories a governmental imprimatur, they were regarded by most citizens and the newspapers they depended upon as merely "interesting."

INTERESTING FROM CALIFORNIA, announced a small bold-faced heading to a story buried in the *New York Herald* on September 15, the day after Ned Beale arrived in Washington. "We have received some late and interesting intelligence from California," the apologetic item ran. "It is to the 1st of July. Owing to the crowded state of our columns, we are obliged to omit our correspondence. It relates to the important discovery of a very valuable gold mine. We have received a specimen of the gold."

The omitted correspondence and sample came from Thomas O. "Paisano" Larkin of Monterey and his letter ran in the *Herald* two days later. The long and rousing dispatch ended with the assertion that "the famous Eldorado was but a sand bank, the Arabian Nights were tales of simplicity!"

The "crowded state of our columns" that James Gordon Bennett mentioned had to do with more interesting and important news than the discovery of a gold mine. The 1848 presidential campaign pushed all news back or out of newspapers that fall: the retirement of James K. Polk, as he had promised, after a single term; the nomination of Mexican War hero Zachary Taylor by the Whigs, Michigan lawyer Lewis Cass by the Democrats, Martin Van Buren in a third party cause; the slavery issue which had grown complex as Northerners realized that California and the other Western lands gained from the late war might fall to the slave-holding South; the fact that the favorite—and subsequently, winning—candidate, General Taylor, owned a hundred slaves.

* * *

IN MID-1848, California's non-Indian population of about fifteen thousand was split almost evenly between native Californios and foreigners—6,500 of the latter Americans. Of the total, nine thousand had gone off to hunt gold. The small exodus began with the men (there were as yet too few women and children to count) in the valleys adjacent to the Coloma sawmill, spread to San Francisco in May, to San José and Monterey in June, and in July to the southern towns, Los Angeles and San Diego in particular.

In the early fall, at about the time the first substantial news of the strike reached New York and Washington, a flow of Sandwich Islanders began disembarking at San Francisco, and others from trade ships from Valparaiso. (When one of these miners returned home with bagful of $25,000 in gold, Chileans clamored at the ticket offices for passage to California.)

Among those coming overland, the most numerous in 1848 were the Mexicans from Hermosillo in the northern state of Sonora, many of them experienced miners, who set up their camps in the southwestern foothills of the Sierra Nevada.

From the north, 150 men and fifty wagons came from Oregon in the fall, led by Peter Burnett, age forty-one, a former storekeeper and self-taught lawyer, hopelessly in debt when he had gone out to Oregon during the "Great Migration" of 1841. He guided his company of pioneers from the Willamette Valley across the Cascades to the rancho run by Peter Lassen, the Danish blacksmith and Bear Flag rebel who had settled on Deer Creek, a hundred miles upriver from Sutter's Fort.

Burnett himself found a camp of ninety miners, a cluster of tents and a lone log cabin at a place called Long Bar on the swift-flowing Yuba River. For $300 he bought a tiny claim measuring twenty feet along the river and fifty feet behind it, built a rocker and began taking out twenty dollars a day in dust. In a month he had enough to pay his debts and in December quit the placers to enter politics.*

A few other land-bound emigrants entered California, these from the Missouri frontier who brought plows, axes, and sticks of furni-

---

*In 1850 Burnett became the first elected governor of California. Among its many claims, Long Bar was "worked" in 1852 by Hubert H. Bancroft, employed there to cut trees and haul wood in the months before he became a prominent bookseller in San Francisco and later, the eminent historian quoted often in these pages.

ture, intending to settle and farm. Some of these pioneers, arriving on
the Humboldt River for a summer crossing of the Sierra, met Henry
Bigler who was taking a party of Latter-Day Saints to Salt Lake City.
A Virginia-born veteran of the Mormon Battalion of the Mexican
War, Bigler had worked for James Marshall at the Coloma sawmill at
the time of the gold discovery and had taken out some gold himself.
From him the newcomers learned of the riches being panned from
the streams and chipped from the hills of the Sacramento Valley and
beyond.

Added to this heterogenous band of early argonauts were a small
number of Chinese, "Celestials from the Flowery Kingdom," the
newspapers called them. The first of these emigrants arrived from
Hong Kong on the trading brig *Eagle* in February 1848, the menfolk
eventually departing for the mines where they hired out as laborers
and hoped to find gold for themselves while washing dirt for others.

In 1848, more than half of the men working the diggings were
Indians, "aboriginals wild and tame, half-naked, eating his grasshop-
per cake, and sleeping in his hut of bushes," as Bancroft described
them. When Spanish explorers and missionaries came to Alta California in 1769, there may have been as many as 300,000 native people
scattered in small bands throughout the province. They were a varied
people: hunters and fishers; makers of acorn bread; insect and grub
eaters; snarers of small game; growers of corn, beans and pumpkins;
basketmakers; boatmen in canoes made of tule and rush and
hollowed-out redwood trunks. In the north, to the Oregon border,
there were Shasta, Modoc, and Northern Paiute; on the coast the
Pomo, Miwok, Costanoan, and Salinan; to the east were the Washo
and Paiute and Shoshone; south and southeast the Chumash,
Gabrielino, Serrano, Mojave, and Yuma. There were probably a hundred other tribes and bands scattered between the Oregon border and
Baja California, between the ocean, the Sierra, and the deserts.

These original natives of California were treated as little better
than slaves during the Spanish mission era and by the Mexicans later,
and were treated worse in the gold era when they were robbed,
cheated, and, for a time, by state sanction, murdered.

Bancroft wrote vividly of them "arrayed in civilization's cotton
shirts, some with duck trousers, squatting in groups and eagerly dis-
cussing the yellow handkerchiefs, red blankets, and bad muskets just

secured by a little of this so lately worthless stuff which had been lying in their streams with the other dirt these past thousand years."

The maltreatment of the Indians was already commonplace by the time of the gold discovery; the vile acts in the gold country by white men toward Mexicans, Chileans, Chinese, and other "foreigners," and the equally hateful treatment of white toward white, began soon enough.

THOSE WHO WERE in the country in the year of the discovery invariably drew distinctions between themselves and those who came later. The first to the mines were Sutter's neighbors in the valleys above and to the east of San Francisco and those who came up from the bay and from Monterey. Added to these were the early Oregon and Missouri emigrants, aiming to settle and farm, and the Sonorans, tireless and peaceable miners making their way into the San Joaquín River country in what became known as the "southern mines."

Thefts among these original argonauts were rare, claim jumping and violence almost unknown. Camp tents lay unguarded, cabins unlocked, often with a sack of dust in plain sight. In 1848 there were only two recorded instances in which a "miner's meeting"—a kangaroo court in the placers—had to be called. One case involved a Frenchman caught stealing horses at Dry Diggings (later appropriately known as Hangtown), the other a Spaniard found at an American River camp with a stolen poke of gold dust. Both men were tried, found guilty, and hanged.

"Every thing was honorable and safe," miner Daniel Knower of Albany, New York, recalled in later years, "until the overland emigrants from western Missouri arrived there. They were a different kind of people; more of the brute order."

Except for the Sonorans and a handful of Cornishmen from south England, the argonauts of '48 were just learning their trade, trudging the trails in the broiling summer carrying a pick and shovel, an old musket and hunting knife, a frying pan, tin cup, roll of blankets, some flour, bacon, coffee, and tobacco. In these innocent days the idea prevailed that the gold found in streams had washed down from the solid beds in the mountains and so the miners sought these phantom lodes with their picks and shovels, starving in the process. Many had yet to learn the simple art of panning a stream for "colors"; few could afford the lumber or had the knack to build a rocker; most worked for others, to make a grubstake to strike out on their own, learning as they labored.

BEING IN CALIFORNIA in '48 and within walking distance of the gold country, did not, except for a few, translate to luck, success, or least of all, riches. So testified Sergeant James H. Carson, who left a spirited chronicle of his experiences as a '48er.

He was a native of Middletown, Virginia, who enlisted in the army in 1839, at age eighteen, and after service at Fort McHenry, Maryland, arrived in Monterey in January 1847, after a five-month Cape Horn voyage. His unit, the Third Artillery Regiment, had among its officers Lieutenants W. T. Sherman and Lucien Loeser.

In April 1848, Carson said the gold news had "carried off many of Monterey's inhabitants" and that he remained an unbeliever until, on May 10, he encountered an old friend who had just returned from the mines. This man, who Carson called "Billy," carried a sack of gold on his back that he had gathered in five weeks' work at Kelsey's, a camp between Coloma and the Dry Diggings. The gold, Carson said, was not in dust or scales but "in pieces ranging in size from that of a pea to hen's eggs." Billy told him, "This is only what I picked out with a knife."

Carson wrote, "There was before me proof positive that I had held too long to the wrong side of the question. I looked on for a moment; a frenzy seized my soul; unbidden my legs performed some entirely new movements of Polka steps. . . ." He said that suddenly he found himself in the byways of Monterey searching for an "outfit" while "piles of gold rose up before me at every step. . . . In short, I had a very violent attack of gold fever."

Precisely when he made his first venture to the mining district is not clear. In June, Carson was among the escorting soldiers who accompanied Governor Mason and Lieutenant Sherman to Sutter's Fort and the diggings at Coloma, Mormon Island, and Weber Creek; in August he was granted a furlough, perhaps as a reward for being among the troops who had not deserted their posts to follow the gold scent. He headed north then, but from his own account, appears to have made at least one prior gold plunge, a trip that may have inspired and provided direction for Governor Mason's tour.

Carson claimed that soon after his encounter with his friend Billy, he bought an old mule, a washbasin, a fire shovel, "a piece of iron pointed at one end"—to dig gold from rocks—plus a blanket, a rifle, "a few yards of jerked beef," and a bag of *penole* (ground corn), and headed out for the places which Billy said rewarded him with a bag of gold.

At Mormon Island Carson began "annihilating earth" with his washbasin, standing knee-deep in water. He made fifty cents from fifty pans and departed, disgusted. But at the Weber Creek trading camp he saw "sights of gold that revived the fever" and he stayed on at Kelsey's and Dry Diggings until his furlough expired.

The '48ers, Carson said, did not work on the Sabbath but used the day to "prospect the neighborhood" while others gambled, using their hard-won dust as stakes, and drank whiskey. "We had ministers of the gospel amongst us, but they never preached. Religion had been forgotten, even by its ministers, and instead of pointing out the narrow paths that led to eternal happiness to the diggers . . . there they might be seen with pick-ax and pan trodding untravelled ways in search of 'filthy lucre.' "

He wrote: "I have worked hard eight hours, and my gains for that time are $12.25; my day's provisions have cost nearly seventy-five cents, leaving a net gain of $11.50. Have I been tasked? No! but when my pick rested, my pay stopped."

Of all the '48ers, Thomas Larkin of Monterey had the perfect seat to observe the early days of the gold rush, the eminence to be trusted as a chronicler of it, and the business sense to make money from it without bending his back with pick and pan. He was forty-six and had been in the country fifteen years as a trader, merchant, occasional smuggler and port tax dodger at the time of the Coloma discovery. With his stores and warehouses established and making money, he had time, beginning in about 1840, to propaganize California, his "contributing correspondent" effusions on the New Elysium on the Pacific published in the *Herald* and the *New York Sun*, with reprintings in other papers as well.

His "Paisano" letters of 1848 were stirring in their depictions of the California populace fleeing to the mines as if swept there by a tidal wave. He worried, extolled, exaggerated, and to a degree, educated, at least insofar as he portrayed the excitement of the race for riches within California. He rarely wrote of the commonest experience of the '48er and those to follow—failure.

While communicating on the successes of others, Larkin made his own gold fortune with typical Yankee shrewdness. He entered into merchant partnerships, and set up stores and gold exchanges in San Francisco and New Helvetia. He bought schooners to ply the Sacramento carrying trade goods from the bay to the mines and bought and sold as well in Mazatlán, the Sandwich Islands, and even Canton. He invested in hundreds of lots in Benicia and on the Sacramento where the boomtown named for the river would soon spring to life. He employed men to work the diggings and seemed to have the Midas touch in this as in his other business ventures.

In July, he reported that two of his workers on the Yuba River were taking out $100 in gold a day—"for killing work . . . the hardest labor that God ever willed that white man should perform"—and by mid-August said they had accumulated 209 pounds of gold "nearly clean and about 150 to 200 lbs. not clean." He wrote of the Yuba operation again on August 16 from New Helvetia, saying he found his two employees washing an average of $500 in dust a day with $10,000 "on hand."

Larkin's buccaneering rapacity is no better illustrated than in his complaint on the laziness of his "Injun workers" while gloating over the piratical profits made on the merchandise he was selling to them: "We sell high to Indians—Serapas [serapes] from 60$ to 100$—Shirts 16$ . . . all our goods will bring from 300 to 500 percent profit."

While neither man made more than passing reference to it, in his frequent trips to New Helvetia that summer, Larkin and Sutter must have met, dined, and talked frequently. They were among the paramount '48ers, each ideally situated to reap immense profits in gold in the hush before the noisy multitude of argonauts reached California.

With his considerable pre-1848 wealth and his partnership with other monied men, Larkin was well on his way to a new fortune; John Sutter stood nearer than Don Tomás on the brink of riches, but being Sutter, could not close the gap.

SUTTER SAID THE gold discovery "ruined my hard, restless, and industrious life." For years he had banked on an American migration, by sea and across the Sierra, funneling through New Helvetia, as the the key to his success, the answer to his chronic indebtedness. But during the 1846 conquest of the province by American soldiers, sailors, and volunteers, he had a taste of what such an influx might bring and found it bitter. Frémont's gang of ruffians had stolen from him, usurped his authority, and reduced him to servitude when they occupied his fort. He lamented to H. H. Bancroft, thirty years afterward, that he had been "at the mercy of the rabble" then and again when his lands were overrun by gold hunters. He said he regretted that he had not closed up the fort and moved to Fort Ross, with its higher and healthier location, its rich soil and abundant timber, a place where the gold-crazed adventurers could not rob him. Or, he said, he might better have sold New Helvetia, paid his debts, and fled the country altogether.

He had managed to amass a large sum of gold, as much as $20,000 worth, hiring Indians and others to work his claims. The rents he charged for living quarters and shops at the fort brought in $2,000 a month, and other gold came in from the store he opened at Coloma, but the bills he had begun accumulating from the moment he set foot in California in 1839 staggered him. Among old debts, he had yet to pay the Russians the $30,000 plus massive interest owed for the purchase of Fort Ross and the property at Bodega Bay. Among new losses, he said the Coloma sawmill, seat of all his current misery, had cost his investment of $10,000, the failed flour mill $25,000. Intruders stole his millstones, the bells from the fort, gate weights, hides from the tannery, salmon barrels, even some of the fort's cannons. He said his property was left exposed when gold was discovered, and his men all deserted. "The country swarmed with lawless men. Emigrants drove their stock into my yard, and used my grain with impunity. Expostulation did no good. I was alone. There was no law."

With his ledgers chaotic, his creditors closing in, and his dreamed-of empire crumbling, Sutter found some solace in awaiting the arrival of one man to whom he owed an unpayable debt, his oldest son, Johann Augustus Jr.

Nearly fifteen years had passed since Sutter had abandoned his family in Switzerland to take passage to America. He had kept up contact, if desultorily, with his wife Anna and their children—John, Anna Eliza, Emil Victor, and Wilhelm Alphonse—and seems to have sent money home on occasion. At some point in 1846, apparently after John Junior expressed an interest in joining his father in California, Sutter welcomed him and sent the passage funds. After some delays, John was due in San Francisco in the summer of 1848, and Sutter had plans for him.

There is a bothersome gap in the record on John Jr.—often called August to avoid confusion with his father. Before his advent in California, Sutter bragged endlessly about him, claiming the lad had received a fine education, was a talented linguist and experienced in business. He did not offer an explanation of how his son, now age twenty-one, had managed all this in a family left destitute, but August was to prove worthy of his father's confidence.

He arrived in San Francisco in late August on the sailing vessel *Huntress*. With his father away "at the mines" and a week's time involved in getting a message to him and waiting for him to return to the fort, the young man had time to survey his father's domain and reflect on what he had heard about "the Captain" en route. Seven years after the reunion, August wrote, "It is impossible for anyone to imagine with what contradictory feelings I set out for Sacramento in my father's schooner, that craft then happening to be in port. All rumors made a very definite impression on my disturbed mind. Having never heard that my father was a drunkard and a victim of disorderly habits, I could not and would not believe it without proof." He also heard "strange reports" and "altogether contradictory rumors" in San Francisco about the Captain's business affairs. Some informants told August that John A. Sutter was the richest man in California. "Others, to the contrary," he said, "told me confidentially that because of his loose and careless manner of transacting business, he was on the brink of ruin." Instead of being associated with honorable and trustworthy men, Sutter Senior was surrounded by a parcel of immoral rogues, said these last informants, and "instead of aiding him, the rascals would only accelerate and accomplish his utter moral, physical, and financial ruin."

He learned quickly: "Now I saw with my own eyes how business was conducted," he said. "Anything belonging to my father was at every man's disposal . . . Indians, negroes, Kanakas, white men—all indiscriminately applied to my father and easily obtained credit from him which entitled them to any provender or stores in and about the fort."

He had "a week of terrific anguish and uncertainty" awaiting his father's return but when Sutter at last rode into the fort, their reunion was, August said, "affectionate and sincere. Both of us wept. . . . I soon forgot all I had heard, and was unreservedly happy to be with him at last. We spoke a long time of my mother, my brothers and my sister; of family matters; of times gone by."

Sutter promised he would soon send for Anna and the other children; meantime, he had work for his son, beginning by appointing him his chief clerk and keeper of the ledgers, succeeding John Bidwell, who had departed to ranch and mine gold on the Feather River. The books were the expected nightmare: "I could never clearly ascertain the state of affairs, so confusing were the entries," August said. "Moreover, they had been neglected for some six months."

When it was learned that he was second-in-command at the fort, August said every man in his father's employ "wanted to acquire my confidence and friendship. Every man had a different tale; each blackened the other fellow with hearty zest."

In October, in a clever and patently illegal move to buy time to ward off bankruptcy, Sutter deeded to August all his real estate—the fort, a lot he owned in San Francisco—and his personal property as well, pledging, the son remembered, "that I would pay all his debts as soon as possible, as he was insistent on this point." The urgency of the transaction seems to have been generated by a lawsuit lately filed against Sutter by William A. Leidesdorff, the businessman and onetime United States vice consul in Yerba Buena, now agent for the Russian-American Fur Company. He was suing for the $30,000 owed for the Fort Ross and Bodega Bay properties and had papers drawn up by San Francisco legal authorities to attach all of Sutter's properties.

After the deed work, Sutter departed for the mines and his trading post at Coloma, leaving his son free to settle all legal and financial matters.

In January, with Peter Burnett, the Oregon pioneer lawyer as Sutter's counsel, the Fort Ross note was paid in full with $10,000 in gold, the balance from the sale of lots on the Sacramento property. Soon after, the $7,000 owed the Hudson's Bay Company, in arrears for a decade, was settled and miscellaneous other debts as well.

In the space of ten months, Sutter was able to retire to his 1,200-acre Hock Farm and its spacious frame-and-adobe house on the Feather River. He even had enough money to engage his countryman and onetime majordomo Heinrich Leinhard to travel to Switzerland, pay the family's debts there, and escort Anna and the other three children to California.

For the first time in his adult life, the erstwhile Potentate of the Sacramento was free of debt.

AT ABOUT THE time August Sutter arrived on the Sacramento, the letters by such prominent '48ers as Walter Colton and Thomas Larkin to eastern newspapers were growing increasingly feverish with overgilded accounts of gold discoveries.

Colton wrote prolifically even after the collapse of the newspaper he founded. His letters, datelined "Monterey, Upper California," were published in the *North American and United States Gazette*, the *New York Tribune*, *New York Daily Union*, *Boston Courier*, *Boston Daily Advertiser*, *Baltimore Sun*, *Cincinnati Daily Enquirer*, and *Arkansas State Democrat*, among other papers.

Like Larkin, Colton mastered the technique of recounting fabulous tales told by unidentified miners. "I have just been conversing with a man who in six days gathered five hundred dollars worth," he would write. He would tell of certain "Monterey men" who, after hiring thirty Indians, "divided seventy-six thousand and eight hundred and forty-four dollars," after seven weeks' work; and of another man who "worked on the Yuba sixty-four days and took out $5,356."

He also flew off into many ludicrous flights of fancy. "Only the women remain," he wrote, "and they will, it is expected, start soon. Their cradles will answer admirably to wash out gold in, and the little fellows in the meantime must amuse themselves with the ingots which the mothers dig."

Colton had heard of the gold discovery in May, regarding it then as "a flash of a firefly at night," but on September 20, gathered some friends and pushed north to the mines, where, he wrote, "I jumped from my horse, took a pick, and in five minutes found a piece of gold large enough to make a signet-ring." The next day he said he was "tearing up the bogs" with the other diggers, standing up to his knees in mud, splitting ledges apart and finding "particles of gold, resembling in shape the small and delicate scales of a fish."

The successful miner, he wrote, was "like the leader of hounds in the chase—the whole pack comes sweeping after, and are sure to be in at the death." He estimated there were fifty thousand people "drifting up and down these slopes of the great Sierra, of every hue, language, and clime, tumultuous and confused."

He became poetic: "I have walked on the roaring verge of Niagara, through the grumbling parks of London, on the laughing boulevards of Paris, among the majestic ruins of Rome, in the torch-lit galleries of Herculaneum, around the flaming crater of Vesuvius, through the wave-reflected palaces of Venice, among the barbaric splendors of Constantinople, but none of these, not all combined, have left in my memory a page graven with more significant and indelible than the gold 'diggins' of California."

He concluded the gold region of California was so abundant that "ten thousand men in ten years could not exhaust it."

The *North American and United States Gazette* editor remained skeptical of many of the reverend's perorations, adding a note to one of Colton's letters: "It [California] needs some deposits of the precious metals as some offset to the howling sterility of nine-tenths of California; but we will back a coal mine in Pennsylvania against all the gold mines of the new El Dorado."

Larkin, meantime, almost matched Reverend Colton's effusions.

"At present, the people are running over the country and picking it [gold] out of the earth here and there, just as 1,000 hogs, let loose in a forest, would root out ground nuts," claimed Larkin in a letter from Monterey dated August 29, 1848, and published in the *New York Journal of Commerce* in October. "Some get eight or ten ounces a day, and the least active one or two. They make the most who employ the wild Indians to hunt it for them. There is one man who has sixty Indians in his employ; his profits are a dollar a minute."

He continued, reporting on the ignorance of the wild Indians doing all the work while, presumably, their employers lounged on the riverbanks: "The wild Indians know nothing of its [gold's] value, and wonder what the pale-faces want to do with it; they will give an ounce of it for the same weight of coined silver, or a thimbleful of glass beads, or a glass of grog. And white men themselves often give an ounce of it, which is worth at our mint $18 or more, for a bottle of brandy, a bottle of soda powders, or a plug of tobacco."

A man named Childs, apparently Larkin's agent in the east, wrote him in late September, "Your letter and those of others have been running through the papers all over the country, creating wonder and amazement in every mind."

*   *   *

IN THE WINTER of 1848, with heavy rains preceding numbing arctic winds from the Sierra Nevada, at least eight thousand miners were huddling around their campfires and in their thrown-together hovels and log huts in the diggings.

Many grimy, bearded, threadbare, sun-browned men, most of them sick and disappointed, made their way down to San Francisco with whatever gold they had taken out, to await warmer weather. In the already raucous town, as in the camps above, they squandered their dust drinking and gambling, or spent it buying impossibly high-priced provisions for new season at the placers.

Only a handful had earned enough to "retire," but the '48ers, probably ten thousand men in all, had taken nearly a quarter-million dollars in gold from the rivers, streams, banks, arroyos, slopes, and hillsides of the Sierra Nevada, and from the Missouri border to the Atlantic the voices of doubt dwindled as the year closed. The Colton and Larkin reports, among hundreds of other newspaper letters and dispatches from California, some even more stridently fabulous, had made an impact, even more so the arrivals in Washington of Ned Beale and Lucien Loeser with their tea caddies and satchels of gold and the president's acknowledgment of the discovery in his message to Congress.

In Cincinnati, a twenty-two-year-old composer named Stephen Foster unknowingly wrote a marching song for the army amassing, a minstrel show ditty titled "Oh! Susanna":

> *I come from Alabama with my banjo on my knee;*
> *I'se gwan to Louisiana my true lub for to see.*
> *It rain'd all night de day I left,*
> *De wedder it was dry;*
> *The sun so hot I froze to def,*
> *Susanna, don't you cry.*
> *Oh! Susanna, do not cry for me;*
> *I come from Alabama,*
> *Wid my banjo on my knee.*

And an aspiring gold miner named Jonathan Nichols of Salem, Massachusetts, who sailed for California on a vessel named *Eliza* toward the end of 1848, reworked the lyrics:

I soon shall be in Frisco
And then I'll look around,
And when I see the gold lumps there
I'll pick them off the ground.
Oh, Californi-o
That's the land for me!
I'm going to Sacramento
With my washbowl on my knee.

At year's end the prevailing question in the minds of those determined to go out and get rich was simply, "How do I get there?"

III

JOURNEYS

Then blow ye winds hi-oh,
For Califor-ni-o,
There's plenty of gold
So I've been told
On the banks of the Sac-ra-men-to.
—Anonymous, 1849

EIGHT

DOUBLING THE CAPE

THE PADDLE-WHEEL steamer *California* slipped its moorings in New York Harbor on the morning of October 6, 1848, and thrashed the water out past Bedloe's Island, Sandy Hook, and the New Jersey shore while Captain Cleaveland Forbes pored over his charts of the forthcoming 15,000-mile voyage via the Strait of Magellan to the Pacific coast. His ship, "a stately lady," the newspapers called it, carried a crew of thirty-six, five hundred tons of coal, some bags of mail, and six passengers bound for Rio de Janeiro and Valparaiso.

The voyage of the *California* to California marked the brief interval between the lingering doubt that the gold discovery was more than a flash in a tailrace and the realization that it was a sensationally rich strike. The ship departed New York a month after Lieutenant Beale arrived in Washington, bringing news and gold from the commander of the Pacific Squadron, and two months before James K. Polk gave the gold matter a presidential endorsement in his message to Congress.

The steamer had been built for a more mundane mission than carrying gold hunters. It was launched to carry mail under a federal subsidy and to inaugurate passenger service between the Atlantic and Pacific seaboards. As it happened, by the time the *California* reached the Pacific side of the Isthmus of Panama, the rush for California gold had begun and the ship would have the double distinction of being the first steam-and-sail vessel to reach San Francisco and the first to convey "Forty-niners" to the gold fields.

The keel of the *California* had been ceremoniously laid on January 4, 1848, twenty days before the gold discovery, at the yards of the noted clipper-ship builder William H. Webb in New York. As the hull rose it became clear this was to be a vessel of strength and beauty. Built of choice oak and cedar, 203 feet from stem to stern, 33½ feet in the beam, it weighed 1,057 gross tons and cost $200,000, a colossal sum in the 1848 ship industry. Classed as a brigantine, three-masted and equipped with a full suit of sails, the *California*'s gleaming black hull was reinforced by diagonal iron straps to withstand the battering of the seas and the incessant vibrations issuing from its engine and the two twenty-six-foot paddle wheels amidships. Copper sheathing below the waterline was installed to prevent damage by teredos ("shipworms," actually elongated sea clams capable of boring holes in oak hulls).

The big one-cylinder engine that turned the wheels had been manufactured by the oddly named Novelty Iron Works of New York. It was steam powered from seawater by two coal-fed boilers, the fuel, five hundred tons of it, stored in a coal hold together with a complete set of replacement machinery. The ship also carried a year's provisions for its crew and what was expected to be a small number of passengers, most of them departing at Rio and Valparaiso.

A black-painted hull and a single tall, black funnel billowing black smoke; a white upper works, red paddle wheels, gleaming brass rails and housings—the spectacular *California* drew admiring waterfront throngs as it churned down the Jersey shore, at a coal-conserving eight knots, to the open sea where sails were unfurled to snag the south-driving wind.

For over two months the voyage passed uneventfully, the equator crossed on October 24, the Brazilian coast reached on November 2 in a record twenty-six-day run. By then, Captain Forbes had taken to his bed with some undiagnosed illness and the ship spent twenty-three days at anchor off Rio de Janeiro, taking on fresh water and making repairs before steaming south toward the Strait of Magellan. An historic ordeal, threading the strait occupied six days of battering storms, cross-currents, tide rips, and a long, wallowing anchorage off a Chilean prison colony aptly called Fort Famine before the ship broke free and began riding the long Pacific swells up the western coast of South America.

On December 20, eight days after punching through the strait, the *California* anchored in Valparaiso harbor where the still-ailing Captain Forbes hired a merchant ship master to assist him. A trickle of gold news had reached the Chilean capital and there were some aspiring argonauts there hoping to buy passage to San Francisco. But since Forbes had been ordered to take on no passengers before reaching Panama, he ordered the anchor up to steam on to the port of Callao, arriving there on December 29, eighty-three days out of New York. At the Peruvian coastal town the no-passenger order was rescinded and there began a drastic change in the leisurely nature of the *California*'s maiden voyage.

The shipping office at Callao had been crowded if not besieged since October, after Lieutenant Loeser, emissary of the military governor of California, brought in the first substantial news of the gold strike. When a delegation of Peruvians with their bedrolls, bags and portmanteaux, picks and shovels and fistfuls of money, begged for berths on any vessel departing for Mazatlán and points north, Captain Forbes relented and took aboard sixty-nine passengers who could afford stateroom space.

The *California* reached the harbor of Panama City on January 17, 1849, where a mob of fifteen hundred men, a few with their wives and children, packed the beach and jetty clamoring for passage to San Francisco. Worse for Captain Forbes, over seven hundred of the clamorers were Americans who had purchased and were entitled to space on his vessel.

There were three steamers—the *Georgia*, *Ohio*, and *Illinois*—ferrying passengers from New York to Chagres, Panama's main Atlantic port. To reach the Pacific side, the travelers had to move up the sluggish, malarial Chagres River by dugout canoes with hired paddlemen, then continue on foot and with pack animals through the jungle to Panama City. What neither the Atlantic- nor Pacific-side shipping companies could have foreseen was the shocking effect of the gold news between the *California*'s departure on October 6 and its arrival in the Bay of Panama on January 17. In this period, the office of the Atlantic Company in New York had been inundated by the gold-hungry, wallets in hand, and tickets to California quickly sold out (scalpers sold steerage vouchers for $400 and up), not only for passage to Chagres but for the *California* and the two other ships that were to follow it on the Pacific side, the *Oregon*, and the *Panama*. In the two months following the *California*'s departure, at least seven hundred paid ticket holders were expecting to board her or the ships following.

The "Great Madness," which Sutter's biographer Julian Dana said began with the invasion of New Helvetia in the spring of 1848, was nowhere better illustrated than in Panama City in the dangerous days between January 17th and 31st, 1849. Those tumultuous two weeks of the *California*'s anchorage fairly defined Dana's phrase for Captain Forbes and his crewmen.

The ancient, delapidated town, oldest European settlement in the Americas, its nights loud with parrot and monkey noises, its days an enervating stew of steamy heat and the ripe odors of waste and decay, was a perilous place even without an angry mob of ticket wavers. Here, where once Columbus probed, where Balboa ruled, and Francis Drake and Henry Morgan plundered, had erupted a green hell. Deadly fevers lurked in the offal and sewage in its rough streets; its byways were alive with rats and feral dogs and their human kin, the cutthroats preying on the hapless newcomers wandering about looking for a drink, a meal, and a pallet to sleep on while awaiting ships bound for San Francisco.

When the seven hundred paid-up Americans learned of the Peruvians already occupying staterooms on the *California*, they, and a good many of the eight hundred or so other hopefuls surging through the Panama City waterfront, stormed the Pacific Mail Steamship Company's ticket office demanding that the agent evict the interlopers.

What magnificent diplomatic maneuvering took place in those frantic days, and who was responsible for it, has never been explained, but the *California* escaped, burdened but unscathed. Somehow, four hundred passengers, one hundred and fifty over its berthing capacity, were boarded and given to understand they would need to find spaces by their own ingenuity. Many found a bed on a coil of rope on the maindeck, and some, it was said, paid a thousand dollars to a scalper for a place to sleep in steerage. Others were content to sit on a square of deck and sleep hunched over on their knees.

To resolve the issue of the Peruvians aboard the steamer, the Americans sought out Brevet Major General Persifor Frazer Smith, sailing to Monterey to replace Richard Mason as commander-in-chief of American military forces in the Pacific. This blustering fifty-year-old veteran of campaigns against the Seminoles in Florida and Mexicans in the late war, had careers as lawyer, politician, and soldier, but not then, or later, would he become a diplomat.

In an angry letter he addressed to William Nelson, United States Consul in Panama, Smith took the lawyerly view that since California was now property of the United States, its laws "inflict the penalty of fine and imprisonment on trespassers on public lands." Nothing could be more unreasonable or unjust, he said, "than the conduct pursued by persons not citizens of the United States, who are flocking from all parts to search for and carry off gold belonging to the

United States in California." He added sternly, "As such conduct is in direct violation of the law, it will become my duty, immediately on my arrival there, to put these laws in force."

This rattle of the ceremonial saber, its sentiments destined to commit endless mischief in the gold fields, actually seemed to have some positive effect on the agitation for passage on the *California*. The letter was apparently read aloud or a version of it, styled as a proclamation, posted in the shipping office, and calmed those talking of rushing the ship and evicting the foreigners. Soon after the general's pronouncement, the Chileans were peaceably moved to the main deck where bunks were rigged for them. Ticket-holding Americans took over the staterooms.

The *California* steamed out of Panama Harbor on January 31, "filled to cramnation . . . with passengers and stores and everyone looking out for himself," said Captain Forbes, whose health and temperament had not improved during the tense stay in Panama City. He noted in his log that there were respectable men aboard, but "we also have many of the scum of creation—blacklegs, gamblers, thieves, runners, and drunkards."

The ship took on water and firewood at Acapulco on February 9. The coal bunkers were empty by then and spars, bunks, bulkheads, and anything else that was expendable and flammable had been thrown into the boiler furnace. Then, somebody found a hundred hidden sacks of reserve coal and the anxious skipper got his stokers busy and moved on to San Blas and Mazatlán. At all three ports hundreds of Mexican argonauts were waiting at the quays for the voyage to California but could not be taken aboard.

The big steamer chuffed and churned into Monterey Bay on the 14th to a cannon salute arranged by Governor Mason. Lieutenant Sherman and former consul, now naval agent, Thomas Larkin were rowed out into the bay, climbed the ladder to the foredeck and welcomed Forbes, his crew, and passengers to California.

In the ten days spent in Monterey, Generals Smith and Mason conducted their business while crewmen cut all the wood they could find to fuel the ship's boilers. Meantime, the "scum of creation" Captain Forbes had logged flocked ashore to set up monte tables and sharper outfits and to belly up at Monterey's saloons. One tavern owner said he cleared $2,000 in two days of *California* passenger and crew business. Some who had spent all their savings on the passage to the Chagres and in buying a space on the steamer, put up "For Sale" signs on piles of clothing, tools, and weapons, to find subsistence money.

The ship weighed anchor and departed Monterey at seven on the morning of February 27 and reached San Francisco Bay on the 28th, 145 days out of New York, the first steamship to enter the Golden Gate.

The town of San Francisco had prepared for the event: The ships in the bay, traders and military, were draped with bunting; the Pacific squadron guns boomed a welcome; the townspeople, including hundreds of miners down to civilization from the diggings, flocked to the hills and beaches to wave handkerchiefs. Bands played, boats slipped out from shore carrying town dignitaries who gave overly glowing replies to questions about gold from the newcomers, assurances to calm their misgivings over coming so far chasing their dream of riches. (Of this, Bancroft said it would have been better "had they been able to translate the invisible, arched in flaming letters across the Golden Gate, as at the portal of hell, LASCIATE OGNI SPERANZA VOI CH'ENTRATE—all hope abandon, ye who enter here.")

General Persifor Smith and the other passengers were landed in boats and within hours the entire crew of the *California*, thirty-six men, deserted for the gold fields, leaving behind Captain Forbes, a single engine-room boy, and empty coal bunkers on an empty ship.

While the *California* lay at anchor in San Francisco Bay, the *Oregon*, second of the Pacific Mail Steamship Company vessels to leave New York for California, reached Panama City and took five hundred argonauts on board. When it reached San Francisco on April 1 its captain anchored his ship under the guns of a man-of-war in the bay and placed the more refractory of the crew under arrest. Eventually, with their pay increased from $12 to $112 a month, the *Oregon* was able to return east, the first ship to bring mail, passengers, and gold, back from California.

It galled Forbes that his captain's salary of $250 a month was half what he had to pay to recruit a chief engineer. A head cook cost him $250, and seamen $150 each, monthly. By April, with such expenditures, he had his crew signed, his coal bunkers filled, fifty-four passengers boarded, and departed San Francisco for the return voyage to New York.

★   ★   ★

THERE WOULD NEVER be a distinct pattern to the journeys to California in 1849, the frenzied signal year of the gold rush, but at the beginning of the year, at least five routes to California had been identified, four of them involving sea travel. New Englanders and those from the middle states drifted toward the Atlantic seaports for passage via Cape Horn. Southerners, most often embarking from New Orleans, elected to cross the Isthmus of Panama from the Atlantic port town of Chagres to Panama City on the Pacific. Others in the south took passage from New Orleans to Tampico, Vera Cruz, or Tehuantepéc, and crossed Mexico to the Pacific. Some, fortunately few in number, crossed Honduras, Nicaragua, and even Costa Rica, but had slimmer chances of finding a California-bound vessel on the Pacific side. Midwesterners and westerners followed the overland trails out of Missouri to the Sierra Nevada and across into California.

There were countless variations on these routes. Easterners did not always choose the sea, nor westerners the trapper's trails. A few New Englanders who could not abide the idea of any ocean journey made their way to St. Louis to buy an "outfit"—wagons, draft animals, provisions—to take their chances with the wild Indians said to be lurking everywhere in the western wilderness. Some in the midwest and even west of the Mississippi, imagining the sea lanes were quicker, contrived to get to New Orleans or perhaps back home to New York, Boston, Salem, Norfolk, Philadelphia, Baltimore, or Charleston, often doing so with little or no knowledge of the vastness of the seas ahead or the speed of the vessels plying them. Many '49ers, such as John W. Audubon, son of the eminent naturalist painter, followed well-planned and complex (if generally disastrous) routes from the mouth of the Rio Grande where they began an overland trek across Texas and northern Mexico to southern California, thence north to the mining country.

The voyage of the *California* illustrated two of the commonest sea routes to the gold country.

Cape Horn was well understood by New Englanders, who since 1791 had sent whalers around the southern tip of South America to the Pacific. The '49ers voyages followed the whalers' paths, sailing south from New England to intercept the trade winds, which swept their vessels into the calms and light winds of the horse latitudes at about 30° north latitude, then into the equatorial doldrums and across the equator. The southeast trades carried the ship under Sugar Loaf

Mountain to Rio de Janeiro, usually the first port-of-call, and a favorite, where during the layover passengers toured the city and its cathedrals, parks, and cafés, saw the palace of Emperor Dom Pedro II, and perhaps the slave markets, particularly obnoxious to any abolitionists aboard.

A brief stopover might be made at the island of Santa Catarina, five hundred miles down the coast from Rio, where vendors sold melons, pineapples, milk, and other delicacies not enjoyed since leaving home. After some hours ashore, sails bloomed and the ship headed toward the Southern Cross, the Falkland Islands, and the critical business of "doubling the cape."

To landlubbers this "doubling" had a romantic sound, a sting of salt spray far more delectable than a mere sailing around a cape or promontory. But those who fought the protean storms, the shrieking, sleet-filled winds and writhing seas at 56° south latitude by 67° 16 minutes west longitude, from the Dutch who named it in 1616 onward, bestowed little but curses on it. As well did the terrified passengers, when, with their compartments awash in the icy seas cascading down from leaking decks, they lashed themselves to their bunks, slid around the frozen planking, and were knocked off their feet by the hammer blows of wind and sea.

William Bligh and the crew of the *Bounty* spent a month trying to batter their way around the high headland in 1788, finally surrendering and turning east for Africa's Cape of Good Hope. During the War of 1812, the American naval captain David Porter's frigate *Essex* fought through the passage with great suffering to his crew and ship, and wrote, "I would advise those bound into the Pacific never to attempt the passage of Cape Horn if they can get there by another route."

But in 1849, sixty-five years before the oceans were connected, there were few alternatives.

The Strait of Magellan, a winding, stormy slot two to fifteen miles wide, 350 miles long, and bordered by high cliffs between the southern tip of South America and the island of Tierra del Fuego, was a slightly better course, depending on the season. Some ships at anchor below the tablelands of Patagonia, waiting for weirdly unpredictable currents, fogs, squalls, and williwaws—short, ferocious, headwinds— to clear, allowed passengers to explore ashore, to collect mussels and wild celery, and to hunt deerlike guanicos, foxes, rabbits, and rhea birds.

Patagonian Indians, living in hide lodges on the shore and hunting seals and otters from their canoes, were feared as cannibals and avoided.

Few of the '49ers' ships chose the strait over the Horn but among all-sea courses, those were the choices. A popular ship-board song among Cape Horners summed up the experience:

> *We lived like hogs penned up to fat,*
> *Our vessel was so small.*
> *We had a "duff" but once a month,*
> *And twice a day a squall.*
> *A meeting now and then was held*
> *Which kicked up quite a stink;*
> *The Captain damned us fore and aft*
> *And wished the box would sink.*

By 1849, the cape and strait routes were well-traveled and mapped, if no less miserable and dangerous to sailor and certainly to the uninitiated passenger. Commonly, the Pacific-bound vessel, after touching at Havana and Rio on its leisurely run south, watered again in the Falkland Islands before the trying days negotiating the southern tip of South America, and once free of Horn or strait sailed up along the western South American coast. Anchorages might include Talcahuano, Chile, a mud village with a good harbor; certainly Valparaiso, a city of cobblestoned streets, a population of thirty thousand, and many waterfront curio shops, fruit stands, groggeries, and brothels; and the Peruvian port of Callao, generally the final stopover before reaching Panama City.

Juan Fernández Island, a former Chilean prison colony four hundred miles west of Valparaiso, became a favorite disembarkation place for the argonauts. The boomerang-shaped island, twelve miles long by four wide, was well known to Cape Horn sailors, and fascinated Cape Horn passengers. The craggy, volcanic upthrust from the ocean floor served as a primitive home to the Scots castaway Alexander Selkirk who lived there four years after being branded a troublemaker and put ashore in 1705 from the privateer *Cinque Ports*. (His story was immortalized by Daniel Defoe in the 1720 novel *The Life and Strange Surprising Adventures of Robinson Crusoe of York, Mariner*.)

J. Ross Browne, an Irishman and onetime police reporter who

headed for California via Cape Horn in 1849, visited the island four months out of Boston and later wrote a book about it. He wrote that in 1849 about a dozen Chileans lived there with a single American, one William Pearce, a former whaler from Maine who was landed there suffering from scurvy from the whaleship *Gideon Howland* out of New Bedford. Brown said the island was popular among South Pacific voyagers since it was overrun with horses, cattle, dogs, goats, and hogs, and lush with herbs, fruits, and vegetables—spearmint, wild oats, barley, beets, and radishes; peaches, cherries, quinces, figs, apples, and pears. Fresh water and firewood was also readily available.

The greatest attraction, Browne said, was Selkirk's cave, twelve feet deep, the inside walls covered by the names of adventurers who had visited it over the decades.

THE CAPE HORN voyage was expensive, costing as much as $600 for a reasonable berth, thus eliminating it as a route for what newspapers called "the vagabond element"—apparently meaning the poor as well as the footloose. The route was lengthy as well. The Forty-niner faced a passage of 13,000 to 18,000 miles, depending on detours, rarely accomplished under four months, often taking as much as six months between departure from an Atlantic seaport to arrival in San Francisco Bay. This tedious journey did not change materially until the the early 1850s, when clipper ships cut the passage to under ninety days.*

As late as November 1849, an advertisement in the *Boston Courier* described "The splendid, *fast-sailing*, A-1 bark *Orion*, 450 tons, Henry C. Bunker, of Falmouth, master, coppered and copper-fastened," as sailing on November 12 for California. The ship, somewhat luxurious with its spacious " 'tween-decks cabins" and two large "houses" on the maindeck, carried ninety-two passengers, most from Massachusetts, and twenty-three crewmen. Captain Bunker, a fifty-two-year-old former whaling master who had spent most of his life at sea, ran a taut ship. The *Orion* reached Rio on January 14, Cape Horn on February 19, and San Francisco on May 5, 1850—a creditable voyage. But it covered 19,102 sea miles, 166 days sailing time (175 days total),

---

*Similarly, the trans-Panamanian railway was not completed until 1855, by which time the gold rush, at least for individual enterprise, was over.

somewhat longer than the average of 168 days for all vessels departing New England to reach the Golden Gate.

For even the most adventuresome of travelers, the voyage around the Americas was a test of fortitude. The prisonlike confinement between ports, the cramped, damp quarters, the incessant groaning of timbers, the pounding of sea and wind, and seasickness ("Paying tribute to Neptune") were inescapable. Less expected were the foul food and fouler water, the latter so stagnant and rancid-smelling the casks were often "sweetened" with molasses, the stink minimized with vinegar, the resulting brew called "switchel." Common dining fare included "lobscouse" or "scouse," a hash of salt meat, potatoes, and crumbled hardtack; "hashamagundy," an odoriferous mix of turnips, parsnips, and fish parts; "dandy funk," shingle-tough sea biscuit (also called "ship's bread," both euphemisms for a form of marine hardtack) cooked with molasses, raisins, and cinnamon; kegged salt pork and beef, moldy cheese, and an occasional treat such as applesauce.

Passengers, in calm seas at least, found ways to break the tedium. They stood at the rail looking for whales, dolphins, and flying fish; fished for bonito or whatever would swallow a hook; wrote in their diaries, held prayer and debating sessions, gambled, played checkers, dominoes, chess, and backgammon.

For all the miseries found on them, the sea routes to California boomed. The all-sea voyage was relatively safe, certainly safer than the malarial Isthmus of Panama and the cholera ravages and backbreaking toil of the overland trails. There were fewer than fifty casualties on the Cape Horn route in 1849, some brought about by diseases brought aboard, some from accidental drownings.

Shipboard travel also had the advantage of offering the passenger cargo space to bring along bulky trunks and luggage, boxed stores and luxuries, even machinery and furniture.

Most '49ers sailed in blunt-bowed, three-masted barks with the forward two masts square-rigged, or two-masted schooners and brigantines. But all along the Atlantic seaboard, every vessel with a mast or more was refitted, these ranging from condemned hulks with rotted keels, ketches, schooners, brigs, genuine steamers, and seventy of New England's whalers. Temporary decks and tiers of open bunks were rigged up on deck, provisions thrown aboard, ads placed in the papers that the ship was available to passengers bound for the gold fields.

Remarkably, none of the Cape Horn vessels, no matter how dilapidated, sank.

Between mid-December 1848 and mid-January 1849, sixty-one sailing vessels, averaging fifty passengers each, departed from New York, Baltimore, Boston, Salem, Philadelphia, and Norfolk; in February, sixty ships sailed from New York, seventy from Philadelphia and Boston, and eleven from New Bedford, bound for Cape Horn, Panama, and California. The passenger fleet continued to flourish through the year: Between the winter of 1849 and the spring of 1850, 250 vessels sailed for California from these eastern ports.

Meantime, the terminus of these voyages, San Francisco Bay, clogged with shipping. In the nine months following the arrival of the *California* in February 1849, 549 vessels, nearly half of them from the Atlantic states, sailed through the Golden Gate to discharge their passengers (over 30,000 by February 1850), on the wharves of the teeming town. From the jackstraw tangle of mastheads in the bay fluttered the jacks of most of the nations of Europe and South America, and of the Sandwich Islands, Mexico, and China. "All styles of nautical architecture may be seen," a San Francisco newspaper reported, "from the 'Gundalor' to the low, rakish-looking schooner, up to the magnificent ocean steamer, and from the Chinese junk to the most perfect symmetry and proportions of some of our men-of-war."

Just as the commanders of these ships could not keep their men from deserting to the mines, the fleet of vessels that came in '49 had to make do with recruiting, at high prices, crews for the return voyage. J. A. Swan, a colorfully observant miner lucky to have arrived in California before the gold discovery, wrote that everybody in the country was making money and that there could be small wonder that soldiers and sailors were fleeing their posts. "Uncle Sam's soldiers grumbled among themselves about the hardships of standing guard, polishing muskets and pipe-claying belts when they might be busy in the mines putting gold into leather bags," he wrote. As to the navy: "The tars howled about the evils of holystoning dirty decks and about being forced out of dry hammocks on stormy nights to trim sail—all when they could be swinging a lazy pick and drinking as much grog as a sailorman could hold without having their backs clawed by the 'cat' for doing it. . . . They preferred flapjacks and the musical jingle of nuggets in a poke to hard biscuits and a bos'n's whistle in a man-o'-war."

⋆   ⋆   ⋆

A NEW ENGLANDER named Octavius Howe compiled records of 124 "companies" which sailed or traveled overland from Massachusetts to the California mines in 1849 and provided some valuable findings. Of the 124, twenty-two parties chose the trails out of Missouri, 102 took all-sea routes⋆, ninety-six around Cape Horn, six through the Strait of Magellan. The average length of the all-sea voyage was 168 days, ten of them spent in port; the shortest time was made by the *Civilian*, 143 days, via the strait; the longest by the *Acadian*, 267 days via the Horn. (The longest time taken rounding the Horn was forty days by the brig *Pauline*.) The smallest ship to make the journey was the *Tobacco*, twenty-eight tons, the largest the *Edward Everett*, seven hundred tons. A good speed for any vessel was ten to twelve knots; a reasonable expenditure for passage was $500, including provisions. The parties ranged in size from five to 180 members.

The idea of traveling in "companies," born of the idea that there is strength in numbers, began nobly among those planning their journey to California but was recognized as futile once the every-man-for-himself gold fields were reached. The parties, sometimes called "outfits," often combined the funds of men actually going to the mines with the stay-at-homes willing to invest for shares of any gold discovered. The eastern seagoing parties were most often hastily thrown together and destined to hastily fall apart, often before the voyage was over, and certainly after.

The companies bore such impressive names as the Kennebec Trading and Mining Company and the Mattapan and California Trading and Mining Company, some including "dredging" in their title, giving the impression they intended raking up the gold from stream and lake bottoms.

Among the most impressive and ambitious of the New England outfits was the Boston and California Joint Mining and Trading Company, which sailed from Boston Harbor on January 13, 1849, on the aforementioned *Edward Everett*. The ship was named for Harvard's president, who presented the company with a one-hundred-volume library and the Horatio Alger–like admonition, "Take your Bible in

---

⋆Curiously, Howe omitted mention of companies who crossed Panama or the southern overland routes.

one hand and your New England civilization in the other, and make your mark on that country."

In the party were merchants, manufacturers, artisans, medical and divinity students, no less than eight sea captains, a mineralogist, a geologist, and four physicians. Among them were also a sufficient number of musicians to give nightly band concerts, and plenty of learned men for lectures. They set up a dispensary and library on board, stocked the ship with trade goods, enough foodstuffs and clothing to last two years, enough lumber to build two houses, and all manner of mining equipment. This elaborate and expensive company of gentleman miners dissolved soon after reaching California.

Daniel Woods, a Massachusetts Forty-niner, started out with a company of forty men—"of all professions and pursuits of life, young and old, grave and gay, married and unmarried"— calling themselves the Camargo Company. The party went broke and split up after many ordeals in the mines. In 1851 Woods wrote, "While at San Francisco I had the opportunity of obtaining information respecting the companies which had been formed in the States. Not one of these, so far as I could learn, continued together."

By mid-January, 1849, there were at least five California-bound mining companies organized in London at a time when virtually every European port was readying vessels bound for America. These British associations sold shares for as much as $1,000 each, bought ships, some of which carried wooden houses in sections, millworks, and other heavy machinery. Capital was recklessly advanced to the companies by "gold societies," rich men stricken with the fever but unable or unwilling to go themselves. Virtually all the loans were lost and few of the companies survived the voyage to California.

THE GOLD NEWS had reached England on October 10, 1848, on the Royal Mail steamer *Europa* and precipitated a lively newspaper debate on the authenticity of the reports. The editor of the *Times* of London buried an item about it among sundry commercial notices with the comment, "We need hardly observe that it is necessary to view these statements with great caution."

The *London Daily News*, the paper founded by Charles Dickens, ventured, "We must hear more of this El Dorado before we bestow upon it our serious consideration. There are some textures which will not bear many weeks washing, and the gold mines of the Sacramento may be one of them."

The *Times* sneered at President Polk's address to Congress in December, vastly exaggerating his few words on the gold discovery in California: "Paragraph after paragraph glitters with gold and groans with bullion. . . . A mint is forthwith to be established on the western coast, which is to deluge Asia and Polynesia with glittering tokens of the fortunate Republic." The writer ended his ridicule by predicting that a quarter million Englishmen had already gone or soon would depart for the gold fields.

In the winter of 1848, ominous news in European newspapers crowded out the California gold sensation. A cholera epidemic was sweeping the continent, with thousands of cases being discovered weekly and an estimated two thousand victims dead by the end of November, about the time the disease reached the United States.

Cholera had crossed the Atlantic before. An Asiatic strain that rampaged through Europe in the 1830s came to America on the customary route, in the fetid bilges and steerage compartments of passenger ships. It scythed through the eastern seaboard and rose and fell in spasmodic outbreaks over two decades as it swept westward.

Little was known of it except its sudden, catastrophic effect on the human body, the violent diarrhea, vomiting, and dehydration, the bone-wracking chills and fevers, the skin turning a clayey color, presaging death. Remedies advised by apothecaries and physicians— doses of laudanum, application of clysters and mustard poultices to the belly, calves, and soles of the feet—did no good.

The cholera bacterium, *Vibro cholerae*, unknown in the time, throve wherever poor sanitation existed, spread in water tainted by sewage, in "fecal-oral contact" as investigators later called it, and its deadly path knew no boundaries. It killed in cities where garbage, and human and animal excrement, ran in gutters and seeped into wells and other water sources; it killed in campgrounds and anywhere else where people congregated and emptied their bowels in or near their water supply. It could spread from a handshake and in any circumstance of poor hygiene.

The cholera outbreak of 1849, which did not subside until 1855, thus encompassing the entire gold rush era, is believed to have arrived in America on two ships from the French port of Le Havre. The *Swanton*, a passenger vessel which sailed in late October for New

Orleans, was apparently a plague ship since in the year following its arrival, four thousand of the city's populace died of the disease. The cholera lingered, became pandemic, and eventually claimed a third of the New Orleans citizenry before mysteriously dying out.

The steam packet *New York*, which debarked from Le Havre in November 1848, carrying 250 passengers, reached New York Harbor on December 1. Seven cholera victims had died aboard the ship en route and forty more within a few weeks of its arrival. By the end of the summer of 1849, five thousand New Yorkers had succumbed.

By then the outbreak had crept westward, invading St. Louis and the Missouri border settlements of Independence and St. Joseph, and the migrant camps along the Missouri and Platte Rivers. There, in the wet spring and early summer of '49, five thousand Oregon-bound pioneers and hope-filled argonauts died and were buried in the forlorn graves that became a familiar feature of travel along the overland trails. Before the epidemic ran its course it killed 30,000 men, women, and children across the states and territories.

Except for a few isolated cases, cholera did not reach the California mining camps until the fall of 1850, when it cut a year-long swath, carrying off fifteen percent of the populace of Sacramento—the town that grew up around the embarcadero of Sutter's Fort.

In truth, the casualties were probably much higher than guessed long after the gold rush ended. The California mining camps were perfect petri dishes for incubating cholera and were rife with unindentified diseases and unexplained deaths from the beginning of their occupation.

Of the thousands who disembarked from ships into San Francisco in 1849, estimates are that one in twenty died within six months, most of them in the camps where men felt no constraints of civilized living, least of all cleanliness; where their wretched habits turned rivers and streams into latrines; where they lived, and died, amidst fetid sloughs of garbage and excrement; where it was not uncommon for "died of the dysentery" to serve as an epitaph for half of a party of miners working a remote waterway.

Aside from the more readily diagnosable of mining camp ailments such as scurvy and venereal disease, and the recognizable deaths by gunshot, knife wounds, hanging, and "misadventure" (accidents), thousands of death certificates made by physicians in the diggings and at the "pest houses" of San Francisco carried vague causal remarks.

People were listed as having died of "ulcerated bowels," "destitution," "exposure to the elements," "rheumatism," "Panama fever," "phythisis" (consumption), "acute pneumonia," "insanity," and the odd finding of those who died alone with no marks of disease, violence, or misadventure on their corpses, "suicide."

Many of these most certainly died of cholera.

NINE

THE ISTHMUS

JULIUS PRATT OF Connecticut had contracted the fever in the autumn of '48 and with twenty other "good, intelligent Yankee men" formed up a company to mine gold in California. Now, in March 1849, all were anxious to get underway before the nuggets and dust played out. They had studied maps and the one depicting the territory west of Missouri labeled much of it the "Great American Desert." This clearly was not a route for well-bred Yankee men, and the all-sea, Cape Horn passage seemed "too long for our adventurous spirits," Pratt wrote sixty years later. And so they placed their collective finger on the throat of Central America and felt the pulse of Panama.

The Cape Horn and overland routes were as much as six months from California, the newspapers said, but the Isthmus of Panama was a "shortcut." Ticket agents said so, too, and were selling "through" fares, passage on sail and steam vessels from New England or New Orleans to the port of Chagres on the Atlantic shore of the isthmus, and from Panama City on the Pacific side to San Francisco. The agents claimed that the whole journey could be made in six weeks. True, the tickets were pricey—$80 to $100 to Chagres "in saloon" (a large cabin accommodating several passengers), another $20 for boat transport up the river, $250 from Panama City to San Francisco, also in saloon, or $100 for a smaller, "second cabin"—say $300 total for decent shipboard quarters.

This seemed reasonable to Pratt and the others. They had planned their excursion to the gold fields to the fine detail. Most in the party were married men, all were respected citizens of their New England communities. They had enlisted a physician, had representatives of various other useful trades and professions, were in "robust health" and "fond of adventure." Each man had subscribed to a code of conduct and to articles of agreement for two years of "service in the gold country." Each man was restricted to seventy-five pounds of clothing and personal effects, packed in a rubberized, watertight bag; each took along a carbine, a revolver, and an assortment of portable camp gear—bedroll, half-shelter, folding chair, mess kit, and the like. The doctor was responsible for bringing a medicine chest and a set of surgical instruments.

They packed two bags of dimes for expenses on the Isthmus because somebody had heard that dimes were rated as *reales* in Panama. Daily rations were to be purchased along the way as needed and so they sent ahead on two vessels departing on the Cape Horn route bags of flour, sugar, coffee, cheeses in sealed tins, and similar nonperishable provisions, plus a cookstove, farming tools, tents, lanterns, and extra arms and clothing, all to be warehoused in San Francisco until claimed by Pratt or others of the company. By the time these bulky stores reached California, the company expected to be long established in the mines.

Most of the twenty were churchgoers and and packed books of sermons and similarly uplifting reading matter, and a collection of "glees" and other music for the singers in the party, of which Julius Pratt was one.

Each man had put up $500 in cash in addition to the purchases necessary in putting together his kit and weaponry. Whatever remained of the $10,500 in pooled funds, after expenses, plus all profits cleared in the mines, was to be divided evenly among the party members.

They were aware that the Panama route had certain disadvantages, even dangers. It required at least two ship journeys, maybe three. Some of the New England vessels discharged passengers in New Orleans where they proceeded on a second steamer the 1,500 miles to the port of Chagres. Then when they reached the Pacific side of the isthmus they would board a third ship bound for California, 3,500 miles from Panama City.

Also, the *New York Herald* had carried a scary story about the Panama route, written by a correspondent who had been to Chagres, where argonauts began the isthmus crossing. "The climate there is, without doubt, the most pestiferous in the whole world," the writer said. "The coast of Africa, which enjoys a dreaded reputation in this way, is not so deadly in its climate as is Chagres. The thermometer ranges from 78 degs. to 85 degs. all the year, and it rains every day." The article ended as it began, on an ominous note: "Many a traveler, who has incautiously remained there for a few days and nights, has had cause to remember Chagres; and many a gallant crew who have entered its harbor in full health, have, ere many days, found their final resting-place on the dark and malarious bank of the river."

Elsewhere they read that physicians were advising that those traveling to Chagres, and on the river by that name, take two to four grains of sulphate of quinine, the specific for malaria, in a glass of wine as a preventative, to avoid the sun when possible, eschew native fruits and oysters, and wear flannel next to the skin by day and night.

Pratt and his party were not afraid of the purported horrors of Panama; they were hardy, dauntless men, had a physician to administer quinine and planned to "be civil to the natives," as another newspaper writer advised.

They looked at the map, at the skinny strip of land separating the two oceans: They would go to Panama, get a boat, ride the river to the Pacific Ocean, and buy tickets for a steamer to take them to the diggings.

JULIUS PRATT'S FATHER, "a man of iron, of indefatigable industry, cherishing an implacable hatred of all forms of laziness," manufactured fine ivory combs with ingenious machinery he had himself designed. His small but prosperous shop was located in the village of Meriden, halfway between New Haven and Hartford, Connecticut, close to the Pratt cottage where Julius was born in August 1821.

The senior Pratt's workday commenced an hour before dawn and ended at nine P.M. every day save Sunday; Mother Pratt worked an hour more, caring for their children, cooking for and managing the workers who were quartered as boarders in the comb shop and warehouse.

Puritanical piousness gloomed the household. The Pratts regarded most forms of amusement as sinful. There were few occasions to smile, none to laugh. "My knowledge of right and wrong," Julius remembered, "was often acquired from the end of birch twigs."

He attended Yale College in 1838, was "rusticated"—expelled— for a year after participating in a prank in which students locked a professor in a faculty office, but graduated in 1842 "and proceeded to engage in the battle of life." He taught school in Alabama, and in 1843, married his childhood sweetheart, Adeline Barnes of New Haven, over his father's initial objection that she was a "city girl" and as such would make "an extravagant and unprofitable wife."

Young Pratt bought a brick cottage in Meriden and the couple began their forty-three-year marriage as he reentered his father's firm at a salary of $1,000 a year, still under a shadow for his disgraceful conduct at Yale.

At age twenty-eight, Julius was tall and lean, straight-backed with a high-domed head, shock of thick dark hair, big nose and brushy moustache comfortably appropriate for his wide, expressionful face and steady brown eyes.

On a trip to New York he found the place astir with gold excitement, swarming with schemes advertised for conveying argonauts to California, the big harbor filled with hulks and ruins of vessels being slapped with paint and decorated with bunting and advertised as soon to sail by the "best routes to the gold fields."

Since his comrades had selected him to head their Panama party he shopped for a ship in New York and chose a little brig of 140 tons named *Mayflower* which was advertised "for Chagres." It carried forty-five passengers when it sailed on March 22, 1849, Pratt's people given "cabins" extemporized in the hold by fitting up two- and three-tiered bunks along the bulkheads.

Just as the *Mayflower* sailed past Sandy Hook, disaster struck in the form of a terrific northeast gale that tumbled crew, passengers, baggage, barrels, ropes, and shredded sail around the deck in sopping confusion. The main boom and topmast crashed down on the roof of the wheelhouse, knocking the helmsman off his feet. Pratt, his men, and the other argonauts aboard reeled to their berths with blanched faces, spewing seawater and their breakfasts as the brig smashed into the swells, heaving and heeling, sluing into troughs, rocketing up, teetering on wave after foamy wave, then plunging down again.

In the midst of the storm the *Mayflower*'s master said to anybody listening that their chances were about even on weathering or foundering, but the wind abated after an eternal forty-eight hours and the brig drifted south under a clear sky and reached the Isthmus of Panama on April 13 without further incident.

The Chagres waterfront exuded a loathsome effluvia made up of sweating stevedores, fish, excrement, and nameless, rotting debris bobbing in the water. Even without the stench, the air, hanging like a sodden blanket over the bay, pier, and town, seemed risky to breathe. More worrisome were the loungers on the beach, an indolent, insolent crew of Panamanian Indians and a jetsam of drifters, dark as lascars, jabbering in exotic tongues and pointing at the sun-reddened, white-skinned outlanders trundling down the gangplanks.

Before hiring boats—flat-bottomed craft called *bungos*, hewn from huge mahogany trunks and shaded by palm-leaf awnings—to take them upriver, the company members, now organized along military lines with Pratt their "captain," fetched weapons from their baggage. Whispers from the Chagres wharf had warned them of what lay ahead and most of the scuttlebutt indicated that the native boatmen were a lazy but volatile lot.

Pratt's party and others anxious to get ahead started out on the river on April 15 in ten *bungos* with thirty natives to paddle and pole them. The sluggish Chagres cut a swath through a rank, green wall of jungle, the boatmen singing monotonous chants to the dip of their paddles, "and the wild beasts on the shore responding with savage howls," Pratt said. Deep in the night the boats swung ashore at a spot where a scattering of native-built grass-and-reed huts hugged the riverbank and there the travelers crawled into their pallets for a night of sweaty, fitful sleep, swatting flies and mosquitos, listening to squawking birds, chittering monkeys, and the guttural noises of larger beasts aprowl somewhere uncomfortably close.

At breakfast, a quarrel broke out between the *bungo* men and some of the passengers. The natives were insisting on more money and threatening to quit. Pratt called the affair a "mutiny," and it was a tense and potentially lethal business especially, as Pratt testified, "after we formed our company into line behind the natives and drove them into the boats at the muzzles of our guns. . . ."

On the fourth day on the river they reached the primitive village of Gorgona, and found a crowd of exasperated men anxious to spread the news. Panama City, they said, was crowded with ticket-holding argonauts from all over the world expecting to find transport to California. Many were sick with fevers. There were no ships, sail or steam, available.

A N   I N C E S S A N T   D O W N P O U R drove them from Gorgona and Pratt and his men spent three weeks in a muddy camp on the banks of the Chagres where they questioned every man returning on the swampy road before deciding to move on to Panama City, dividing the party into detachments, each with rented pack mules to carry their bags and provisions.

Pratt's memoir is undetailed on the weeks he spent in Panama City, as if it pained him to remember them, but at some point, a week or two after entering the town, they learned of an all-sail coal storeship, the *Alexander Humboldt*, anchored three miles offshore. Counting deck space, there were 360 spaces available on the ship and 440 were being sold for as much at $200 each no matter who held "through" tickets. The Pratt company paid up and boarded the day before the ship was due to depart. They found the hold and decks packed tightly with miners, many among them gaunt with fever and starvation, who had spent their last dollar for a sleeping space on deck or in one of the boats hanging from davits inside the rails.

The crowding was intolerable and Pratt, grown confident as "captain" of his militarylike party, led them and others, all armed, to confront the ticket agent to "adjust the passenger list." The agent, a Frenchman, must have heard of the angry crowd gathering on the beach and retreated to his office in a three-storied building fronting the Panama City plaza, finally emerging on his balcony to "a volley of Anglo-Saxon anathemas" from the infuriated mob below. When quiet was restored and the grievance stated, Pratt said, "The Frog was profuse in protestations, promising to arrange matters to our satisfaction."

Pratt found a spot on the deck and slept on an inflatable mattress and a waterproof blanket he had brought along to shed rain and sea spray. "Probably there is no prison in the United States where we could have found so little real comfort as we experienced on that ship," he recalled bitterly decades later.

The *Humboldt* drifted three weeks amid perverse currents and calms before finding enough wind to depart the Bay of Panama, and another forty-eight days were passed "on this prison ship," Pratt said, "our rotten and wormy provisions and our intolerable nasty water almost exhausted," before the coaler hove into Acapulco's harbor on July 7, 1849.

THEY WERE ANXIOUS to move on, had already spent close to four months just getting to the southern coast of Mexico. The ticket agent's lie about a three-week journey from Chagres to San Francisco had faded along with all other traces of their naive, adventure-filled dreams.

They recaptured some of their optimism upon learning that the steamer *Panama* was due in Acapulco in a matter of days but since the *Humboldt* was readying to depart, Pratt decided not to give up the party's spaces on it. He wanted to stay behind with Dr. Paddock, the company physician, and planned that the two would take passage on the *Panama* and reach San Francisco ahead of the others where he could claim their warehoused goods and perhaps get established in the mines before the balance of the party arrived.

At dusk about a week after the *Humboldt* sailed with his companions aboard, the *Panama* entered Acapulco's harbor and sent a boat ashore with some bags of mail. Pratt was waiting at the jetty when the mailboat tied up and said he "extorted a promise from the mate in command that he would wait until my comrade and I could get our effects and return with him to the steamer."

This plan, like so many others he had devised, failed. By the time Pratt and Dr. Paddock returned to the beach with their bags, the mailboat had departed to the *Panama*. The two waited over an hour for its return, then sought out the American consul in the town who informed them that Mexican authorities had forbade any passenger boat coming ashore until the steamer passed quarantine regulations.

The *Panama* skipper could not wait, ordered steam up, and slid out of the harbor.

At last, in September, the paddle-wheeler *California* arrived off Acapulco. This was the vessel that had been mobbed at Panama City the previous January and Pratt was told that its passenger complement already exceeded the "legal limit" and that there was "strife aboard for food and sleeping space." After much argument, however, the captain relented. He would take Pratt and the doctor aboard if they would accept "a sailor's ration of salt pork and hardtack" and "roost wherever we could find a space." Pratt agreed instantly.

On about October 1, 1849, he wrote, "seven months after leaving home, we passed through the Golden Gate and stepped ashore upon the promised land."

PRATT'S EXPERIENCES ON the Panama route to California were maddening but not unique; indeed, compared to others, he suffered little except lost time. He traveled with a well-heeled party and did not lose a man. Behind, on the malarial paths from the port of Chagres to the Pacific side of the isthmus, and in and about Panama City, lay countless perils he and his comrades had managed to avoid.

The *New York Herald* writer who compared the Panama route to the plague coasts of Africa had not exaggerated. In 1849 it would have been difficult to pinpoint a deadlier stretch of territory in the world than the seventy-five-mile trans-isthmus crossing. Epidemics lurked in the steamy rain forest, mangrove swamps, and squalid riverside villages, behind every stand of palm, mango, teak, and banana trees, in the canopies of dripping vines, creepers and hanging mosses. Yellow fever prospered there, as did myriad other always debilitating, often fatal, diseases, commonly and euphemistically called "complaints" when recorded by physicians passing through with their satchels of worthless nostrums. In the days before bacterial and viral infections or insect and animal hosts were understood, before the most elementary of sanitation measures were taken, these medicos wrote of argonauts suffering from "acute ague," "parasitic infection," "lung congestion," "bloody flux," "black vomit," "jaundice," "epigastric distress," "fulminant fever," "foul water fever," "Chagres fever," and "Panama fever." Among the real fevers endemic in Panama were yellow, dengue, typhoid, and malaria. Cholera (probably the "Panama fever" so often mentioned in argonaut journals), if not already indigenous to the isthmus in 1849 was certainly introduced there early in the year with the first shipload of California-bound passengers to reach Chagres from New Orleans.

PRATT'S FIRST ACT ashore in San Francisco was to find the shipping agent to whom he had consigned his party's cargo of goods and equipment, sent ahead on two trade ships more than seven months past. The vessels had not yet reached California, the agent said, but yes, Pratt's companions had arrived in the bay a month ago and were working somewhere in the mines up on the Sacramento.

With only this vague information to guide him, the comb maker's son began his search by buying space on a lumber sloop headed up the Sacramento River. The town now bearing the river's name had been platted by John A. Sutter Jr. and Sam Brannan in the fall of 1848, and sprawled on the embarcadero of Sutter's Fort, a mile and a half west of the fort proper.

For four days Pratt wandered the "incongruous chaos of board cabins and tents . . . the greatest community of desperadoes and criminals on the face of the earth," confronting grimy miners down from the hills and streams to the north and east, questioning shop-keepers, expressmen, whoever spoke English, on the whereabouts of his company.

At last he found six of his party in a camp on the river, the men sick with scurvy and diarrhea, surviving, he said, "on a diet of raw onions at one dollar each and raw potatoes at one dollar per pound." (Both vegetables are antiscorbutics and were probably prescribed by a town physician). Two of the men were employed as carpenters at an upriver rancho at an ounce of gold a day, the barest of subsistence wages, and the rest of the company, Pratt learned, had found work in the diggings thirty miles up along the American fork.

He bought two horses from the personal cash reserve he had brought with him from Meriden, and took one of the invalid partners with him on a day-long ride along the river. The others of the company were faring poorly, Pratt said, all washing dirt from a gulch and finding a few dollars in dust a day.

He did everything he could to keep the company together but in 1849, California was no place for men to be dependent upon others.

He spent much of his dwindling reserve money buying a large wagon and five mules, assembled his men, their baggage and skimpy provisions, and started on the trail toward the settlement of Stockton, fifty miles south of Sacramento. This tent town, which took its name from the commander of Pacific naval forces during the war with Mexico, had sprung up in 1849 with a sudden population of 1,000, and sported several saloons and gambling parlors. Pratt had picked up a tip that there was gold to be found on the Stanislaus River, directly

east of Stockton in what were being called the "southern mines," and
that the town had a regular commerce by sail and steam vessels with
San Francisco and served as a winter station for miners.

He used one of Frémont's books as a guide and with his forlorn
party pushed south to the Stanislaus, a tributary of the San Joaquín
River, in a thunderstorm, making only three miles a day and spending
most of the time coaxing the mules to work and loading and unloading the wagon to free it from mud holes. When they reached the
Sierra foothills and the headwaters of the river they found an oak and
elm grove and set about building a cabin.

Pratt needed to get to San Francisco to determine if the party's
spare equipment, clothing, and provisions had arrived, and so
returned to Stockton and hired a boat to taken him downriver.

The ships, now nine months out of New York, still had not
arrived.

He hired a room and waited, "hearing occasionally from my company at the mines through traders who went back and forth with
pack mules," he wrote. "They were not earning enough to pay for
their provisions and so I arranged to send, partly by a boat and partly
by ox team, enough to keep them supplied."

The ships arrived toward the end of 1849★ but too late to assist
Pratt's failing party. "After three months' experience in gold washing . . . the more intelligent and conscientious of our company had
reached the conclusion that it was inadvisable to continue the organization," Pratt said wistfully. "So, after a division which gave to each
member the necessary outfit for digging and washing, and one
month's ration, we dissolved and each one became free to pursue his
own way individually."

He returned to San Francisco and sold off the goods so laboriously
shipped around Cape Horn, realizing enough to pay all the debts
accumulated during the nine months since their departure and to pay
back to the stockholders sixty percent of the original capital. He sold
a cookstove and fixtures that had cost $60 for $400; a farm wagon and
harness costing $90 found a buyer offering $500; a lot of cheeses
sealed in tin costing 16¢ a pound, sold for $1.50 a pound.

★Pratt offered no explanation for the nine or more months that passed before his company's cargo reached San Francisco. He wrote his memoir sixty years after the event and
may have been mistaken on the date the consignment arrived.

⊰ Henry P. Huntington ⊱

AMONG THE PASSENGERS who boarded the *Humboldt* at Panama City in the summer of 1849 was a twenty-eight-year-old peddler-entrepreneur named Collis Potter Huntington, a tinker's son born in Harwinton, Connecticut, in 1821. Raised in poverty, he labored as a farmhand through his boyhood, worked as a store clerk in Oneonta, New York, hawked jewelry in Ohio and Indiana, collected bills in the southern states, and sold butter in New York City. During his stayover in Panama City, waiting with the others for a ship to San Francisco, he rented a small schooner and shipped beef, potatoes, and sugar from the Colombian coast into the Bay of Panama, and had $4,000 in cash by the time he bought a berth on the *Humboldt*.

"I tried mining as thorough as any man did in this country," he said of his advent in California. "I worked nearly a whole day in the mines and I made up my mind it would not pay me. I came back to Sacramento to start in business."

He became a shrewd trader in mining equipment and hardware with a partner named Mark Hopkins and, with Hopkins and two dry-goods merchants, Charles Crocker and Leland Stanford, became one of the the "Big Four" financiers behind the Central Pacific Railroad. Among these men, Huntington, the lobbyist and fiscal genius, was the least liked and least likeable, often compared to various sea denizens—"soul of a shark," "ruthless as a crocodile"—and his later railroad interest, the monopolistic Southern Pacific, was widely regarded as an "octopus."

The financier died in 1900, immensely rich and as immensely despised as the perfect self-caricature of the American robber baron. Ambrose Bierce, who campaigned against the "railrogues" for William Randolph Hearst's *San Francisco Examiner*, provided an epitaph for him:

> *Here Huntington's ashes long have lain,*
> *Whose loss was our eternal gain,*

> *For while he exercised all his powers*
> *Whatever he gained, the loss was ours.*
>
> Born only thirty-five miles northeast of Julius Pratt's birth-
> place of Meriden, Connecticut, and in the same year, the two men
> were thrown together on the *Humboldt* in the Bay of Panama, en
> route to San Francisco, yet apparently did not meet. If they had,
> Pratt would certainly have mentioned Huntington in his mem-
> oirs.

A BOOK PUBLISHED not long after Julius Pratt's return to Meriden
proved, if he needed more proof than his own ordeal supplied, that
the gold rush was as diabolical a game of chance as any devised in the
meanest gambling hell of San Francisco. Published in two volumes by
Putnam's of New York, *Eldorado* was engagingly written by a *New
York Tribune* correspondent named Bayard Taylor, a published poet,
European traveler, and member, at age twenty-five, of the old New
England literati. The English edition received a glowing review by
Charles Dickens, and in England and America it sold better than such
other literary productions of 1850–1851 as Elizabeth Barrett Brown-
ing's *Sonnets from the Portuguese*, Emerson's *Representative Men*, and
Herman Melville's *Moby-Dick*.

Taylor was born in Kennett Square, Pennsylvania, thirty miles
south of Philadelphia, on January 11, 1825, his Christian name deriving from Senator James A. Bayard of Delaware, an ardent Federalist
and hero of the Taylor family.

Mother Rebecca, a teacher, and father John Taylor, the sheriff of
West Chester, a cattletown a few miles north of Kennett Square, seem
to have recognized Bayard's early literary precociousness and gave the
boy all the latitude he needed to develop it. His mother taught him
not only to read but to love reading, his father stood by proudly
watching the two read to each other and was so certain of his son's
brilliance that he took the boy to a noted phrenologist for another
kind of "reading." The man, a "Doctor" England, ran his fingers over
the topography of Bayard's cranium and said the fourteen-year-old
would be a poet and a traveler.

The lad did love poetry and travel books, also Gibbon, and David Hume's discourses, which he consumed at age thirteen. He wrote experimental verse in the manner of Sir Walter Scott—a lifelong literary lodestar—and sketched and painted, and read and read. He relived the conquest of Grenada by reading Washington Irving's *Alhambra* over and over, absorbed all of Emerson, Dickens, Byron, Shelley, Keats, Wordsworth, and Tennyson; read Voltaire in French editions (not his "atheistical" works, only his tragedies, he hastened to explain to his watchful mother), and followed the outré stories in *Graham's Magazine* by an admirable writer named Edgar A. Poe, and the editorials by fellow Quaker John Greenleaf Whittier in *The Pennsylvania Freeman*.

He fell asleep with books and magazines littering his bed. The Taylors made certain he read the Bible, something that required no coercion since Bayard loved its sonorous prose and vivid stories of lands he expected one day to see for himself.

In about 1840, he apprenticed as copy boy and typesetter on the *West Chester Village Record* and began sending his poems to such periodicals as the *Saturday Evening Post* and the Philadelphia-based *Graham's Magazine*. The first to be published, "The Soliloquy of a Young Poet," contained such lines as,

> *High hopes spring up within;*
> *Hopes of the future—thoughts of glory—fame*
> *Which prompt my mind to toil and bid me win*
> *That dream—a deathless name.*

And when the author was revealed to be a mere sixteen-year-old, he was considered "as mature as Chatterton," a droll reference to the eighteenth-century English poet who killed himself at about Bayard's age.

The burgeoning poet came to the attention of Rufus N. Griswold, editor of *Graham's*, a onetime Baptist minister who had a small reputation as literary arbiter. He encouraged Taylor to assemble his verse for a book and this maiden effort, opulently titled *Ximenia, or the Battle of the Sierra Morena*, appeared and disappeared in 1844, before the poet's twentieth birthday. Copies were sent to Longfellow and Lowell, and the book did Taylor no harm; indeed, its publication inspired him to begin the life of traveler-poet the phrenologist had predicted would be his lot in life.

By 1844 he had the look and carriage of a poet, He was an athletic six-footer with wavy, shoulder-length brown hair, a high forehead, a hawk's beak of a nose, heavy-lidded brown eyes, and what descriptive writers of the day loved to call a "finely chisled" mouth and jaw, and "a manly presence." These traits, and his conviviality, considered extraordinary in the commonly lonely and internal life of a poet, helped him as he set out on a two-year European *wanderjahre*, the first of a lifetime of journeys.

Upon his return to America he threw his adventures into a book, *Views Afoot*, which ran into six editions in a year and fourteen more by the end of the decade. Horace Greeley, editor of the *New York Tribune*, which had published some of Taylor's letters from the continent, was so pleased with the colorful dispatches he hired the poet early in 1848, at a salary of twelve dollars a week.

Greeley's decision to send Taylor to California probably had nothing to do with the poet's experience as a travel writer and his incessant appeals to be sent to the Pacific. Newspaper readers were clamoring for gold news and the editor appreciated Taylor's eye for detail, ear for what people said, and his companionable nature, perfect to extract everything needed for stories that would sell newspapers.

He gave his writer some instructions, among them, it seems, to keep the story lively and not dwell unduly on any miseries he encountered. Taylor wrote to his fiancée, Mary Agnew, "I am going to tell the truth and I think I shall have a cheerful story to send home. . . . I am light and buoyant hearted."

He sailed on the mail steamer *Falcon*★ on June 28, 1849, and eight days out of New York, the ship reached the harbor of Chagres.

TAYLOR'S DESCRIPTION OF the isthmus crossing stands in starkest contrast to what Julius Pratt, and most others who crossed it in '49, experienced. The others wrote down what they saw when they found time to set pen to paper; Taylor's only work was to write and he wrote incessantly, with a newspaperman's eye for vivid detail, a poet's

---

★This vessel, the first steamer to carry California-bound passengers to the Atlantic side of the isthmus, is believed to have brought the first cholera-infected passengers to Panama from New Orleans toward the end of 1848.

gift for expression, and a gentleman traveler's obliviousness to all but his own comforts.

With a party of five others (about whom, oddly, he wrote nothing), Taylor paid fifteen dollars for a seat in a *bungo* headed upriver to the village of Cruces. He seemed to love the experience. The boatmen, he said, sang "Oh! Susanna" as they poled the canoe through the sun-blazed swamplands with its "splendid overplus of vegetable life," its "rank jungle of canes and gigantic lilies and the thickets of strange shrubs."

In the late afternoon the canoe reached a village of bamboo huts on the right bank of the river, and he and the others "engaged hammocks for the night." Then, after a supper of pork and coffee, he made his day's notes under a thatched roof, by the light of a guttering candle stuck in a bottle.

Near the village of Gorgona, three days on the river, the boatmen began warning the passengers, "Cruces—muchas cólera," so the stay there, where the river ended, had to be brief. Taylor and the others hired horses—"tough little mustangs"—at ten dollars a head and plunged into forests screened by a roof of dripping vines and foliage, struck a stretch of paved road and passed the first of the many cholera victims they were to see, some being tended under trees, others writhing in their saddles. Because they could offer no assistance, they pushed on.

Five days from Chagres they caught the scent of the salt air of the Pacific and passed huts along the path, then stone houses, massive ruined buildings, a plaza, a great church, and an open space fronting the bay that washed the shore of Panama City.

In the comfort of the Hotel Americano that night Taylor wrote, "In spite of the many dolorous accounts which have been sent from the Isthmus, there is nothing, at the worst season, to deter anyone from the journey." This from a man who crossed the isthmus in five days and spent a day and a half in Panama City. He saw the whole Panamanian interlude as little more taxing than a tramp through Heidelburg or any other of his "views afoot" in Europe.

At the hotel, where he got his clothes washed while waiting for his luggage to come uptrail, he learned there were seven hundred gold-hungry people in the city awaiting passage to California. All steamer tickets had been issued and so great was the rush to get to San Francisco that $600 was frequently paid for a berth, double the normal price, and treble that paid by Julius Pratt for space on the *Humboldt*.

For Taylor, whose "through" ticket to California, *Tribune* credentials, and pocket money, allowed him to spend his time in Panama City worry-free, the wait had another pleasant reward. At the Hotel Americano he met the American naval lieutenant Edward Fitzgerald Beale, the courier who had carried the first news of the gold discovery to Washington in September 1848.

The two men became instant friends and the association benefited both. Ned Beale, age twenty-seven, had literary aspirations, regarded poetry as the highest of callings, and had read Taylor's work; Bayard Taylor, age twenty-four, found Beale charming in his insouciance, an admirable man of action who loved literature. Both shared "thoughts of glory—fame" and the hope of "That dream—a deathless name."

Within a day of their meeting, the *Panama*, coal smoke surging from its funnel, steamed into the Golfo de Panama to an anchorage a mile and a half offshore. While hotel porters hustled their bags to the skiff that would take them out to the steamer, Taylor seems to have coolly ignored the angry mob of bypassed argonauts on the beach. He took note of the heat, however, so fervent, he said, "that I was obliged to hoist my umbrella."

As the boat moved out among the pelicans' roosts to the ship, he said, "I was satisfied to leave Panama at the time; the cholera, which had already carried off one fourth of the native population, was making havoc among the Americans." Several of the passengers on the *Falcon*, the ship that had brought him to the isthmus, "lay at the point of death," he said.

When the *Panama* thrashed a path into Acapulco Harbor there was much bustling among the passengers as they anticipated a day in the picturesque town to stretch legs, eat a sumptuous café meal, and see the sights. On the quayside, a cheering knot of Americans watched the steamer anchor and awaited the gig that was approaching from it to the pier, bringing mail.

Among those stranded in Acapulco, and anxious for the boat to tie up, was Julius Pratt of Meriden, Connecticut. Nearly four months had passed since his departure from New York and he had reached Acapulco after a struggle that would have vanquished a man of smaller resolution.

But the *Panama* captain saw no need for a quarantine inspection, ordered the boilers coaled and the anchor weighed, and departed at sunrise. Pratt remained a castaway for another two months.

THE STEAMER TOUCHED briefly at Monterey as it beat its path north along the California coast, and on August 19 entered the Golden Gate, the island of Alcatraz gleaming white with pelican guano straight ahead, Angel Island and the bight of Sausalito on the port quarter, and high through the morning fog, thirty miles inland, rose the peak of Monte Diablo, sentinel of the gold country of the Sierra Nevada.

As it came abeam of the American man-of-war *Ohio*, the *Panama* announced its arrival with a cannon salute and wallowed into the bay in search of a moorage among the bristling multitude of masts.

The warship sent boats out to greet the *Panama* and assist in conveying its passengers ashore, and with Ned Beale at his side, Bayard Taylor, just fifty-one days since departing from New York Harbor, scrambled into a longboat to set foot on California mud. By the time he climbed off pierside, newcomers and teamsters were picking through the jumble of luggage, crates, barrels, and bags, while a furious wind blew down from a gap in the hills encircling the bay, billowing tents and driving dirt and sand up in a scouring tempest.

Taylor's first impression of San Francisco was of the "polyglot horde" he saw en route to finding lodgings. "Yankees of every possible variety," he saw, and "native Californians in serapes and sombreros, Chileans, Sonorans, Kanakas from Hawaii, Chinese with long pigtails, Malays armed with their everlasting creeses [a wavy-bladed Asian knife], and others in whose embrowned and bearded visages it was impossible to recognize any especial nationality."

He and Beale rode in a teamster's wagon to Portsmouth Square, once a cow pen, then a customs house when the town was called Yerba Buena, and took rooms at the City Hotel at twenty-five dollars a week (meals twenty dollars extra). Taylor muscled his trunk and valises up a rickety stairway to a garret containing two cots, some blankets, two chairs, a rough table, washstand with ewer and porcelain basin, and a tiny shaving mirror. There was scarcely space, he said, for a tall man to stand up between the cots, and the room had but a single small window to light it during the day. Still, the garret appealed to his poet's spirit.

During a fast tour of the town led by Beale, Taylor saw a dozen men and several children in front of another hotel "digging up the earth with knives and crumbling it in their hands." Some were finding as much as five dollars a day at this enterprise and the poet surmised that the gold specks they found in the street got here as leakings from miners' pokes and pockets and from store and saloon sweepings. (More than likely, however, the gold had been "salted" in the streets by unscrupulous land speculators.)

The "unnatural value placed upon property" Taylor learned during his first day in town. The Parker House, filled to capacity with lodgers, brought in $110,000 a year renting space, $60,000 of the total from gambling layouts. He heard of a lawyer searching for a place to open an office who was shown a cellar, twelve feet square and six high, renting at $250 a month. And there was the story of a San Francisco citizen who died insolvent in the fall of 1848 with debts of $41,000. The man's lawyers and bankers were delayed in settling his affairs, during which time his real estate holdings had multiplied in value to such a degree that after his debts were paid, the proceeds guaranteed his heirs annual incomes of $40,000 each.★

Beale had a packet of government papers to deliver to John C. Frémont, and on his second day ashore from the *Panama* prepared to depart for San José where the explorer and his wife had taken up temporary residence. Taylor joined him. They prepared pack saddles with camp gear and provisions for the two mules Beale had bought, strapped wicker-covered jugs of water on the animals, armed themselves with skinning knives and pistols, and hiked over the hills toward the southern end of the bay. As they started out they heard the guns of the *Ohio* fire a salvo, "for the obsequies of ex-President Polk," Taylor later learned.

They descended to the foothills of San Bruno and crossed plains of burnt grass and gravelly arroyos to Santa Clara. At a rancho there they ate a *guisado* of beef and onions, drank some rank black tea, and spent a night battling fleas in an outbuilding where they were permitted to throw their pallets on the bare ground. In the morning, they fed the mules from a bushel of wheat purchased from the ranchero for five dollars.

★The deceased was the former vice consul in San Francisco, William A. Leidesdorff. Of the case, Bancroft said, "It is necessary for the living to take charge of the effects of the dead, but it smells strongly of the cormorant, the avidity with which men seek to administer an estate for the profit to be derived from it."

The pueblo of San José, a flourishing town of seven hundred inhabitants and an assortment of adobe homes, tents, and clapboard buildings, lay five miles inland from the southern extremity of San Francisco Bay. Most notable of the town's occupants, the Frémonts had quarters in a borrowed cottage. Beale and the explorer were old friends and comrades-in-arms and greeted each other warmly; Taylor had preconceived romantic notions of the great man, whose exploits were widely celebrated, and was thrilled to be presented to the hero.

The explorer was dressed in buckskins, a short "California jacket," and a great Mexican sombrero. The poet guessed Frémont's age to be thirty-five (he was in fact forty-six) and said, "I have seen in no other man the qualities of lightness, activity, strength, and physical endurance in so perfect an equilibrium. His face is rather thin and enbrowned by exposure; his nose a bold aquiline and his eyes deep-set and keen as a hawk's."

Frémont had just returned from his Mariposa Creek property where his party of miners were, he said, "successfully engaged in gold-digging." On a subsequent visit, Taylor learned the details behind this offhand remark and of the colonel's fabulous turn of fortune.

After an enjoyable day or two in San José and with provisions from the Frémonts' larder, Taylor and Beale repacked their mules and headed out northeast to Stockton, making a night camp en route with their picketed animals, eating stewed beef and tortillas by their campfire.

Taylor found Stockton an unimpressive place except for the twenty-five river schooners at anchor on its riverfront and the fact that a one-story clapboard house in this miners' supply depot cost $15,000.

Beale appears to have returned to San Francisco on one of the Stockton schooners while Taylor decided to visit the diggings on the Mokelumne River, the most accessible placers from Stockton. He spent four days among the miners there, finding it a cosmopolitan scattering of camps where Americans, Frenchmen, Sonorans, and Kanakas were working claims with high hopes and low returns. Some were taking ten dollars a day from the creek and its gulches, others as much as two ounces.

In the Mokelumne camps he saw in full flower two of the scourges of the gold camps, gambling and xenophobic hatred of "foreigners," but passed them by in his relentlessly sentimentalized prose. He wrote with vague criticism of the men who expected instant riches once they dipped a pan in a stream or lifted a shovel of dirt and, with little passion, of the "first colony of miners" on the Mokelumne who "attempted to drive out all foreigners, without distinction, as well as native Californians."

As for the miners, he saw camaraderie and honesty. Admittedly, he said, the Sonorans ("those Bedouins of the West"), who came into the country "in armed bands, to the number of ten thousand in all, and took possession of the best points on the Tuolumne, Stanislaus, and Mokelumne Rivers" were pushed out by the Americans and "Several parties of them, in revenge for the treatment they experienced, committed outrages on their way home." But for all that, he insisted, "The cosmopolitan cast of society in California, resulting from the commingling of so many races and the primitive mode of life, gave a character of good-fellowship to all its members."

IN 1849, THIRTY-NINE thousand people came to California by sea lanes—around Cape Horn, or after crossing the Isthmus of Panama. Twenty-three thousand of this number were Americans. Another forty-two thousand came overland. Of these, nine thousand came from Mexico, eight thousand following trails, or blazing of new ones, across Texas and the Southwest; and twenty-five thousand crossing the Rocky Mountains.

TEN

THE GREENHORN TRAIL

MANY WHO WERE anxious to take the gold plunge decided that the overland trails had significant advantages over other routes to California. Even if starting out from eastern and southern states, the landlocked traveler faced a mere 3,000 transcontinental miles compared to 13,000 to 15,000 via Cape Horn, probably half that much on the isthmus route. And sea travel was expensive in 1849, and fraught with dangers, disease, at least severe discomfort—storms, *mal-de-mer*, bad food, rationed water—and the miseries of Panama were already being documented.

True, there were discomforts to be expected on the emigrant trails west, in particular the most traveled and therefore the best-known of these, the route across the Rocky Mountains. Wild Indians were a worry, and work had to be done every day. There would be nothing like lolling at the rail of a sailing ship, as the seagoing did, admiring flying fish and Saint Elmo's fire. Afoot, one had to make camp, cut wood, shoot game, cook, care for one's animals—all that. But the rewards! Fresh air. Seeing firsthand the immense Western wilderness Frémont had described so vividly in his books. Living off the land. The safety in numbers. The camaraderie of the trail.

Such fancies were not unusual among aspiring argonauts as they made their plans to find a way to California. Those who stayed home never learned the bitter truth; those who reached the western Missouri settlements to begin their journey learned it quickly.

Distances, they learned, we're meaningless; they varied, literally, all over the map, and were dependent upon the routes and detours taken. The *time* it took to get to the diggings was the paramount matter and a wagon party was lucky to travel fifteen miles a day, including stoppages. These could often last a week or more, in crossing rain-swollen waterways and inching up and down steep mountain trails. Those who walked beside their wagons the 2,000 miles from the Missouri rendezvous points to the Sacramento Valley required about the same time to reach California, five months on average, as a Cape Horner sailing from an eastern seaport.

Time burdened all the overlander's plans and efforts from the instant he decided to go to California and began to worry that unless he got there in a hurry the mines might play out. He learned from newspaper stories and "guides" to the gold country that wagon parties traveling the northern trails had to start out from western Missouri toward the Platte River in late April, certainly no later than mid-May. This timing was critical on both ends of the trails to the mines. Out of Missouri, the spring grass had to be high enough for oxen, mules, and horses to forage upon; and the wagons had to reach and cross the Sierra Nevada before the winter snows of mid-October locked the passes. The very least punishment for a late start or a slow progress was to spend the winter in Salt Lake City while others were counting their day's gold take on the Sacramento. The worst consequence was too dreadful to contemplate: being stranded, snowbound, as the Donner-Reed party had been in 1846, on the eastern slopes of the Sierra.

With about five months between good grass and open mountain passes, any hindrance to a fifteen-miles-a-day average westward progress had to be reckoned with. Natural obstacles were figured in, such as rainstorms that turned trails into wagon mires, and detours necessitated in finding a good river crossing or skirting the edge of a buffalo herd, but the most common obstruction, the overloaded wagon, was man-made. A benefit enjoyed by the sea-going miner was taking along a vast amount of baggage, equipment, and stores, to be stowed in a ship's hold. Even the isthmus crossers often landed at Chagres with piles of luggage, trunks, and crates, hiring natives to convey them to Panama City. Weight was no concern to the seagoers but to the overlander it translated to speed, and speed to time. The rule-of-thumb was that each adult on the trail required about five hundred pounds of provisions for the journey and that a wagon carrying 1,500 pounds needed three yoke of oxen—six animals—to keep pace. This lesson was hard-won; many wagons departed with 2,500 pounds weight or more, a matter usually resolved by the time the argonauts reached Fort Kearny, 260 miles out of Saint Joseph, and certainly before reaching Fort Laramie, 650 miles out. Between these two army posts lay a forlorn graveyard of jettisoned goods, some of it dating to 1843 when a thousand people were moving to the Oregon country in "the Great Migration." Now, with 25,000 making their way toward California, the trailsides were a litter of gold-washing machines, cumbersome tools, books, surplus ox yokes and mule collars, wheelbarrows, plows, barrels of rice, beans, flour, and sugar, kegs of nails, and mounds of salt pork. There were also piles of ashes and iron wagon parts where unrepairable wagons had been broken up and burned for firewood, their owners joining other parties or fashioning packsaddles and moving on alone or in pack trains. By 1850, overlanders were starting out with barely adequate outfits, depending upon the growing number of trade posts along the route, these mostly trailside tents or board-and-brush outstations, for provisions and fresh draft animals. These shabby emporia eventually spread from the Missouri border to the Truckee Valley, the gateway to the Sierra Nevada, serving as combination post offices, gambling dens, and blacksmith shops, and sold everything from a bottle of whiskey or a wheel of cheese to an ox, butchered or on the hoof.

By then the whole process of getting to California had speeded up. There were ferry services everywhere, ranging in cost from forty cents per wagon over the Sweetwater to sixteen dollars to cross the Green River; and even bridges were appearing: across the Platte at Deer Creek, the Laramie, the Bear, and the Portneuf River below Fort Hall.

OVERLAND TRAVEL, ALTHOUGH touted as the poor man's opportunity, was not cheap; indeed, it could get very expensive. The sea routes required $300 to $600 in startup passage money, and often three times as much would be spent from start to finish, whether via Horn or isthmus. A farmer already owned some of what was needed to make his way across country—wagons, mules, oxen, stores of crops and garden foods, basic implements and household goods such as hunting rifles, axes, pots and pans, water kegs, and camp gear. But often the farmer uprooted, invested everything he owned, his homestead and land, to finance his journey, taking his wife and children with him in a true "California or Bust" gamble. Historian Bernard DeVoto estimated that an average farm family's "outfit" on the trails west in '49 to be worth $700 to $1,500, the proceeds from selling out.

Those determined to travel overland, but with no farm to sell, faced stiff outfitting expenses in St. Louis or such key western Missouri rendezvous towns as St. Joseph, fifty miles north of Independence, or Council Bluffs, Iowa, where outrageous prices were demanded, and met, for everything from wagons and draft animals to barrels of flour and bags of coffee.

Wagon "companies," structured along military lines and similar to Julius Pratt's party, which pooled resources for ship passage to California, blossomed in the camps huddled on the Missouri border. Their wagon covers bore such names as "Wolverine Rangers," "The Ophir Company," and "Granite State and California Mining and Trading Company," and were often formed with elaborate constitutions and codes of conduct. ("Laid end to end," wrote George R. Stewart, historian of the California Trail, "their articles might have paved the way clear to Fort Laramie; the good intentions, an even longer road. . . .")

Some impecunious Forty-niners managed to travel cheaply, tagging along with such companies and hiring out as hunters, "mechanics"—handymen-laborers—or stock tenders. Others, an estimated 1,500 of them by 1850, either joined a wagonless pack train or simply forged into the plains on horseback with gun and bedroll and a mule or two carrying provisions.

Traveling light and in numbers, always advised by mountain men guides and veterans of the western trails, did not diminish the dangers the overlander faced. The Indian scare, deeply felt by Oregon Trail emigrants in the early 1840s, held in '49, even though it had proven to be the least of the worries of the journey. What few Indians the argonauts encountered in crossing the plains came to their camps out of curiosity, or to barter. In the Nevada desert and along the Humboldt and Truckee Rivers, there were occasional troubles with "Diggers," the migrant's collective name for primitive root-digging Paiutes, Bannocks, and Mojaves, but generally the cattle and draft animals were the only casualties.*

The real perils of the trails were diseases and "misadventures"—accidents. Nine out of ten emigrants who died on the northern trails succumbed in their trailside camps to tuberculosis, smallpox, measles, whooping cough, pneumonia, heart disease, diphtheria, scurvy, fevers—typhoid, Rocky Mountain fever, tick fever, complications from malaria—and cholera, a national epidemic in 1849. This plague struck down some argonauts before they reached St. Louis, others on the steamers carrying them toward the Missouri frontier, and it continued to harry the argonauts on the trails and after they reached the California mines. At least 2,500 emigrants died of cholera en route to California or in the mines, in 1849–1850.

TIME RULED THE overlander's life, but water, with its elemental unpredictability, plagued him to near madness. He was in turn guided by it, glutted with it, suffering from the diseases that lurked in it, or, as would occur soon enough, despairing from the want of it.

---

*According to John D. Unruh in his *The Plains Across* (1979), fewer than 400 emigrants were killed by Indians, of an estimated 10,000 deaths on the Western trails in the pre–Civil War era.

The unusually wet spring in and around the Missouri settlements in 1849 introduced the greenhorn to these water vagaries. The rains created a healthy growth of grass on the prairielands of the Missouri and Platte rivers, but the mud bogged the wagons from the first day out, slowing every train to a crawl, and the sudden thunderstorms, buffeting winds, and bright cracks of lightning frightened people and especially their stock as all stood in open, naked land. The chilly, rain-soaked camps bred rheumatism and pneumonia, and in their fetid latrines, dug too closely to their water supply, cholera thrived.

Daily mishaps in wrestling wagons and draft animals caused skull and bone fractures, but even among accidents, the second principal cause of death for the overland emigrants, one of the most common was associated with water. Drownings occurred with regularity, particularly on such river crossings as the Platte and Laramie, within the first 650 miles of the journey.

SCHEMES TO FLEECE the golden fleecers became an industry within months of the gold discovery as eastern entrepreneurs scurried to devise "labor-saving" devices for western miners. Among these were a variety of "gold-washing machines," dredges, drills, pumps, mechanized mortars and pestles, "deep-water shovels," "quicksilver retorts," gold sifters, nugget locators, "sand crucibles," diving bells, collapsible boats, "goldometers," and other "gold-locating equipment." Newspaper advertisements in late 1849 and thereafter offered tarpaulin hats, rubberized miner's suits, tents, and life preservers, water filters, salt-water soap, "Dirks and Bowie Knives Made Special for Miners," money belts, waterproofed matches, and countless nostrums for the argonautical medicine chest, including the immensely popular and utterly worthless "cholera preventive."

Another example of entrepreneurial ingenuity took the form of "guides" to "the auriferous region" for budding Forty-niners, particularly those who intended traveling overland. These cut-and-paste chapbooks offered all manner of advice, much of it sound since it was extravagantly "borrowed" from the writings of respected explorers and veterans of the trails west; some of it was unproductive, even dangerous.

The *New York Herald* published the first of these guides in four special editions on California, beginning with the December 26, 1848, issue (complete with a fanciful map of the gold fields), and by the new year, *New York Tribune* writer G. G. Foster, who had never been close to California, threw together a slim paperback, *The Gold Regions of California*, which sold briskly and established the template for the guides to follow, particularly in the sources commonly appropriated by the guide makers.

A forty-page pamphlet printed early in 1849, *California, and the Way to Get There; with the Official Documents Relating to the Gold Region*, by one J. Ely Sherwood, contained Thomas Larkin's letters to Secretary of State James Buchanan, Governor Richard Mason's report to army headquarters in Washington, President Polk's message to Congress, a letter from Reverend Walter Colton of Monterey, extracts from dispatches to the New York press from California correspondents, information from Richard Henry Dana's 1840 *Two Years Before the Mast* and from the western exploration books by John C. Frémont.

Frémont's books sold well toward the end of 1848 and thereafter, as did Lansford Warren Hastings's notorious *The Emigrants' Guide to Oregon and California*, first published in 1845. An Ohioan and frontier lawyer, Hastings, at age twenty-four, led an emigrant party to Oregon but later sought to divert travelers on the Oregon Trail to California by urging they take the "Hastings Cut-off" through Salt Lake City and the Utah-Nevada desert to reach the Sierra Nevada. This ill-conceived route, and the wild inaccuracies in his book, contributed to the deaths of thirty-nine members of the Donner Party, trapped in the Sierra snows in the winter of 1846.

The revised Hastings guide described various routes to the California mines, including one from an eastern seaboard port to California via an east-to-west crossing of Mexico. He estimated this excursion to the diggings would average thirty-six days' travel: seven or eight days from New York to Vera Cruz, three days by *diligencia* to Mexico City, another six days by stagecoach to Guadalajara, thence five to seven days to Tepic and San Blas on horseback, and twelve final days, by water, to California.

Hastings was apparently unaware of, or chose to ignore, Ned Beale's ride across Mexico to Washington in August and September, 1848, which took six weeks of hard travel and immeasurable luck through territory crawling with anti-American *banditos*.

Perhaps the most noteworthy of the early guidebooks was *The Emigrants' Guide to California* by the St. Louis newspaperman, Joseph

E. Ware. The fifty-six-page booklet, written in late 1848 and published in St. Louis in early 1849, was dedicated "To the Hon. Thomas H. Benton," the Missouri senator and expansionist, and carried a ladder of type under the title:

CONTAINING EVERY POINT OF INFORMATION FOR
THE EMIGRANT—INCLUDING ROUTES, DISTANCES,
WATER, GRASS, TIMBER, CROSSING OF RIVERS,
PASSES, ALTITUDES, WITH A LARGE MAP OF
ROUTES, AND PROFILES OF COUNTRY, &C.,—
WITH FULL DIRECTIONS FOR TESTING AND
ASSAYING GOLD AND OTHER ORES.

Ware, who had at least been as close to California as Missouri, offered much valuable information and sensible advice. "The distance is great, and in some respects, perilous," he wrote at the outset. He provided such sound tips as "The best place to cross the Mississippi is at Rock Island, or Davenport," and, while misguided in his assertion that the overlander departing Missouri for the gold country could complete the journey in a hundred days, gave such valuable data as: "From St. Louis to Independence, or St. Joseph, distance 450 miles, in [river steamer], cabin six dollars; on deck four dollars."

He advised the argonaut to leave the Missouri settlements by May 1, and said parties of fifty were best and oxen should not be over six years old.

He recommended, "Let your waggons be strong, but light, with good lock chains, and the tire well riveted through the fellowes—if not thus fastened, you will have to wet your wheels every day, to prevent them from coming off." He said an oval circling of the wagons at night was the best configuration for the safety of the train, urged parties to start out at four A.M. daily, and estimated the cost of provisioning a wagon for four people at $670.78. However, he said, "no person should attempt to leave the frontier with more than lbs. 2,500 weight" (without cautioning that such a weight was too much for a single wagon) "or with a team of less than four yoke of oxen, or six mules."

He provided estimates on what foodstuffs each person would consume in the journey to California: a barrel of flour or 180 pounds of ship's biscuit "that is kiln dried"; 150–180 pounds of bacon, twenty-five each of coffee and rice, forty of sugar, sixty of beans, a keg of beef suet "as a substitute for butter"; plus dried fruit, molasses, and vinegar. He cautioned wagonmasters to adopt such policies as "Never allow an Indian to come within your lines under any pretext—they seldom have a good object in view," and made such common sense admonitions to the traveler as "Never bathe if you feel fatigued," and "Let there be no contention or intrigues in your camp."

He advised that the emigrant camps be guarded at all times by sentinels but "no shooting of fire arms should be allowed, as false alarms are frequently raised by such carelessness."

Some of his advice, as the travelers soon learned, was time-defeating. He recommended farmers bring their plows, a set of harrow teeth, scythes, even a small cast-iron corn mill, and miners "a gold washing machine if you can afford it." (Such weighty items invariably became roadside scrap.)

More potentially dangerous was Ware's romanticized picture of the Humboldt River country, describing the river valley as "rich and beautifully clothed with blue grass, herd grass, clover, and other nutritious grasses." He said, "Its course is marked by a line of timber, mostly cotton wood and willow trees, and is unobstructed for three hundred miles, furnishing the requisite for the emigrants' comfort, in abundance."

Neither the succulent grasses or the timberline existed; the Humboldt was a sluggish stream in the best of times—called the "Humbug" by early travelers who most often found it dry—and the country around it was rough brush and desert, an ox, mule, and horse boneyard.

He advised a "spirit of civility and accommodation," and urged, "Take no steps that will not reflect honor, not only upon yourself but your country. . . . Unite with the well disposed to sustain the rights of individuals whenever incroached upon."

Sadly, this last cautioning went unheeded by the overland party Ware himself subsequently joined.

Nothing is known of Ware's life other than his newspaper association and the guide he wrote, and we would not know of his pitiful death were it not for an admirable character named Alonzo Delano, a Forty-niner from Ottawa, Illinois, who in his book, *Life on the Plains and Among the Diggings*, wrote of Ware's fate.

In August 1849, Delano and his party of argonauts reached the

Humboldt River in Nevada, the place Ware had overpainted in his guidebook but did not live to see firsthand. In camp among some other pilgrims Delano met up with an Illinois acquaintance named Fisher who reported the "abandonment by his companions of Joseph E. Ware, formerly from Galena, but known in St. Louis as a writer."

Delano learned that Ware had joined a wagon company of California-bound emigrants as it departed Missouri and fell ill as the train reached the outskirts of Fort Laramie. There, the Illinoisan reported, "instead of affording him that protection which they were now more than ever bound to do, by the ties of common humanity, [they] barbarously laid him by the roadside, without water, provisions, covering or medicines, to die!"

Ware, he said, "contrived to crawl off the road about a mile, to a pond, where he lay two days, exposed to a burning sun by day and cold winds by night, when Providence directed Fisher and his mess[mates] to the same pond, where they found him. With a humanity that did them honor, they took him to their tent and nursed him two days; but nature, over-powered by exposure as well as disease, gave way, and he sank under his sufferings."

Ware gave Fisher his name, home, and occupation, and related the story of his company's heartlessness.

"He was a young man of decided talents," Delano wrote. "Fisher was confident that if he had had medicines and proper attendance he might have recovered."

◀ The Aerial Locomotive ▶

NEW ENGLANDER RUFUS Porter had no plans to go to California and mine gold but thought it an imposition for those who wanted to go that it would take several months to get there. He therefore turned his fertile mind to the problem and wrote a prospectus titled *Aerial Navigation: The Practicability of Traveling Pleasantly and Safely from New York to California in Three Days*. The idea had come to him in 1820, inspired by schemes to rescue Napoleon from his imprisonment on the remote island of Saint Helena. In 1833 and years following he built several small models of the machine but could find no financial backing to construct a full-sized prototype.

The gold rush seemed the ideal opportunity to realize his dream so he proposed to build an 800-foot-long, 14,000-pound steam engine–powered balloon, an "Aerial Locomotive" he called it. It would be made of 8,000 yards of rubberized material stretched over a spruce-wood skeleton and filled with hydrogen. Beneath this behemoth gasbag a 180-foot-long passenger cabin, also fabricated of wood and cloth, would be suspended by steel wires.

Porter estimated the engines would produce a speed of one hundred miles an hour, certainly sixty at full capacity of one hundred passengers. He had worked out the dangers, as well: the fabric envelope would be "arrow-proof"—presuming it would be fired upon by hostile Indians, some perhaps perched on mountaintops. Against a lightning strike, he proposed that "It may sometimes be requisite to throw out one end of a small copper wire to earth, to discharge electricity from the machine"; and in case of tornados or similar bad weather said, "the locomotive may either rise above it, or a grapple may be thrown out by which the machine may be brought to safe moorings."

He envisioned his carefree passengers sailing effortlessly over the western mountains, amused by the grizzly bears and Indians gawking up in wonderment at the apparatus floating across the sky.

Porter, an accomplished musician, landscape painter, portraitist, and inventor, was fifty-three years old when he launched the *Scientific American* as a showcase for his ideas and inventions, but among them, the Aërial Locomotive was never built. There were not nearly enough subscribers and the inventor probably also determined he had been overly optimistic in guessing the speed of such an immense craft against air resistance.

Nathaniel Currier, the New York City lithographer, later celebrated with James M. Ives for their printing collaborations, produced a burlesque likeness of Porter's locomotive embarking for the mines with a legend on the vessel's stern: "Passage $125 and Found (if Lost)." Another Currier production was the

"How They Go to California" print, this one depicting a giant rubber band slinging argonauts from Brooklyn to Sacramento.

Rufus Porter (who died in 1884 at the age of ninety-two) lived to see his dirigible idea inspire others, although the first such commercial airship was not put into service until 1908. It averaged just under twenty miles an hour.

FROM SUCH OUTFITTING towns as Independence, Westport Landing and St. Joseph, in Missouri; Council Bluffs, Iowa, and other waystations and camps, the first three weeks' travel to the Platte River turned out to be a small part lark and a large part test. As the wagons headed west, then northwest, over the corner of Kansas Territory, a land lush in blue-stem grass and wildflowers, the travelers' labors were as yet light, their night camps lighthearted, their progress a steady but tedious clip of fifteen or twenty miles a day. The dragging weight of overloaded wagons was already being felt and mental inventories were taken of what could be carried and what left at the side of the trail.

There were many rivers to cross, among them the Kansas where the ferries were operated by Shawnees and Delawares, eastern tribes moved west by federal decree, and the Little Blue and Big Blue, which led to a ridge of sandhills atop which one could see the sluggish Platte, the argonauts' conduit for the next six hundred miles of their journey.

The most unpredictable of rivers—Bernard DeVoto called it "one of the most preposterous in the world"—the Platte was as ugly and stunted as its name (from the French *plat*, meaning flat, dull, insipid), as often a river bottom as a river, a mile wide between fringes of cottonwoods on its banks, shallow ("an infernal liar—hardly able to float a canoe," one pioneer wrote of it) and deadly with its twists and abrupt turns around the boggy islands rising in its bed. Platte mud and quicksand were diabolical. Oregon Trail emigrants told stories of eighteen yoke of oxen being required to drag a single wagon from one bank to the other, and of yokes of oxen, and the wagons they pulled, disappearing entirely in the Platte's shifting mud-and-sand sloughs.

The argonaut trains, now in buffalo country, and Pawnee and Cheyenne country, swung along the river's southern bank in oppressive summer heat through prairie dog towns and seas of dry grass. Firewood was scarce, the trees on the Platte islands and banks steadily denuded by the emigrant march, but buffalo chips were gathered for the supper fire. The meals were commonly of bread or johnnycakes made with yellow cornmeal, saleratus and molasses; bacon, maybe a buffalo steak or some animal bagged by hunters, perhaps a rabbit, a racoon, or sage hen; and coffee.

The land grew less monotonous as the procession moved west along the river, the prairie yielding to sandhills, and rock formations, on the approach to Fort Kearny, the army post built in 1848 to assist the emigrant parties.

A month after departing Saint Joseph or Council Bluffs, the trains reached the South Platte Ford where the wagons crossed the river to follow the North Platte drainage into Wyoming. Here the fickle river, sometimes nearly dry, sometimes boiling with spring rain and runoff, could require a week of bitter and frustrating labor to cross.

About twenty miles beyond this hair-raising fording, the parties reached Ash Hollow, the first shade they had seen in weeks, and the bank of the North Platte. They traveled now on a slight uphill grade and the summer nights were growing colder as they gained altitude and began to see the stark rock formations they had heard about from old Oregon Trail hands. The most notable of these were Courthouse Rock, a 400-foot mound of volcanic material said to resemble a municipal building in Saint Louis; the 500-foot inverted funnel spire of Chimney Rock, a formation mentioned in more emigrant diaries than any other; and within sight of Chimney Rock, the last of the area's great geological curiosities, Scotts Bluff. This Nebraskan Gibraltar had been described by explorer Sir Richard Burton as "a massive medieval city . . . round a colossal fortress." It loomed over the western horizon and hugged the south bank of the river so closely wagons had to detour around it.

Six weeks out of Missouri the emigrants reached Fort Laramie, the big American Fur Company trading post at the junction of the Laramie River and the North Platte, and the first semblance of civilization seen since the loud towns of the Missouri border. Here a mountain guide told Oregon-bound emigrants a few years past, "It is discouraging to tell you that you have not yet traveled one third of the long road to Oregon." These discouraging words were true for the California-bound as well, and at Fort Laramie the gold hunters began talking about time again. It was now late June; they had traveled 640 miles and had 1,200 miles or more to go before reaching the Sierra Nevada, to cross it before being walled out, or worse, walled *in*, by winter snows.

Independence Rock, greatest of landmarks for the California-bound wagons, was a 128-foot-high oval formation of granite, likened to a stranded whale and called the "Register of the Desert." It overlooked the Sweetwater River, 814 miles from the Missouri border, and was signed and initialed by paint and scratches by thousands of passersby. Time and experience had lent the name: Try to reach the rock by Independence Day to insure a safe passage through the Rockies and a timely arrival at the Sierra Nevada.

The meandering Sweetwater required as many as nine crossings and a scary passage through a two-mile-long canyon with 400-foot walls known as Devil's Gate. Beyond it lay South Pass, a magic name in the annals of western migration since its discovery by a party of trappers in 1812. So named because it lay south of the Rocky Mountain trail blazed by the Lewis and Clark expedition in 1805, the pass was a pleasant disappointment to those imagining a towering slot in the mountains where wagons passed single file to open country beyond. In fact, the pass turned out to be a thirty-mile-wide grassy saddle in the Wind River Range of the Rockies, the ascent of it so gradual that the traveler's only evidence that he was climbing was the thinning air. The summit rose 7,412 feet above sea level.

The trail due west led to Little Sandy Creek, then through desert country to Pacific Springs—the first westward flowing water the overlanders would see after crossing the Continental Divide. At the Green River, most followed the trail south to Fort Bridger, a trading post built by the mountain hero Jim Bridger in 1843, while some followed a "cutoff" across a waterless fifty-mile alkaline lake bed that intercepted the main road to Fort Hall. Still others, in need of provisions and draft animals, detoured to the Mormon trail leading to Salt Lake City.

After visiting the iron-tangy carbonated waters of Steamboat Springs and Soda Springs, the wagons parties reached the former

Hudson's Bay post of Fort Hall, Idaho, usually in late August, then followed the left bank of the Snake River a few miles west of the fort. There, at the Raft River confluence, the California Trail branched off southwestward toward the Great Basin of Utah and Nevada, a sun-tortured wasteland of salt beds, sand, clay, ancient lava flows, and stunted sage, circled by mountains which reflected the sun like a heliograph. Night travel alone provided some relief from the fatiguing heat, and in these wastelands, with the oxen and mules dropping from exhaustion and starvation, the wagons were reduced to carrying the barest assortment of provisions, water, and forage.

Five days spent crossing the basin brought the overlanders to the Humboldt River of northern Nevada, followed to its "sink," a barren spot where the river disappeared in a series of sloughs, swampy meadows and saline lakes. A few miles above the sink, a rough trail called "Lassen's Cutoff" broke off northwest across desert country, crossed the Sierra close to the Oregon border, then dropped south to the Rancho Bosquejo, between the Feather River and the Sacramento, two hundred miles north of Sutter's Fort. The rancho was owned by a colorful Danish blacksmith, Peter Lassen, a veteran of Frémont's California volunteers during the war with Mexico.

Most of the argonauts opted to follow the water, this time the Truckee River which flowed westward a few days' travel south of the Humboldt Sink, there to cross the "Forty-Mile Desert" to Truckee Pass through the Sierra Nevada.

The seventy-mile crossing of the 13,000-foot Sierra was the last test, ending in a week's climb in timber-choked canyons, threading through pine forests and thick brush to a place called Emigrant's Gap where wagons had to be lowered on ropes down forested ridges to the lush western foothills and the valley of the Sacramento.

IN MID-MAY 1849, as the wagons began to roll west of the Missouri line, the *Arkansas Democrat* carried a report from Fort Kearny saying, "The ice is at last broken, and the inundation of gold diggers upon us. The first specimen, with a large pick-axe over his shoulder, a long rifle in his hand, and two revolvers and a bowie knife stuck in his belt, made his appearance here a week ago last Sunday. He had only time to ask for a drink of buttermilk, a piece of ginger-bread and how 'fur' it was to 'Californy,' and then hallooing to his long-legged, slab-sided cattle, drawing a diminutive yellowtop Yankee wagon, he disappeared on the trail toward the gold 'diggins.' Since then wagons have been constantly crossing."

The newspaper editorialized, "Who will sit quietly at home in the States, pining in penury when fortunes are to be had merely for the labor of picking them up in California, the fact being now established that there is gold enough for all?"

According to data kept at Fort Kearny, by the end of June, 1849, 6,400 wagons had passed through the post, and six to eight hundred more started out on the Council Bluffs road, bypassing the fort. The human migration between April and June was at least 21,500, probably as many as 25,000; there were also 60,000 animals in the procession, a few horses and milch cows, 6,000 mules, the rest oxen.

George Stewart, the historian of the California Trail, wrote that "if all the wagons of '49 had been organized into a single close-spaced train, they would have extended for some sixty miles."

ON THURSDAY, MAY 3, 1849, a party of Illinoisans broke camp fourteen miles above Saint Joseph, Missouri, packed their wagons, gathered their stock, and pushed out toward the Rocky Mountains. Of the men in the company, Alonzo Delano stood out among those popping their whips above the backs of their ox teams. Within a year of his westward journey an artist would depict him as a rumpled Ichabod Crane, a newspaper would call him "a noseworthy citizen," another "the Cyrano of California." He did not object to these references to his tall, skinny frame and heroically long nose; rather, he gloried, or at least gave that impression, in his remarkable physical attributes, never lost his humor, and wrote in a manner H. H. Bancroft described as "the overflowing of a merry heart, which no hard times could depress." His infectious good nature and skill with the pen came to earn him many friends, among them Eliza Rosanna Gilbert of Limerick, Ireland, an exceptionally beautiful termagant notoriously known as Lola Montez, the peerless *femme fatale* of her age. Delano was considerably more stricken with Montez than vice-versa, but she liked him and enjoyed his company, and it was a tribute to his homely charm that she did.

He became an argonaut, a "nomad denizen of the world," unintentionally. Except that he was born in Aurora, New York, in 1806,

Delano's life before the spring of 1849 is a blank among the hundreds of pages of his published writings. He refers only obliquely to his residence in Illinois (and like John A. Sutter, scarcely mentions the family he left behind) but must have found Ottawa, forty miles southwest of Chicago, debilitating. He suffered from a recurring fever there and, as it happened, the news of the gold discovery in California reached Ottawa at the time he was deciding on a warmer clime. "Besides the fever of the body," he said, "I was suddenly seized with the fever of mind for gold and . . . I turned my attention 'westward ho!'"

He and his Ottawa friends joined a like-minded group being gathered in nearby Dayton, and after buying oxen, wagons, and provisions, proceeded to Saint Louis, and bought passage on the riverboat *Embassy* to the Missouri border, there to rendezvous with the balance of the Dayton party.

At Saint Joseph, after landing their stock, wagon, stores, and gear, Delano and his Ottawa friends found the rendezvous camp and moved out on May 3, "well-arranged and provided for the great journey before us," Delano said. A captain of the train was elected and the seventeen wagons, each drawn by three to six yoke of oxen, were numbered so that each could take a turn in the lead one day and bring up the rear the next. The company was divided into "messes," each man armed with rifle, pistol, ammunition, and hunting knife. The cattle were cared for by stock-experienced farmers; outriders were selected to scout the trail ahead; night watches were set for the circled wagons and camp and others to keep an eye on the animals. They heard of firewood scarcity en route to the Platte and threw enough in the wagons for several days' cookfires. The single mistake, to be reckoned with after a month of travel, was the overloading of the wagons.

They followed the well-marked trail, stream crossings, and detours for nineteen days and reached Fort Kearny without incident despite Delano's exaggerated assertion that "we did not know where we were—we had no trail to follow . . . and our wanderings and windings resembled those of the children of Israel in the wilderness." Winds and rainstorms slowed them at times, the grass played out to stubble in some areas, wood and game were as scarce as predicted, but they made steady progress: twelve, sometimes eighteen, miles a day.

In the week of May 24, incessant thunderstorms and whipping

winds mired wagons, scattered the draft animals, and forced the companies to dig trenches around their tents and cook their meals over sputtering fires, or more often, to eat their rations cold. Hours, even a day or more, were spent gathering the skittish oxen and mules together, some having strayed ten miles or more from camp in a wind-lashed rain, panicked by booming thunder and lightning strikes.

At the forks of the Platte, the Illinoisans spotted buffalo for the first time during their crossing to the north bank and by June 3 were taking a day of rest-and-repair amidst the luxuriant grass and dry willows of the North Platte bottomlands.

The company camped at Ash Hollow and at the mouth of a ravine discovered a scattering of Sioux lodges on a hillside. "The men were tall, and graceful in their movements," Delano observed, "and some of the squaws were quite pretty, and dressed in tanned buffalo [probably deer] skins, highly ornamented with beads." A tribal elder, he said, approached them, "made some kind of a speech, and invited us into a lodge. . . . Almost the first request made to us was for whiskey, for which I verily believe they would have sold their children— showing conclusively that temperence societies were not yet well organized on the Platte. Of course we had no fire-water for them, and we left them lamentably sober, and encamped about a mile above them, where several came to beg bread, whiskey, and shirts."

THE RAMPARTS OF Fort Laramie lay a mile above the river fording. Delano found the trading post to be little more than a wagon graveyard—a heavy wagon with good running gear could be purchased there for five dollars. There were no fresh provisions in the store, yet so heavy was the overland traffic through the post that a booming enterprise had been made of the fort's "letter drop." For twenty-five cents each, letters left there were supposed to be picked up by an express rider and delivered to a post office east of the Missouri. Delano said this "service" and others like it along the California Trail were "deliberate frauds" perpetrated on the emigrants, and that no letter he or his comrades placed in them ever reached their destination.

Ferrying wagons across the Platte to its north fork turned out to be more of an ordeal than even the direst of warnings conveyed. One ferriage twelve miles above the Illinois camp was so crowded with wagons that "several days" was the estimated wait in line; moreover, the grass in the area was exhausted and trailside water holes corrupted with alkali. "Look at this!" one pond sign warned, "The water here is poison and we have lost six of our cattle. Do not let your cattle drink on this bottom." Of this, Delano said that from the North Platte until his party left the Humboldt many weeks later, "we were obliged to use great precaution in allowing the cattle to drink; and never before we had ascertained the character of the water." Animals who strayed and drank tainted water, he said, most often died on the spot but if found in time, vinegar, even bacon, was forced down their throats to neutralize the alkali in their stomachs. Miraculously, some of the beasts survived these radical measures.

After scouting several ferries to the North Platte, one with 250 wagons waiting in line, another, operated by Mormons, with nearly the same number backed up, Dayton company members decided to raft their wagons, belongings, and provisions across and let the animals swim to the north bank. The rafts consisted of canoes lashed together with a platform on top. Ropes were attached to each end of the canoe base and forty men were required to wrestle the clumsy thing across the shallow fording place and back again for the next load.

At Independence Rock overlooking the Sweetwater River, Delano and his friends examined the names scratched on the naked granite, some of them dating back to 1836. After this excursion, they pitched their tents, posted their guards, turned the animals out to graze, built their fires, and feasted on antelope steaks. "Dear Reader," Delano wrote in his journal, "if you are an Epicure, for heaven's sake, walk to California across the plains, and you will learn to enjoy with a zest you know not, the luxury of a good meal." Of that first night on the Sweetwater, he noted, "Fatigued as I was, a hyena might have tugged at my toes without awaking me."

They were now over eight hundred miles from the Missouri settlements and lingered three days at the Sweetwater. They were loath to leave the recuperating river, the hunting and fishing and such diversions as picking up bright chunks of mica from the water's edge and testing them with nitric acid which "instantly dispelled the pleasing hallucination, and proved that Sweet Water Valley was not the valley of the Sacramento."

Five days later, Delano wrote, "we ascended a steep hill from the bottom land and then found a good and almost level road to the South Pass," its gradual ascent and steeper decline on its western terminus, Delano said, made the more memorable for its leading to Pacific Spring, "the first water which flows into the Pacific ocean." Crossing the Continental Divide gave the traveler a vista to the north of a broken mountain plain leading to the Wind River Range twenty or thirty miles distant, and to the west a large basin with a rim of peculiar table hills and ridges, easy to ascend.

A mile after crossing Little Sandy Creek, a branch of the deep and treacherous Green River, the company reached a fork in the trail and had to decide on which direction to proceed. The safest route, with good water and graze along it, was also something of a detour, a drop southwest to Fort Bridger where a traveler might find supplies and even "recruited" oxen, worn-out animals traded in at the fort whose strength had been restored by rest and pasturage. The other choice, and the one selected by Delano and his men, was the Sublette Cutoff, named for a Rocky Mountain trapper who once had partnered with Jim Bridger. This was a dangerous path across an alkali lakebed with no water or grass to be found in the fifty-mile crossing. Its sole virtue—and it was an enticing one—was that it saved eighty-five miles from the Fort Bridger route.

A "guidebook" Delano carried wisely urged those taking the Sublette shortcut to fill all water casks and bottles at the Big Sandy and to start across the desert at four in the afternoon and travel all night without camp. The Illinois men found good grass along the river, filled their water barrels, threw "all superfluous articles" off the wagons and rolled into the alkaline plain, the wagons throwing up a dense curtain of gray dust. An hour into the journey they were blessed by a light rain shower that settled the choking dust and as the day closed they caught up with other wagons, horsemen, others astride mules, many others afoot. "As the night wore heavily on, all sounds of mirth or of loud profanity ceased, and the creaking of wheels and the howling of wolves alone were heard," Delano wrote.

At five in the afternoon of July 2, the Illinoisans reached the Green River. They had walked fifty-five miles in twenty-four hours, and after unyoking their oxen and turning them out to forage, Delano said he celebrated his forty-third birthday, "the hardest one of all my life," by falling on his blankets to be "lost in utter unconsciousness till morning."

The ferry across the Green, a large, oar-driven scow capable of carrying two wagons each trip across, was backed up two days and Delano had to sign a register and wait until the company's name rose to the top. The river, a hundred yards across, afforded little forage or firewood so the company moved away from the fording place to find pasturage and cottonwoods, the delay giving Delano and his companions the opportunity to visit other camps and find old friends met earlier along the trail.

The trail to Fort Hall passed through the valley of the Bear River, two to four miles in width, the hills covered with bunch grass, firs, poplars, and aspens, and led to Soda Springs (which Delano called "Beer Springs"), the mountainsides above them white with carbonate of lime. The gassy springs, Delano said, were "one of the greatest luxuries on the whole route," equal to to the purest soda water in the world, "and though good without any additional concomitants, with lemon-syrup, or sugar, they are delicious."

On the 16th the entire Dayton-Ottawa company reached the banks of he Portneuf River, and two days later camped outside the walls of Fort Hall.

TWO WEEKS OF steady travel took them into the heart of the Great Basin and on July 29, the company found a cool stream and stopped to fill barrels and enjoy the shade of the few willows along its bank. During the rest, the men had their first encounter with what Delano called "Digger [probably Paiute] Indians." He said that as he approached them one "offered his hand and pronounced in good English, 'How de do,' followed by 'Whoa haw!'" These words, and such phrases as "Goddamn you!", the Indians had learned from emigrants and teamsters passing through their lands and were employed by them as common greetings to all whites.

The Indians were friendly, but as the company moved deeper into the Great Basin and began following the Humboldt River on the last day of July, they became problematical.

The Humboldt, so named by Frémont in 1845 honoring the eminent German geographer, and previously known as Ogden's River and Mary's River, was thirty feet wide with a good current and unbrackish water at the point intersected by the Illinois party, and flowed through a valley between high and barren mountains. They found good forage there, and sage hens, ducks, and geese, along its brushy shoreline.

At a noon halt on the river on August 1, a horseman rode into their camp and Delano discovered the man to be an Ottawa acquaintance, Charles Fisher, who had sold his wagon and oxen at Fort Laramie and pushed on alone with a mount and pack horse to the Humboldt. Such serendipitous coincidences, seemingly amazing given the vastness of the territory west of the Missouri frontier, were in fact not rare on the northern California Trail where the argonauts were traveling the same road and passing, or being passed, by friends from their state and sometimes even their hometown. Even so, Fisher's appearance was "an agreeable surprise," and since he had started out a month after Delano and his party, he was able to bring some news from the settlements and confirmed the stories drifting into the camps that cholera was decimating the wagon trains along the Platte. Fisher reported that many argonauts were forced to abandon their plans to cross the Sierra before the passes were snowbound, and had decided either to winter in Salt Lake City or "return to the States."

Fisher also told Delano "the lamentable case" of the abandonment some miles east of Fort Laramie of Joseph E. Ware, author of the *Emigrant's Guide to California*.

Delano was horrified by the story: "What misery has not California brought on individuals?—and this is but one of the many tales of suffering which might be told."

As the Illinoisans followed the Humboldt, averaging fifteen miles a day, signs of Indian hostility began to appear as the grass thinned and the draft animals had to range further from camp to graze. The wagons began passing oxen carcasses bristling with arrows, partially slaughtered and with haunches of meat spirited away by the raiders. "The Indians," Delano wrote, "seemed to have as cruel a taste for beef as the Irishman's cow had for music, when she ate Paddy the piper, pipes and all."

The river was narrowing now, twenty feet across, its waters muddy and saline—the old "Humbug" showing its true colors. Just three years past, Kit Carson arrived at Fort Laramie on one of his several cross-country journeys as dispatch rider, and warned wagonmasters to enter California by way of Oregon since there wouldn't be a blade of grass on the Humboldt. This prediction seemed true enough to Delano and his people: The ashy, arid plains spreading out from each bank of the river bore nothing but stunted sage and greasewood bushes. Reports filtering back from wagons a day ahead told the tale that there was no grass at the Humboldt Sink, that the Truckee Canyon was steep and potentially deadly, and that there was a forty-mile grassless and waterless stretch to cross, a man- and beast-killer as pitiless as the Sublette Cutoff, before the next oasis some miles from the southern edge of Lake Tahoe. Everyone was urged to cut what grass they could find and stuff their wagons with it, and fill every water barrel and bottle before moving, at night, to avoid the crippling heat.

Some potentially good news arrived as well, for those willing to take a chance. The argonauts knew of a detour to the north that was said to lead to a good, even "easy," route across the Sierra and ending in the Feather River gold country a considerable distance north of Sutter's Fort. Stories about this "cutoff" were mixed. One man claimed to have ridden thirty miles into it and said there was grass in the first ten miles, plenty of grass and water thereafter; others claimed there was neither grass nor water on the first thirty-five miles of the cutoff, two full days of wagon travel, and that it led to Oregon and not to California. There was some truth in all the testimony and two matters were agreed upon by all: the detour was probably infested with aggressive Indians, and it was 135 miles longer than the route through Truckee Pass.

Most of the Dayton-Ottawa company decided to try the northern route, variously called the Applegate Trail, after the Oregon pioneer Jesse Applegate, or the Lassen Cutoff, and on August 15, left the Humboldt sixty-five miles above the sink, and moved northwest across a plain of wild sage to intersect the trail.

After a day's travel the sage thinned out, the grass vanished, and what water they found appeared in muddy seepages in the foothills of volcanic mountains. The cutoff parties were already fearful they had made a fatal mistake but on the 17th, the company came across a huge hot spring, the water at its edge cool, drinkable, and bathable, at its center "hot enough to boil bacon." The ponding water formed a natural basin at the foot of a mass of black volcanic cinders like the waste from a colossal blacksmith's forge.

The company rested a day, allowing their stock to roam.

On August 25, the Sierra Nevada stood before them—not, as they had imagined, a towering wall of granite defying their passage, but a series of ridges and snow-capped peaks broken by defiles, valleys, basins, ravines, dry lakebeds, hot springs, mountain brooks, and meadows of ripe grass.

By September 10 they had crossed it without incident and reached the Feather River, and a week later, upon climbing a hill saw "the long-sought, the long-wished-for and welcome valley of the Sacramento." Delano wrote, "How my heart bounded at the view! how every nerve thrilled at the sight! It looked like a grateful haven to the tempest-tossed mariner."

Ahead lay the rancho of Peter Lassen, the Danish pioneer for whom the cutoff had been named, and a trading post, consisting of three adobe buildings surrounded by "gangs of naked Indians of both sexes, drunken Mexicans, and weary emigrants," Delano said, which "did not give me a very flattering impression." The impression did not improve when he checked the prices at Lassen's store: flour at $50 for a hundred pounds, sugar the same, cheese at $1.50 a pound, beef, $35.

But there was no time to complain; all the argonauts, Delano said, "were anxious to find where the best mines were, and were busy seeking intelligence." Companies were splitting up, some men heading directly to the diggings along the Feather River, or south to see if there were any opportunities on the Sacramento or the American fork; others heading to Sutter's Fort and the town of Sacramento that had sprung up there, to buy supplies.

⊰ Seeing the Elephant ⊱

IN APRIL 1796, the first live elephant seen in America went on display at the corner of Beaver Street and Broadway in New York City. The young, eight-foot-tall animal, shipped from Bengal, India, drew crowds for months, people coming to New York from such distant places as Pennsylvania and Virginia to pay a penny or two to the exhibitor, one Jacob Crowninshield, for a glimpse of the most exotic beast in the country. To be able to say "I saw the elephant" was the sign of an initiate, a cosmopolite.

Fifty years after the debut of Crowninshield's pachyderm, during the great Westering movement of the 1840s, the phrase had survived but with a more metaphorical usage. To the emigrant headed west, whether on the overland trails or on shipboard, "going out to see the elephant" meant expecting to gain new experiences. The Forty-niner saw the elephant in Indians, prairie dogs, buffalos, and Gila monsters, saw it in the parrots and monkeys of the Isthmus of Panama, and in the Saint Elmo's fire crawling up the rigging of a vessel sailing around Cape Horn.

But it signified more than seeing new things. Western historian Dee Brown wrote that seeing the elephant also "meant going west with one's eyes wide open, expecting to find marvels and wondrous fortunes only to be monstrously defrauded in the end."

In San Francisco in the summer of 1850, a popular burlesque of mining life titled *Seeing the Elephant* was performed by pioneer showman David Gorman "Yankee" Robinson, who had toured the east with his temperance play *The Reformed Drunkard* before sailing to the Pacific in gold rush days. Attesting to the negative weight the phrase had taken on, *Seeing the Elephant* featured the ballad "The Used-Up Miner," with this refrain:

> *Oh, I'm a used-up man,*
> *A perfect used-up man,*
> *And if I ever get home again,*
> *I'll stay there if I can.*

"Seeing the Elephant" was also a favorite gold rush ballad, now as forgotten as "Crossing the Plains," "Coming Around the Horn," "The Fools of Forty-Nine," "The Ballad of the Happy Miner," "There's a Good Pile Coming, Boys," "Joe Bowers," "The Hog-Eye Man," and "I'm Sad and Lonely Here."

In addition, there was an Elephant House restaurant in Sacramento that thrived in 1849 by advertising "Hash, low grade, 75 cents; Hash, 18 carat, $1; roast grizzly, $1; a square meal, $3."

ELEVEN

LORD AND LADY

SOMEWHERE ON THE Humboldt River in August 1849, Israel Shipman Pelton Lord, a Chicago physician, surveyed his company of argonauts and, with a few exceptions, found them to be a gang of rascals. They were twelve hundred miles from their jump-off camp across the Missouri River from Saint Joseph, but no more than a hundred miles out he had noted in his voluminous journal that "They are by turns, or all together, cross, peevish, sullen, boisterous, giddy, profane, dirty, vulgar, ragged, mustachioed, bewhiskered, petulant, quarrelsome, unfaithful, disobedient, refractory, careless, contrary, stubborn, hungry, and without the fear of God and hardly of man before their eyes."

Although he never would have acknowledged it, Dr. Lord's checklist of the foibles and weaknesses of his comrades on the Oregon-California Trail fit three-quarters of his own peculiar nature. He was, by turns or altogether, cross, peevish, sullen, petulant, quarrelsome, refractory, contrary, and stubborn, to which could be added cantankerous, opinionated, and imperious. He was innocent of the other failings he enumerated because he was a clean shaven, teetotaling, nonsmoking, nongambling, nonswearing, nonwomanizing Baptist fundamentalist.

In a lesser man, the sum of these characteristics might have produced the perfect template for the intolerably superior, invariably friendless, holier-than-thou specimen that haunted many a wagon party on the western trails in the 1840s. But Israel Lord had gifts that rescued himself and his compatriots from such a fate. He was a superior physician, for all his quirky homeopathic beliefs; he wrote brilliantly—better, probably, than he ever realized; had an irrepressible sense of humor, often macabre, always waspish; and he had a great heart—he was the kind of man who could not pass a trailside grave without jotting down the name and particulars on the crude headboard and reflecting on the fate of the person beneath it, could not see a dying ox without penning a verse to commemorate the nobility of the beast and its thankless service to its often ignoble master.

Like Julius Pratt and Henry Huntington, he was a Connecticut native, born in the town of Haddam in 1805, apparently in a family of means. He studied medicine in the period 1826–1830, married and moved to Chicago where he practiced traditional medicine until 1842 when, after the death of his infant daughter, he converted to the system of homeopathy. This medical concept, which originated in Germany in 1796, turned away from such harsh "curative" remedies as bleeding and the indiscriminate use of opiates and mercuric compounds, to the administration of small doses of select medicaments and plasters, and such external treatments as body rubs and baths. Eventually he would publish books and articles supporting his medical beliefs, works such as *Abuse of the Obstetric Forceps, Alcohol*, and *Intermittant Fever.*

In the spring of 1849 he left wife and family in Chicago to join a company of gold hunters, at $200 per "passenger." He began his journal on May 6 by writing, "We left a dead man by the name of Middleton on the levee at St. Louis, and thought we had left all the cholera with him. We were grievously disappointed, however. At noon, a deck passenger from Tennessee, a boy, was taken and died the next day. On the eighth a fireman died. On the ninth a deck passenger, and a negro below died. . . ."

Cholera preoccupied him; he witnessed, and treated, many stricken with the disease, saw many others succumb to it, and wrote down his observations and recommended treatment. "The cholera is a rapidly fatal disease, when suffered to run its course unrestrained," he said, but maintained that it was "more easily controlled than most diseases when met in time" and that "A single dose of laudanum, with pepper, camphor, ammonia, peppermint, or other stimulants, usually effects a cure in a few minutes." Pain in the bowels, cramps in the calves of the legs, coldness of the skin, and sweating, might call for repeated doses, the medicines to be accompanied by "friction, mustard plasters, and other external applications."

He insisted that homeopathic remedies produced "uniform success." He jotted in his notebook, "One drop of tincture of camphor every five minutes will restore warmth to the skin more certainly and speedily than a larger dose, or than any medicine we used; and I presume we had on board [the river steamer] ten or twelve different medicines, put up and labelled 'Cholera Specific.' "

He and his small party departed Saint Joseph on June 1 and made good time, up to twenty miles a day, and on August 25 Lord and the abundance of rascals he was thrown amongst were camping on the Humboldt, still a month from the mountains. "This morning Col. Wm. Hamilton, son of Alexander Hamilton of Revolutionary memory, passed our camp," he wrote in his thickening journal. "He is a small, active, smart looking man, apparently fifty, and was once undoubtedly a very handsome man. His exterior is now not of the smoothest, though a decent hat would much improve it. He is wearing, or rather is capped with an old, rusty, torn, shockingly dilapidated, part of a straw hat. . . . He has a four-horse team of fine looking animals, and has oats to feed them, bought from Salt Lake City at one dollar a bushel and threshed them himself at that."

(Five weeks later he would encounter Colonel Hamilton again, or at least hear about him, in Sacramento City, under sorrowful circumstances.)

"Who says 'Hurrah for California'? Not many here, for most are heartily tired of the journey," he wrote on September 5 as his party followed the Humboldt to its sink and to the hot springs and volcanic badlands beyond. At one camp Lord called the "Gate of Desperation" he saw dead and dying cattle abandoned by the trains ahead of his own, watching one ox "his side to the sun, his nose to the gravel on the side of the ravine, ruminating on his hard fate. . . . His bones seemed to bend out and his wrinkled skin to swell, and a sound like the shrill whistle of the wind through a broken casement, changing to a low prolonged rumble and roll of a bass drum, became a low muttering articulation of sad repining." As soon as he had time he wrote a verse on the animal and its kin and what they stood for among the gold hunters.

The Illinois party gained the Feather River on October 17 and from a rise caught a glimpse of the Sacramento thirty miles to the west. Peter Lassen's rancho, reached at the end of the month, Lord described as a couple of houses built of sun-dried brick covered with logs and shakes and "surrounded with filth. Bones, rags, chips, sticks, horns, skulls, hair, entrails, blood, etc. etc."

A day before he arrived there he heard of an example of mining camp justice: "A Wisconsin gentleman (?) was hauled up to a tree day before yesterday and thirty lashes with a braided rawhide rope applied by a strong arm to his bare back, for stealing a revolver." And while in camp at Lassen's he was called to the tent of a dying man—afflicted with typhus, Lord believed. The victim was in extremis and died: "His troubles are past, his fears ended. . . . Cold and heat and hunger, and sickness no more afflict him, nor has the gold of California any charm. He is where gold glitters not and precious stones are as the dust of the earth."

 Israel Lord's Ode to an Ox

Too sure they've left me here to die,
An old and hungry ox;
Where not a blade of grass can grow
Among the climbing rocks.
They've left me here to starve and die.
Without a lock of hay.
And they've burned my yoke and bows and gone
to Californ-i-a.

They cracked their whips and rolled along
And left me all alone;
And "O Susanna" was the song,
That chased the rascals on.
And "O Susanna, don't you cry,"
Was still the doleful lay,
That cheered the rogues as they marched on
to Californ-i-a.

I know not who Susanna is,
Nor why she shouldn't cry.
It's hard that one can't weep when left
Among the rocks to die;
But I—I cannot weep, my brain
Is scorched and dried away,

And rattles in my skull like gold
Of Californ-i-a.

They may kick and maul and beat me now,
But they'll find it is "no go."
For my neck will never bear a yoke,
Nor my shoulders press a bow.
If an ox's ghost e'er runs at large,
I'll be revenged some day
For I'll haunt the rascals as long as they live
In Californ-i-a.

(From *"At the Extremity of Civilization": An Illinois Physician's Journey to California in 1849* © 1995 by Necia Dixon Liles, published by McFarland & Company, Inc., Jefferson, N.C.)

SARAH ELEANOR BAYLISS, born in Stratford-upon-Avon in 1819, would have no memory of the town or its fame as Shakespeare's birthplace, nor of the celebration throughout England of the birth that same year of Princess, later Queen, Victoria. When Sarah was but six weeks old, the Baylisses bundled her up and took her aboard a ship bound for America.

She grew up in New York State and received an "old academy" education, presumably a private school for girls, and was a well-read, deeply religious young woman when she married Josiah Royce, about whom we know little more than that he was a farmer's son and, from Sarah's occasional testimony about him in the occasional journal she kept, a capable, brave, and caring man.

Until she was sixty, Sarah Royce gave her "Pilgrim's Diary" little thought. It was a relic of a bygone day, suitable for storage in a cedar-lined chest along with pressed flowers, locks of baby hair, and packets of letters tied with fading ribbons. But for her son's urging, she might not have retrieved those rough and simple notes of her adventure "across the plains" except perhaps to show the rare grandchild curious about the old days when people ventured from their homes to chase gold in California.

When she took up her notes to expand on them, thirty years had passed since she, her husband Josiah, and their two-year-old daughter Mary had pushed off toward the setting sun with a wagon, three yoke of oxen and two milch cows, but she found those days rushing back, those days when they had ventured west seeking something better than they had.

The Royces were residing in Iowa, twenty miles west of the Mississippi, when they pulled out on the last day of April 1849, for Council Bluffs, where they would begin measuring the distance to California.

Little Mary turned out to be a miracle child—an uncomplaining traveler, "happy as a lark all day," and able to sink to sleep on her blanket-covered straw tick "as serenely as though she were in a palace, on a downy pillow." Sarah, however, was apprehensive. She felt keenly but kept to herself her "oppressive sense of homelessness." She did not complain; she cooked, labored shoulder-to-shoulder with Josiah, cared for the child, read a few pages daily from Frémont's *Travels* and her Bible and slept little. She said "an instinct of watchfulness kept me awake."

They reached Council Bluffs at the end of May and there fell in with other wagon parties awaiting ferriage across the Missouri. By the time they were all ready to depart, on June 10, 1849, the Royce family was listed as part of an organized company of argonauts with a captain in charge and a set of punctilios to obey. They, and others, attempted to add to the rules a provision to make the Sabbath a day of rest, but this idea was disallowed. The season was too far advanced, they were told, for such a luxury.

Their party was eight days behind Israel Lord's, which had departed Saint Joseph on June 2, but the Royces and the other wagon folk with them made good progress following the Mormon Trail along the north bank of the Platte and reached Fort Laramie in a month. There were Indian scares in the high plains where Sioux, Cheyenne, Pawnees, and Poncas followed the buffalo herds through the grasslands. Travelers were warned that it had become common for Indian bands to bully emigrants and scare them with their warpaint and sullen threats as they tried to exact tolls for every wagon passing through their lands.

But this danger was yet to come, and the Royces reached South

Pass on August 4 unmolested. There, at latitude 42 degrees 26 minutes, over 7,500 feet above sea level, where the Continental Divide debouched into a wide plain of sand and sage, Sarah thanked God for their safe journey thus far. She wanted to build a small stone monument—her "Ebenezer," a "stone of help" such as Samuel built to thank God for his victory over the Philistines—but there were no stones and no time, so a prayer had to serve.

After a drop southeast from the roiling current of the Green River, the Royces reached Fort Bridger on August 13, now detached from the company they joined at Council Bluffs, and had decided to forego the long and out-of-the-way detour to the north required to reach Fort Hall, and to push on west to Salt Lake City, then westerly again to the Humboldt.

They were traveling light and fast, had no other slower wagons ahead to impede them, and thus entered the Mormon capital at a good pace. There was no time for extended rest, only time to replenish their foodstuffs and graze their stock. The example of the Donner train was a daily reminder of the consequence of attempting to cross the Sierra in winter, and so, on August 30, despite protestations from Mormon merchants and veterans of the California trail that it was already too late, they continued on.

The Indian warning the Royces had heard at Fort Laramie materialized on September 11 as they neared the Humboldt. They were, she remembered, "moving quietly along our way, no living creature, save our plodding team and our own feeble company, within sight," when a party of Indians appeared suddenly between two low hills. As they approached the wagon, she said, "we saw they were all armed; and presently, several arranged themselves in a sort of semi-circle closing the road. . . . I saw we were completely in their power. Their numbers and their arms were enough to destroy us in a few moments."

The standoff lasted nearly an hour, with the tribesmen yielding no ground, drawing together to "consult with puzzled looks," while some blocked the ox team. Finally, Josiah grew weary of the impasse and, as Sarah described the moment, "raised the big ox-whip, shouted to the cattle, and rushed them forward so suddenly that those nearest Indians instinctively stepped aside, then [with Josiah] pompously exclaiming 'I'm going to move on' . . . we were once more in motion."

The seconds crawled past. They fully expected to be waylaid again as they passed through several narrow defiles that day, but night came and they set up their camp without another sighting of the "enemy," she said.

To whites, Indians were the "enemy" everywhere in the West.

AT THE HUMBOLDT Sink, amid brittle sagebrush and the carcasses of cattle, "miles out on the desert without a mouthful of food for the cattle and only two or three quarts of water in a little cask," Sarah Royce told of feeding mattress straw to the oxen and of the water cask running so low she vowed to drink none herself so that her husband and child would have a sip. She depended on God for their survival. "He would never leave us," she said. "He came so near that I no longer simply *believed* in Him, but *knew* His presence there." A few hours later, she wrote, "when my little one, from the wagon behind me, called out, 'Mamma I want a drink'—I stopped, gave her some, noted that there were but a few swallows left, then mechanically pressed onward again . . . repeating, over and over, the words, 'Let me not see the death of the child.'"

The hand of Providence Sarah Royce saw protecting her little family was nowhere more in evidence than at a point a short distance from Truckee Pass, the place where, almost exactly three years before, the Donner Party, upon reaching the granite wall of the Sierra, had rested five fatal days before plunging on into the mountain blizzards that killed thirty-five of them. Now, at this lamentable site, on Friday, October 12, 1849, two horsemen approached, cantering down the pass, "clad in loose, flying garments that flapped like wings on each side of them, their broad-brimmed hats blown up from their foreheads." They had the appearance, Sarah said, of "coming down from above, and the thought flashed into my mind, 'They look heaven-sent.'"

The lead rider approached Josiah. "Well, sir, you are the man we are after! . . . You and your wife, and that little girl, are what brought us as far as this." He said they belonged to a relief company authorized by the United States government in California to "help late emigrants over the mountains." A company ahead of the Royces told the horsemen of the lone wagon and family of three struggling toward Truckee Pass.

"I stood in mute adoration, breathing, in my inmost heart, thanksgiving," Sarah wrote.

The Royces left their wagon behind, packed their provisions and belongings on the oxen and the mules the relief riders brought along, and rode on borrowed horses across the pass ten days before the mountains were blocked with snow.

On October 24, they reached a high ridge and looked down at the silver ribbon of the Sacramento River threading through its lush valley.

"California, land of sunny skies—that was my first look into your smiling face," she wrote joyously. "I loved you from that moment, for you seemed to welcome me with a loving look into rest and safety."

ALONZO DELANO HAD arrived on the Feather River with four dollars in his pocket and would soon settle in Grass Valley, northwest of Lake Tahoe and across the divide from the far northern mining district. There, in October 1850, a miner named George McKnight stubbed his toe on an outcropping of white quartz while out searching for a stray cow. A piece of quartz he picked up had threads of a yellow substance in it and McKnight, who knew a thing or two about gold, took the specimen to his cabin, pounded it to dust and washed the dust in a pan. It turned out to be gold, a particle of a fabulous lode of gold.

None of what McKnight found managed to find its way into Delano's pockets, nor was he successful when he tried his hand at trading with the Indians and land speculation. At banking and journalism, however, he found his personal mother lode.

"California proved to be a great leveler of pride," he wrote in later years. "It was a common thing to see a statesman, a lawyer, a physician, a merchant or clergyman engaged in driving oxen or mules, cooking his mess, at work for wages by the day, making hay, hauling wood, or filling menial offices." False pride, he said, quickly evaporated. "I have seen the scholar and scientific man, the ex-judge, the ex-member of Congress or the would-be exquisite at home, bending over the washtub, practising the homely art of the washerwoman; or sitting on the ground with a needle, awkwardly enough repairing the huge rents in his pantaloons or sewing on buttons."

ISRAEL LORD WANDERED the gold camps of the Feather River country for a month before paying a visit in December 1849 to

Sacramento City. He found the boomtown a congeries of tarp-roofed buildings, tents, streets and winding footpaths of mud and muck. Littering every square foot of ground were boxes, barrels, wagons, piles of lumber, glass bottles, rusting, discarded machinery, "and plunder of all sorts, heaped and scattered and tumbled about in 'the most admired confusion.'"

The saloons, with their monte tables where "Common laborers, mechanics, etc., will risk a whole day's earnings on the turn of a card," appalled him. These dives, with their "Drinking, smoking, playing, betting, swearing, lying, cheating, swindling, robbing, stealing, piles of money . . . and cigars by the bushel," defined for the physician "dens of iniquity." He wrote that "Occasionally you will find a man of mind, a moral and intellectual man, and a thinking man" in the gold camps and towns, but said they "are hidden, overwhelmed by the putrid tide whose impurity would contaminate the wash of the Augean stables, and push the reeking impieties of Sodom a backward step from hell."

No ethnic group escaped his contemptuous eye. The Indians were unspeakably filthy and ignorant; the garb of the Chinese, their "pig tail cues," and "flat mockery of a basket hat," was a "tout ensemble which defies pen and pencil"; the Sandwich Islanders, while "most singular and interesting," he figured to be but a generation removed from cannibalism: "One cannot divest himself of the idea that, whilom, their fathers may have luxuriated in steaks of good English—not beef—but sailors"; and he found few specimens of his own kind much above his description of one of the men in his overland party, an "unprincipled, quick-tempered, obstinate, ignorant scoundrel," or another he described as "a great—I was about to say ass, but I will say Irishman."

He engaged a room on the levee in a one-story hotel, part of which had been partitioned off for a saloon. The main sleeping quarters had three tiers of bunks: a meal cost two dollars, and four bits bought a cigar or a drink. "People die here, I reckon," he wrote with ponderous irony, "for 38 were buried day before yesterday, and nobody committed murder or suicide. When I went to bed last night, or rather this morning, I found a man in the berth at my feet raising blood from the lungs. There were at least two quarts in the pan before him. People can afford to employ physicians here. Only an ounce [of gold] a visit, or $16."

Lord stayed through the December flood that inundated the country between the Feather River and Sacramento City, then, with five partners "made our first essay at gold digging as a business" on a fork of the Yuba River not far from a claim worked by Alonzo Delano, taking out eighteen dollars between them for over a half day's labor. They raised their take to twelve dollars a day each before moving on. "Plenty of gold everywhere except where you are," Lord wrote.

In July, he was enduring 107 degrees of heat in a short-lived camp called Stringtown and proposing that California be renamed "Humbugnia" with Frémont appointed governor *in perpetuo.* "It is a worthless country for anything but gold; and even for that, every day is accumulating evidence of its depreciating value."

On September 30, 1850, he added to his journal, "The cholera is approaching us slowly from both east and west. It will make a charnel house of Sacramento when it comes." This turned out to be a prescient statement for the disease probably arrived in San Francisco within a week of the doctor's prediction, brought from Panama on the steamer *Carolina.* There had been fourteen deaths on the vessel en route but for unknown reasons San Francisco customs agents did not quarantine it and the disease rapidly made its way upriver. There were twenty cholera deaths in Sacramento by October 25 and so many others fell ill the Odd Fellows lodge set up a temporary hospital for victims and donated coffins to families of the dead.

Cholera claimed about nine hundred lives before the end of the year.

Lord does not appear to have been in attendance at the death in Sacramento that October of Colonel William S. Hamilton. The Illinoisan had met the handsome, trail-weary officer on the Humboldt River in August 1849, and remarked in typical Lordly fashion on the colonel's "exterior" and how it could have been improved by "a decent hat." The doctor must have learned of Hamilton's death from others since his diary entry, except for its dilation on Burr, is briefer than would have been the case if he had been at the bedside. On Monday, October 7, 1850, he wrote: "Died today at a quarter to 12 of heart disease—Col. Wm. S. Hamilton, youngest son of Alexander Hamilton who years by gone was swept from the political arena by the fiendlike malice of Aaron Burr. Take him all in all no worse man than that same Aaron Burr has ever polluted the American soil. Don't talk of Benedict Arnold. He was a meteor which glared and blazed and flashed and vanished. Burr was a planet, dense, dark, portentous, madly yet steadily rushing on to jostle in its errant course every other body within its influence."

THAT FALL OF 1849 after they crossed the Sierra, Josiah, Sarah, and Mary Royce found their first gold camp, called Weberville★, situated on Weber Creek, under twenty miles from the Coloma discovery site. Both tent camp and creek had been named for Charles M. Weber, a native of Hamburg, Germany, who, among other pioneering accomplishments, founded the town of Stockton in 1845.

In partnership with some other miners, Josiah wagoned in provisions from Sacramento City and opened a tent store in the camp, while, Sarah wrote, "On all sides the gold-pans were rattling, the cradles rocking, and the water splashing." The back of the tent was curtained off for living quarters, a big cookstove occupying most of the space.

She worked at the store counter while her husband and the others labored in the diggings. Payment for supplies at the Royce store was most often offered in gold dust. While the majority of her customers were of "a better sort of men," others she characterized as "Roughly-reared frontier-men almost as ignorant of civilized life as savages. Reckless bravados, carrying their characters in their faces and demeanor." Still, she said, while she kept busy at her counter and "in near communication with all these characters, no rude word or impertinent behavior was ever offered me."

Her husband was prostrated by an attack of "cholera-morbus" but recovered, and Sara, too, took to her bed with a fever. When the two were able, they loaded a wagon and set out for Sacramento City and arrived on New Year's Day 1850 at Sutter's old fort, a place she said she had read about "away back in the Empire State, when, in laughing girlhood, I used to threaten I would go and see some day, and stand on the Pacific shore."

By the time the Royces visited there Sacramento had upwards of thirty stores, a print shop, billard hall, bowling alley, six saloons, and a

---

★Sarah Royce called the place "Weaverville" and there is such a place, but it is two hundred miles north of Sacramento in the Trinity Mountain country. California historian Joseph Henry Jackson states that the Royce's camp was "Weberville" and that "some tongue had corrupted his [Weber's] name to 'Weaver.'"

blacksmith shop. Lots which first sold for two hundred dollars were now costing as much as $30,000.

The floods of early January, which put 80 percent of the town under water so high boats could enter the second story of the City Hotel, drove the Royces to San Francisco. They stayed for a time at Montgomery House, then to a tenement "occupied by a number of the most respectable and companionable people in San Francisco." Sarah was never happier than in those days among new-found churchgoing friends in the boisterous city by the Golden Gate.

MOST LANDBOUND FORTY-NINERS favored the northern trails to the Sacramento Valley—the Platte–South Pass–Humboldt–Sierra Nevada route. The advantages seemed incontrovertible and were spelled out in overland guidebooks. These trails, at least as far as Fort Hall in Idaho, 1,200 or more miles from the Missouri frontier, had been blazed by Oregon country emigrants in the early 1840s. The main Oregon Trail would be "peopled," if not crowded, and therein lay safety. Water, grass, and timber on the main road, and the California Trail and its variations beyond Fort Hall, ranged from good to adequate. The northern trails afforded waystations, places to rest and recuperate, "recruit" draft animals, and buy supplies.

But if the advantages of the Oregon and California trails seemed to outweigh all the overland alternatives, the southern routes—dimmer paths across Texas, Mexico, New Mexico, and Arizona—had their adherents, especially among newspaper editors who saw the migration as a chance to tout their state or town as a vital crossroad to the gold fields.

"We are at a loss to conceive any good reasons why the emigrants who are now leaving the eastern states should take the northern route to California," an *Arkansas State Democrat* editor wrote in October 1848, and asked why other emigrants would elect "the dangerous, costly, and circuitous route through the pestilential atmosphere of the Isthmus of Panama." Between these two extremes, which he called "the Scylla and Charybdis of these modern voyagers," lay a southern overland path "free alike from the blighting influence of the frosts and snows of the northern region, and the withering effects of gentle breezes under whose wings is hidden the deadly malaria of equatorial climes." The shortest route to the Pacific, he claimed with the

heated zeal and elaborate exaggeration of a civic booster, lay
"through a country among whose hills is heard continually reverber-
ating the joyous laugh of spring, and whose valleys wear the warm
smile of eternal summer! To come down to plain prose, the route to
California through our state via Santa Fé and the Old Spanish trail, or
by way of the Gila river, is the only route which can be safely taken
by emigrants after the first of May."

Such claims, more often the ones in plain word-of-mouth prose,
had their effect: In the spring and summer of 1849, three thousand
argonauts from twenty-five states assembled at Forts Smith and Van
Buren, on the western boundary of Arkansas, and plunged west along
the Canadian River toward Santa Fé.

But the notion of a quick march across the Southwest to the gold
fields had no basis in fact: No overland route to California was either
quick or safe, and the southern paths west held special miseries for the
venturer on them. A clearer picture of them was provided by a correspondent for the *Missouri Republican* who wrote from Santa Fé on
July 15, 1849, "Hundreds of emigrants have passed through this place
on their way to California. . . . Hundreds are arriving daily and
departing, and nearly all are destitute of the necessary means to see
them through." No facts or reason gave them pause, he wrote, and
predicted that the trail out to Tucson and the Gila River "will be
marked out and Macadamized by the bones of the victims of a
nation's insanity."

The expanses beyond Santa Fé were mysterious, largely
unmapped, known only vaguely even by trappers, Indians, and wan-
derers come up from Mexico on dim trade paths.

Some Forty-niners followed General Kearny's line of march out of
fabled Santa Fé, down the Rio Grande to the adobe hamlet of
Socorro, then south and west across the desert above Tucson to the villages of the Pima people, and along the Gila to the fording of the Colorado River at Fort Yuma. The final leg of the journey was a straight
westward desert trek of ninety miles into the outskirts of San Diego.

Most of the argonauts lured to the Southwest chose a wagon trail
blazed by Captain Philip St. George Cooke of Kearny's Army of the
West who made an epic march to California with five hundred volunteers called the Mormon Battalion. Cooke's force moved out of
Santa Fé in October 1846, with a dozen wagons and oxcarts, marched
down the Rio Grande and made a trail to Tucson considerably south

of Kearny's. They struck the Gila in late December and struggled into San Diego in January.

Among the first of the Gila River argonauts reached San Diego in August 1849, and were fortunate to find passage to San Francisco on the steamer *Panama*. One who observed these men, "lank and brown as is the ribbed sea-sand," was Bayard Taylor, en route to the gold fields to report for Horace Greeley's *New York Tribune*. The Gila men, he wrote, showed "the rigid expression of suffering."

A few weeks later, as Taylor was hiking from San Francisco to Monterey, he met others who had entered California from the deserts to the east of San Diego—"wild, sun-burned, dilapidated men, but with strong and hardy frames." He said many spoke of the kindnesses of the Pima Indians, the pilfering by the Yuma and Maricopa bands they encountered, but said they passed through Apache country with no problem other than "a little thieving."

Nearly all, Taylor reported, had been seven months getting to California from their starting place.

TEXAS NEWSPAPERS PROMOTED two overland routes to California, each more torturous than its advocates admitted.

One of these had wagons rolling west from Brownsville, Corpus Christi, and San Antonio, to the lower Rio Grande, thence either southwest across Mexico to the Mexican seaport of Mazatlán or via the northern Mexican states of Coahuila and Chihuahua, up to the Gila River and onward to San Diego. The other ran from San Antonio to the Gila, passing through Paso del Norte (later Ciudad Juárez, Mexico) or, opposite it on the Rio Grande, the village of Franklin (later El Paso, Texas), then across New Mexico to Tucson, and along the Gila River to San Diego.

One segment of the Gila River passage had a reputation uglier than the poisonous lizard that lived in the river's valley. Generations of trappers searching for beaver grounds, Kearny's dragoons, Forty-niners—anyone who ventured there—attested to the horrors of the crossing of the eighty-mile wasteland between Tucson and the Pima Indian villages, a burning and virtually waterless tract of bleached animal bones, stunted greasewood, sage, and cactus, and a river of gluey mud. Here, as with the Oregon Trail and California Trail, emigrants threw out all superfluous weight along the roadside, a litter of goods and provisions mixed with the carcasses of mules, horses, and oxen left to the buzzards in the 120-degree heat and violent dust storms. Louisiana judge Benjamin Hayes wrote after his experience there in 1849, "I consider the crossing of this *jornada* of eighty miles an era in my life and shall never forget it to the day of my death."

The traveler who got across found relief among the Pimas, friendly farm folk who offered their water, pumpkins, melons, and vegetables to the passersby and saved countless lives through their generosity.

An estimated three thousand argonauts departed east Texas that year, and after journeys ranging from four to six months arrived in San Diego to search for a vessel bound for the Golden Gate.

THERE WERE A bewildering number of southern routes, each one with its detours, cutoffs, and variant paths, every one of them appearing advantageous, every one laden with unimagined perils. The best of the southern trails in American territory were those with some previously dug wagon ruts, paths blazed by traders from Missouri in the 1820s and later Bent's Fort, to Santa Fé, and by Kearny and Cooke between Santa Fé and San Diego. The worst was that taken by a few hundred gold seekers, one party accurately called the Sandwalking Company, who ventured out of the Mormon settlements in southern Utah in the summer of 1849. Some of these argonauts, leaving as late as September, hoped to make up for their late start by taking a "cut-off" southwest across the Nevada and California deserts to Walker Pass in the southern end of the Sierra, and across the mountains directly to the diggings.

The chimerical shortcut led the party into the wastelands subsequently called Death Valley. There they wandered for weeks in valleys of sand; weird, waterless canyons of fantastic bleached rock formations, salt columns, alkaline lakebeds and tainted seepages.

After a desperate two-week crossing of the Panamint Range, the remnant of the party, wraiths from the desert, reached a California rancho where in a few days they recovered from the ordeal and continued on to the mines.

A GLANCE AT a map told many in the east and south that a trans-Mexico passage was the shortest route to the Pacific: Tampico to

Mazatlán looked very good, five hundred miles, straight as a belt across the waist of Mexico; or Vera Cruz through Mexico City and northwest to Guadalajara and San Blas—emulating Ned Beale's celebrated west-to-east ride in the summer of '48—was only one hundred fifty miles more. Of course, it would be a pack mule and horse journey, no ox-wagons to bog down such a sprint across country. And sea travel would be required to the eastern Mexican ports, and again on the Pacific side up to San Francisco.

Among the first argonauts to act on such ideas was the Manhattan-California Overland Association, described by its captain and chronicler, A. C. Ferris of Hackensack, New Jersey, as "a company of two hundred adventurous spirits . . . eager to dig our fortunes from the mines in the shortest possible time." The plan, Ferris said, was simple: to go by sea to Vera Cruz, buy pack animals and horses, and journey overland to the Pacific coast at San Blas or Mazatlán "and in the absence of vessels at these ports to continue to journey two thousand miles by land through Mexico and Lower and Upper California to the mines."

They chartered the 200-ton brig *Mara* and boarded on Wednesday, January 31, 1849, suited out in wide-brimmed hats, boots, buckskins, and red flannel shirts, and kissing wives and sweethearts as if trooping off to war. In their quarters they stowed blanket rolls, tin pans for washing gold, shovels, picks, crowbars, camp kettles, frying pans, tin plates and cups, daguerrotypes of wives and mothers, locks of hair, Spanish language how-to books, a number of patent gold washers, and some musical instruments. Most of this miscellany, Ferris said, was "early scattered along the Mexican trails or in the chaparral, or perhaps sold to the natives for a few small coins." To the company's arms—rifles, carbines, shotguns, revolvers, and bowie knives—"we clung closely all the way."

They sped down the bay singing a variation on Stephen Foster's song on the quarterdeck—

> *Oh, Susannah, don't you cry for me;*
> *I'm bound for Californy with my tin pan on my knee.*

and the somewhat premature refrain:

> *But the happy time is over;*
> *I've only grief and pain,*

For I shall never, never see
Susannah dear again.

After the landing at Vera Cruz, the company spent their first night in Mexico at a windowless "caravansary," spreading their blankets on the floor amid the burros, mules, and horses, and spending the night tormented by fleas. "Nothing could parallel this first night in Mexico but a page of Dante's *Inferno*," Ferris said.

As they prepared to follow Winfield Scott's route to Mexico City, passing over the battlefields of the late war where, as they learned, "bleached skeletons lay still unburied," the Manhattan company was informed, Ferris said, that "the whole country was yet in a state of demoralization, and guerillas and robbers infested almost every mile of the way." Besides this, "merchants of intelligence in Vera Cruz warned us that we were almost sure to be robbed and murdered, that if we should escape this fate we could not find provisions on our journey for men or beasts, and that we would most surely break down our animals, and be glad to resort to horse or mule meat to sustain life."

As a result of these reports, "Fifty of the most pronounced and boastful among our company took a return passage on the vessel for New York."

The company needed horses and pack mules and dickered with Mexican traders for them. Ferris said the animals made available to *los Yankees* included, "not only the halt and the maimed, the lame and the blind, but some of the most vicious and worthless brutes that were ever collected together—galled and chafed, sore-backed, buckers, jumpers, and balky," and paid twenty-five to forty dollars each for the picks of the miserable lot. Each man carried two blankets, mining tools, a camp kettle or frying pan dangling from saddle, plus a bag of cups, spoons, and metal plates, the chronicler wrote, and with a rattle of tinware and some shouted orders they marched out of Vera Cruz on February 28, 1849. "Don Quixote and Sancho Panza joined to Falstaff's regiment would not have presented half so motley a group," Ferris wrote.

To escape the malarial seacoast, the party moved north and camped on the outskirts of Jalapa, a pretty place set in a mountain-ringed valley. A visit to the town plaza by too great a number of Ferris's men produced a dangerous moment when a crowd gathered and some rushed the Americans, scaring their horses and forcing them to pull their sidearms while they rushed through to an open street.

Upon reaching the heights of Cerro Gordo they camped upon the battlefield where Mexican President Santa Anna made a stubborn fight in April 1847, against Winfield Scott's army of 8,500 men. "We kindled our camp-fires, and, dipping water from its sunken pools covered with slimy green vegetation, we drank our coffee under the shade of the same trees where the desperately wounded lay to die," Ferris wrote. "All around us lay scattered uncoffined bones, and ghastly skulls looked down upon us where in mockery they had been secured among the branches."

As they worked their way up toward Mexico's central plateau, discarding gold washers, spare picks and shovels, and cook pots en route, they passed through numerous villages where "the señoras and señoritas greated us with kindness but the men followed with frowns and threats and with the significant gesture of a finger drawn across the throat." They were able to purchase bananas, sweet potatoes, even some pork and beef on occasion, the latter cut into long strips and sold by the yard; and at certain haciendas bought "the universal national dish of tortillas and frijoles," served with coffee at three cents a meal. But on other days, after riding forty miles, when asking for food they were told, "*Nada, Señor, nada. No hay tortillas. No hay frijoles,*" and had to make do with shooting wild turkeys and jackrabbits.

At some places they were called *ladrones* and moved on uneasily, swiveling in their saddle to keep an eye on their backtrail. At Buena Vista, where Zachary Taylor's force had a close call against Santa Anna in a two-day fight in late February 1847, they found shelter in a hacienda. Across the valley of Mexico and in the plaza of the ancient town of Montezuma, they failed to remove their hats in front of a great cathedral and had them knocked off by an angry crowd.

They passed through the magnificent city of Puebla, saw its cathedral, built in 1649, its eighteenth-century theater, great fountains and statues, and survived the fury of thunderstorms at nearly 10,000 feet, close to the Continental Divide. There they fought for breath, shook with ague and "crouched helplessly upon the ground, dazed by the lightning and shocked by the thunder."

They pushed on, descending into the valley of Mexico, flanked by the great volcanos, their maws capped by gauzy clouds. "It was a sublime experience," Ferris said, "to ride down that mountain height—

Mounts Popocatépetl and Ixtaccihuatl both looking down upon us, and the great valley and City of Mexico in full view below us, and a thunder shower with its dark nimbus clouds and forked lightning full in the sunshine under us."

None of the members of the Manhattan-California Overland Association came to Mexico as tourists; the country was a series of stepping-stones to the Pacific and to the California gold fields and so they spent little time in the old capital among its wonders. They were 280 miles inland from Vera Cruz and had 400 miles more to travel to reach the western coast, so they crossed the causeway over Lake Texcoco, camped at twilight and before daybreak resumed their march.

With one sad exception they reached San Blas uneventfully.

In Guadalajara, 360 miles northwest of the capital, one of the company, a young man from New Jersey, shot himself dead—apparently a suicide. Ferris said, "We extemporized a coffin from some rude boards, prepared the body for burial, and I read over him the burial service, and waiting till the town was silent, in midnight darkness, we silently stole out of town and buried him in a secluded spot."

In the coastal village of San Blas the men found the two-hundred-ton brig *Cayuga* at anchor and taking on passengers to California. The company, now thinned to 120 men, paid eighty dollars each for the voyage to San Francisco plus thirty more each for "sea stores" that included jerked beef so tough and gristly it had to be attached to ropes and towed behind the ship for two days before it became chewable.

On the eighty-fourth day out of New York Harbor, the Manhattan-Californians set sail for San Francisco. Thirty days later, on May 14, 1849, they passed through the Golden Gate.

THE DAY AFTER A. C. Ferris and his band departed for Vera Cruz and their 114-day expedition to San Francisco, Daniel B. Woods, a schoolteacher and minister, and a assemblage of men calling themselves the Camargo Company gathered at the foot of Arch Street in Philadelphia. They had their gear with them, these forty Forty-niners Woods described as "men of all professions and pursuits of life— young and old, grave and gay, married and unmarried" and they sailed that morning on the barkentine *Thomas Walters*. They were not bound for Ciudad Camargo, the Mexican hamlet on the lower Rio

Grande from which they took their name, but for Tampico, and from there a ride across Mexico to Mazatlán, and another sea passage to the Golden Gate.

The bark wallowed the sea lanes for three weeks before reaching the mouth of the Rio Panuco and an anchorage under the brow of the promontory on which Tampico lay.

After visiting the American consul in the city, they obtained *cartas de seguridad* (letters of security), supposed to assist them in dealing with town and village authorities while traveling across Mexico. They next hired a guide, bought horses and mules, and on March 8 mounted up and rode along the banks of the Panuco River toward the Sierra Madre Range and San Luís Potosí.

They crossed the "Andes of Mexico" without serious incident, rode and walked across the tableland of the Central Plateau and its thorny thickets of prickly pear and mesquite, its palms, cypresses, and palmetto groves, volcanic peaks, and terrific dust storms, stopping in villages for food and forage.

At San Blas, which they reached on April 12, Woods wrote, "Our company, which had hung together in fragments was dissolved. Men alone are not social beings; and in the numerous attempts to bind them together in California gold-mining associations are as vain as the attempt to make a rope of sand."

On June 25, 1849, aboard the Scottish bark *Collooney*, Woods and the others reached San Francisco, 145 days out of Philadelphia.

ANOTHER ILL-MARKED AND ill-understood Mexican route that attracted some argonauts had the single advantage of eliminating the need for ocean travel, and a world of disadvantages—perils learned only by the journey on it.

This was the northern Mexico path from the Lower Rio Grande following that river across the northern Mexican states of Nuevo León, Coahuila, Chihuahua, and Sonora, up to intersect the Gila River west of Tucson, thence across the deserts into San Diego.

Among the first, and certainly the most prominent of the Forty-niners to chance this primitive pathway was John Woodhouse Audubon, youngest son of the acclaimed ornithologist and artist, and himself a talented naturalist, painter, and musician.

He was born in Kentucky in 1812 at a time when his Haitian-born father was engaged in a sawmill business in the southern wilderness and going broke at it, and fifteen years distant from publishing his masterpiece, *The Birds of America.*

In 1848, upon returning from a trip to Europe, John Woodhouse learned of the gold discovery of California and joined a military-styled unit being formed by Colonel Henry L. Webb, brother of the editor of the *New York Herald.* This citizen-soldier, who had served in Mexico in the recent war, advocated an overland route west from the gulf coast of Texas and Audubon Senior applauded the idea, seeing the journey as a rare opportunity for his son to sketch and collect specimens of birds and mammals during the journey.

In January 1849, when he signed on with the "Colonel H. L. Webb California Company," Aububon was thirty-six, tall, lean, and athletic, with dark, curly, shoulder-length hair and side whiskers and so accustomed to "the backwoodsman's life" that Webb appointed him second-in-command of the expedition.

The company of ninety-eight men had strong financial backing: $27,000 in cash and certificates of deposit put together by a group of New York financiers, many of them friends and sponsors of the senior Audubon, who expected to see their investment recouped and profits made once Webb and his men reached Eldorado and began amassing gold.

Most of the company were New Yorkers, with little or no experience outside their homes and offices. They were to provide their own horses and personal belongings, all else to be supplied from the company treasury.

After buying provisions and ammunition in New Orleans, the party departed on March 4 on the *Globe* steamer for Brazos, a village near the mouth of the Rio Grande, then proceeded to Brownsville, and 125 miles upstream to a point of debarkation on the Mexican side of the river opposite Rio Grande City. While Webb rode off to Camargo to buy mules and visit with the town *alcalde,* Audubon found time to do some of the work his father had urged on him by "collecting" a thrush, a green jay, a cardinal, a dove, and two woodpeckers, sketching them and drying their skins to be packed in his specimen case in papered layers.

After three days in camp, John Lambert, a Connecticut lawyer and one of five Lamberts in the Webb party, fell violently ill with stomach cramps and vomiting, diarrhea, and alternating chills and fever. The expedition's physician, John B. Trask, knew the symptoms and administered his cholera specifics (which would have been endorsed by Dr. Israel Lord): mustard plasters, massage of the limbs, teaspoonsful of brandy, and sips of camphor. Lambert seemed to improve during the day—"the composure of cholera," Aububon called it—then suddenly died. Two of the company bought a coffin in Rio Grande City and buried their companion on the American side of the river with fifty of the men in attendance.

During an overnight stay in Rio Grande City, Audubon, who in Webb's absence had charge of the company's money, was talked into turning over close to $15,000 of it to a hotel bartender for safekeeping. When he tried to retrieve the cash the next day the saloon man claimed that another member of the party had already claimed it. For this lie the man was taken out and chained to a mesquite stump with a guard posted over him. He was given time to confess or be hanged; eventually about half the gold coins were recovered.

They were hopelessly behind schedule—"two full months behind our reckoning," Audubon said, "and on a route of which I never approved, but which, when I took command, we were already compelled to pursue." In the ten weeks since departing New York, they had moved no farther than Mier, a riverside village thirty miles above Rio Grande City. They had buried ten men, and another twenty, including Colonel Webb, had quit the company and departed for New Orleans and home.

Audubon himself was weakened by cholera symptoms but rallied enough at Mier to oversee the sale of all but one of the company's wagons, and all its spare stock and goods. Forty-eight men of the original Webb California Company agreed to push on with Audubon in command of what was now a pack mule train. They took with them only the necessities of survival in the rough country ahead, and after a month's recuperation in Mier, moved out along the river on April 28.

Even with a single wagon, the pace was agonizingly slow—ten days to cover the hundred miles to Monterrey, far behind the rate of a full wagon party on the Oregon and California Trails.

Two more men died of cholera in Parral and were buried in the desert, and after selling their remaining wagon Audubon led the party he now regarded as "accursed" westward across the mountains into the state of Sonora. They made one eight-day journey in the searing desert heat, draining their stock of water before finding relief in one of the many *poblados* and tiny mining settlements scattered, with great distances between them, along their route.

On September 9 they entered the town of Altar and two weeks later, gaunt, weak, their clothing in rags, their animals half dead, reached the Pima Indian settlements on the Gila River where they recuperated before moving on to raft across the Colorado.

During the last agonizing leg of the journey Aububon surrendered the last of his cumbersome painting materials and specimens. "My arsenic [the preservative for his bird skins] is broadcast on the barren clay soil of Mexico, the paper in which to preserve plants was used for gun-wadding, and, though I clung to them to the last, my paints and canvases were left on the Gila desert of awful memories."

They stumbled into San Diego in mid-October 1849, and four months later, the surviving members of the group scattered over the southern mines from Stockton to Mariposa, the Colonel Webb California Company dissolved.

≋ The Rough Diamond ≋

BIOGRAPHER SYLVAN MULDOON says William Stephen Hamilton was "somewhat of a runagate, if we are to judge his character by the standards of conventional aristocracy." The man Israel Lord met in a bleak camp on the Humboldt River in the summer of 1849, if not a vagabond, did lead a life equal to all the subtle imaginations of a fiction writer.

He was born in New York City in 1797, the fifth son of Alexander and Elizabeth Schuyler Hamilton, and was a schoolboy when his father was killed in a duel with Aaron Burr at Weehawken, on the Jersey shore, on July 11, 1804.

William entered West Point at age sixteen but because of chronic absenteeism did not graduate and wandered west to Illinois where he worked as a surveyor and practiced law. He fought as a colonel of volunteers in campaigns against Winnebago Indians on the northern Mississippi in 1827, and in the Blackhawk War in Illinois in 1832. At the time he decided to join the argonauts to California he was owner and developer of lead mines and smelters in Wisconsin.

He departed Saint Louis in the spring of 1849 with two wagons and joined a train bound west from the Missouri frontier. He left no account of his journey, and Dr. Lord's meeting him on the Humboldt is the only clue to Hamilton's route to California. His biographer states Hamilton reached the Sacramento Valley in the late summer and began prospecting in the "Weaver Creek" [Weber Creek] vicinity—the same diggings in which Sarah Royce and her family made a home—and that in a year he accumulated something close to $12,000 in gold from his claim on the creek's south bank.

He died on August 7, 1850, in Sacramento, at a time when the town was in the grip of a cholera epidemic, and was buried with fifty cholera victims in an unmarked mass grave. In 1889 he was reburied in the Sacramento City Cemetery. General Schuyler Hamilton, William's uncle, arranged for a modest obelisk-shaped monument, with a medallion attached, to be placed over the grave.

Hamilton was described by a contemporary as five-foot-seven, about 160 pounds, slight as his father, "quite handsome, a true gentleman," a Whig, and an admirer of Daniel Webster and Henry Clay. An obituary in the *Alta California* on October 18, 1850, stated, "His nature was frank, generous and manly. His ready wit, well-stored memory and uniform good humor made him a choice and agreeable companion."

Schuyler Hamilton called William "The Rough Diamond," and those words were included on a plaque by the grave installed by the Sacramento chapter of the Daughters of the American Revolution.

ELDORADO

Gaily bedight,
A gallant knight,
In sunshine and in shadow,
Had journeyed long, singing a song
In search of Eldorado.
—Edgar Allan Poe, 1849

TWELVE

GATEWAY

JOHN C. FRÉMONT sailed in and out of San Francisco Bay many times on American trade vessels and warships during the military campaign in California in 1846. He was a thorough-going landsman but learned to love the fog-veiled beauty of the entrance to the finest natural harbor on the Pacific coast of North America. Long before gold was discovered a hundred miles beyond its headlands, he called the roadway into the bay the "Golden Gate."

Others before him admired the place and guessed at its significance after Juan Rodríguez Cabrillo passed by it in 1542, Sir Francis Drake in 1579, and the merchant-adventurer Sebastian Vizcaíno in 1602. The bay itself was first seen in 1769 when Captain Gaspar de Portolá, the Spanish governor of Baja California, led an overland expedition into the northern wilderness. His advance scouts saw a great body of water they thought an inland sea, but found to be an enormous inlet of the great western ocean and a harbor so spacious one of the missionaries in the party wrote that "not only all the navy of our most Catholic Majesty but those of all of Europe could take shelter there." A similar view was expressed in 1841 by the American naval explorer Charles Wilkes who, with a wondrous myopia, found little other than the magnificent harbor to recommend California to expansionists in Congress.

While San Francisco Bay was considered the greatest prize of the war with Mexico, the significance of the growing town that lay inside it, at the end of the big thumblike peninsula, remained as lost as when John Sutter first saw it when his brig *Clementine* passed through the Golden Gate in 1839. It was, as H. H. Bancroft wrote, an "ill-favored site" but "topographically marked for greatness, rising on a series of hills, with a great harbor on one side, a great ocean on the other, and mighty waters ever passing by to the outlet of the wide-spread river system of the country."

From 1839 until 1847, a year before the gold discovery, the bay was rarely visited by more than one trade ship or whaler at a time; indeed,

in all of 1847, a total of six vessels anchored there, and between April
of that year and April 1848, only eleven—a bark, a brig, and nine
whalers—wallowed in to anchor off the mud flats fronting the village.

In August 1846, in the waning months of its history as Yerba
Buena, the settlement had 459 residents, three hundred of them
Americans or Europeans, of which 273 could read and write. These
figures were compiled by one Edward Gilbert, an officer in Colonel
Jonathan D. Stevenson's First Regiment of New York Volunteers, an
assortment of riffraff recruited in New York for the Mexican War.
Gilbert also counted 157 buildings of varying size and function there,
41 of them "places of business."

In January 1847, Lieutenant Washington A. Bartlett of the United
States sloop-of-war *Portsmouth* was appointed *alcalde* of Yerba Buena,
and on the 30th of the month, issued an announcement that the place
would henceforth be known as San Francisco. The news appeared in
Sam Brannan's newly launched *California Star* a little more than six
months after the American seizure of the town by a detachment of
sailors from the *Portsmouth*, John B. Montgomery commanding. To
commemorate the event the village plaza became Portsmouth Square
and the main path along the waterfront was named Montgomery
Street.

Another of Bartlett's accomplishments was the appointment of
Jasper O'Farrell to make a survey, drawings, and a plat of San Francisco, complete with streets named for heroes of the late war. The
thirty-one-year-old Dubliner had landed in Alta California from a
whaling ship in 1843, became fluent in Spanish and went to work for
Sutter as a surveyor and mechanic. He knew the town and tramped
over every foot of it for Bartlett, making meticulous notes and drawings among the tents, corrugated iron stores and warehouses, the random clots of adobes and driftwood squatters' shacks thrown together
amid the feeble grass and windblown dwarf oaks above Yerba Buena
Cove.

By May 1848, the dreary canvas hamlet that Jasper O'Farrell
mapped stood on the eve of an astonishing transformation; it was a
boomtown awaiting. This was the month in which the frenetic Sam
Brannan reached the mines at Mormon Island, took a look at the
furious work going on there and became instantly convinced that
there was more gold in the Sacramento River system "than all the
people in California could take out in fifty years."

The town now consisted of two wharves and two hundred buildings, including two small hotels, twelve commercial stores, a billiard parlor, and a tenpin bowling alley. These rough structures were spread out in a ragged crescent along the slope of the Clay Street hill while Montgomery, along the cove, was strewn with the customary waterfront complement of sailors and waterfront knockabouts, and piled with bales, boxes, and barrels of shipped merchandise. This chaos was overseen by bustling stevedores (being paid an astronomical $30 a day by shipmasters) and anxious merchants with their manifests and bills of lading.

Beach lots on the cove were selling for $600, a laughable price a few months past, but now space and building materials were as coveted as the gold that had driven all prices skyward. Lumber, as precious a commodity as common sense in San Francisco in gold rush days, sold for up to a dollar a board foot, so expensive it was often purchased only for the supporting joists and roof beams for "rag houses" of canvas. The newspaper correspondent Bayard Taylor told of a friend who had shipped lumber costing him $1,000 from New York to San Francisco and sold it for $14,000. Ready-made wooden edifices were made from the hulks of old sailing ships, such as the *Niantic*, a whaler out of Sag Harbor hauled up in the mud at the foot of Commercial Street, a hole cut in her hull, a roof roped over her deck, to make a warehouse. Eventually, 148 beached ships served as store and warehouse space; one became a bank, another a Methodist church, and the brig *Euphemia* was transformed into the city's first prison.

Even the physical configuration of the town was changing as sand and earth were carted from nearby hills to the waterfront and dumped into the bay, filling in the cove of Yerba Buena. Soon a dozen wharves jutted into the bay, the longest extending 2,000 feet across the low-tide mud flats to a deep-water anchorage. Brick buildings were rising and entrepreneurs and monied operators like Collis Huntington were making huge profits from shovels and blasting powder. Even greater profits lay in real estate, and in hotels, saloons, gambling layouts, and brothels. Profits were even made in trading coinage for the contents of the miner's poke: *Se compra oro de polvo*— WE BUY GOLD DUST—was a ubiquitous sign in Spanish and English in San Francisco's gold rush days.

By February 1849, one year after the gold discovery, the town population had risen to 2,000, by the end of the year to 20,000, and in early 1850 to 30,000 (including 2,000 women, a generous proportion of them "of base character and loose practices," according to Bancroft). The eleven vessels from eastern seaports which passed through the Golden Gate between April 1847 and April 1848, increased seventy-fold by April 1849.

Until 1850 when street lamps first appeared there, San Francisco glowed from the lamps in canvas dwellings and saloons, a thousand of them erected in the latter half of '49, warmed by potbellied stoves and therefore instant fire traps. Along the mud streets, rickety framed buildings and residences appeared overnight, as did hotels, one of which was shipped in sections from Baltimore.

Among the best San Francisco hotels in 1849, the Parker House lay on the east side of the sandy flat called Portsmouth Square and housed the Jenny Lind Theater, the town's first, and rented rooms and tables to professional gamblers at $1,800 a month. The 100-room Union Hotel on Kearny Street opened in 1850 at a cost of $250,000 and featured crystal chandeliers and a good many garish art works in rococo frames. Other favorite hostelries were the Oriental, the Broadway, the Frémont, the Ward House, the Graham House, and the St. Francis.

IN LATE AUGUST 1849, John Sutter ventured down to San Francisco Bay and after a short visit ashore boarded the chartered merchant brigantine *Frémont*, southbound for Monterey.

With ratification of the treaty signed at Guadalupe Hidalgo, Mexico, in May 1848, California had become a region of the United States but Washington lawmakers had stalled on granting it territorial status. Now, Congress had adjourned again without resolving the issue and Sutter had been elected one of forty-eight delegates to draw up a constitution and devise a government for the *state* of California.

The Monterey convention had been ordered by Acting Governor Bennett Riley of Maryland, a sixty-one-year-old brigadier general of the army, "a grim old fellow and a fine, free swearer," a contemporary said of the battle-scarred veteran of the War of 1812, the Blackhawk campaign, and the recent war with Mexico. The general had no experience in either military or civil governance but needed none to understand that California was in peril. It might have survived a longer period of lawlessness when settlers were trickling in, finding tracts of squatter land, tending a few head of cattle, raising crops, minding their business, and causing no trouble. But now a horde of gold hunters had arrived, thousands of others were on the march, and in their wake a legion of camp-followers, gamblers, and villains of every stripe on the run from their crimes in the east. There were good reasons to form a government before gold was discovered, but gold had made it imperative.

Monterey as yet had no hotel or even a restaurant when the delegates began arriving in late August, and so some of the delegates chose to sleep under the stars at Point Pinos, wrapped in blankets and serapes, others were taken into the homes of the wealthier Californios and such eminent American residents as Thomas Larkin, whose wife, and Frémont's Jessie, served as hostesses.

The assembly opened on September 3, 1849, in Colton Hall, a two-story, white stone, balconied building erected by Walter Colton, the former town *alcalde*, naval chaplain, and correspondent to the eastern press. The commissioners represented all populated areas of California, from San Diego north to the Trinity River mining camps of the Oregon border country. Of the forty-eight men, thirty-seven were Americans, twenty-two from free states, fifteen from slave states. Four, including John Sutter, were foreign-born; nine were under age thirty; fourteen were lawyers, twelve *rancheros*, seven merchants. Six were eminent Californios—members of the conquered populace now pledged to help form an American government. Among these, Mariano Guadalupe Vallejo still smarted over his mistreatment at the hands of the Bear Flaggers who imprisoned him for two months at Sutter's Fort in the summer of '46. Longtime settlers included Sutter, Larkin, Don Abel Stearns of Los Angeles (a Californian since 1829), Lansford Hastings, the Scotsman Hugo Reid, future Union general Henry W. Halleck of New York, who served as an aide to Governor Riley, and Kentuckian Robert Semple of Benicia, frontier doctor and printer, "a giant in height if not in intellect," Bancroft said of him, who was elected president of the convention. Delegate William H. Gwin of Tennessee, recently arrived in California specifically to be elected one of the state's first senators, brought with him the New York and Iowa state constitutions which he had reprinted in San Francisco to supply copies for assemblyman.

Selected as secretary of the convention was the Irishman John

Ross Browne, onetime Cincinnati police reporter, secretary to the secretary of the United States Treasury, and author of a book about Juan Fernández Island, which he had only recently visited en route to California via Cape Horn.

The most difficult issue facing the delegates was determining California's eastern boundary, a contentious matter that nearly wrecked the convention. A big-state faction, led by William Gwin, wanted to set the boundary at the Rocky Mountains and envelop all the lands ceded by Mexico in the Guadalupe-Hidalgo treaty. Others, "small-staters," urged the Sierra Nevada be recognized as the eastern state line. After several days' debate, often acrimonious, a compromise was reached fixing the eastern line roughly as it stands today.

The Iowa state constitution served as the model for California's. The document prohibited slavery, lotteries, and dueling, allowed women to control property in their possession before their marriage, extended the vote to white male citizens of the United States, and those of Mexico who had accepted citizenship, providing the voter had reached age twenty-four and had resided in California for at least six months. A proviso permitted the legislature, by a two-thirds vote, to admit to suffrage Indians or Indian descendents. A system of public schools was designated as "required," and the state executive, legislative, and judicial branches were delineated.

In their forty days of work, the delegates even adopted a state seal, a crowded circle drawn by Major Robert S. Garnett of Riley's staff. It busily depicted San Francisco Bay, the goddess Minerva in the foreground with a grizzly bear at her feet, the Sierra Nevada in the background, a mining scene in the middle distance, and the word "Eureka" atop a belt of stars. General Vallejo was disturbed by the presence of the bear in the design. He did not wish to honor the "Osos," the Bear Flag–waving Yankee ruffians who had invaded his Sonoma home and arrested him. He suggested that the bear in the seal be shown as held in check by a lariat in the hands of a vaquero. Secretary Robert Semple put the matter to vote and it was defeated.

Delegates ignored the idea of an interim territorial status. After the constitution and other documents were signed by the commissioners on October 13, 1849 (during which ceremony Sutter is said to have leapt to his feet and shouted, "This is the happiest day of my life!"), Governor Riley ordered a thirty-one-gun salute fired to announce the birth of the thirty-first state.

The constitution was submitted to voters on November 13, and was accepted by a vote of 12,064 yeas, 811 nays, out of a total citizenry of about 107,000, 76,000 of them Americans. Peter H. Burnett, the onetime Oregon lawyer and Sutter assistant, was elected governor. Sutter himself, who had once fired Burnett, received 2,201 votes, Burnett 6,716 out of the 13,000 cast, and after the vote count was declared over, General Riley proclaimed the end of military rule.

When the new legislature met on December 20, John C. Frémont was elected to the United States Senate on the first ballot and William M. Gwin on the second.

California was admitted as the free thirty-first state on September 9, 1850, with the signing of the bill by President Millard Fillmore.

WHEN THE NORTHERN delegates to the constitutional convention returned through the Golden Gate late in October 1849, they could scarcely credit the changes that had befallen San Francisco in the mere two months they had been absent. More than five hundred ships swayed at anchor in the bay, virtually all of them deserted, crews, often officers as well, off to the mines. There were new squatters' shacks, saloons and brothels at the foot of Telegraph Hill, hundreds of tents flapping in the breeze, some corrugated iron stores and brick buildings under construction, new dry goods and hardware emporiums, restaurants, new hotels, a theater or two, an opera house, even a bull ring.

Barges were unloading stores and merchandise on the mud beaches; Long Wharf, the extension of Commercial Street, was living up to that name with a parade of drummers called "Cheap Johns" yelling at passersby to buy something. Portsmouth Square, a cowpen not long ago, was bright and loud welcoming the tavern and gambling trade as did the byways of Sydney Town, northeastward around Telegraph Hill, Little Chile to the north of it, the French Quarter along Jackson Street, and Little China on Sacramento Street.

With so many sailing vessels and steamers vying for space in the bay, each flying identifying pennants and flags, the news of their arrivals had to be relayed inland by semaphore from Rincon Point on Telegraph Hill. (The semaphore signals became so familar that one night at a San Francisco theater, an actor threw his arms outward while delivering the line, "What means this, my lord?" From the audience came the shouted answer: "Sidewheel steamer!")

The sidewheeler became the favorite vessel among Forty-niners, especially if it turned out to be one the Pacific Mail steamers. Those coming to San Francisco from the diggings often did so expressly to see if the "P.M." had brought a letter from home. The miners squandered their gold at the gambling tables and in restaurants offering outlandishly priced "fancy" plates of canvasback duck, oysters, beef, brant, plover, salmon, and turtle; paid a whore an ounce for a few minutes talk or up to $400 for a night together; shelled out $37.50 for a night at the Saint Francis or six dollars for a flop in a reeking dormitory; paid an ounce for a turn in a public bath, forty dollars for a quart of bad whiskey, and one to five dollars for a two-month-old New York newspaper. They would also happily pay for a place in line to get their mail.

In 1849 there were 17,000 post offices east of the Mississippi but none in California until Washington sent an agent to make arrangements for the establishment of postal routes and offices along the Pacific seaboard. The agent arrived in San Francisco in February 1849, and swiftly reported his news to Washington. He could not hire postmasters at the pay scale designated by the government since labor was in short supply in San Francisco and what men remained there could command five times the offered salary. Property prices for post office sites were astronomical, far beyond the money suggested by the government. And, plans for post offices in outlying areas of California, such as Los Angeles, San Diego, and Monterey, needed to be delayed, all mail meantime to be funneled directly to San Francisco for sorting and delivery.

As a result of these findings few events created as much excitement as the arrival of a mail steamer through the Golden Gate. Lines at the San Francisco post office were so long hawkers sold pies, cakes, and newspapers, while others carried cans of coffee up and down the lines, or sold tripod stools for the exhausted patrons. Adults, and children, who got up before dawn and found good spots in the line, sold their places to miners for an ounce of gold and more.

On the last day of October 1849, the *Panama* came through the Golden Gate bringing three months' accumulation of eastern seaboard mail. Forty-five thousand letters in thirty-seven huge canvas bags, plus bales of newspapers, were hauled up to the little San Francisco post office that night, where eight clerks locked themselves in the building to sort the items alphabetically while weary patrons banged on the door. New York *Tribune* writer Bayard Taylor offered his services as "clerk-extraordinary" and "was at once vested with full powers and initiated into all the mysteries of counting, classifying, and distributing letters." The post office, he wrote, was a small, one-story, frame building about forty feet long with two public "windows," one for receiving and distributing domestic mail, the other for foreign business. The *Panama*'s bags were hauled in at about nine P.M., the doors and windows closed, "and every precaution made for a long siege." Knocks on the doors, taps on windows, and beseeching calls were ignored as the clerks labored steadily until, after forty-four hours of work, the windows were opened.

By then, Taylor said, the line extended all the way down the hill into Portsmouth Square and on the south side across Sacramento street to the tents among the chaparral.

TAYLOR ALSO WITNESSED San Francisco's transformation between his arrival in the city on the *Panama* on August 19, 1849, after a tour of the mines with Ned Beale, and after covering the Monterey constitutional convention for the *Tribune*. That winter he took a $30 steamer trip down from Sacramento and reached San Francisco in a golden sunset.

The city astonished him. "Of all the marvelous phases of the history of the Present, the growth of San Francisco is the one which will most tax the belief of the Future," he wrote. "Its parallel was never known, and shall never be beheld again." On his first tour just four months past, he said, "I found a scattering town of tents and canvas houses, with a show of frame buildings on one of two streets, and a population of about six thousand." Now, he wrote effusively, "I saw around me an actual metropolis, displaying street after street of well-built edifices, filled with an active and enterprising people, and exhibiting every mark of permanent commercial prosperity."

He commented on the prices for lodgings and meals—$150 a month at the Saint Francis ("the best in California"), $250 a month, without board, at Ward House, $35 for a meal at a decent restaurant.

He found the mud streets "little short of fathomless," and said one could not walk any distance without getting at least ankle-deep in muck.

(The streets were far worse than Taylor reported. Animals suffocated in them, human bodies were found entombed in mud on Montgomery Street and at Clay and Kearny a sign warned "This street is impassable, not even jackassable." Sidewalks were often fashioned from jettisoned cargo. One on Montgomery that led to the mail steamer office was formed of boxes of Virginia tobacco, each box containing one hundred pounds of it, worth seventy-five cents a pound; and tons of iron, sheet lead, cement, and barrels of salt beef were sunk in San Francisco's infamous mud.)

The poet-reporter wrote of heavy gales blowing in from the bay, and steady cold rains with the temperature sinking below fifty degrees. "It was impossible to stand still for even a short time without a death-like chill taking hold of the feet," he said.

Perhaps adhering to Horace Greeley's admonition not to write too negatively, Taylor did not mention that the prevailing west winds were in fact a blessing in that they carried off some of the city's stink of sewage, fish, and rotting produce. Nor did he mention that San Francisco's primitive drainage system and miasmatic atmosphere formed a perfect breeding ground for disease, or that the town was plagued by fleas. They were designated "quicks" to distinguish them from the other infestation, lice, which Daniel Knower, the Forty-niner from Albany, New York, said "pulled twelve oars on a side and was known under the generic appelation of 'slow,' the very thought of which causes a shiver even now."

Another of San Francisco's 1849 boomtown features omitted by the *Tribune* correspondent was its enormous rat population, its "headquarters" at Clark's Point, just north of the Broadway Wharf. Daniel Knower wrote that the clews of sailors' hammocks were rife with them and darts tipped with paper wings and a sail needle were used to kill them as sport. (Some of the rat species were as large as alley cats and as voracious, notably the white, pink-eyed rice rats, brought in ship bilges from Batavia.) A decent rat terrier, Knower said, was worth his weight in gold dust. Poison was spread liberally but the vermin compounded the problem when, driven by pain and thirst, they found their way to the town's wells, polluting them.

Small wonder, then, that San Francisco in 1849 and '50 was a hotbed of disease—rat-borne typhus, cholera, pneumonia, dysentery, various agues and fevers, and countless undiagnosible ailments including various forms of insanity. Bayard Taylor wrote of fifty "hopeless lunatics" at San Francisco's City Hospital, "some of them produced by disappointments and ill luck, and others by sudden increase of fortune." (To be sure, there were infinitely more of the former than the latter.)

Another Taylor, Methodist minister William Taylor, who went out to San Francisco in 1848 to save souls and spent seven years in the city as a street preacher, told of spending part of each day with the sick and dying in City Hospital. "The most prevalent and fatal disease in California at that time was chronic diarrhea and dysentery, a consumption of the bowels, very similar in its debilitating effect on the constitution as consumption of the lungs," he wrote in his memoirs in 1896. "Men afflicted with this disease have been seen moping about the streets, looking like the personification of death and despair, for weeks, till strength and money and friends were gone, and then, as a last resort, they were carried to the hospital to pass a few miserable weeks more in one of those filthy wards, where they often died in the night without any one knowing the time of their departure." Each morning, the minister wrote, nurses passed through the wards and reported the dead. Then a plain coffin, a supply of which was kept handy, was brought to the cot of the deceased, and the victim carried outside to the dead cart, the driver of which was seen daily plodding through the mud to the graveyard near North Beach, with from one to three corpses in his tumbril.

One "very genteel-looking man" who died of cholera in the hospital in 1850, seemed to the preacher to be the prototype of the tough, independent, and fearless argonaut who came west for riches and died broke but unbroken.

"My dear brother," Taylor asked the man, "have you made your peace with God?"

"No sir, I can't say that I have."

"Do you not pray to the Lord sometimes to have mercy on you, and for the sake of Jesus to pardon your sins?"

"No, sir."

"Have you ever prayed?"

"No, sir, never in my life."

"You believe in the divine reality of religion and that we may have our sins all forgiven and enjoy the conscious evidence of pardon, do you not?"

"Yes, sir; I believe in religion, and think it a very good thing to have."

Taylor said the man was calm and composed and knew that "He was then poised on an eddying wave of death's dark tide, which on its next swell would whirl him out of the bounds of time into the breakers of eternal seas beyond." The preacher said he saw the man's peril, "and pulled with all my might to bring the lifeboat of mercy by his side. I got very near to him, and entreated him to try to get into it and save his soul, but I could not prevail on him to make an effort. Under the force of the ruling habit of his life he coolly said, 'Well, I'll think about it.'"

DANIEL WOODS, THE Massachusetts teacher-minister who reached the Golden Gate in June 1849, after crossing Mexico from Tampico to San Blas, returned to the bay in September. He had spent three months in the mines, had gained precisely $390 in gold for his labors, and hoped to collect some letters from home. He rode a borrowed mule to Sacramento City, bought a steamer ticket to San Francisco, spent three weeks there waiting for mail from home, and found much that horrified him.

"Stretched away before me is the world of San Francisco," he wrote, "and what a world! How the tide of human life flows and dashes upon its shores! Crowds every day arrive, and other crowds every day leave. Old friends meet, exchange a few words, and hasten on to the shrine of Mammon. Multitudes die, and the waves close over them, and they are forgotten."

He toured gambling dens ("A volume could not describe their splendor or their fatal attraction"), attended religious meetings in tent chapels, and witnessed many tragedies and horrors.

"Yesterday a young man from New England left his tent in 'Happy Valley' [a residential area on Yerba Buena Cove below the Market Street Wharf]," he wrote, "and went to a retired place, untied his cravat and hung it upon the bushes, took a razor from its case, and put the case upon his cravat, and then deliberately cut his own throat. Pecuniary losses, it is supposed, was the cause."

San Francisco was "a moral whirlpool. . . . Civilized, semibarbarous, and savage—American, European, Asiatic, and African. . . . I hazard the assertion that in no other part of the United States can there be found so many persons abjectly poor in proportion to the population."

He mused on opportunities lost while he bent his back in the diggings: "In the spring of 1849, the single article of saleratus [baking soda] sold for $12 a pound; it could be purchased in New York for 4 cents. One hundred dollars invested in this single article, deducting all expenses, would yield at least $25,000." And he had time to calculate the failures of the mining "companies" formed with such youthful enthusiasm and high hope as they sailed and walked toward the gold fields of California. The fourteen companies he investigated, presumably including his own Camargo Company, numbered 344 miners. The total days of labor of the 344 amounted to 35,876 (about three and a half months per man), and the amount of gold "taken out" was $113,633. The average income for each day's labor came to $3.17.

Woods's own average of four dollars a day, less than a quarter of what was considered a "living wage" in the diggings, was thus above average for "company men."

Despite these devastating calculations, Woods returned to the mines, although without significant success, and on November 26, 1850, sailed for home, reaching New York after an absence of two years and eight days, sixteen months of which he had spent in the mines.

His failures had not soured him but he had advice for those planning a gold venture in California: do not overplan and overprepare; have at least $150 in cash by the time you reach the diggings; leave all machinery behind; avoid companies organized at home; leave the work of prospecting to experienced miners and be content at first to work rather than explore; be careful of your health; throw aside your wet garments and put on dry ones; guard against immoral influences: "I think *intemperence* may be named as, next to gambling, the prevailing vice of California," he said, after which he named licentiousness and profanity.

Above all, wrote Daniel Woods after he returned to his classroom and pulpit: "Your motto must be 'Hope on, hope ever!'"

THIRTEEN

THE DIGGINGS

Neither James Marshall nor any other of John Sutter's sawmill employees knew what the thimbleful of bright specks collected from the Coloma millrace represented. Was it what soon became called "a flash in the pan"—a dab of gold in a world of dross—or had the land of Califía, an American Ophir, been uncovered? When Sutter wrote to General Vallejo on February 10, 1848, "I have made a discovery of a gold mine, which, according to experiments we have made, is extraordinarily rich," it was the hopeful boasting of a chronic debtor. He had discovered nothing, and on the date of his letter, seventeen days after Marshall spied the glitter in the race, no more than a dozen sawmill workers were chipping riverside rocks with their jackknives. Vallejo, who knew Sutter well, blessed the Swiss's good fortune while passing off the news as "a piece of pleasantry."

And how rich could the gold mine be without knowing the extent of it? Was it a mine, singular, located on the south fork of the American River, apt to play out quickly, or was Coloma the heart of a vaster field, a belt, an "auriferous zone," as newspapers came to call it, rich beyond imagining?

Such is the allure and power of gold that the configuration of California's gold country took shape in a miraculously brief time. In the early months after the strike, those who were fortunately situated in northern California, or who came north from military stations in San Diego and Monterey, aimed their boots, horses, and mules toward Sutter's Fort, the American River, and Coloma. But, since every neophyte gold hunter was also an instinctive *prospector*, eternally searching for something better, the sawmill area diggings were supplanted by other placers★ within a few weeks of the Marshall discovery. These new strikes were made along the Sacramento and its branches, the American, Feather, and Yuba (each with three forks), the uplands

---

★Placer gold, the kind James Marshall saw and for the first three years thereafter the principal kind "mined" in California, is gold found on or near the earth's surface.

between these rivers, and the western scarps of the Sierra Nevada. While such explorations were proceeding in what became known as the "northern mines," others were drawing miners south of Sutter's Fort, in the San Joaquín River valley and along that river's network of tributaries, these mostly Indian and Spanish-named streams such as the Cosumnes, Mokelumne, Calaveras, Stanislaus (Anglicized from Estanislao, the Spanish name for a Walla Walla Indian chief), Tuolumne, Merced, and Mariposa.

As early as May 1848, ninety days after discovery, the waterways and ravines for thirty miles east and west of Coloma, and some distance north and south, were being worked by an estimated eight hundred miners.

In June, Thomas O. Larkin estimated there were two thousand men in the northern mines, half of them working the streams and feeders of the American River, the others dispersed to the north and east of Coloma.

In the first week of July, when Military Governor Richard B. Mason made his inspection of the diggings, he visited Weber Creek, east of Coloma, and reported that four thousand men were extracting daily as much as fifty thousand dollars in gold from the Sierra foothills.

By the time of Mason's visit, John Bidwell, Sutter's confidante and majordomo, struck a rich gold deposit thirty miles north of Coloma. Now age thirty, Bidwell, who had crossed the plains in 1841 and went to work for Sutter as soon as he reached the fort, was a man of substance even before the strike—he had acquired his own land grant in the Feather River country in 1847 and was developing his "Rancho Chico" there. But Bidwell's Bar, near the junction of the south and middle forks of the Feather, made him rich.

Bidwell's successes were followed by exploration of the Feather's main branch, the Yuba, and the first party of miners to test the gravel on its banks took out $75,000 in dust and nuggets between July and September, 1848.

The northernmost of the 1848 diggings lay in the Trinity River valley, two hundred miles north of New Helvetia, discovered by another Sutter employee and former Bear Flag rebel, Pierson B. Reading. The Trinity stream and bench gravels were so rich the tiny camp grew into a sizable town, Weaverville, named for one of its more prosperous prospectors.

To the south, the discovery year ended with work on the tributaries of the San Joaquín River: the Tuolumne, and soon, the Merced and the Mariposa. These placers, in scrub oak country a few hundred feet above sea level, were most often dry, the rivers and gullies running with snow runoff and rainwater in winter months but parched in the long summers. Elaborate ditching and fluming would be required to divert water to the claims.

The northern mines, at elevations of 5,000 feet and more (6,500 at certain points on the Yuba River), were pierced by swift-flowing waterways with steep-sided ravines, but there were also "dry diggings" in the north and ditching and flume building were common miner labors in most of the gold country.

At the head of navigation on the San Joaquín, and with regular steam and sail traffic to San Francisco, Stockton became the supply base for the southern diggings.

Sacramento City, which rose up from the Sutter's Fort embarcadero, served as the main depot for the northern mines.

Thus did the general outline of California's gold country take shape: the central part of it a 200-mile-long oval, from the north fork of the Feather River down to the Mariposa, by fifty or sixty miles wide, with scattered camps and diggings, some of them quite productive, as far north as the Klamath Mountains on the Oregon border, as far south as the Mojave Desert, as far west as the Pacific shore, and east into the Sierra Nevada range. And, embedded in the main gold oval, from Mariposa in the south to a point a few miles above Placerville, lay the richest deposit, a 120-mile-long system of linked gold-quartz veins and schists called "the Mother Lode."

CAMPS MUSHROOMED, THE typical one starting with a scattering of streamside tents. Then, depending on how productive the "prospect," a tarp-roofed trade store sprung up with some outrageously priced foodstuffs, picks, pans, twists of tobacco, and packets of Seidlitz Powders, and gold scales made of sardine cans with silver Mexican *reales* as counterweights. Soon a tent saloon materialized, with boards across barrelheads serving as the bar to belly up to and a table outside for the monte game. If the claims "panned out," produced enough gold, the tents would become shanties, the variety of goods in the trade store expanded, the saloon and gambling games prospered, and the location became semipermanent, maybe growing to townhood. When the claims dwindled in productivity the place would be unceremoniously abandoned, its denizens scattered to other streams and hills to locate a better prospect, make a new camp, and start over again.

Among the significant towns that flourished in the first year of the gold rush, Sacramento and Stockton, the supply stations for the northern and southern mines, were destined to endure. The most prominent settlement north of Sacramento was Marysville, at the junction of the Feather and Yuba rivers, a few miles above Sutter's Hock Farm retreat. The town site was founded in 1844 as a rancho on land illegally leased by Sutter to Theodor Cordua, a native of the duchy of Mecklenburg, Germany. Marysville (the name derived from Mary Murphy Covillaud, a survivor of the Donner Party) became the home port for steamboat traffic on the Feather River, with a sloop making regular trips down to Sutter's Fort and on to San Francisco.

Placerville, between the south fork of the American River and Weber Creek, started out in mid–1848 with the unlovely name Dry Diggings when a party of Sutter's workers found some gold-bearing dirt there in the summer drought. Like the other dry mines to the south, Placerville's fortunes fluctuated with the seasons, between the winter's flow of water and prosperity and the summer's drying up and doldrums. But the camp had another distinction, that of holding the first "miner's meeting," a kangaroo court in the outback of California, and this circumstance created an enduring nickname.

In Dry Diggings in January 1849, a gambler named López was accosted by five men in the deep of night, held at gunpoint and robbed. López managed to wake the camp, the "skulkers" were captured with the booty and trussed up to await daylight. A judge and a twelve-miner jury found the men guilty and sentenced them to thirty-nine lashes with a stout rope. (The "forty lashes save one" punishment was a common one for thieves in the diggings.)

After the sentence was carried out, three of the culprits, two Frenchmen and a Chilean, were recognized as escapees from a murder and attempted robbery on the Stanislaus River a few months earlier and were retried on these charges. The three presented no defense, understandable since they were only semiconscious from the flogging and were unable to stand up, speak, or comprehend English. The judge, after hearing the evidence, surveyed the two hundred miners gathered for the open-air judicial proceeding and asked for their verdict. "Hang them!" was the shouted answer.

The hapless trio were strung up from a convenient oak and "Hangtown" was born. The name, never officially bestowed, was not to be denied even when the state legislature granted the town the name Placerville in 1850. "Hangtown Gals," a ditty by some wandering troubador of the placers, gave the name a dance hall familiarity:

Hangtown gals are plump and rosy,
Hair in ringlets, mighty cozy;
Painted cheeks and jossy bonnets,
Touch 'em and they'll sting like hornets!
(Chorus)
Hangtown gals are lovely creatures
Think they'll marry Mormon preachers;
Heads thrown back to show their features,
Ha, ha, ha! Hangtown gals!

Between June and August, 1848, miners at Dry Diggings dug, per man, three ounces to five pounds of gold daily. Bancroft said the "three hundred Hangtown men were the happiest in the universe."

ANOTHER TOWN OF consequence in the northern mines was Downieville, on the north fork of the Yuba River in the Sierra foothills fifty miles east of Bidwell's Bar. The place was settled through the efforts of the Scotsman William Downie, who caught the gold fever while living in Buffalo, New York, signed on as a seaman on a Cape Horner out of New Orleans, and reached San Francisco in June 1849. In Sacramento City he gathered together a party of eleven men—seven of them blacks (of whom several were believed to be fugitive slaves), one an Indian, and one a Sandwich Islander playfully called "Jim Crow"—and moved north to the Yuba.

The story of the Downie party's success, part gold camp myth and part truth, began with Jim Crow's catching a fourteen-pound salmon and boiling it in a cookpot. In dumping out the water, he found some gold specks in the pot bottom, told his partners, and all fanned out along the fork and began washing sand and chipping at rock crevasses. They retrieved seventeen ounces of gold the first day after the salmon pot discovery, twenty-four the next, and forty on the third day including a single pan of washed dirt that yielded $225 in dust and flakes.

The party settled down on the claim for the winter, with some of the men departing for Sacramento to buy provisions while Downie and the others built a log cabin and continued to work the river. Downie himself took out a pound or more of gold each day, often as much as twenty or thirty ounces, and became a rich man before the break in the cold weather.

Word of the Scot's success, no doubt assisted by the chest thumping of his workmen dispatched to buy goods in Sacramento, spread quickly and by the spring of 1850, Downieville lay sprawled along both banks of the Yuba fork with 3,000 miners hunkered in the water and on the rocks.

The Yuba claims were some of the richest of the gold country. At Durgan's Flat near Downieville, four men extracted $12,900 in gold in eleven days, $80,000 in six months, from a claim sixty feet square; Tin Cup Diggings, in the same vicinity, was so named after the three men working the claim made a rule not to quit the day's work before filling a tin cup with gold dust and nuggets; and in 1850, upstream from Downie's diggings, somebody found a nugget weighing twenty-five pounds.

Colorfully named camps magically appeared and disappeared on the Feather River and its main branches, the Yuba and Bear: Helltown, Kanaka Flat, Dutch Flat, Poker Flat (whose outcasts were immortalized in Bret Harte's 1869 story), Whiskey Flat, Goodyear's Bar, Cut-Eye Foster's Bar, and Spanish Bar, a deposit twelve miles northeast of Coloma that eventually yielded more than a million dollars.

WHILE SOME GOLD hunters were penetrating farther north than Downieville, toward the valley of the Trinity River and even the foothills of the Klamath Range, rich placers were uncovered on the Cosumnes River in 1848 by José de Jesús Pico, a Californio from San Luís Obispo. He hired ten laborers, led them to San José, across Livermore Pass to Stockton, and on northeast to the Cosumnes. After four months' work, Pico was able to pay off his workers and net a tidy fortune of $14,000.

Good prospects were also found on the Mokelumne and Calaveras and in the sandy hills and shrublands between these San Joaquín tributaries.

The three-forked Stanislaus gave rise to diggings at Murphy's Camp where John Murphy, age twenty-three, found a good prospect trading cheap goods for gold among the local Indians; at Sullivan's Bar, named for Irish ox teamster John Sullivan, who took out $26,000 in gold from his Stanislaus claim and subsequently opened a bank; and at Jamestown where a San Francisco lawyer, George F. James, dabbled in selling land, then, after disputes with Mexican miners in the area, left the town he named for himself for less contentious places.

Rhode Islander Henry P. Angel opened a trading post on the Stanislaus in 1848 and Angel's Camp became the locale of one of the gold rush's finest tales, some of it probably true. The story is of a onetime storekeeper with a name hard to invent, Bennager Raspberry, who went out hunting in the Stanislaus hills. While arming his muzzle loader he got the ramrod wedged in the barrel, aimed at a squirrel and pulled the trigger. The ramrod landed in the roots of a manzanita bush and when he pulled it out found a small piece of gold-bearing quartz clinging to it. Using the ramrod to dig, he took out $700 in gold, came back the next day with better tools and dug out $2,000 worth and on the third day, $7,000 in manzanita root nuggets. What became of Raspberry is not recorded, but presumably he took his three-days' income and retired.

The richest of the southern mines were those at the Sierra headwaters of the Tuolumne River, where the camp, later town, of Sonora reached a population of 5,000 before the close of 1849.

Between October 1848, and March of the following year, an estimated 4,000 men came up from the Mexican border state of Sonora to California's San Joaquín Valley. They "shared the distemper" of the gold rush, Bancroft said, but unlike most of the other sharers, were experienced miners and quarriers, their homeland historically rich in gold, silver, copper, tin, and lead.* When the Mexican miners found gold on the Sierra slopes between the Tuolumne and Stanislaus Rivers and called their camp Sonora, word of it reached Monterey

---

*The name Sonora is from the Spanish word meaning "sonorous" or "resounding," said to derive from the noise made in mining the state's rich ore and marble deposits.

and points north and south in a hurry. Gold seemed to have an intrinsic telegraph system: No new discovery could be kept secret, and news of each new strike raced to all corners of the country with astonishing and quite mysterious speed.

The experiences of Antonio Franco Coronel, a school teacher in Los Angeles, illustrate the early successes at Sonora. In August 1848, he gathered a party of thirty men and at least one woman, apparently with no specific destination in mind, traveled up to San José and crossed the southern Coast Range to the San Joaquín River. At some point on the journey toward the Sierra foothills, Coronel met a priest, Padre José María Suárez del Real, who was returning home with a quantity of gold he said he mined at the "Stanislaus camp"—the newly discovered diggings at Sonora. Coronel and his laborers crossed the San Joaquín and followed either the Tuolumne or Stanislaus to the Sonora camp where they found a number of other Californios, some miners from New Mexico, and a few Americans, working the placers along with the Sonoran discoverers.

The Los Angeles men seem to have had goods to trade with the local Indians and questioned them about the location of the gold they were bringing in. One of Coronel's men, Benito Pérez, an experienced miner, took one of the natives, called Augustin, to find the Indian placer and the two passed the night near the rancho where Chief Estanislao once lived. Early the next day, they were joined by six other of Augustin's band and made their way east to a place called Cañada del Barro where they began to dig with sharpened stakes, Pérez with his hunting knife. In a short time they dug out three ounces of *chispas* (sparks)—small nuggets.

Pérez told Coronel the mine was rich and in a short time the Angelino leader, working, he said, "with two dumb Indians," hacked and shoveled out forty-five ounces of coarse gold from Cañada del Barro. A few yards away, one Dolores Sepúlveda picked up a nugget weighing twelve ounces, and a Santa Bárbaran named Valdéz, dug three feet down, discovered a pocket, and picked out enough gold to fill a large towel. He sold his claim to another man who in eight days took out fifty-two *pounds* of raw gold.

Meantime, Coronel left his servants at his claim and inspected another nearby bar with a Sonoran miner named "Chino" Tirador. Each marked out a claim. At four feet, Tirador found a pocket and for eight hours dug gold out of it with a horn spoon, throwing the *chis-*

pas into a wooden tray that became so heavy he had to drag it along the ground.

Coronel had less luck with his claim. With a laborer's help, he took out a mere six ounces that day but Tirador, who may have been experienced as a miner but had a serious ignorance of the worth of gold, sold his nuggets and dust for the more spendable Mexican silver. Coronel bought seventy-six ounces from the Sonoran at the rate of $2.50 an ounce and wrote that by the time Tirador returned to his unmarked claim the next morning, others were working it. The Sonoran abandoned his mine, purchased a bottle of whiskey "for a double-handful of gold," spread a blanket on the ground, and opened a monte bank. By ten that night he was both drunk and penniless.

Coronel later became mayor of Los Angeles.

Sonora grew quickly to a wild and dangerous place. Those who saw it in its raucous heyday said it had bigger lumps of gold, more drunks, gamblers, and "Cyprians" (prostitutes: from Cyprus, Aphrodite's birthplace), than any settlement in the diggings, north or south, and the most cosmopolitan population.

The valley of Woods Creek, a branch of the Tuolumne below Sonora, became a spectacular example of the area's international flavor. The valley was a gorgeous place with wild oat meadows rolling off to the horizon and a meandering creek shaded by live oaks running through the fields. Mexican miners and their families lived there in tents and brush shelters decorated with silk flags and trappings, and rode shaggy California ponies on gold- and silver-edged saddles. In the central camp could be heard the songs, horns, and thumping guitars of amateur musicians and the shouts—"*Agua fresca! Agua fresca! Cuatro reales*"—of the women at their tables arrayed with *dulces*, dried fruits, cakes, hot meat and chile *gorditas* and *burritos*, and drinks cooled with Sierra snows. Scurrying along the creekbed were Chileans, Argentinos, and Peruvians in ponchos and flat-brimmed *gaucho* sombreros, "John Chinaman" in his quilted jacket, blue cotton breeches, and beehive hat. There were lascars there, sailors from East Indian trade ships, wearing bright Madras kerchiefs around their heads, piratelike, each with a menacing *kris* stuck in his belt; and Kanakas, Californios, Yankees, Englishmen, Irishmen, Frenchmen, Germans, and several bands of California Indians.

Frank Marryat, an English sportsman, artist, and adventurer, who came to San Francisco after publishing a popular travelogue on his

experiences in Borneo, visited Sonora in 1851, at the camp's boisterous apogee. He said, "The habits of the people here are noctur-
nal. . . . Greenwich Fair might be spoken of as a sober picture of
domestic life compared to the din and clamor that resounded through
the main street." He explored "gambling houses of large dimensions,
but very fragile in structure, built of a fashion to invite conflagration,"
and found in "booths and barns" candle chandeliers "throwing a glittering light on the heaps of gold that lay piled on each monte table,
while the drinking bars held forth inducements that nothing mortal is
supposed to be able to resist."

In his tour of the mines Marryat also provided a spirited description—"a scene of mining life as perfect in its details as it was novel in
its features"—of a camp on the middle fork of the American River
ominously named Murderer's Bar.

"Immediately beneath us the swift river glided tranquilly, though
foaming still from the great battle which a few yards higher up, it had
fought with a mass of black obstructing rocks," he wrote. "On the
banks was a village of canvas that the winter rains had bleached to
perfection, and round it the miners were at work at every point."
Many of the men were waist-deep in water, toiling together to construct a race and dam to turn the river's course, he wrote; others were
entrenched in holes, like grave diggers, working down to the
"bedrock." Some were on the brink of the stream washing out
"prospects" from tin pans and wooden *batteaus*; and others worked
with the Long Toms, the water for them conveyed by sluices from the
river. Many were digging coyote holes, "from which from time to
time their heads popped out, like those of squirrels to take a look at
the world," and a few worked with hand augers, dissatisfied with
nature's work, and preparing to remove large rocks with gunpowder
placed in the bored holes. "All was life, merriment, vigor and determination, as this part of the earth was being turned inside out to see
what it was made of," he said.

It was Marryat, in his book *Mountains and Molehills* (published in
1855, a few months before the author died of a stroke at age twenty-
nine) who told one of the abiding tales of the gold rush.

This was an incident occurring in the southern mines, somewhere near the banks of Carson Creek, a branch of the Stanislaus
River, in which a miner died and his comrades decided to give him
a dignified funeral. An argonaut who had been a clergyman in his

past life was located to officiate and after the dead man's friends had several "drinks all around," the entourage proceeded in a well-oiled assemblage to the gravesite. There the body was lowered and the preacher began an extemporary prayer-elegy which ran somewhat overlong.

As the divine declaimed, Marrayat reported, some of the men absentmindedly began fingering the loose dirt thrown out of the grave hole. "It proved to be thick with gold, and an excitement was immediately apparent to the kneeling crowd. Upon this the preacher stopped and inquiringly asked, 'Boys, what's that?', took a view of the ground for himself and, as he did so, shouted 'Gold! Gold!—and the richest kind of diggings! The congregation is dismissed!' "

The dead miner, the Englishman said, "was taken from his auriferous grave to be buried elsewhere, while the funeral party, with the minister at their head, lost no time in prospecting and staking out new diggings!"

FOR TEN GENERATIONS and more, Californians, native-born and emigrant, enjoyed their sun-washed province unhindered by serious governance or law. In those halcyon times, the legal *pronunciamentos* of Spanish and Mexican *jefes políticos* sent out to the province were ignored by the tiny, scattered populace. Lawlessness worked in a time when wealth was measured in land, cattle, and horses, when Californians exchanged their cowhides and tallow for the goods brought to their shores by the trade ships of the world. In a time when there was little actual money in use there were few actual laws in force, and few lawbreakers.

Gold changed all that. Into the country came what Bancroft called the "less desirable elements," among which he listed: "the ungainly, illiterate crowds from the border states, such as Indiana Hoosiers and Missourians, or 'Pike County' people, and the pretentious, fire-eating chivalry from the south." Of the southerners, these, "While less obnoxious at first . . . proved more persistently objectionable, for the angularities of the others soon wore off in the contact with their varied neighbors, partly with the educated youths of New England."

The influx included, he said, "fugitives from trouble and dishonor" lured to California for its remoteness and its gold, "graceless scions of respectable families, never-do-wells, men of wavering virtue and frail piety," and drunken, nomadic brawlers and sharpers who doted on bullying Indians.

Real crime, the historian claimed, took root in the winter of 1849–50, a time when starvation and sickness struck the camps— cholera, fevers, bowel complaints, rheumatism, scurvy, and pulmonary disease—ailments deriving from exhausting labor, from standing in cold water, or on wet ground under a withering sun; from the poor shelter of flimsy tents and beds on damp soil; from poor food, poor or nonexistent personal hygiene, and living amid sewage.

With an evil element arriving, and crime blossoming, suddenly, laws were needed, even if made up on the spot, as indeed was most often the case throughout the diggings and throughout the gold rush.

IN THE EARLY months after its discovery, no one seemed to know what gold was worth and the first rules of the camps centered on establishing the value of what was being panned, sifted, dug, shoveled, and carved from the earth.

Many early miners brought their pokes and bottles of gold dust to traders in San Francisco or to a brushwood post in the tules and sold it for as little as four dollars an ounce, rarely more than twice that. Coinage was so rare that an ounce of gold was often exchanged for a single Mexican silver dollar.

Until he learned about the white man's limitless capacity for cupidity, the Indian miner was routinely swindled when he came to trade, his gold balanced with lead slugs and paid for by the "Digger ounce," the reference not to gold "digger" but the white epithet for all of California's native people. Forty-niner Daniel Knower recalled a time when he bought supplies from a Coloma storekeeper, handing over his bag of dust to pay the bill. He found he had been over-charged three or four dollars and informed the clerk of the discrepancy. The man weighed the gold again and apologized: He had weighed it on scales used in trade with Indians. "It needs no comment to know that the Christian man is not always superior to the Indian in integrity," Knower opined.

Nor were Indians the only swindled miners. Sergeant James Carson wrote of a merchant called "Dutch John" whose brushwood store in the diggings displayed crackers, sardines, a few knives, some tobacco, "and two barrels of the youngest whiskey I have ever tasted."

The counter, Carson said, was a barrel on which sat a broken tumbler, a tin cup, and a "junk bottle of the ardent." Dutch John had no scales: "A drink was paid for by his taking a pinch of gold dust with his thumb and forefinger from the miner's bag, or, sorting out a lump the size or value of a dollar." This was an advantageous maneuver for the storekeeper, Carson said, since, "Before taking the pinch from the bag, John's finger and thumb could be seen sliding down his throat for the purpose of covering them with saliva, to make the gold stick. . . . The amount of such a pinch was four to eight dollars!"

In 1849, the Philadelphia Mint paid about $17.50 for a troy ounce of gold, depending on its purity, the fineness of the bullion expressed in thousandths. With unalloyed, twenty-four-carat gold, reckoned at 1,000 thousandths, California gold ranged from 825 to 950 thousandths, most of it between 870 and 900, with silver constituting most of the alloy.

Eventually, the exchange rate in the mines settled at $16 per common ounce. When a day at the diggings produced an ounce, it was worth ten times the average daily wage of a worker "in the states."

The claim, the place where gold had been found or where the search for gold was going on, was contentious ground and required rules and legalities: title and registration by an official "recorder," and some mechanism for settling disputes. In the beginning the rules governing claims were arbitrary and varied from camp to camp. The size of a claim might depend on the richness of the diggings in which it was located. Some claims in productive mines were limited to ten feet square (one such, at Jackass Hill, a few miles west of Sonora, yielded $10,000 in surface dirt in a few weeks), others were measured at fifty feet along a streambed, a hundred feet in poorer districts. Generally, a claim extended fifty to a hundred feet along the "thread" or center of a river or stream channel and behind the bank far enough for the miner to work. The landward corners of the claim were marked by stakes decorated with rags or tin cans.

In the early days of the rush, a claim could be marked by leaving a few tools on it and continued possession required a minimal amount of work on it; a day a month the common rule. Registration cost a dollar with the recorder, often appointed by the miners themselves, inspecting the site and alloting it a number, painted on a stick or tin pie plate.

Claim matters eventually became complicated. In the opening two years of the gold rush, miners were restricted to a single claim at a time, with no proxy ownership permitted. The sale or transfer of a claim, like any real estate transaction, required deeding. Disputes over ownership were settled by the recorder, the nearest *alcalde*, or by a camp committee.

California mining camps were dangerous places for the naive, weak, or careless, and painful, sometimes fatal, for the breaker of camp-made laws. Petty thievery called for floggings, shaving head and eyebrows, even cropping of ears for repeat offenders. Murder, and theft of anything worth over $100, could result in execution by hanging.

The most notorious capital sentence in the mines, more hotly debated than the triple execution at Hangtown in January 1849, took place in July 1851 at Downieville, on the Yuba River, with the condemned a representative of the most highly regarded segment of the populace—a woman.

Variously called Juanita and Joséfa, she was said to be Mexican, Chilean, or perhaps Peruvian, called a "dance-hall girl" by some, a harsher name by others. Distilled from the many versions of her crime, it appears that on the night of July 4, 1851, a Scottish gambler named Cannon and a companion named Lawson were walking home after an Independence Day celebration and passed the adobe shack where Juanita lived with a man called José, a card dealer at a dive called Craycroft's Saloon. Some said Cannon and Juanita were "involved," others claimed Cannon and his partner were drunk, but whatever the case, they smashed in the door of her cabin and left, reeling down the road. The next morning, so it was told, Cannon and his friend returned to apologize and pay damages—an unlikely scenario—but before the Scot could say a word, Juanita plunged a knife into his heart. (Another version has it they were passing the house and José emerged and accosted them, demanding payment for the damages, and as Cannon was about to strike José, Juanita rushed between them. Cannon then called her a *puta*, whereupon she knifed him in his chest.)

At the miner trial that followed, a crowd of 2,000 (two-thirds of the population of Downieville) gathered, and viewed Cannon's corpse, on display with his red flannel shirt pulled open to show the fatal wound. Juanita was sentenced to death, even though many recoiled at the idea of executing a woman, especially in so confusing a case. Moreover, a physician, Cyrus D. Aiken, testified that the girl was "with child," a diagnosis that caused some hangers-on to suggest that the doctor be hanged with Juanita.

Finally, three other Downieville doctors examined her and declared she was not *enceinte*, and the verdict was handed down "That she suffer death in two hours."

A scaffold was knocked together on the Yuba bank near the bridge across the forks and Juanita was taken to it at four in the afternoon. She climbed the steps unassisted and coolly supervised her skirts being tied down. Some reported that her hands were not tied and that she held up her braids so that the noose could be placed around her neck.

Her last words were *"Adíos, señores."*

José the gambler was found not guilty and ordered to leave town in twenty-four hours.

The *Sonora Union Democrat* editor wrote that the execution was "the greatest possible crime against humanity, Christianity and civilization."

DANIEL WOODS OF Massachusetts, who reached California in June 1849, wrote of an attempt to codify gold camp laws and reduce the number of hasty Juanita-like verdicts. This experiment occurred in January 1850, at Jacksonville, a camp on the Tuolumne River in the southern mines named for Alden M. Jackson, a New England lawyer who was well-liked for settling claim disputes and drawing up legal papers. The governing articles Jackson composed called for election of an *alcalde* and sheriff, criminal trials by a jury of eight "American citizens," and laws to conform "as near as possible to those of the United States." The document restricted claims to twelve feet in width, "running back to the hill or mountain and forward to the centre of the river or creek or across a gulch or ravine," and stated that "parties hold claims by leaving a pick, shovel, or bar—but should the tool or tools aforesaid be stolen or removed, it shall not dispossess those who located it, provided he or they can prove that they were left as required." Another provision held that "no man [will be] permitted to hold two claims at the same time; no party permitted to throw dirt, stones, or other obstructions on located ground adjoining."

For theft of articles valued less than $100, the new laws decreed that the guilty party's head and eyebrows would be "close shaved," and the thief banished from the camp within twenty-four hours. Hanging was prescribed for "theft of a mule or other draught animal," or of gold dust, or money in other forms, or provisions or goods valued at over $100. Hanging was also the penalty for any perpetrator or "abettor therein" to the crime of murder.

A significant rule that exemplified the virulent xenophobia among the American miners stated that "No person coming direct from a foreign country shall be permitted to locate or work any lot [claim] within the jurisdiction of the encampment."

Juanita of Downieville would not have benefited from the ink spilled by attorney Jackson; indeed, no "foreigner" would have escaped the noose for killing a white man, no matter the malefactor's gender or circumstances.

"Murders, thefts, and heavy robberies soon became the order of the day," James Carson said of the mining districts in 1849 and thereafter. "A panic seized that portion of the diggers who had never been out of sight of marm's chimbly, and who went cringing about in fear." The veteran soldier wrote that although most of the miners carried personal firearms, they preferred settling their disputes in a miner's meeting, and "whipping bare backs, cutting off ears, and hanging."

"We were not blessed at that day with statutes as unintelligible as a Chinese bible, or with hordes of lawyers who for a pittance would screen, under the informalities of indictments or proceedings, villains from just punishment," he said. "I am not an advocate of unlawful trials by the people but those who know the purifying influence of Judge Lynch in 1849, and of the vigilance committee in 1851, will join me in saying that their institution and their firm devotion to the cause of right, alone saved California from becoming the theatre of strife and bloodshed unknown before in the history of the world."

Addressing himself to those who had yearnings to come out to the diggings, he asked, "Do you want to live independent and happy, in one of the best climates in the world? If you do, come to California, and *make it your home*," but added, "those who are coming to this country for the purpose of making fortunes by swindling, robbery, or theft, my parting advice to them is to *bring their coffins along*."

*   *   *

SCOTSMAN HUGH REID, who ranched in California years before
the rule of gold took over the country, made a tour of the diggings
late in 1848 and attested to their risks. Upon returning to Monterey
he wrote a letter to a friend, cautioning him, "Don't go to the mines
on any account. . . . [They are] loaded to the muzzle with vagabonds
from every quarter of the globe, scoundrels from nowhere, rascals
from Oregon, pickpockets from New York, accomplished gentlemen
from Europe, interlopers from Lima and Chile, Mexican thieves,
gamblers of no particular spot, and assassins manufactured in Hell for
the express purpose of converting highways and byways into theaters
of blood; then last, but not least, Judge Lynch with his thousand arms,
thousand sightless eyes, and five hundred lying tongues, ready under
the banner of justice to hang, half, and quarter any individual who
may meet his disapprobation."

⋹ Roaring Camps ⋺

IN THE COURSE of the gold rush, 1848 through the early 1850s,
over 500 camps and settlements sprang up in the California mining country. In a 1970 bulletin, the California Division of Mines
and Geology listed 337 camps that survived long enough to produce a significant amount of gold. At least 200 others vanished
completely, their precise locations in dispute to this day. Most
were abandoned after what gold they offered played out, their residents packing their tents, picks, and shovels and moving on to
other flashes-in-the-pan. Many of the tent-and-lantern settlements were "piped away"—eradicated by hydraulic monitors; a
handful progressed into cities and towns, and some survived as
permanent, if sleepy, hamlets.

At the summit of its glittering, chaotic life, the gold country
consisted of villes, towns, burgs, cuts, gulches, hills, camps, flats,
runs, diggings, hollows, canyons, and slides—a cornucopia of
names which H.H. Bancroft said were "as a rule both appropriate
and expressive, although tinged too much by the looseness and

harebrained recklessness of the flush times, with their characteristic abjuration of elegance."

Among the most offensive of the camp names were Greaser Flats and Nigger's Bar; patently inelegant were Gouge Eye, Plugtown, and Chicken Thief Flat.

Drunkard's Bar, the more specific Whiskey Hill and Brandy Bar, and the all-encompassing Delerium Tremens, celebrated one of the two chief vices of the camps. (A tip of the hat to teetotalers were Temperence Flat and Milkpunch, although the names were likely used ironically.) Honoring the other great miners' vice were Poker Flat, Euchre Flat, and Keno Flat.

Animal names were common favorites: Coon Hollow, Skunk Gulch, Mad Mule, Jackass Flat, Dead Mule Canyon, Hog-Eye, Red Dog, Dogtown, Otter, Quail, Grizzly, Wildcat, Stag, Badger Hill, and the marvelous Ground Hog Glory. Some camps were named for the vermin and insects infesting them: Rattrap Slide, Lousy Level, Centipede Hollow, Mosquito Valley, Fleatown.

There were four Missouri Bars plus an Alabama, Massachusetts, and Michigan Bar, Iowa and Wisconsin Hills, Georgia Slide, Nevada City, Illinoistown, a Washington, Boston, and Bangor, and such international places as Frenchman, Dutch, Chinese, and Kanaka Flats, Canada Hill, Irish Hill, and Malay Camp.

Many names reflected the miners' frustration and failure: Mud, Humbug, and Graveyard Canyons; Bogus Thunder, Quack Hill, Helltown, Hell's Delight, Condemned Bar, Murderer's Bar, Poverty Bar (there were four of these), Cut Throat, Loafer Hill, Liar's Flat, Poverty Flat, Chucklehead Diggings, Dead Man's Gulch, Poor Man's Creek, Squabbletown, and Growlersburg. Far fewer names were optimistic: Rich Bar, Rich Gulch, You Bet, Confidence, Diamond Springs, Fine Gold, Fair Play, Mount Bullion, and Pleasant Valley.

Bret Harte and other writers celebrated such settlements as Angel and Chinese Camp, Poker Flat, Sierra Flat, Roaring Camp, Hangtown, Jenny Lind, Sandy Bar, and Red Dog.

Some of the camp names defied translation; a good many told of the miners' keen sense of mordant humor: Henpeck Flat, Pancake Ravine, Slapjack Bar, Rawhide, Sardine, Greenhorn, Yankee Jim's, Rough and Ready, Git-Up-and-Git, Nutcake Camp, Blue Tent, Shirttail, Sweet Revenge, Coffee Gulch, Backbone, Volcano, Bully Choop, Jim Crow, Blizzardville, Boomo Flat, Shingle Springs, Skidoo, Pinchemtight, and, perhaps best and most inexplicable, Randy Doodler.

FOURTEEN

PAYDIRT

JAMES CARSON WROTE of the "divining art" of prospecting by telling the story of an old man who owned a rich claim in a ravine in the Hangtown district. Carson and some friends gathered at a brush-wood shanty, where by the light of a bullock tallow candle the grizzled miner began "making suspicious-looking circles, and odd-looking marks on the ground." Periodically the prospector would deal himself a hand from a greasy, dog-eared pack of cards, following which he sauntered out into the open air to gaze long into the inky vault above, "as if consulting some lucky planet for further information."

At dawn, armed with a knife and pick, the old man headed for the hills with a long line of eager diggers following him. After a half-mile hike, they came to a sudden halt when the man cast down his pack, looked at the sun, and took his bearings. Then, "with comic gestures and pantomimic manners," he stepped cautiously, as if creeping up on some wild game, stooped "to listen to sounds from the earth, then smilingly looked back at his followers, finger to his lips to enjoin silence."

Carson said his "slight belief in necromancy was fast cooling off" when the old miner reached a ravine, picked out a spot and drove his pick into the ground. "This was a signal for a general onset, and in a few moments over twenty picks were making the stones and iron earth fly in every direction, the closer to the wizard the better."

But with the sun sinking and no gold uncovered, the miners began deserting the "wizard" to return to camp. The prospector explained to those who remained that he had missed the gold pocket by some baffling miscalculation, but that he was close and would soon make the strike.

"Curses deep and long were heaped on him and his science," Carson said, but this was followed by "a general good laugh all round, and drinks at the old diggings, and the circumstance was soon forgotten."

Another failed venture the sergeant described involved a device he saw demonstrated at Murphy's Camp on the Stanislaus. It resembled a plumb-bob, was called a "goldometer," and of the owner Carson said, "no monarch was ever looked up to or hailed with the same feelings of delight as that motley group hailed our hero, as he stepped forth."

The goldometrist (it is not clear if he was selling the apparatus or had brought it to the diggings for his own use) strode majestically off toward a flat space in the camp with such an air of confidence, Carson said, "Had anyone dared to have pronounced the device a humbug at this moment, he would have been cried down as a heretic, a disbeliever, a defamer of science and revelation."

"Our philosopher," as Carson called the man, came to a halt on the flat, and "adjusted his machine with mouth and nostrils extended, and eyes fixed on the magic ball." The witnesses "tremblingly awaited its slightest move. When the ball commenced swaying to and fro, and then bobbing up and down, a hundred pick-axes struck the earth at once, and a hundred voices shouted, 'This is my claim.'"

A hundred holes were sunk, Carson said, but none panned out. The philosopher told the men that the gold was not on the ledge but *under* it and "blasting tools appeared and as much as twenty or thirty feet of solid rock was dug through before their belief in the goldometer grew faint, and they became back-sliders from the true faith."

There followed "disrespectful diviners" using as goldometers twigs with potatoes, bars of soap, and cans of oysters suspended from them, "and many unscientific things which so disgusted the inventor that he soon left those inhospitable regions."

Although Carson loved the humor of such situations, in fact, California's miners were susceptible to any scheme, would follow anyone perceived to have the "golden touch" in locating new diggings, would believe in any contraption, no matter how preposterous, said to detect gold, and would abandon their claims to chase any rumor promising easy pickings.

Of all the gold country will-o'-the-wisps, the most memorable was promulgated by a man named Thomas Robertson Stoddard (or Stoddart), described as "a gentleman of respectability," who told of a fabulous lake he discovered high in the Sierra near the headwaters of the Feather River. He said he was prospecting with a partner in the mountains in the late summer of 1849 when they were attacked by Indians and he sustained an arrow wound in the heel. He never saw his partner again but many days later managed to drag himself, half-starved, into a mining camp on the upper Feather. As he recovered from his wound and privations he told his saviors that before the Indian attack he had stumbled upon a lake whose shores were strewn with lumps of gold. He promised the miners who had nursed him back to health that he would lead them to the lake as soon as the winter snows permitted travel.

Naturally, the "news" could not be contained, and by the spring of 1850 the Gold Lake tale had become so often repeated that newspapers were embroidering on it. (A Sacramento paper reported that Indians in the Gold Lake area routinely used golden fishhooks and arrowheads.) Dr. Israel Lord, working the Yuba River diggings in June that year, wrote: "The country seems all alive about the Gold Lake humbug, though no one seems to know anything in particular."

Other stories surfaced concerning Stoddard himself. He seems to have claimed to be, or a newspaper writer made him out to be, a former Royal Navy officer who had been wounded in the 1840 bombardment of Acre, Syria, while serving on the warship *Asia*; and a journalist and school teacher who crossed the plains to California in '49 and reached the Yuba River camps where his subsequent adventures began.

That summer of 1850, Stoddard set out with twenty-five men and several hundred uninvited hangers-on from Marysville, and led the entourage northeast to Downieville on the north fork of the Yuba. He seemed certain of his directions and destination but when he reached the western scarps of the Sierra became confused and finally admitted he was lost. The more charitable of his followers said a winter landslide had erased the trail and perhaps had inundated the lake; others said Stoddard was a liar, a fraud, or a madman—maybe all three.

He appears to have returned to Marysville in the late summer but soon thereafter vanished from gold country annals.

Those who had followed Stoddard fanned out in search of a decent claim and some found paydirt at Nelson Creek, a tributary of the middle fork of the Feather, and three German miners did even better on the north fork. These prospectors discovered cracks in the rocky riverbed packed with fine gold and were said to have extracted $36,000 in four days of work with pick, shovel, pan, and rocker. The Germans tried to keep their diggings a secret but reports escaped, as word of such discoveries invariably did, and were whispered along the argonaut telegraph until the claim was densely populated. The Feather River camp, 120 miles northeast of Sutter's Fort, became known as Rich Bar and turned out to be an outcrop at the timbered base of a hill so abundant in gold that claims were limited to plots ten feet square.

A distinguished citizen of Rich Bar sonorously named Louise Amelia Knapp Smith Clapp, described the place in 1851 as "a tiny valley, about eight hundred yards in length and thirty in width . . . hemmed in by lofty hills, almost perpendicular, draperied to their very summits with beautiful fir trees; the blue-bosomed 'Plumas' or Feather River . . . undulating along their base."

In a memorable series of letters home, later published under her pen name "Dame Shirley," Mrs. Clapp said the town sprang up "as if a fairy's wand had been waved above the bar" and that it consisted of about forty "tenements," round and square tents, plank hovels, and log cabins, with a common "local habitation" formed of pine boughs covered with old calico shirts.

The strike at Rich Bar was genuine, gained by good prospecting and educated guesswork, its gold wrested from the outcrop by muscle and sweat. Gold Lake, like all tales of easy riches, was as mythic as the Seven Cities.

FEW OF THE rumors and none of the goldometers or prospector-wizards ever turned up gold, but the blind-pig-and-the-acorn variety of luck occasionally did. The real instances of fluke riches were exceedingly rare but were so endlessly elaborated upon in the retelling that what few facts served them often vanished. Frank Marryat's yarn of the diggers on Carson's Creek panning gold from the

dirt thrown out of the preacher's grave may have been the invention
of a gifted storyteller—he titled his book *Mountains and Molehills* and
appears to have made the former from the latter on several occasions—but the story had believable elements. After all, an article of
faith among California miners stated that any dirt in the "auriferous
region" of the Sierra Nevada had gold-bearing potential. Further,
Carson's Creek ran close to Carson Hill (both named for Sergeant
James H. Carson, who discovered gold in the vicinity in 1848), and
Carson's Hill was in the Mother Lode belt where, in 1850, a wandering prospector picked up a fourteen-pound chunk of gold lying on
the ground and started a stampede. Carson Hill yielded $2,800,000 in
gold in ten months and as late in 1854 added another page to gold
country annals.

In November that year a miner named James Perkins and four
partners had quit the day's work in their coyote hole, which was
barely producing "wages"—an ounce of gold a day. The last man to
emerge from the shaft spotted a huge gleaming rock nearby, rubbed
the dirt from it and called out to the others. He had uncovered
what became known as the Calaveras Nugget, the largest single
lump of gold ever found in California. It weighed a bit over 195
pounds and, melted down and cleaned of impurities, was valued at
$43,534.

Daniel Woods told of incidents in July 1849 that defined the role
chance—or happenstance, serendipity, fate, or luck—played in gold
hunting. He wrote of two Irishmen at Salmon Falls on the south fork
of the American River who, one morning before breakfast, took out
$422 from a vein seven inches wide and ten feet below ground in a
stratum of hard clay. Woods says he witnessed their success for he was
working three yards from them and was getting fifty-cent pans,
"which is considered encouraging." He also observed two foreign
miners working side by side who began to question the size of their
individual claims. They sought out an American, Woods wrote, "who
happened by, and who had not yet done an hour's work in the mines"
to settle the question. "He measured off ten feet, allowed by custom
for a claim, and took for his trouble a narrow strip of land lying
between the two claims. In a few hours, the larger claims were abandoned as useless; the new-comer American discovered a deposit
which yielded him $7,435."

Woods, who on a lucky day was fetching twenty dollars from the

Salmon Falls placers, concluded that "the chances of making a fortune in the gold mines are about the same as those in favor of our drawing a prize in a lottery."

THE LUCKLESS, HAPLESS miner, representative of the overwhelming majority of the brethren of the diggings, stood on the fringes of fortune, never quite stepping across the line separating him from such a man as George McKnight of Grass Valley in the northern mines. In July 1850, this man stubbed his boot toe on an outcropping of rock while searching for a lost cow, picked up a fragment of rotted quartz veined with gold, took it to his cabin, pounded it to dust in an iron skillet, and washed the gold in a pan. The place where he found the quartz became known as Gold Hill and the boom started by the wandering cow and George McKnight, about whom nothing is known but his name and his luck, lasted a century. Gold Hill, Massachusetts Hill, Ophir Hill, and other quartz veins were opened and Grass Valley became the richest district in California, yielding an estimated $300 million in gold before operations there were closed down after a *century* of production.

There were extensive quartz-gold veins from Grass Valley south to the Mariposa diggings, and thousands of miners were at work sinking shafts to bedrock to find them. At first, miners' cabins became miniature quartz mills where tools no more sophisticated than George McKnight's hammer and frying pan were employed. Then large iron mortars and pestles came into use, the quartz dust treated with quicksilver to amalgamate with the gold. In the south, where a great many Sonoran miners were at work, a Mexican quartz-crushing system was revived. This was the *arrastra*, a configuration as old as Scripture in which a mule was attached to a pole and walked in circles dragging a granite boulder, to pulverize quartz ore lying in flat, rock-paved depressions in the ground.

By 1851, crushing or "stamp" mills made their appearance in the mines, the first of these operating by small steam engines; later water-powered mills, and mills with iron balls revolving in a set of iron pans, came into use.

For it to pay, quartz mining required drilling, blasting, and heavy machinery—hoists, ore cars, stamp mills, and the like. Even with the latest industrial equipment, the yield of gold was often only twenty dollars *per ton* of quartz ore. For the average miner, working for a mining company invested in extraction equipment was dangerous and paid below the normal placer claim average. Moreover, quartz work was even more fickle than aboveground mining. Quartz veins had a maddening tendency to peter out abruptly, and often, when the shafts were dug deeply, water rose in them and pumps had to be transported overland while work stopped and investments evaporated.

So many quartz-gold companies and combines failed, a wag issued an announcement of the formation of the "Munchausen Quartz Rock Mining and Crushing Company" accompanied by a prospectus. In presenting its stock as available, the "Company" announced claims of sixty feet each, "beginning at a blazed dogwood tree on the right bank of the River Styx, adjacent to the residence of Charon, the ferryman, extending to a large bee-gum tree on the left shore of the River Lethe, one half mile from the lake of Avernus, beyond which no auriferous quartz has ever yet been discovered." To work these claims, the paper stated that "Skillful Siberian miners have been obtained at an immense expense, through the agency of one of our distinguished Board of Trustees, P. T. Barnum, Esq."

Most of the quartz-gold operations failed. Gold Hill and its satellite mines in Grass Valley were fabulous exceptions, as was a discovery down at the southern terminus of the gold country, on a branch of the San Joaquín River.

IN JUNE 1847, John Charles Frémont waited at Sutter's Fort for the order by his commanding officer and chief nemesis, General Stephen Watts Kearny, that they would begin their overland march to Missouri. The general had already notified his Washington superiors that upon reaching Fort Leavenworth he would have Lieutenant Colonel Frémont arrested and sent on to the capital for court-martial. Kearny had not yet informed Frémont of the charges against him but they were grave: insubordination and mutiny.

Before leaving Monterey with his small force of volunteers for the journey to Sutter's Fort under Kearny's orders, Frémont was planning his return to California. He saw his future in what he expected to be a new state of the American union, and talked the matter over with Thomas O. Larkin, the former United States consul.

The two were uneasy friends. Larkin, as duplicitous as Frémont, had covertly championed the American annexation of Alta California while continuing to befriend Mexican authorities, as he had done since landing in Monterey in 1832 and starting the mercantile business that made him rich. Frémont's brashness and lethal temper during the course of the Bear Flag rebellion and subsequent events of the takeover Larkin found ugly and dangerous. He was often at odds with the explorer, and for his part, Frémont found Larkin too much the pussy-footer, too loathe to align himself publicly with the conquering Americans, too Sutter-like in protecting his business interests with Mexico. Even so, Frémont respected the merchant's business expertise and wide circle of influential friends, both Mexican and American.

As the result of their talks, Frémont gave Larkin $3,000 in bank drafts with which to purchase a rancho, specifically a piece of land near Mission San José at the southern end of San Francisco Bay.

Larkin acted with alacrity on his assignment but ignored the specified location of Rancho Frémont, a matter the explorer learned while waiting at Sutter's Fort to begin the march to Missouri, ignominiously bringing up the rear of Kearny's column.

A few days before departure, a messenger from Larkin delivered a document to Frémont. The paper was signed by former governor Juan B. Alvarado and deeded to the explorer ten square leagues of land, seventy square miles, to a "rancho" somewhere in the high Sierra wilderness of the San Joaquín River valley, forty miles from the pristine Yosemite timberlands. The place was called Las Mariposas but the lovely name could not conceal certain facts the explorer learned at Sutter's Fort: The land lay a hundred miles from the Pacific in a region unfit for farming or raising cattle—too wildly cold and blizzard-prone in the winter—and overrun by hostile Cauchile Indians.

He read the deed, grew furious at Larkin's ignorance of clear instructions, and indignantly wrote the merchant refusing the Alvarado lands and insisting he would have a tract of property near Mission San José or his $3,000 returned.

A peculiar train of events followed Frémont's message: Larkin did not act upon it and Frémont did not press the issue.

Two clues seem to point to Larkin as a culprit in the Las Mariposas matter. Jessie Benton Frémont, in some notes quoted many years afterward, referred to the Larkin purchase of the Alvarado tract as "a curious error," and added, "By another curious error, Larkin became possessed about this same time of the very olive orchard and lands Colonel Frémont had directed him to buy, and for which he had substituted the Mariposa property." Then, twenty-four years after the transaction, Juan Alvarado wrote that Larkin "and his agent despoiled me of the Mariposa Ranch . . . worth 20,000 times the price I obtained for it . . . but I was in the grip of my creditors."

Whatever the case for Larkin's culpability in the matter, he would have reason to regret not buying the Mariposa rancho for himself and deeding the San José olive groves to the explorer.

Between November 1847, and January 1848, Frémont faced court-martial in Washington and, despite defending himself brilliantly, was found guilty of disobedience and mutiny, and sentenced to dismissal from the army. President Polk rescinded the sentence, but Frémont resigned his commission and in the winter of 1848 led his fourth exploring party into the western wilderness, this one seeking to find a railroad route across the Rocky Mountains along the 38th parallel. The expedition ended disastrously when eleven of his thirty-three men were trapped by heavy snows in the San Juan Mountains of New Mexico and died, Frémont and the survivors crawling into Taos to recuperate.

Some weeks after resuming their journey to California via the southern route, the explorer and his men fell in with a group of Sonorans on the Gila River and learned that gold had been discovered at Sutter's mill. "Then and there," wrote Larkin biographer Reuben Underhill, "by some strange powers of reasoning, Frémont decided that gold must exist on the Mariposa lands."

He hired forty men, mostly seasoned Sonoran miners, and set out with them, a cattle herd and supplies, to Rancho Mariposa. Jessie wrote later the Mexicans were to provide labor and have their food furnished in exchange for a share in any gold recovered—a "grub-stake."

Frémont was due for a turn of luck and found it at Mariposa. There were rich placer deposits in the creek beds of the property, especially along a little creek called the Agua Fria, where flakes and nuggets were scooped up in cups and frying pans, and gold dug from crevasses with jackknives. It was a reenactment of the opening days of the discovery at Coloma, with a marked difference: The Mariposa deposits were part of a great *Veta Madre*, a 120-mile-long, 2-mile-wide Mother Lode deposit of gold-bearing quartz pockets that ran from the canyons of the American River south to the Merced, a tributary of the San Joaquín, which ran through Frémont's lands.

Leaving his Sonoran workers under the supervision of a trusted lieutenant, Frémont departed the mines to carry the news of their riches to Jessie, temporarily ensconced in a San Francisco hotel.

Bayard Taylor of the *New York Tribune* met the colonel in the city in September 1849, and learned details of the strike. Frémont said that even after the placers had waned, a mile-long vein of reddish quartz, rich in gold, had been discovered on his property.

News of the bonanza inevitably leaked. Reuben Underhill wrote, "Each time this hero of the trail [Frémont] entered the Golden Gate, a derisive Fate greeted him with a laurel wreath in one hand and a brickbat in the other." The brickbat this time was the invasion of the Mariposa countryside by an army of gold-hungry miners.

In the winter of 1849, Daniel Woods visited Frémont's gold camp and said it was "now quite a settlement" but was unable to make a prospect there. Nor could Julius Pratt, the Connecticut comb-maker's son who made his way from Stockton to the Stanislaus River fringes of Frémont's lands that winter, coincidentally reading one of Frémont's journals en route. With two professors, one an eminent geologist, the other a former college instructor, Pratt made a tour through the mines, starting out on horseback for the southern end of the great quartz vein, described by the geologist as "the spinal column of the gold-producing system of the Sierra Nevada." They followed the course of the vein north for about one hundred miles, Pratt said, "experiencing many adventures," to the Stanislaus River settlements where Pratt had some miner friends. There, he said, he "handled many nuggets, varying in size from a pea to a hen's egg." He handled them but found none for himself.

Frémont was as helpless to stem the invasion as Sutter had been the year before—neither man had control of the mineral rights to their lands—so the explorer had to make the most of his own claims. As it turned out, Fate's laurel wreath was mightier, at least for a time, than the brickbat. Jessie Frémont told friends that their share of the first placer "cleanup" at Mariposa reached them in San José where they were residing in a rented cottage. The gold, she said, was packed in buckskin bags, each containing a hundred pounds of dust and nuggets. Since there were no banks nor vaults in the village, she said, "we hid it under the mattress for a few days." After moving to Monterey where her husband set up his headquarters, she told intimates, "the bags of gold began to accumulate in inconvenient quantity in dust, lumps, rich bits of rock. We emptied trunks and used them for treasure chests."

Always the colorful writer, Jessie also wrote that Thomas Larkin, accidental author of their riches, "did all in his power to regain possession of the Mariposas but Colonel Frémont declined to return it for the $3,000 he had paid."

On January 1, 1850, the Pacific Mail steamer *Oregon* departed San Francisco for Mazatlán and Panama. Aboard were senators-elect Frémont and Gwin, Jessie Frémont, the newspaperman-poet Bayard Taylor, a score of merchants and prominent businessmen, several army and navy officers, and $2 million in bullion, many thousands of it the property of the Frémonts. They took the mule trail route across the isthmus, both falling desperately ill with "Chagres fever" in the process, but reached Washington in March and recuperated under the care of Jessie's father.

In something of a triumphal return to the scene of his court-martial ignominy two years past, on September 10, 1850, the day after California was officially admitted to the Union, Frémont took his seat in the Senate with the radiant Jessie looking on from the gallery.

FRÉMONT'S FORTUNE LASTED seven years, through his defeat as a presidential candidate of the young Republican Party in 1856. In the words of Reuben Underhill, "A careful scrutiny of his dramatic career, with its many vicissitudes, especially subsequent to his golden period, suggests incapacity, lack of executive ability, of financial forethought and shrewdness. . . . Here was a tract of land, vast in extent, limitless in its potentialities for mineral, agricultural, and pastoral wealth; yet this man of dreams . . . failed utterly to keep it in his grasp."

WALTER COLTON WATCHED the flood of gold chasers swamping California in 1849 and wrote, "All have come here with the expectation of finding but little work and less law!"

Of law only, the expectation was met.

At Hangtown, a prospector named Shufeld eloquently summed up what it took to be successful in the mines when he wrote home: "There is gold here in abundance but it requires patience and hard labor, with some skill and experience to obtain it. If any man has his health and will work, he can make more than ten times as much here as he can in the states in the same length of time."

Some of the misapprehension concerning the physical labor required to find and recover gold was traceable to the overwrought reports by Colton, Larkin, and others in California at the time of James Marshall's discovery. To read the early newspaper stories that appeared in the east, all a person needed to qualify as a miner was a washbasin, pick, shovel, a split ox horn to serve as a spoon, and a sturdy jackknife for "crevassing": digging gold out of cracks in rocks. There were descriptions of Sonoran miners sieving gold from streams using nothing more complicated than a fine-woven willow basket, and of "dry washing" by tossing a blanket piled with "paydirt" in the air and letting the wind blow the "chaff" away from the heavy gold dust. The correspondents wrote of "free gold," found as dust, *chispas*, scales shaped like cucumber seeds, pea-size and boulder-size nuggets, and quartz pieces seamed with gold in intricate, lacy patterns, all of it "easy pickings."

Too seldom mentioned was the physical misery required to just work a claim, both to learn if any gold was present in it and to extract it when found.

Placer mining required back-, leg-, and arm-work, mindless, enervating stoop-labor performed under a searing sun, knee-deep in water, or in a fog of dust in a dry ravine or on a bald hillside.

Panning, the most rudimentary of placer work, was known by the Georgians and North Carolinians who came to California and taught their tricks to others. The common gold pan cost twenty cents in the east and sold at Sam Brannan's store at Sutter's Fort for eight to sixteen dollars. Fabricated of iron with a rolled rim, the typical pan was three or four inches deep, eighteen inches across at the lip, sloping down to ten or twelve inches at the bottom. To employ it the miner squatted at streamside or a few feet into the waterway, submerged the pan and filled it with dirt and water, then, holding it by the rim gyrated it and stirred it with his fingers to throw out pebbles. Water was added regularly, and with more gyrating and stirring, the load was reduced to a few of the smallest pebbles and perhaps a streak of sand and particles of fine gold. This material was dried in the sun or by campfire and the lighter materials blown off, the gold, with its heavier specific gravity, remaining.

A strong-backed and persevering miner might handle a hundred pans in a ten-hour day but fifty was considered a decent average. (When not in use to wash gold, the pan served to fry bacon and flapjacks, feed the mule, and wash the face and blistered feet.)

A labor-saving device used almost from the beginning of the gold rush, also introduced by experienced southern miners, was the "rocker" or "cradle." This wooden box vaguely resembled a baby's cradle, its top and foot end open, its sides flared outward. The device was usually about 3½ feet long, twenty inches wide, and eighteen deep. Dirt was shoveled onto a perforated iron tray or "riddle" in the rocker, and dippers or buckets of water were added while the cradle was rocked. Fine gravel, sand, and gold sifted through the tray holes onto a sloping canvas apron on which wooden cleats, called "riffles," were tacked down. The riffles trapped the "settlings"—fine sand and gold particles—while allowing the detritus to be washed away.

Mining authority Otis Young said, "It was a crude device, but it worked, and even an unskilled ribbon clerk could cobble a rocker together in short order. It eliminated squatting haunch-deep in icy mountain streams for hours on end, as panning had required. The pan was forthwith retired from every use but prospecting and cleanup."

Even so, operating a rocker was laborious. One miner wrote of carrying three hundred buckets of dirt to the cradle in a day, each bucket yielding about 25¢ in gold. The day's earnings of $75 was then divided with his two partners, giving each $25. "Not bad," he said, "but not as good as the work should have produced."

The "Long Tom" came into use late in 1849. It was a deep wooden trough, ten to thirty feet long, a foot or two wide at the bottom, eight to sixteen inches deep. At the end of the trough a curved-up, perforated riffle was nailed, under which lay a "riffle box." The Tom, operated by six or eight men, was placed on an easy grade and supplied with a constant flow of water. Dirt was shoveled in, stirred, rocks thrown out by hand, and, as with the rocker, particles of gold washed down and settled behind the cleats. A miner stationed at the riddle cleared away the "tailings" and stirred up the fine dirt accumulating there. Sometimes the gold washed by cradle or Long Tom was so minute and so liable to be washed away, a box containing a vial of quicksilver was attached to the end of the riffle to save the gold by amalgamating it with the mercury. (Often, too, a drop of quicksilver in a gold pan saved a dollar's worth of butterlike gold particles.) The mercury was later "cooked," vaporized, to retrieve the gold particles.

A Long Tom could wash ten times more dirt than the cradle but required hundreds of bucketfuls of water per man per day, so the more partners involved in its operation, the better the chance for a decent day's gold yield.

SINCE PLACER MINING depended upon water, the early gold country claims were invariably streamside—producing the classic image of the prospector hunkered down, his pan dipped in water and his pack mule waiting patiently nearby.

In a brief time, however, placers were discovered on elevated ground and the dirt and gravel had to be transported to water, often a long distance, where the gold could be washed from the dirt. In the early Chinese Camp diggings in the southern mines, troops of "Celestials" groaned under sacks of ore brought up from eighteen-foot-deep shafts and carried to a muddy streamlet where they were deposited in heaps to be washed in rockers.

(The richest gold veins were deep in the ground, near bedrock, requiring the digging of these shafts, called "coyote holes," with pick, spade, and crowbar, some of them 150 feet deep, and all of them dangerous since few had bracing timbers.)

In the never-ending search for water and quicker working of pay-dirt, Long Toms were extended to sluices, some of them several hundred feet long and capable of processing a hundred cubic yards of gravel daily. A piece of carpeting at end of the sluice snagged the gold not trapped in riffles and a quicksilver deposit on the carpet produced an amalgamate to preserve the tiniest of gold particles.

Bringing the dirt to the water was replaced whenever possible by reversing the process, and countless diggers remembered the grueling work of building flumes, some of them more than a thousand feet long. These wooden aqueducts were constructed by cleating a string of wooden troughs together and their purpose was to carry water down from the Sierra so that work might be carried on year-round. In the northern mines, there were some 1,500 miles of ditches and flumes by 1858; in the central district, 2,175 miles, and in the southern mines, 796 miles.

Daniel Woods was working the dry diggings at Hart's Bar on the Tuolumne River in May 1850, when he was elected secretary and treasurer of the Draining and Mining Company, a band of twenty miners determined to build a "canal," a clay and timber aqueduct to bring water to the claims. Mud for the canal was carried in wheelbarrows (Woods figured each barrow covered fourteen miles a day) and the lumber whipsawed from logs cut and rolled down the mountain slopes.

By September, the canal was completed—630 feet long and 16 feet wide with supporting piers sunk in the ground. For a few days, the artificial waterway worked: $415.75 was washed out, using rockers, on one particularly good day. But when the rains came, the contraption began leaking. The thunderstorms raised the river, source of the canal water, eight feet until it poured over the aqueduct. Finally, Woods wrote, "Gently and gracefully it [the wooden structure] yielded, swayed forward, and moved away with the ease and rapidity of a thing of life. Thus, in one moment, we saw the work . . . swept away and rendered useless."

When the company gold was divided up at the end of November, each member had earned an average of $7.28 from the project.

Woods also witnessed the use of "submarine armor" on the Tuolumne, an experiment "soon abandoned as useless," and Daniel Knower of Albany was present on the middle fork of the American River when a similar apparatus was lowered into the river. "It was a diving armor that had been used in the Gulf of Lower California to go down in the deep waters to hunt for pearls," he wrote. The diving suit had been brought to the mines by a party of men who invested $8,000 in the scheme, "expecting to make their fortunes by getting into the deep water of the gold rivers." Miners quit their work to watch the operation, but, Knower said, the diver failed to find any gold and when he left to go further down the river to try another location, he bilked a storekeeper of $800, ostensibly for a partnership in the diving scheme. Said Knower of the schemer, "I have no doubt he came to grief like all evil-doers."

A RUINOUS USE of water in the California gold country began in 1853 with the introduction of hydraulic mining, a massively violent method of exposing gold-bearing rocks on mountain slopes and hillsides. The system employed giant pivoting hoses called "monitors" braced on a rig that permitted one man to operate the eight-inch nozzle. The hoses, capable of knocking a man off his feet 200 feet away, blasted water at a 100-mile-an-hour force against the rocks, using millions of gallons a day. The runoff polluted streams, the gravel and a thick mud called "slickens" carpeted farmlands and overflowed rivers. The Yuba, once crystal clear and almost thirty-five feet deep at Marysville, became so choked with mud and waste from hydraulic operations that it rose nearly level to the streets and even protective levees could not prevent the town from flooding. The inundation from the monitors deforested square miles of lush timberlands, devegetated farms by washing topsoil away, and did incalculable flood and erosion damage before hydraulic mining was outlawed in 1884.

A melancholy phrase often used to explain the disappearance of a mining camp was that the place had been "piped away"—eradicated by the hammering monitors.

Charles Nordhoff, the Prussian-born travel writer, wrote in 1872 of the ravages of this method of mining: "They washed away hills, they shoveled away broad, elevated plains; dozens of square miles of soil disappeared and were driven off into lower valleys that they might exhume the gold.

"If you want to know how a part of the surface of our planet looked some thousands of years ago, here is a good opportunity; for what two or three men with torrents of water wash away into the Yuba River in a few weeks must have taken centuries to accumulate." The Yuba, he said, "once contained trout, but now I imagine a catfish would die in it."

Naturalist John Muir, founder of the Sierra Club, wrote in 1894 of the "dead rivers of California," streams and rivers that had vanished, their basins drained, the traces of their channels choked with gravel. At Murphy's Camp he wrote, "The hills have been cut and scalped, and every gorge and gulch and valley torn to pieces and disemboweled."

The Miners' Ten Commandments

James H. Hutchings (1818–1902), an Englishman and failed Forty-niner, staked a profitable claim in 1853 with his broadside, "The Miners' Ten Commandments," designed to be folded and mailed home. He sold 100,000 of them and used the profits to launch *Hutchings California Magazine*, a mixture of local writers and illustrators, which reached a circulation of 8,000. He became one of the first white settlers in the Yosemite Valley and opened the valley's first hotel there.

"A Man spake these words, and said: I am a miner, who wandered 'from away down east,' and came to sojourn in a strange land, and 'see the elephant,'" the broadside began. "And behold I saw him, and bear witness, that from his trunk to the end of his tail, his whole body has passed before me; and I followed him until his huge feet stood still before a clapboard shanty; then with his trunk extended, he pointed to a candle-card tacked upon a shingle, as though he would say Read, and I read. . . ."

The commandments contained such admonitions as:

Thou shalt have no other claim than one.

Thou shalt not make unto thyself any false claim, nor any likeness to a mean man, by jumping one.

Thou shalt not go prospecting before thy claim gives out. Neither shalt thou take thy money, nor thy gold dust, nor thy good name, to the gaming table in vain; for monte, twenty-one, roulette, faro, lansquenet, and poker will prove to thee that the more thou puttest down the less thou shalt take up; and when thou thinkest of thy wife and children, thou shalt not hold thyself guiltless—but insane.

Thou shalt not remember what thy friends do at home on the Sabbath day, lest the remembrance may not compare favorably with what thou doest here.

Thou shalt not think more of all thy gold, and how thou canst make it fastest, than how thou wilt enjoy it, after thou hast ridden rough-shod over thy good old parents' precepts and examples. . . .

Thou shalt not grow discouraged, nor think of going home before thou hast made thy "pile."

FIFTEEN

A VAGRANT LIFE

HUBERT HOWE BANCROFT arrived late in the diggings but came to know miners and their labors firsthand. His experiences, and the miners he came to know, proved invaluable decades later when he wrote voluminously of the gold rush.

Born in Granville, Ohio, in 1832, Bancroft learned the printing trade in his teens in Buffalo, New York, before returning to Ohio where he peddled books from a farm wagon. He sailed for California in 1852, made the Panama crossing, and that summer joined his father and brother, who had gone out the year before and were working the placers at Long Bar, a settlement near Marysville.

Hubert, who stood six-foot-two with a chesty, powerful build, did not mind the labor, cutting trees and hauling wood and ore with a mule team at Long Bar and later at Rich Bar on the Feather River. Indeed, it was a joyous time for the callow twenty-year-old: He was reunited with family members, seeing a new land he was certain had a bright future, and feeling like a pioneer. "Behold us now! My father and me, tramping over the plains beneath a broiling sun about the middle of June, each with a bundle and stick, mine containing my sole possessions," he wrote in a 1891 memoir. "My feet blistered; my limbs ached; water was to be had only at intervals; the prayed-for breath of air came hot and suffocating. . . ."

Years later, when he wrote of the trickle of emigrants who came into California prior to the American takeover, he characterized them as "mere filibusters . . . entitled to none of the sympathy or honor which the world accords to revolutionists who struggle against oppression." The majority of these trespassers, he said, were deserters from merchant ships, adventurers, "Reckless, daring, and unprincipled men, with nothing to lose," plus political opportunists looking for glory, wealth, and power under American hegemony—"men who looked upon Californians as inferiors who needed to be taught the beauties of freedom and a superior civilization."

But of the Forty-niners and the flood of gold hunters who followed, so many of them reckless, daring, opportunistic haters of "inferior" races and nationalities, he adopted a kindlier tone. "They were a self-reliant class, these diggers," he said, "of rough, shaggy appearance, bristling with small-arms at the belt, yet warm-hearted; with mobile passions and racy, pungent language; yet withal generous and gentle. Cast adrift on the sea of adventure in motley companionship, each man held life in his own hand, prepared for storm or shoal, and confident in finding means and remedies when needed."

This romanticized view was later compounded by Mark Twain, who arrived in California in 1861, too late to witness the real gold fever but in time to make mawkish observations on those who had been stricken with it. They formed, he wrote, "an assemblage of two hundred thousand *young* men—not simpering, dainty, kid-gloved weaklings, but stalwart, muscular, dauntless young braves, brimful of push and energy, and royally endowed with every attribute that goes to make up a peerless and magnificent manhood—the very pick and choice of the world's glorious ones."

The kindly frontier lady Sarah Royce, who caught her first glimpse of California in October 1849, and fell in love with it, observed miners in Weberville and Sacramento City and called them "Roughly-reared frontier men—almost as ignorant of civilized life as savages." They were, she said, "Reckless bravados, carrying their characters in their faces and demeanor."

Whether or not rough, shaggy, stalwart, muscular, dauntless, peerless, or magnificent, men—specifically young men, most in their twenties and thirties—dominated the gold rush. About a quarter of them were born outside the United States; among the Americans, probably half were from New England and New York, Yankees with little prior contact with non-Yankees, certainly not with Indians, Mexicans, Latin Americans, and Asians. Many, particularly the easterners, had gathered up a substantial sum of money, as much as two years' salary at home, to follow their gold dream, spending much of it for transportation and in "outfitting" too elaborately.

Most who came to the gold fields, more adventurous than ambitious, intended to stay but briefly. Unlike the Oregon Trail travelers of the 1840s, the Forty-niners, with some significant exceptions, were neither pioneers nor settlers. They intended to find as much gold as they could and go home triumphant to family and friends. Their optimism wore thin en route to California and in the early days of their quest in the mines as they experienced cholera epidemics, starvation, evil weather, boredom, and homesickness. What sense of adventure remained eroded further after the death of a comrade, something virtually every miner witnessed since deaths were commonplace on the overland trails, on the isthmus crossing, and in the diggings. Within six months of reaching California, one out of five argonauts died.

The Virginian James H. Carson experienced all the emotions of the gold rush, from his "frenzy" when he saw a sack of gold a friend brought back to Monterey in May 1848, to his deep melancholia over lost friends and his own failing health.

After five years working the placers, this normally exuberant soldier-miner grew meditative about his brethren of the pick and pan. He remembered standing under a pine tree at the lonely grave of a Virginia friend who had "left all the endearments of home, and with a heart buoyant with expectations, sought the far off land of gold." The friend fell ill and died and "No sobbing mourners followed in his funeral train, no church bell tolled for his departure, or grey-haired pastor chaunted a prayer for the departed," Carson wrote, and only "a few comrades bore him to the romantic spot where now he rests. His blanket was his winding sheet; the cold, cold clods his coffin lid."

The sergeant himself was soon to sleep thus lonely.

He received his army discharge in November 1849, after ten years' service, and moved into the gold country, coming to know the southern mines so well he accompanied the army engineers on the first topographical survey of the Tulare Basin, a marshland in the San Joaquín Valley.

In 1853, with new gold discoveries opened at Guyong in New South Wales, and at Ballarat and Bendigo in Victoria, Carson wrote of California miners quitting their claims to chase the gilded rainbow in Australia. There were 100,000 miners swarming the Sierra foothills that year but he was forced to admit, "California is herself no more. The mines are too much crowded for all to do well. Many men, ay, the majority in the mines, have not made their board this winter."

That year, California produced $67 million in gold and elected James H. Carson to the California state legislature, an honor he could not fulfill.

In the course of the topographical survey he had contracted a debilitating fever and never recovered from it. He spent months in hospitals in Monterey and Stockton, writing while recuperating. In 1852, the Stockton-based *San Joaquín Republican* published over thirty of his articles on his mining experiences, and his letters were published in book form in Stockton as *Early Recollections of the California Mines* in the same year.

He died of "chronic rheumatism" (probably a misdiagnosis) at Dr. Bateman's Hospital in Stockton on December 12, 1853, at age thirty-two, a few weeks after his election as state representative. His widow and daughter arrived from the east a month later, destitute, and were assisted by a generous "subscription" from among his miner comrades.

Carson had some success in gold mining—though little from the diggings named for him—but seems to have spent all he earned. The editor of the Stockton newspaper paid his hospital bills and the expenses in having him buried in the Tulare Valley.

AS A FORTY-EIGHTER, in the gold rush from first to last, and a shrewd and intelligent observer, Carson's recollections of the treatment of California's true natives, its Indians, were poignant and pathetic.

They labored for their miner-employers and were routinely cheated and mistreated, he said. Traders had special scales to bilk them of their hard-earned dust, and charged them $20 a yard for calico, six ounces of gold (almost $100) for a blanket. "They came from the bug and acorn hunting grounds, naked as nature had made them," he wrote, and had no concept of the value of gold, at least early in the game, before older mission Indians educated them. Many of the natives doted on fancy shirts and strutted around wearing a dozen at a time; others fell in love with garish sashes and outsized Mexican sombreros, "and in many instances the wearer of the hat would have his naked heels adorned with a huge pair of California spurs."

The miners feared the Indians of the plains and mountains between Missouri and the gold fields but regarded California's natives as little more than subhuman nuisances, "diggers," eating acorns, roots, and grubs, living in the Stone Age. This pitiless view was expressed by former proslavery Congressman Thomas Butler King of Georgia, the "confidential agent" of the Zachary Taylor administration who came to California in 1849 to take part in establishing the state government. He described the Indians he saw as "degraded objects of filth and idleness," and said they were destined to disappear as whites took over the land—a prognostication already being enacted as he wrote his screed; indeed, a process that had been taking place since the first Spaniards landed on the California coast in 1769.

The estimated 300,000 Indians of that era, spread in diverse and often elaborately advanced cultures from the Oregon border to the Mojave country, were reduced to 50,000 by 1848, their arts, crafts, religions, survival skills—their ways of life—dead or dying long before.

In the opening year of the gold rush, more than half of California's natives were working in the mines, for Mexican or American masters, and faring no better than they had when slaving for the Franciscan fathers or Californio dons. In truth, they fared worse. While their salmon streams, acorn groves, and timberlands were being destroyed by mining operations, the Indians were dying from new diseases, from malnutrition, from whiskey, and from legislatively sanctioned murder.

A few months after the gold discovery Walter Colton of Monterey wrote of "The diamond-brooched gentleman and the clouted Indian working side by side, lovingly, as if they had been rocked in the same cradle." But a few weeks later, the *New York Journal of Commerce* published a letter dated Monterey, August 29, written either by Colton or Thomas Larkin, that gave a truer picture: "At present, the people are running over the country and picking it [gold] out of the earth here and there. . . . Some get eight or ten ounces a day, and the least active one or two. They make the most who employ the wild Indians to hunt it for them. There is one man who has sixty Indians in his employ; his profits are a dollar a minute.

"The wild Indians," the writer said, "know nothing of its [gold's] value, and wonder what the pale-faces want to do with it; they will give an ounce of it for the same weight of coined silver, or a thimbleful of glass beads, or a glass of grog."

Those natives who learned the white man's ways and retaliated by horse stealing and cattle rustling were killed by loosely organized "state militia" posses. In the 1850s more than a million dollars in state bonds were issued to pay the cost of local volunteer campaigns for "the suppression of Indian hostilities"—a form of legalized, and subsidized, murder.

In 1851, no less a personage than Peter H. Burnett, lawyer and judge and first governor after California statehood, proclaimed "That a war of extermination will continue to be waged by the two races until the Indian race becomes extinct. . . . While we cannot anticipate the result with but painful regret, the inevitable destiny of the race is beyond the power and wisdom of man to avert."

As late as 1866, the *Chico Courant* editorialized, "It has become a question of extermination now. . . . It is a mercy to the red devils to exterminate them, and a saving of many white lives. Treaties are played out. There is only one kind of treaty that is effective—cold lead."

ALL RACES AND ethnic groups fared better than the native races in California in the gold rush, but none other than whites fared well.

In 1847, there were nine black men and one black woman in a San Francisco population of 459; by 1852 there were 2,000 black men and women in the state—Afro-Latins from Mexico, Chile, and Peru, and some from the West Indies, with American blacks accounting for about 1 percent of the state's populace.

In the early years of the gold rush, slavery was abided because it was rare, but white slaveowners in the diggings were anathema. Ordinary miners hated seeing these men idling while their human chattels worked their claims or were hired out as laborers, cooks, and domestic servants, providing another source of revenue for their lazy owners.

Runaway slaves were sought, with rewards offered, in notices in the California newspapers as early as 1847 but abolitionists were also at work, boarding ships in the harbors and informing slaves who were heading home with their masters that the laws of California had declared them free.

Except among the abolitionists and the politest of society, gold rush blacks were called "niggers" in the same noxious manner Mexicans and Latin Americans were collectively "greasers," the Chinese "chinks."

Probably the most eminent black man in California in the 1840s was William A. Leidesdorff, a businessman and United States consul in Yerba Buena. His associates considered him white but he was of West Indian and Danish-African ancestry ("son of a Dane and a mulatress" in Bancroft's words) who as a young man became a merchant captain in New York and New Orleans before reaching California in about 1843.

The best known among black men of the gold rush was the mountaineer Jim Beckwourth, although much of his status as a celebrity was due to the lucky circumstance of his finding a worshipful chronicler.

A native of Fredericksburg, Virginia, Beckwourth was sent to school in St. Louis, apprenticed to a blacksmith there, and in 1823, at age twenty-five, ran away to join a Rocky Mountain Fur Company brigade. By 1826, he was said to have been "adopted" by the Crow people of the Yellowstone River country, became a warrior and a "chief" called Medicine Calf, and a fur trader with the tribe.

He joined General Kearny's march to Santa Fé in 1846 as a courier and in 1849 settled in California, working traps and as a laborer-miner.

He was described as "a tall and muscular mulatto" by his first biographer, T. D. Bonner, a wandering newspaperman whom Beckwourth met at the Rich Bar camp in 1854. The two drank together as Beckwourth spun his history and Bonner took it down. Louise Amelia Clapp, who wrote about Rich Bar under the pen name "Dame Shirley," and who met both men, said, "The more they drank, the more Indians Jim would recall having slain, his eloquence increasing in inverse ratio to the diminishing rum supply, and, at last, he would slap the Squire [Bonner] on the knee and chortle, 'Paint her up, Bonner! Paint her up!' And Bonner painted her up for the joy of posterity."

In 1856 Beckwourth was run out of California for horse stealing. Afterward, he kept a store in Denver and operated a ranch.

He died in 1867 among the Crow people who had adopted him.

AT THE END of 1848 there were seven "registered," that is, counted, Chinese in California; by 1852, 25,000 "Celestials" (from China's appellation, the Celestial Empire) were concentrated in the gold country and in San Francisco where they constituted the largest foreign population element.

Many of these emigrants were from the Pearl River delta near Canton in southeastern China, where shipping agents wooed them with flyers describing California's "Gum Shan" or Golden Mountain, and offering passage for as little as forty dollars.

A contributing factor to Chinese immigration to California was the T'ai P'ing Rebellion of 1849–64. This long, bloody civil war, a revolt against the existing dynasty of the country and attempt to replace it with a government containing elements of Western Protestantism, started in Canton, and spread to Nanking and Shanghai, causing thousands of Chinese to flee their country.

They were tireless workers, much in demand as laborers, carpenters, cooks, and house servants, but in the mines, where resentment of foreigners was epidemic, the Chinese were favorite butts of abuse. They took work at lower wages than others; wore pigtails, baggy trousers, and "coolie" hats made of split bamboo; carried buckets and bags of belongings suspended from a bamboo pole across their shoulders; preferred opium over whiskey, dried fish over beef, rice over beans, and tea over coffee; had a sing-song language and a "heathen" religion. In the diggings they often worked abandoned claims, sifting tailings and dumps, then were driven off if the waste gravel produced a bit of gold. A common phrase in the mines for a particularly worthless prospect was "one even a Chinaman would pass by."

The Chinese had no legal rights, could not vote, and could not testify in court for or against a white. They were beaten, even killed, and their gold stolen without punishment until federal courts struck down anti-Chinese state and municipal laws in the 1870s.

They were clannish, living in their own isolated pockets of the camps, never abandoning their dreams of returning home, although few were ever able to. They further attempted to escape the hatred of the white man by forming "tongs," fraternal organizations, but these tended to promote internecine rivalries that occasionally devolved into real fights among disputing tongs.

The best-known of the gold rush tong "wars" took place in the summer of 1854 in a little valley near Weaverville in the far northern mines. The dispute involved two tongs, indentified as the Cantons and the Hongkongs, which had been quarreling for months. After a Canton leader was killed, his tong issued a challenge to the other and a "battle" was scheduled by mutual agreement to take place in one month.

That July, every blacksmith in Weaverville and surrounding camps was busy making weapons—spears with three prongs or curved hooks affixed to fifteen-foot-long foot poles; stabbing and hacking swords, and shields of iron or plaited straw.

The law officer in the area, a Sheriff Lowe, tried to head off the battle but to no avail. The two "armies" drilled and paraded, then on the day of battle, July 14, assembled at Five Cent Gulch near Weaverville. Both sides heralded their advent with horns and gongs, each force carrying heavy two-handed swords, pikes, daggers, shields, and bright banners on long poles.

A throng of two thousand white miners gathered to watch as the armies marched and countermarched for two hours, hurling insults and threats, and finally clashed. Some accounts of the fight say the Cantons outnumbered the Hongkongs 400 men to 130, but the Hongkongs forced the Cantons into an untenable position, their force split by the crowd of spectators, and defeated them. At least seven men were killed in the ten-minute battle.

There was another tong battle, in September 1856, at Chinese Camp near Sonora between two factions, the Sam-Yaps and Yan-Wos, the dispute said to be over a claim on the Stanislaus River. Pikes, swords, salmon-spears, and muskets were carried by the opposing tongs. They clashed on September 26 and the hundred or so shots fired resulted in casualties of four dead and four wounded.

The *San Francisco Bulletin*, true to the sentiment of the day, reported, "It was a very bad battle as so few were killed."

IN THE VAGRANT life of the white California miner there seemed no end of opportunities to test his innate confidence in his God-given superiority. Indians were backward, indolent, pathetic; blacks little more than slaves, same with the heathen Chinese; and the Kanakas were mere Hawaiian savages, probably cannibals not long past. The white foreigners—English, Australian, German, French, Italian—were tolerated, although not without suspicion. Of the French, variously called "Frogs" or "Keskydees," the latter for their incessant question, "*Ou'est-ce qu'il dit?*" ("What is he saying?"), many had ended up in California as the result of a clever stratagem.

News of the California gold strike reached France while the country was in the grip of revolution. King Louis-Philippe abdicated in 1848; workers rose in revolt in Paris; and Louis Napoleon, nephew of Napoleon I, was elected president of the new French republic in December, and after a coup in 1851 became Emperor Napoleon III.

California's riches inspired a tactic in mid-1850 to rid France of thousands of out-of-work poor (and perhaps potential political enemies) by shipping four thousand of them to the gateway to the California gold fields. The dreamed-up device for this seemingly benevolent deportation was a lottery in which tickets were sold at one franc (twenty cents American) each; the goal was to raise seven million francs in order to finance the prize for each winning number: a paid passage to San Francisco.

La Société des Lingots d'Or opened a sumptuous office on the Boulevard Montmartre, exhibiting ostensible gold bars in its windows. Alexandre Dumas *fils*, the twenty-five-year-old son of the author of *Les Trois Mousquetaires* and *Le Comte de Monte-Cristo*,* wrote a promotional pamphlet for the lottery and tickets were sold in England, Italy, and Spain, as well as France. In the end, nearly 4,000 lottery winners, mostly Frenchman, traveled to San Francisco, but too late to find any gold. Hundreds were stranded in California and had to seek help from the French consulate for passage home.

SOME OF THE intolerance in the mines, particularly that directed toward Mexicans and South Americans, was attributable to the anti-Catholic and anti-immigrant movement in the eastern United States. The agitation was exemplifed in the rise in the 1840s of the political party called the "Know-Nothings," formed as a reaction to the breakup of the two national parties over the slavery issue. The organization, officially the American Party, took its popular name from the password "I don't know" used in its local lodges. Its members campaigned for the exclusion of Catholics and foreigners from public office, and for a mandatory twenty-one-year residency requirement before immigrants could be granted citizenship.

---

*Dumas *père* later wrote a novel set in the gold rush, *Un Gil Blas en Californie*, the story in the form of a memoir of a young Frenchman in the mines of the Sierra Nevada.

Mexicans, the largest of the "foreign" contingents in the mines, most of them Catholic, were special Know-Nothing targets.

The anti-foreign, particularly anti-Mexican bias was expressed plainly by army Brevet Major General Persifor F. Smith when he was en route to Monterey in January 1849, to replace Richard Mason as commander of the Pacific military forces. While the steamer *California* lay off Panama City, Smith wrote to the U.S. consul in Panama, on the subject of "trespassers on public lands" and stated that "nothing can be more unreasonable or unjust" than noncitizens of the United carrying off gold belonging to the United States in California.

The unnamed places these trespassers had departed were clearly Mexico, Chile, and Peru, for it was these countries that came to General Smith's attention when gold hunters from them were overrunning such vessels as the one he was taking to Monterey.

General Smith's sentiments were publicly expressed by the *Alta California* on August 2, 1849: "The desire to expel foreign 'vagrants' is very general."

Probably most of the antipathy toward Mexicans was traceable to the recent war. The common thinking among Americans ran that just three years past, Mexico owned California, but lost it in war and now California was American by right of conquest. Further, while Mexicans had no significant role in discovering gold in their former province these conquered people were now infesting the mines, reaping rewards they had not earned.

"Those we have injured we hate," Bancroft wrote of this, "so it was with Mexicans and Americans in California. We had unfairly wrested the country from them, and now we were determined that they should have none of the benefits."

Enmities, of course, were nurtured on both sides of the border. John Woodhouse Audubon, as urbane a gentleman as ever joined the gold rush, confessed to a "hatred of everything Mexican," reflecting an attitude common among those who chose the trans-Mexico route to California. These travelers were despised and harassed by the citizenry of the war-torn land and Audubon's everlasting resentment grew from the time he and his sick, dwindling company were crossing the Chihuahua desert in the summer of 1849, and were harassed by bandits on several occasions.

Another source of irritation among the American miners centered on the Mexicans who came up to the southern California mines in such numbers that their headquarters camp in the dry diggings was named for their home state of Sonora. Worse, these men came from a rich mineral district of Mexico, were skilled horse and mule handlers, and knew how to mine gold. They were so good at it, in fact, that their work inspired the California legislature to pass a "Foreign Miners Tax" in April 1850, covering all non-Americans in the mines but leveled expressly at the worrisomely flourishing Mexicans. The monthly tax of twenty dollars in effect legalized the Know-Nothing philosophy in vacuous prose: the tax was defined as "a small bonus for the privilege of taking from our country the vast treasure for which they [foreigners] have no right."

Any doubt that the act was aimed at specific "foreigners" was removed when it was refined and expanded in 1855 and baldly named the "Anti-Greaser Act" until some sensitive legislator had the hateful word expunged from the record.

Eventually the tax was reduced to three dollars a year. Bancroft wrote that "The reduction gave fresh courage to the Mexicans, who with the Mongols [Chinese] constituted almost the exclusive prey of the collector." However, the historian said, the adjustment "brought little relief from Anglo-Saxon persecution, with the attendant seizures of tempting claims and maltreatment, exclusion from camps and districts and not infrequent bloody encounters."

Claim-jumping and violent behavior on the part of Americans occurred chefly in the central and northern mines where Mexicans were fewer in numbers and unable to put up a resistance. Many of the miners in these districts abandoned their claims and joined their countrymen in the San Joaquín River valley, where the Mexican population was large enough to fight back.

There, around the town of Sonora and its thriving gold claims and camps, rose an extraordinary character, a man so entangled in legendry as the "Robin Hood of Eldorado" that in the century and a half since he made some kind of mark on the gold rush, neither historians nor folklorists can agree on who he was or what kind of mark he made.

He was believed to have been named Joaquín Murieta, although there appears to have been at least five "Joaquíns" wanted for banditry in 1852, named, with probable spelling errors, by the California legislature as Joaquín Muriati (subsequently rendered as "Murieta"), Joaquín Valenzuela, Joaquín Carillo, Joaquín Botellier, and Joaquín Ocomorenia.

Probably a Sonoran, Murieta was believed to have staked a rich claim on the Stanislaus River early in '49 and to have been evicted from his claim by Americans who were said to have raped his wife, hanged his brother, and tied Murieta to a tree and flogged him nearly to death.

He became an outlaw, the story goes, and for about three years left a bloody trail of retribution throughout the gold country, at times accompanied by as many as eighty confederates, robbing stagecoaches and horseback travelers, holding up mining camps and settlements, and, so it was told, "generously sharing the stolen gold with his perse-cuted countrymen."

Devotees of the Murieta legend claim he killed every one of the men who had driven him from his claim and abused his wife, and every one of the mob which flogged him and hanged his brother. Most of the culprits were allegedly captured alive and dragged behind horses until shredded to death on rocky roads. Nor was the American white man his sole antagonist. One of his exploits, the story goes, was tying together the queues of half a dozen Chinese miners before cutting their throats.

In 1852 the California legislature offered a $5,000 reward for his capture dead or alive. This lonely fact is accompanied by the yarn that Murieta rode into Stockton just as a deputy sheriff was posting the reward poster to a tree and wrote at the bottom of the notice, "I will pay $1,000 myself," and signed it J. Murieta.

Early in May 1853, the legislature authorized Harry Love, deputy sheriff of Los Angeles, to form a company of twenty-five state "rangers" to protect the mining camps from rampaging bandit gangs. While not specifying Murieta, the lawmakers defined the mission of the rangers to capture "the five Joaquíns" and fixed the pay of the pursuers at $150 a month for three months.

Love was accompanied by a gambler named William Burns, who had been friendly with Murieta and consented to betray the bandit for a few hundred dollars.

According to several accounts, on a July night in 1853, Love, Burns, and seven rangers came upon Murieta and a confederate called

"Three-Fingered Jack" sitting at a campfire near Lake Tulare in the southern San Joaquín Valley. Three-Fingered Jack died in the first fusillade but Murieta leaped on a horse and fled into the darkness. A chance shot brought the horse down and a volley of seven bullets struck the bandit king who allegedly, despite grievous wounds, threw down his rifle, raised his hands and cried out to Harry Love, "Shoot no more. The work is done," whereupon he sank to the ground and died.

Murieta's head was severed and placed in a bottle of spirits by Love's rangers and taken to San Francisco. On August 18, 1853, a notice appeared in the town newspapers confirming the whereabouts of the grisly trophy:

JOAQUÍN'S HEAD
Is to be seen at King's
Corner of Halleck and Sansome Streets.
ADMISSION ONE DOLLAR

Many who saw the exhibit said the head was not Murieta's, that it probably belonged to an innocent Indian killed by the rangers. Among those who looked at it and declared it a fraud was James W. Marshall, Sutter's gold discoverer, who claimed to have known the bandit. Murieta's alleged widow also denied the head in the jar was Joaquín's. She was convinced her alleged husband had escaped into Mexico and, anticipating such a flight, had sent ahead a great herd of horses and $50,000 in gold to his old home in Sonora.

This supposed testimony went nowhere and eventually the head ended up in "Dr. Jordan's Museum of Horrors" on Montgomery Street and was among the treasured artifacts destroyed in San Francisco's earthquake and fire of 1906.

H. H. Bancroft added some weight to the Murieta legend by writing that this principal of all the Joaquíns "had higher aims than mere revenge and pillage. . . . It is easy to see that he regarded himself as a champion of his country rather than as an outlaw. He was only a few months more than twenty-one years old when he died and his brilliant career of crime occupied him less than three years."

Many other historians, however, believe that Murieta was largely fictitious, his history the creation of novelist John Rollin Ridge, a half-Cherokee writer who came from Georgia to California during the gold rush. Ridge's famous book, *The Life and Adventures of Joaquín Murieta* (published in California in 1854) was patently a dime novel but much of it was adopted as factual by numerous popular writers and even such serious historians as Bancroft.

Joseph H. Jackson's sensible summation of the story was that whatever truth lay behind the outrages committed on Murieta and his family, "they parallel things that did happen to many a Mexican. Whatever Murieta did or did not do—and there is no way, now, to disentangle fact from fiction—he and many another like him may well have been forced to an extra-legal way of life by the brutal treatment that Americans in general accorded all foreigners, especially Mexicans, who presumed to think they had any rights in California gold."

CHILE, THAT LONG strip of land on the western coast of South America between the 17th and 57th parallels of latitude, contributed 7,000 of its citizens to the California gold rush, the second largest contingent, after Mexico's, in the early months after the gold discovery. Cape Horn ships routinely anchored at Valparaiso and Talcahuano (port for the city of Concepción), and the gold news reached the country in August 1848.

Many Chileans were experienced hard-rock miners, as knowledgeable as the Sonorans in placer mining, and in reading gravel and quartz formations. They were therefore instantly suspect and grouped with all the other "greasers" as outlanders stealing Yankee gold.

The most notorious act against the Chileans occurred in December 1849, when a band of American miners confiscated some claims in a ravine of the Calaveras River known as "Chili Gulch." About twenty Chileans opposed the takeover, and in their attempt to arrest some of the interlopers and take them to Stockton for a legal judgment, killed two of the Americans. Several of the resisters were captured and dragged before a kangaroo court where some were sentenced to head-shavings, ear-loppings, and banishment from the mines, and three were sentenced to death by firing squad—a new twist on gold country executions. On January 1, 1850, the condemned were shot one at a time so that the ringleader, a man named Terán, would witness the deaths of the others before he fell under a hail of fifteen bullets.

＊   ＊   ＊

THE ESTEEMED CALIFORNIO, General Mariano Guadalupe Vallejo of Sonoma, who welcomed American emigrants to his native country and survived the indignities of the Bear Flag Revolt, reflected sadly on the invasion of vagrant gold seekers to his beloved Alta California. Those he saw, he became convinced, were not people seeking a new start in life; in his view, they were the dregs of society. No group or nation escaped his bitterness.

"Australia sent us a swarm of bandits who on their arrival in California, dedicated themselves exclusively to robbery and assault," he said. "The Mormons, lascivious but very industrious people, sent the ship *Brooklyn*, loaded with emigrants, who professed a religion which is in open conflict with good taste and with moral and political soundness. Peru sent us a great number of rascals, begotten in idleness and schooled in vice, who debased themselves for lucre. Mexico inundated us with a wave of gamblers who had no occupation save that of the card table, no motive but the spoliation of the unwary."

France, he said, sought to be rid of "several thousand lying men and corrupt women, and embarked them at the expense of the government on ships which brought them to San Francisco."

Italy sent musicians and gardeners. "The former, of course, lost no time in fraternizing with the keepers of gambling houses and brothels."

Chile, he said, "sent us many laborers who were very useful and contributed not a little toward the development of resources of the country. . . . it is only to be regretted that so many of them were addicted to drinking and gambling. . . ."

"China poured upon our shores clouds and more clouds of Asiatics and more Asiatics. These without exception came to California with the determination to use any means of enriching themselves by 'hook or crook' and returning immediately to their own country. . . . Chinese women . . . keep the hospitals filled with syphilitics."

Vallejo, oddly, had nothing to say of the infestation of American adventurers and outlaws who plagued the towns and mines more fully and fatally than any other nationality.

Of all the Americans who came to California, he grew to despise Yankee lawyers above the rest: "The escaped bandits from Australia stole our cattle and our horses," he said, "but these legal thieves, clothed in the robes of the law, took from us our lands and our houses, and without the least scruple, enthroned themselves in our homes like so many powerful kings."

V
DEPARTURES

Gold begets in brethren hate;
Gold in families debate;
Gold does friendship separate;
Gold does civil wars create.
—Abraham Cowley, *Anacreontics*, 1663

SIXTEEN

DAME SHIRLEY'S WORLD

THE YANKEE MINER despised "foreigners" and professional gamblers, no matter their national origin, and like Vallejo, he had no truck with or trust in lawyers. He was also wary of bankers, politicians, or any man wearing a suit; and he had little good to say about "Pikes."

Bancroft mentioned them too, writing that "among the less desirable elements," in the mines "were the ungainly, illiterate crowds from the border states, such as Indiana Hoosiers and Missourians, or 'Pike County' people. . . ."

"Pike" was originally applied to men from Pike County, Missouri, but on the trails west and in the gold country it became a term of derision for any rustic Missourian, Arkansan, or Deep South backwoodsman—the "hillbilly" of later times—all of whom were believed to be illiterate and ignorant of the simplest niceties of civilization.

The British artist J. D. Borthwick, who roamed the California diggings in the early 1850s, made a small study of Pikes in the placers and described them in his journal: "They were mostly long, gaunt, narrow-chested, round-shouldered men, with long, straight, light-colored, dried-up looking hair, small, thin, sallow faces, with rather scanty beard and moustache, and small, grey, sunken eyes, which seemed to be keenly perceptive of everything around them." The Pike men, he wrote, were "slow and awkward, and in the towns especially they betrayed a childish astonishment at the strange sights occasioned by the presence of divers nations of the earth. Till they came to California many of them had never seen two houses together, and in any little village in the mines they witnessed more wonders of civilization than ever they dreamed of."

He did admire that they "could use an ax or rifle with any man" and said that two of them "could chop the timber and build a cabin in a day and a half."

In the 1850s, an anonymous poetaster immortalized a pair of Pikes in what became nearly as popular a gold rush song as "Oh, Susanna" or "Clementine."

Oh, don't you remember sweet Betsy from Pike,
Who crossed the big mountains with her lover Ike,
With two yoke of oxen, a large yellow dog,
A tall Shanghai rooster and one spotted hog. . . .

Ike the Pike may have been regarded sourly by his neighbors, but to every man in the mines, any Betsy was sweet.

WALTER COLTON OPINED in 1849, "There is no land less relieved by the smiles and soothing caress of woman than California." He went on, as he always did, "If Eden with its ambrosial fruits and guilt-less joys was still sad till the voice of woman mingled with its melodies, California, with all her treasured hills and streams, must be cheerless till she feels the presence of the same enchantress."

By "enchantress," Colton meant the "respectable" woman, and entombed in his hyperbole lay a simple truth: in California in gold rush days, women were scarcer than folding money; and in the mines proper they were scarcer than a hundred-dollar day.

Of the 30,000 emigrants on the western trails in 1849, virtually all of them California-bound, about 3,000 were women. At the close of 1849, California's total population approached 100,000 (excluding Indians), and fewer than 8,000 of these were women. Of these 8,000, Bancroft states, "barely two percent were in the mining districts."

Peter Burnett told a story, no doubt true, of a young man in a mining camp who asked his uncle for the loan of a mule so he could ride forty miles to another camp where, he had learned, a woman had made an appearance.

In the diggings, Bancroft wrote, men would not only travel from afar to catch a glimpse of a newly arrived female, but would "handle in mock or real ecstasy some fragment of female apparel. . . . Even in the cities passers-by would turn to salute a female stranger while the appearance of a little girl would be heralded like that of an angel, many a rugged fellow bending with tears of recollection to give her a kiss and press a golden ounce into her hand." And Mark Twain, in his 1872 book, *Roughing It*, told of dining in San Francisco with a Forty-niner's family and spoke with his daughter, age two or three at the time their ship sailed through the Golden Gate. They were walking the streets, with a servant leading them and carrying the child, Twain reported, when a "huge miner, bearded, belted, spurred, and bristling with deadly weapons," just down from the diggings, barred their way, stopped the servant and gazed at the girl, saying reverently, "Well, if it ain't a child!" He snatched his leather sack from his pocket and said, "There's a hundred and fifty dollars in dust there, and I'll give it to you if you let me kiss the child!"

One of the earliest appeals for women to come to California appeared in a letter and editorial published in the *New York Herald* on January 20, 1849, and dated "Monterey, Upper California, August 27, 1848," seven months after the gold discovery. The letter, signed by Benjamin Park Koozer, a private in the Third U.S. Artillery Regiment at Monterey, was written to a friend and stated that Koozer's company had been reduced from 172 to 20 men due to desertions to the gold fields. With news of the end of the war with Mexico, the private wrote, "I am on the fence as to whether I will desert or not, as I can easily make $150 per day at the mines." After advising his friend to "bundle up your traps and come to California," he ended his letter, "Bring your wife along, for a good wife is the scarcest article in California."

The *Herald* editorialized on January 20, "Now, as most of the emigrants who have lately started for that region are young and enterprising men, and few of them married, we think the best shipment that could be sent hereafter to the gold diggings would be a consignment of young ladies." After a few such consignments, the editorialist wrote, "there would be an excellent chance for clearing off the 'upper shelves'—all those of doubtful age, even verging to and perhaps including a large portion of the old maids."

The writer, perhaps editor James Gordon Bennett Senior, himself, said that "The riches of the mines, and the scarcity of the ladies, persuade us that twenty or thirty cargoes of unmarried women, reaching the Eldorado of money and men, in six or eight months from this time, would be snapped up with more avidity than a similar shipment from England was, in our early history, by the settlers of Virginia."

Of one of the *Herald*'s favorite California correspondents, the writer said, "The Rev. Mr. [Walter] Colton, who is now wading up the shores of the Sacramento, and exploring the ravines of the Sierra Nevada, would make more by marriage fees, if the unruly Christians would only wait for the ceremony, than he could ever do by gathering the raw material."

One who read such newspaper material, looked beyond its tongue-in-cheek humor and felt inspired by the problem, was New Yorker Elizabeth Farnham, a onetime Sing Sing Prison matron, who saw the scarcity of unwed women in California as a potential business opportunity. Late in 1848, after her husband died suddenly in San Francisco and left his affairs in disarray, the widow decided to take passage to the Golden Gate, there to settle Mr. Farnham's debts and collect whatever monies might be due her from his estate. In the weeks she spent preparing for the voyage she learned of the scarcity of marriageable ladies in California and decided to organize a company of them to join her on the journey.

On February 2, 1849, she published a notice to explain her requirements. She sought unmarried women at least twenty-five years old. Each candidate needed to bring from her clergyman or town authority testimonials on her education and character, and each recruit would be required to contribute $250 to defray expenses of the voyage and for "suitable habitation once reaching San Francisco until they are able to enter upon some occupation for their support."

She needed, she said, 100–130 women to enroll and intended that the party would also "include six or eight respectable married men and their families." With the funds in hand she intended to charter the 500-ton steamer *Angelique* "and fit it up with everything necessary for comfort on the voyage." The ship would be ready to sail from New York on April 12, no later than the 15th, 1849, she said.

Horace Greeley's *Tribune* predicted that Mrs. Farnham's "band of female missionaries will be numerous enough to accomplish much in the way of refining and improving the rough California community."

She had convinced others of the efficacy of her mission and was able to append endorsements to her appeal from such notables as Greeley, William Cullen Bryant of the *New York Evening Post*, and Henry Ward Beecher, the influential minister of the Plymouth Congregational Church in Brooklyn. The *Herald*, which had published the Koozer letter and editorial, praised the effort as "an excellent movement" and predicted, "It is not improbable that the ships containing the feminine cargo will be boarded at a distance from land, and every young woman engaged before the vessels reach the harbor of San Francisco." The presence of "a number of respectable women in California would exercise a most happy influence on the morality of that country," the *Herald* writer continued. "It would prevent the male population from degenerating into a state of semi-barbarism."

Mrs. Farnham received over two hundred letters responding to the circular but fell ill during the planning and was unable to continue promoting and organizing the venture. As a result, by the time she had recovered enough to make the voyage, the entire scheme had collapsed and she traveled to the Pacific with her two sons and a regular complement of steamer passengers.

Even so, the Farnham plan was enthusiastically publicized in the eastern press and called attention to California's peculiar problem.

ESTIMATES OF THE number of women in San Francisco in 1849 and the early 1850s vary madly, the confusion due largely to the insistence of some writers in separating the "respectable" females—mostly miners' wives—from the "others." The others, at least in the beginning, were vastly in the majority.

Herbert Asbury, historian of the underworlds of New York, New Orleans, and the Barbary Coast of San Francisco, estimated that there were no more than 300 females in San Francisco for a year after the gold discovery and that two-thirds of these were harlots from Mexico, Peru, and Chile, occupying tents and board shanties around Clark's Point and on the eastern and southern slopes of Telegraph Hill.

He says that in the first six months of 1850 about a thousand women, mostly prostitutes, arrived in San Francisco from France—the *demi-monde* from the bagnios of Paris, Marseilles, and elsewhere in Europe, and from the eastern and southern United States, principally New York and New Orleans. The French women, experienced *belles horizontales*, often attended by their pimps, called *macquereaux*, or "macks," were much sought after as partners at fancy dress and masquerade balls. Some of these "Californicators," as one newspaper wag dubbed them, even became "respectable" by marrying prominent citizens, giving rise to a popular rhyme:

> *The miners came in Forty-nine,*
> *The whores in Fifty-one;*
> *And when they got together*
> *They produced the native son.*

Actually, the first prostitutes to reach San Francisco in '49 came from Valparaiso, Chile. Some of these women married miners but most were destined for "Fandango Houses," the cheapest brothels in the town.

José Fernández, the first *alcalde* of San José after the American takeover, said of these first "sporting women": "They did not pay passage on the ships, but when they reached San Francisco the captains sold them to the highest bidder. There were men who, as soon as any ship arrived from Mexican ports with a load of women, took two or three small boats, or a launch, went on board the ship, paid to the captain the passage of ten or twelve unfortunates and took them immediately to their cantinas, where the newcomers were forced to prostitute themselves for half a year, during which the proprietors took the bulk of their earnings."

China, like Chile, received news of the gold discovery before the end of 1848, and at the height of the rush, San Francisco's Chinatown had hundreds of girls imported for prostitution. They were sold to brothel-keepers for $300 to $3,000, depending upon their age, physical condition, and beauty.

Bancroft says that in 1850 more women arrived in California "although composed largely of loose elements," from Mazatlán, and San Blas, "on trust, and transferred to bidders [pimps] with whom the girls shared their earnings." Many came from Australia, he wrote, and French women were brought out to preside at gambling tables, presumably because their exotic accents and Gallic charm drew crowds. Indian women, too, were "freely offered at the camps and the number was increased by kidnapped females from the Marquesas Islands." Upon the landing of these new arrivals at the San Francisco wharves, steamer agents would cry out, "Ladies on board!" and proprietors of "public resorts"—saloons and gambling parlors—would board the vessels, the historian said, "to offer flattering engagements."

There were, naturally, "good" women coming in as well. Some, such as Elizabeth Farnham had planned, and found ways to earn a fair living supplying other needs than those of the flesh. Most of the work was "domestic": Laundresses were in high demand in the towns and diggings during times when some miners had to ship their filthy clothing to the Sandwich Islands or even to China and wait six months for their return. Women also hired out as seamstresses, camp cooks, and housekeepers, and a few opened shops and trade stores, supplementing their husbands' chancy income from the mines in the manner of Sarah Royce and her husband at Weberville.

IN JANUARY 1850, there arrived in San Francisco a particularly gifted woman who was anxious to take a look at "that most piquant specimen of brute creation, the California 'Elephant.'" Louise Amelia Knapp Smith Clapp saw it and memorialized it so brilliantly that contemporaries such as Bret Harte, Mark Twain, Josiah Royce (son of Sarah), Alonzo Delano, H. H. Bancroft, and a regiment of writers and historians that followed her owed her an unpayable debt.

She set down her record of the gold rush in twenty-three luminous letters to her sister Mary Jane, whom she addressed by the family nickname "Molly." Written between September 13, 1851, and November 21, 1852, the correspondence described her life at Rich Bar and nearby Indian Bar on the north fork of the Feather River, about 120 miles northeast of Sacramento. Because of her razorish wit, her alertness to the fractions as well as the whole of life in that speck of a place among the immensity of the diggings, and her sense of the essential sad futility of the gold hunger, Rich Bar came to epitomize the entire Eldorado adventure.

The letters, clearly intended for publication as well as for communication to her beloved sister, subsequently appeared under the *nom de plume* "Dame Shirley" in a short-lived San Francisco literary journal, *The Pioneer: or, California Monthly Magazine*.

Born in Elizabeth, New Jersey, in 1819, the daughter of a schoolmaster and related to Julia Ward Howe, Louise Smith grew up in her father's hometown of Amherst, Massachusetts, in the time of a New England literary renaissance. As a teenager, orphaned and living with family members, she attended a female seminary and subsequently Amherst Academy, and is said to have become acquainted with Emily Dickinson, Helen Hunt Jackson, and other Boston-area poets and novelists.

In 1848, Louise married Fayette Clapp, a recent graduate of the Boston University School of Medicine. Dr. Clapp, five years her junior, seems to have been in delicate health and with the news of California gold in eastern newspapers, thought the climate of the Pacific coast might cure him of his agues and biliousnesses. Louise was delighted at the prospect of seeing the Pacific Ocean and so the

newlyweds packed their trunks, boarded the steamer *Manila* and
sailed from New York Harbor in August 1849, bound for Cape Horn
and the Golden Gate.

After a year in San Francisco, where her husband's croups and
fevers worsened in the foggy dampness, they decided to move inland
and in June 1851, Dr. Clapp set out with a friend to Rich Bar, the
diggings discovered the previous summer by gold hunters straggling
home from their futile search for "Gold Lake." Clapp hoped the good
mountain air would invigorate him and that he might discover good
mining investments at the camp as well as open a profitable medical
practice.

Prospects turned out to be better than he expected and he bought
lodgings, returned for Louise in September, and provided her with
household help. This was an unusual thing in the vagrant life of a
mining camp, but a well-off New England physician and his genteel
wife were unusual residents.

In her first letter to her sister, in which she used her pen name, a
combination of a childhood nickname with a vaguely British-
sounding title preceding it, she said: "I can figure to myself your
whole surprised attitude, as you exclaim, 'What in the name of all
that is restless, has sent 'Dame Shirley' to Rich Bar? How did such a
shivering, frail, home-loving little thistle ever float safely to that far
away spot, and take root so kindly, as it evidently has, in that barbarous
soil?" She supplied an answer: "You know I am a regular Nomad in
my passion for wandering."

En route by wagon to the camp she saw a band of Indians, a dozen
men and their women "with an unknown quantity of pappooses,"
and received the first blow to her Eastern conception of the Noble
Savage. She was struck by "the extreme beauty of the *limbs* of the
Indian women of California," she said, and the "silken jet" of their
hair, "Though for haggardness of expression, and ugliness of feature,
they might have been taken for a band of Macbethian witches." She
was appalled by "the general hideousness of the faces of these
'squaws,'" the disgustingly filthy chemises of a certain "wild-wood
Cleopatra." The Indian women "are very filthy in their habits," she
wrote, adding that "if one of them should venture out into the rain,
grass would grow on her neck and arms."

Because of the miner traffic in and out of Rich Bar and Indian
Bar, Louise observed and sometimes met white and black Americans,

Californios, Mexicans, Chileños (all Spanish-speakers she called
"Spaniards"), Frenchmen, Swedes, Sandwich Islanders, Englishmen,
Italians, and Germans: "You will hear in the same day, almost at the
same time, the lofty melody of the Spanish language, the piquant pol-
ish of the French . . . the silver, changing clearness of the Italian, the
harsh gargle of the German, the hissing precision of the English,
the liquid sweetness of the Kanaka and the sleep-inspiring languor
of the East Indian. To complete the catalog, there is the *native* Indian,
with his gutteral vocabulary of twenty words!"

Of the black men at Indian Bar, she wrote of "Ned Paganini," proprietor of the Humbolt [sic] Hotel, and the mountain man Jim Beckwourth. Of the latter, she wrote: "He is fifty years of age, perhaps, and
speaks several languages to perfection. As he has been a wanderer for
many years and for a long time was principal chief of the Crow Indians, his adventures are extremely interesting."

Rich Bar had a combination inn, restaurant, and general store
called the Empire Saloon and Rooming House in the only two-story
building, and the only building with glass windows, in a camp trying
to be a town. The Empire had been built as a brothel-saloon combination, with monte tables and a bar built of rough planks roofed with
flapping canvas. At Dame Shirley's advent in Rich Bar, the Empire
barroom was decorated with scarlet drapery—"that eternal crimson
calico," she called it—fluted and puckered into rosettes at the corners,
and the bar itself was of planed and sanded pine behind which was
hung a magnificent mirror, shelves of decanters, vases of cigars, and
jars of brandied fruits. In the gambling rooms she found rough coun-
ters piled with an assortment of wares: velveteen coats, shoes, flannel
shirts, bolts of calico, and such comestibles as hams, preserved meats,
oysters, potatoes, and onions. There were stacks of cheap novels there
but also less-well-thumbed copies of works by Shakespeare, Spenser,
Coleridge, Burns, Keats, Shelley, Dickens, and even a copy of Isaac
Walton's *The Compleat Angler*, all of which she bought and read.

The gambling at the Empire shocked her. "The Monte fiend
ruined hundreds!" she wrote to Molly. "Shall I tell you the fate of
two of the most successful of these gold hunters? From poor men,
they found themselves at the end of a few weeks, absolutely rich.
Elated with their good fortune, seized with a mania for Monte, in less
than a year, these unfortunates—so lately respectable and intelligent—became a pair of drunken gamblers. One of them at this pre-

sent writing, works for five dollars a day and boards himself out of that; the other actually suffers for the necessities of life—a too common result of scenes in the mines."

But whatever she found that was ugly, she discovered tenfold more that was noble and exquisite in her surroundings: "I wish I could give you some faint idea of the majestic solitudes," she wrote, "where the pine trees rise so grandly in their awful height, that they seem looking into Heaven itself." On the trail to Rich Bar, she said, "Hardly a living thing disturbed this solemnly beautiful wilderness. Now and then . . . a golden butterfly flitted languidly blossom to blossom. Sometimes a saucy little squirrel would gleam along the sombre trunk of some ancient oak, or a bevy of quails, with their pretty tufted heads and short, quick, tread, would trip athwart our path."

She wrote lyrically of "the ceaseless river-psalm" of the Feather and its forks where "A hundred tiny rivulets flash down from the brow of the mountains, as if some mighty Titan, standing on the other side, had flung athwart their greenness, a chaplet of radiant pearls." She saw stately deer, roadrunners, lizards "jerking up their impudent little heads above a moss-wrought log," and rattlesnakes. She admired the "still, solemn cedars, the sailing smoke-wreath and vaulted splendor above," "The feathery fringe of fir-trees" that "glitter like emerald," the daphnes, irises, violets, pale wood anemones, tiger lilies, wild roses, buttercups, flox, and privets; and certain "eldritch bushes . . . of a ghastly whiteness" which "reminded me of a plantation of antlers."

There were four other women at Rich Bar, she discovered, and naturally came to know them all.

Mrs. Bancroft, "landlord" at the Empire, cooked with a two-month-old baby kicking and bawling in a makeshift cradle made from a champagne basket.

"Mrs. R—" lived with her husband in a three-room "canvas house" and was much admired by the miners. One of them told Louise, "Magnificent woman that. A wife of the right sort she is. Why, she earnt her old man nine hundred dollars in nine weeks, clear of all expenses, by washing!"

Nancy Bailey, a tiny, birdlike woman, shared a dirt-floored cabin with her miner husband and three children. She died of peritonitis soon after the Clapps' arrival and was carried to her grave in a coffin with a green Monte cloth as a pall.

And "Indiana Girl," the first woman to arrive at Rich Bar, ran the Indiana Hotel—little more than a shack with pallets on the floor—with her father. She was a huge woman and, said Louise, "The far-off roll of her mighty voice, booming through two closed doors and a long entry, added greatly to the severe attack of nervous headache under which I was suffering when she called." This "gentle creature," she said, "wears the thickest kind of miner's boots, and has the dainty habit of wiping her dishes on her apron! Last spring she walked to this place and packed fifty pounds of flour on her back down that awful hill—the snow being five feet deep at the time."

Several miners were smitten with Indiana Girl, including "Yank," a cabin storekeeper up the bar who had "the most comical *olla podrida* ["rotten pot"] of heterongenous merchandise that I ever saw. There is nothing you can ask for but what he has—from crow bars down to cambric needles; from velveteen trowsers up to broadcloth coats of the jauntiest description." In addition, she said, Yank had the greatest collection of greasy, yellow-covered novels on the river.

Dr. Clapp's "office" at Rich Bar lay at the end of a footbridge of mossy, bark-wrapped logs that had been thrown athwart the bar of the Feather. "When I entered this imposing place," Louise recalled, "the shock to my optic nerves was so great that I sank, helplessly, upon one of the benches which ran divan-like, the whole length (ten feet!) of the building, and laughed till I cried." The floorless cabin, she said, had in one corner a crude tablelike fixture, on which was arranged the doctor's medical library, consisting of half a dozen volumes, and some shelves, "which looked like sticks snatched hastily from the wood-pile and nailed up without the least alteration," holding "quite a respectable array of medicines."

Even in so primitive a setting, her husband practiced serious medicine, even to performing a successful amputation of the crushed leg of a young miner.

The Clapps' home cabin lay upstream from Rich Bar at a place called Indian Bar and Louise did her best to make it homey. She described to Molly the twenty-foot-square room hung with a gaudy chintz, and a curtain dividing off a portion of the space to serve as a bedroom. The fireplace was built of stones and mud, the mantelpiece fashioned from a wooden beam covered with strips of tin "upon which still remain in black hieroglyphics, the names of the different eatables which they formerly contained." A two-foot-square hole served as a window, "innocent of glass," and covered with a cloth. The cabin was ingeniously illuminated, she said, "with three feet of a log on one side of the room removed and replaced with glass jars, formerly holding brandied fruits, the spaces between daubed with clay."

No image, photograph or drawing, of Louise seems to have survived. In his *San Francisco's Literary Frontier*, Franklin Walker describes her as "a small, fair, golden-haired bluestocking from New England, a dainty adventurer with a sturdy soul who was wearing her yellow curls down to her shoulders when she stepped from the *Manila* after rounding the Horn in '49."

Louise described herself as an "obstinate little personage, who has always been haunted with a passionate desire to do everything which people said she could not do." She proudly wrote Molly on November 25, 1851, "I have become a mineress; that is, if having washed a pan of dirt with my own hands, and procured therefrom three dollars and twenty-five cents in gold dust (which I shall enclose in this letter), will entitle me to the name. I can truly say, with the blacksmith's apprentice at the close of his first day's work at the anvil, that 'I'm sorry I learned the trade,' for I wet my feet, tore my dress, spoilt a pair of new gloves, nearly froze my fingers, got an awful headache, took cold and lost a valuable breastpin, in this my labor of love."

Louise Amelia Clapp became a student of gold mining, learned the lore of the diggings, and wrote excitedly to her sister on arcane features of "Nature's great lottery scheme."

Miners generally congregated in "companies" of six or more, she wrote, and named their group after their home area—the Illinois, the Bunker Hill, the Bay State Company. "Our countrymen are the most discontented of mortals. They are always longing for 'big strikes.' If a 'claim' is paying them a steady income, by which, if they pleased, they could lay up for more in a month than they could accumulate in a year at home, still, they are dissatisfied, and in most cases, will wander off in search of better 'diggings.'"

She admired those who came to the diggings from across the plains and said she "always had a strange fancy for that Nomadic way of coming to California." She dreamed of lying down under starry skies, hundreds of miles from human habitation, and to rise up on dewy mornings "to pursue our way through a strange country, so wildly beautiful, seeing each day something new and wonderful." Such enchanting ideas, she said, were erased by the cruel reality of seeing women arrive in the Feather River camps "looking as haggard as so many Endorean witches; burnt to the color of a hazel-nut, with their hair cut short, and its gloss entirely destroyed by the alkali, whole plains of which they are compelled to cross on the way." She learned in talking with the emigrants that "You will hardly find a family that has not left some beloved one buried upon the plains," and told of "a young widow of twenty, whose husband died of cholera when they were but five weeks on their journey. He was a Judge in one of the Western states, and a man of some eminence in his profession. She is a pretty little creature, and all the aspirants to matrimony are candidates for her hand."

ONE CONTINUING FEATURE of Dame Shirley's letters that must have shocked her sister was the startlingly vivid description of violence that Louise either witnessed or wrote from information supplied by others.

On December 15, 1851, she wrote of miners' justice in the case of two men arrested on suspicion of having stolen $1,800 in gold dust from their partners. Hard evidence was lacking and the miners were acquitted and quickly decamped from Indian Bar for Marysville. Then, a few weeks later, one of the men, a Swede, returned to the area, loafing around the saloons, drinking heavily and pretending to be searching for a claim at Rich Bar. The miners whose dust had been pilfered laid a trap for him, preparing a coyote hole with brush and rocks in it covering a money belt. The pit was soon rifled, the money belt cut open, and when the plotters confronted the Swede, who went under the name "William Brown," he confessed. He told the men where they could find $600 of the missing dust, under the blankets of his bunk, and said his partner had taken the rest "to the States."

A miner's meeting was called and the thief sentenced: "That William Brown, convicted of stealing, etc., should, in one hour from that time, be hung by the neck until he was dead." Actually the Swede was allowed three hours to prepare, Louise said, and spent them writing letters to friends in Stockholm. By the time the noose was placed around his neck he was drunk, helped by some friend who smuggled whiskey to him in his guarded room.

"The execution was conducted by the jury, and was performed by throwing the cord, one end of which was attached to the neck of the prisoner, across the limb of a tree standing outside of the Rich Bar graveyard," Louise wrote. "Then all, who felt disposed to engage in so revolting a task, lifted the poor wretch from the ground; in the most awkward manner possible. The whole affair, indeed, was a piece of cruel butchery. . . . In truth, life was only crushed out of him, by hauling the writhing body up and down several times in succession."

She said the Swede hung on display for several hours during which time it began snowing and when those "whose business was to inter the remains, arrived at the spot, they found him enwrapped in a soft, white shroud of feather snow-flakes, as if pitying Nature had tried to hide from the offended face of heaven, the cruel deed which her mountain children had committed."

On August 4, 1852, she wrote her sister, "In the short space of twenty-four days, we have had murders, fearful accidents, bloody deaths, a mob, whippings, a hanging, an attempt at suicide, and a fatal duel." She wrote of a Mr. Bacon who kept a ranch about twelve miles from Rich Bar who was murdered and robbed by his black servant, a man named Josh, who had worked for several families in the settlement. A volunteer posse apprehended Josh in Sacramento and found he had some of Bacon's gold in his possession. The black man was brought back in chains to Rich Bar where he was sentenced to be hanged: "And so he 'died and made no sign,' with a calm indifference," Louise wrote. "The dreadful crime and the death of 'Josh,' who having been an excellent cook, and very neat and respectful, was a favorite servant with us, added to the unhappiness."

Much of the violence she reported had nationalistic overtones: "For some time past, there has been a gradually increasing state of bad feeling exhibited by our countrymen . . . toward foreigners. In this affair, our countrymen were principally to blame, or rather I should say, Sir John Barley Corn, for many of the ringleaders are fine young men, who, when sober, are decidedly friendly to the Spaniards."

In the winter of 1852, in a troubled time when deep snows were preventing mule teams from bringing supplies to the claims, resulting in the Clapps and others subsisting on flour, "dark ham," salted mackerel, and "rusty" pork, she wrote, "A few evenings ago, a Spaniard was stabbed by an American. It seems that the presumptious foreigner had the impertinence to ask very humbly and meekly

of that most notable representative of the stars and stripes, if the latter would pay him a few dollars which he had owed him for some
time. His high mightiness, the Yankee, was not going to pay up with
any such impertinence, and the poor Spaniard received, for answer,
several inches of cold steel in his breast. Nothing was done and very
little was said about this atrocious affair."

One atrocity she witnessed may have had a historic significance in
the mythology of early California.

She wrote her sister of the growing xenophobia of the miners, of
the monthly tax imposed on non-Americans for the right to stake
and work claims, and the savage reprisals, against the "Spaniards," in
particular, she witnessed at the hands of vigilance committees. One
of these was a mass flogging that apparently took place at Indian Bar.

"Oh Mary! Imagine my anguish when I heard the first blow fall
upon those wretched men. I had never thought that I should be compelled to hear such fearful sounds, and, although I immediately buried
my head in my shawl, nothing can efface from memory the disgust
and horror." She described one of the victims as "a very gentlemanly
young Spaniard who implored for death in the most moving terms.
He appealed to his judges in the most eloquent manner—as gentlemen, as men of honor; representing to them that to be deprived of
life was nothing in comparison with the never-to-be-effaced stain of
the vilest convict's punishment to which they had sentenced him."
All this was to no avail, she said, and "Finding all his entreaties disre-
garded, he swore a most solemn oath, that he would murder every
American that he should chance to meet alone, and as he is a man of
the most dauntless courage, and rendered desperate by a burning
sense of disgrace . . . he will doubtless keep his word."

Some historical writers believe that this letter inspired the flogging
scene in *The Life and Adventures of Joaquín Murieta* by John Rollin
Ridge, the 1854 novel that started the Murieta legend. Gold rush historian Joseph Henry Jackson states that the Dame Shirley letters were
in the possession of Ferdinand Ewer, the Harvard-educated editor of
The Pioneer of San Francisco, when Ridge was "researching" his book
on Murieta and that Ridge frequently visited Ewer's office.

NOT ALL HER letters to Molly were exclusively on incidents and
impressions of the California mines. For such a self-professed free

spirit and resolute chance-taker, Louise occasionally adopted the attitude of a true Victorian woman—even writing like Queen Victoria,
who was much given to underlinings for emphasis—when considering what was ladylike and what was not.

Amelia Jenks Bloomer, a Seneca Falls, New York, temperance
leader, introduced female pantaloons, subsequently named for her, in
July 1848, as a protest against hooped skirts and similar awkward garments for women. Chances are Louise learned of this development
before she left Massachusetts, but what incident at Indian Bar inspired
her to protest the "ladies' rights" movement in the east is unknown.

She wrote to Molly, "How *can* women—many of whom, I am
told, are *really* interesting and intelligent, how *can* they spoil their
pretty mouths and ruin their beautiful complexions, by demanding
with Xantippian *fervor*, in the presence, often, of a vulgar, irreverent
mob, what the gentle creatures are pleased to call their 'rights'? How
can they wish to soil the delicate texture of their airy fancies, by pon-
dering over the wearying stupidities of Presidential elections, or the
bewildering mystifications of rabid metaphysicians? And, above all,
how *can* they so far forget the sweet, shy coquetries of shrinking
womanhood, as to don those horrid 'Bloomers'? As for me, although
a *wife*, I never wear the————, well you know what they call
them. . . . I confess to an almost religious veneration for trailing
drapery, and I pin my vestural faith with unflinching obstinacy to
sweeping petticoats."

In later years, divorced from Dr. Clapp and less wedded to Victorian ideas of ladyhood, Dame Shirley became an an admirer of the
social reformer Margaret Fuller.

IN THE WINTER of 1852, Louise Clapp's "whole world" at Indian
Bar was "dead broke," with shopkeepers, restaurants, hotels, and gambling dens closed and only about twenty miners remaining to work
the played-out claims.

In her last letter, dated November 21, 1852, she fretted over the
prospect of spending another "dreadful winter at Indian Bar," yet
when it came to moving, wrote, "My heart is heavy at the thought of
departing forever from this place. I like this wild and barbarous life; I
leave it with regret. . . . Yes, Molly, smile if you will at my folly; but I
go from the mountains with a deep heart sorrow. I look kindly to this

existence, which to you seems so sordid and mean. Here at last I have been contented. . . . You would hardly recognize the feeble and half-dying invalid, who drooped languidly out of sight, as night shut down between your straining gaze and the good ship *Manila* . . . in the person of your now perfectly healthy sister."

≋ Levi's & Studebakers ≋

LEVI STRAUSS, BORN in Buttenheim, Bavaria, in 1829, had a successful business as a clothier in New York before sailing around Cape Horn for California in 1852 to join a brother-in-law in a dry-goods business.

He had a stock of cloth with him on the voyage and sold most of it to the passengers en route, landing in San Francisco with a single bolt of canvas tenting material remaining. According to one story, its veracity unknown, Strauss met a miner on the waterfront who bought the canvas to make a pair of heavy trousers. This encounter may have been the inspiration for the industry to come. With a tailor-partner from Nevada, Strauss patented a design for durable, bibless, work trousers with copper reinforcing seam rivets that came to be called Levi's, and by the end of the century his San Francisco plant, employing five hundred workers, was grossing $1 million a year.

Strauss died in 1902.

JAMES LICK, A Pennsylvanian of Dutch ancestry, came to California from Lima, Peru, seventeen days before James Marshall's gold discovery. He brought with him an iron safe filled with $30,000 in gold coins, his savings from a twenty-five-year career as a piano-maker in South America, and began buying lots in San Francisco, at first paying $16 for each. He kept buying them until September 1848, when they were selling at $3,000, and by the fall of 1849, after spending less than $7,000 of his savings, had become the richest man in town, richer even than Sam Brannan, and infinitely more eccentric.

Lick tried his hand in the Mormon Island mines briefly, but his talent was as a financier in land development. For many years, he dressed like a hobo, lived in a shack, and drove a rickety wagon around his properties in northern California. Among his philanthropical works was a bequest of $700,000 to build Lick Observatory on Mount Hamilton, California.

He died, still rich, in 1876.

PHILIP DANFORTH ARMOUR of Stockbridge, New York, walked to California in six months and started work as a ditch digger in the mining camps. He saved $8,000 in five years and opened a butcher shop in Placerville. When he moved to Milwaukee a few years later he continued to build his business into the great Armour & Co. meat packing empire.

JOHN M. STUDEBAKER also began his fortune at Placerville in 1852. He was the son of a prominent wagon-maker in South Bend, Indiana, and had his own modest wagon shop there before his California days where he began work making wheelbarrows for miners. He, like Armour, saved $8,000 in five years, returned to Indiana and joined his brothers in forming the largest and most famous carriage works in the world, and subsequently the Studebaker Automobile Company.

SEVENTEEN

SODOM-BY-THE-SEA

"STRETCHED AWAY BEFORE me is the world of San Francisco—and what a world!" wrote Daniel Woods, the Massachusetts Forty-niner who spent sixteen goldless months in the mines. "How the tide of human life flows and dashes upon its shores! Crowds every day arrive, and other crowds every day leave. Old friends meet, exchange a few words, and hasten on to the shrine of Mammon. Multitudes die, and the waves close over them, and they are forgotten."

At the end of 1850, when he was waiting to board the French ship *Chateaubriand* bound for Panama, he described San Francisco as "a moral whirlpool. . . . Often, Phoenix-like, arisen from its ashes. . . . Civilized, semi-barbarous, and savage."

As he prepared to return home, Bayard Taylor made notes on the city's sartorial progress, how well certain businessmen were doing with the gold they were reaping from the ill-dressed, but he could not wholly avoid the grimmer side of San Francisco life. He wrote of the fevers, agues, and attacks of dysentery that afflicted the citizenry, and of City Hospital with its "hopeless lunatics, some of them produced by disappointment and ill luck, and others by sudden increase of fortune."

Taylor stood in wonderment at the spectacle in the gaming rooms of San Francisco's El Dorado Saloon; Woods said of the gaming parlors, "A volume could not describe their splendor or their fatal attraction." Indeed, virtually all who came to San Francisco and the mining settlements during the gold rush agreed that rats, lice, and cholera paled as scourges compared to the disease of gambling that drove so many men to madness, murder, and suicide.

Julius Pratt of Connecticut, who also failed to find gold in '49, said as he prepared to return home in the spring of 1851 that with San Francisco's populace numbering over 30,000, "Thousands of men organized in bands or wholly disorganized, were arriving from every part of the world. . . . Hundreds of outlaws and professional gamblers opened their saloons at every point where men congregated. . . . Money was scattered everywhere as if by the wind."

The English traveler Frank Marryat was awed by the gambling epidemic he witnessed at Sonora in the southern mines; Dame Shirley was shocked by the waste and tragedy gambling created in her beloved Rich Bar and Indian Bar; the eminent Californio Mariano Vallejo, from his estate in Sonora, cursed the day the gamblers came to his native land.

Like the whores, the gamblers came in 1849, from New Orleans, Natchez, Memphis, St. Louis, and other open towns, and found San Francisco to be a sporting man's paradise.

In the 1854 *Annals of San Francisco*, the authors state, "Gambling was *the* amusement—*the* grand occupation of many classes—apparently the life and soul of the place in gold rush times." Around the gaming tables, they wrote, "the players often stood in lines three or four deep, everyone vying with his neighbors for the privilege of reaching the board and staking his money as fast as the wheel and ball could be rolled or the card turned."

The year before this was recorded, San Francisco had 537 saloons, virtually all of them gambling dens, as were the forty-eight places listed as "kept by bawds."

Gaming places were called "spreads" by the man in the street, and the best of the bad lot of them were palatial hotel-saloons, with imported chandeliers, gilt mirrors, thick (most often scarlet) carpeting, a band or orchestra platform, and immense mahogany bars decorated with paintings of beefy, languorous nudes—"meretricious pictures of naked ladies," Daniel Knower called them. In these establishments, food, and often drinks, were free, to the big players at least, and barkeeps were kept busy washing and filling tumblers in answer to the dealer's bell announcing that the roisterers at his table were thirsty again. Another bartender duty at such places was operating the "blower," a square, funnel-shaped box into which gold dust was poured in a trickle onto a balance tray. A puff of air was blown across the gold stream to rid it of fine sand and other impurities.

Knower recalled the gambling spreads he visited in the city as filled with a motley assortment of classes and nationalities: "Mexicans in dirty serapes jostled the preacher with his soiled white necktie, and the lawyer touched glasses at the bar with his red-shirted client from the mines," he said. Nor was age a deterrent. In all but the uppermost of the upper-crust halls, twelve-year-old boys bellied, or chinned, up to the tables if they had the coins to be plucked by the cheroot-smoking dealers yelling "Do you bet?", the origin of the expression "You bet!".

Every opportunity for a man to go broke was made available in the saloons and gambling parlors of San Francisco in the days of the gold rush. The games, and there were a bewildering number of them, ranged from the more-or-less honest and sophisticated to patent, streetside swindles.

Faro grew to be the great gold rush game, especially favored by American and English players. So named for the King of Hearts being called "the Pharaoh," it was also called "Tiger" from the Bengal tigers decorating the cloths or backdrops of a faro layout. ("Bucking the tiger" was playing the game against the house, or "going for broke"—broke being the common affliction among faro players). The oilcloth faro spread depicted the thirteen cards of a suit and players bet on the order in which certain cards would appear when taken singly from the top of the dealer's spring-loaded box.

Monte, originally "montebank," had some similarities to faro but used a "Spanish deck" of forty-eight cards (the tens missing) and had many variations. One was for the player to select two of four cards laid face-up on the table and bet on one to be matched before the other as the deck was dealt a card at a time. The game fell into disrepute, especially with the rise of the sharper's version, "three-card monte." This variation was played with three cards, usually face cards, shown to the bettor, then thrown down by the sleight-of-hand master serving as dealer while a bet is made on the position of the "winning card."

Three-card monte differed little from the "thimble rig," in which the manipulator hid a pea under one of three thimbles, more commonly nutshells—hence "the shell game." The bettor tried to guess where the pea was located—invariably making the wrong guess. The prevalence of crooked monte dealers gave rise to the common use of "mountebank" to mean charlatan or fraud.

The street-corner barrelhead or upended crate where the thimble rigger or three-card monte sharp hawked his game to passers-by was nether end of the array of gambling games offered in San Francisco in gold rush days.

Vingt-et-un, called "Van John" in England, and "twenty-one" or "blackjack" in America, was favored for its simplicity and the belief that with a "straight" dealer, the bettor had a chance to win.

Rouge-et-noir (also called *trente-et-quarante* among the cognoscenti, and "red and black" among the miner bourgeois) was played at a table marked with two red and two black diamond-shaped spots where the stakes were played.

Roulette and craps tables were always three-deep in waiting bettors; lotteries were popular and ticket drawings drew throngs; and at the bar the gambler could lose his dust at chuck-a-luck, played by turning a cone- or horn-shaped tin cage containing dice and betting on certain numbers turning up. The game gave rise to the word "tinhorn," a gambler with little style or means. From "piking," or betting against the odds in the game of monte, came the word "piker." It had nothing to do with the Pike County Missourians but instead, after monte games fell into disfavor, came to mean a timid bettor.

Minor interest was given to lansquenet, a German card game, the name deriving from *landsknecht*, a lance knight or mercenary soldier; keno, a lotto game, the forerunner of bingo; and diversions such as rondo, and strap-and-pin, the rules for which do not seem to have survived. Another of these oddities was called "tub and ball," and thanks to Daniel Knower we know how it was played. "The meanest among many cut-throat games," he said it was played with a four- or five-inch ball rolled in a tub lined with velvet. "The ball was covered with different colored spots about the size of a quarter-dollar and whichever color is uppermost when the ball stops wins," Knower said, adding that the ball was always suspected of being rigged by "a mysterious combination of springs, etc." known only to the unscrupulous manipulator.

Bets on the games, depending on the elaborateness of their headquarters, ranged from fifty cents in a dive to hundreds or even thousands in a fancy gaming house or saloon. As in every gamblers' town, San Francisco generated countless stories of fortunes wagered on the turn of a card.

Knower witnessed one incident in which a miner brought a $5,000 bag of dust to a monte table, bet $1,000 on a certain card and lost. "While I was looking at him in the course of half an hour, he lost it all." A minister named E. A. Upton recorded in his diary at the end of 1849 a much rarer story: "A young man just returned [to San Francisco] from the mines with his entire summer worth, amounting to 150 ounces gold, went into a gambling establishment and lost all but eight ounces when his luck turned and he won it all back again together with six ounces in addition, then he quit. . . ."

Frank Marryat, who had traveled the world and seen its seamiest places, pronounced San Francisco during the gold rush, in particular its gambling degradation, as "Sodom-by-the-Sea."

SAN FRANCISCO'S FIRST notable gambling emporium, built early in 1849, was the two-story Parker House facing Portsmouth Square, a block or so west of the Washington Street Wharf. Empresario Robert A. Parker invested $30,000 in the structure, at first, planning it as a hotel. After miners began thronging the town with their gold pokes, searching for liquor and a game of chance, Parker began leasing space to gamblers and the astronomical prices he charged were indicative of the profits to be made both by gamblers and their landlords. Ten thousand dollars *a month* rented the second floor of the Parker House with three faro tables, two for monte, a roulette wheel, and a private game room where particularly high rollers could play a night of poker—too slow a game for the average miner—or whatever was their pleasure.

The El Dorado, the first gambling house opened after the gold discovery, appeared practically overnight under a canvas tent on the corner of Kearney and Washington at Portsmouth Square and was soon converted into a large square room of rough boards and a few private booths partitioned off with muslin drapes. Within a few months, its success insured by the steady influx of thirsty, gold-squandering miners, a more substantial structure went up. Its walls were covered with bunting, flags, huge cut glass mirrors, and costly paintings of nude women in various lewd poses. On a raised platform at one end of the main barroom, singers and musicians appeared, and when they were not on stage an "orchestrion," a complex barrel organ–like device that gave a faintly discernible imitation of a full-blown orchestra, wheezed and bellowed through the day and night.

Behind the El Dorado's opulent bar operated jovial "Professor" Jerry Thomas, inventor of the Tom and Jerry and the Blue Blazer, and later author of *The Bon Vivant's Companion, or, How to Mix Drinks*.

Bayard Taylor visited the saloon in 1850 and described the crowds gathered around its eight gaming tables: "Copper-hued Kanakas, Mexicans rolled in their serapes, and Peruvians thrust through their ponchos, stand shoulder to shoulder with brown and bearded American miners. The stakes are generally small, though when the bettor gets into a 'streak of luck' as it is called, they are allowed to double [their bets] until all is lost or the bank breaks." Along the end of the room, he said, was a spacious bar, "supplied with all kinds of bad liquors, and in a sort of gallery, suspended under the ceiling, a female violinist tasks her strength of muscle to minister to the excitement of the play."

On or near the Square were other notable gambling places: Dennison's Exchange, which adjoined the Parker House, the Empire, the Rendezvous, the Verandah (where a one-man band performed daily), the Mazourka, the Arcade, the Fontine House, the Varsouvienne, the Ward House, the Alhambra (a female violinist there received two ounces of gold daily in salary, plus tips), and the Águila de Oro (Golden Eagle) where a "Negro Chorus" introduced Southern spiritual songs to California.

Also renowned was the Bella Union which offered a variety of entertainment for its drunks and gamblers—a Mexican quintet of two guitars, two harps, and a flute; a Virginia minstrel show, and a singer-fiddler named Charlie Schultze who introduced the Hawaiian song "Aloha Oe" to California and to its melody sang a lyric titled, "You Never Miss Your Sainted Mother Till She's Dead and Gone to Heaven."

SAN FRANCISCO OFFERED other pleasures and entertainments than those found in smoky saloons and gambling halls, or watching bull-and-bear fights, cock fights, prize fights, and horseraces. Circuses came to town occasionally, and equestrian shows, and many visitors down from the mines as well as full-time denizens of the town enjoyed a sojourn away from the mud, stink, and noise of the streets and sought a quiet place to think, maybe to have a picnic with wife, children, and friends. A favorite such spot was Mission Dolores in the south central part of the peninsula. Properly Misión de la Nuestra Señora de los Dolores—Mission of Our Lady of Sorrows—the church there, built in 1776, was a noble ruin, described by Bret Harte as possessing a "ragged senility contrasting with the smart spring sunshine." It was an easy wagon or horseback trip, high enough for a good view and breeze, and historically inspiring.

But for every such innocent diversion there were a hundred others in the city drawing a thousandfold the number of weekend pick-nickers.

In June 1849, a wandering English lawyer, newspaperman, and entertainer named Stephen C. Massett rented building space on Portsmouth Square, borrowed a piano, and opened a one-man show, the first formal stage presentation in the town independent of the saloons and gambling parlors. As "Jeems Pipes of Pipesville," Massett sang his own compositions, including a falsetto mimicking of an opera diva, and did impersonations and monologues in a Yankee dialect. He charged three dollars admission, cleared as much as $500 a night, and had a comfortably long run.

The more formal launching of San Francisco's theatrical era took place in 1850 with curtain-raisings at such theaters as Washington Hall, the National, the Dramatic Museum, the Adelphi, Dr. Collyer's Athenaeum ("with prurient model artist exhibitions," Bancroft says), and the Jenny Lind, built over the burned-out hulk of the Parker House.

Tom Maguire, the man who spent $100,000 to build the Jenny Lind, became not only San Francisco's greatest theatrical empresario, but was remembered throughout the gold country, and later to Nevada's Comstock Lode, for the performers he brought to the camps and the disasters he endured.

He was a New Yorker by birth and had worked as a hack driver and bartender before discovering his talents as a gambler. In San Franciso in 1849 he amassed a small fortune from his dazzling card-play and was able to buy the fire-devastated Parker House and its land. On the property he built a new saloon and gambling hall, devoting the second floor of the building to his dream—a theater named after the celebrated Swedish Nightingale. (Sadly, although on an American tour with P. T. Barnum as her promoter, Lind did not venture far from the eastern seaboard.)

The new Parker House and Jenny Lind Theater opened in September 1850—and promptly burned down. Maguire rebuilt and nine days before the grand new opening, it burned down again. In all, he lost six buildings in two years but, between fires, his saloons and theaters were so profitable the *San Francisco Herald* was able to report in 1851: "Mr. Thomas Maguire, so often burnt out and as often rising with energies unsubdued by misfortune, is now engaged in constructing a building which will be an ornament to the city."

Among the actors Maguire brought to San Francisco were Joseph Jefferson, Edwin Forrest, David Belasco, Madame Modjeska, Charles Kean, Edwin Booth, and James O'Neill, father of the playright Eugene O'Neill. The showman, who was said to be illiterate, had a passion for Shakespeare and produced California's first *Hamlet*, *Macbeth*, and *The Merchant of Venice*, as well as the operas *Carmen* and *Faust*, Japanese acrobats and jugglers, minstrel and burlesque shows, and such yeasty melodramas as *The Widow's Victor* and *The Spectre Bridegroom*.

Of all of Maguire's dramatic productions, the most notorious and successful was *Mazeppa*, a story of a Cossack hero told in poetry by Byron and in drama by Pushkin. Playing the part of the youthful Ivan Mazeppa, the New Orleans–born actress Adah Isaacs Menken was sensational in the most memorable scene of the play. Wearing flesh-colored tights, creating the illusion that she was nude, she was lashed to a live horse and delivered her lines, her wrist over her brow in lamentation, as the animal sauntered across the stage.

After the last of the fires that destroyed his saloon-theaters, Maguire built an opera house of stone and brick but in the mid-fifties, deep in debt, was forced to sell it to the city for $200,000 for use as a city hall.

He had some successes during the silver booms in Virginia City and Carson City, Nevada, but suffered many reverses as well, including gambling losses. In the mid-1880s, still an imposing, handsome, and elegantly dressed man-about-town, Maguire sold all his San Francisco properties and drifted back to New York City.

He died there, penniless, in 1896.

DAVID GORMAN "YANKEE" Robinson of Maine came close to matching Tom Maguire in his dramatic successes. A Yale graduate and physician, Robinson had toured the east with his temperance play *The Reformed Drunkard* before coming to San Francisco to set up a medical practice and drugstore on Portsmouth Square. In May 1850, he opened a modest "Dramatic Museum" on Montgomery Street, which, like nearly everything in the city at one time or another, burned down. With a partner, he rebuilt. The Little Dramatic Theater on California Street opened on July 15 for vaudeville skits, satires, stories, and songs. Robinson was immensely popular as a comic performer despite giving temperance lectures between curtain calls.

After another fire, he took a troupe of performers to Marysville and Nevada City, and following the success of this undertaking he returned to San Francisco. There, with another associate, he borrowed $65,000 and built a new theater between California and Sacramento Streets. The American Theater opened in October 1851, the largest (seating 2,000) and most opulent in the city. Great Corinthian columns framed the entrance, elegant draperies decorated the walls, golden chandeliers blazed light across the rooms, and a "sun" of hammered gold leaf revolved under its central dome.

"Yankee" Robinson made a considerable coup in 1853 by engaging Lola Montez to perform at the American.

THE GREAT *FEMME FATALE* of her era, Lola reached San Francisco on May 21, 1853, on the steamer *Northerner* out of Panama. Her advent at the end of the gold boom was sadly fitting. She was only thirty-five and, in Joseph Jackson's phrase, "ripely handsome," but she was approaching the end of her gaudily spectacular career.

Born out of wedlock as Eliza Rosanna Gilbert in about 1818 in Limerick, Ireland, she attended school in Bath, England, but hid as much of her early history as she could and constructed several engaging life stories to replace the banal truth. She seems to have married an army officer at age fifteen, left him soon after, and in Europe picked up the rudiments of acting and stage performance, these greatly augmented and made palatable to her audiences by her natural beauty. She was an inch or two over five feet, weighed a little over a hundred pounds, and even in her middle age had a flawless complexion. A miner who saw her in California said "her hair was like a raven's plumage." Her perfect oval face and prominent high cheekbones drew attention to her deep blue eyes—"Oh, my stars, what eyes," the miner said, "large, dark, liquid, and veiled eye lashes which, like mists before the sun, prevent them from dazzling one entirely."

In the 1840s, according to numerous misty reports, she learned some Spanish dances in London, and thereafter represented herself, with a noticeably affected accent, as "Doña Lola Montez," a native of

Seville, the daughter of a Spanish patriot. She performed her dances with rattling castanets, flowing *mantilla*, and a flared red and black skirt which revealed her shapely calves when she spun across the stage.

By the time she sailed for America in 1851, she had a reputation as a notorious courtesan, said to have had affairs with Nicholas I of Russia, Alexandre Dumas *pere*, Prince Henry of Reuss in the Grand Duchy of Baden, King Ludwig I of Bavaria, an Irish lord, several other eminent Europeans and army officers, and Franz Liszt. Of the latter, James Varley, a recent Montez biographer, says she and the pianist-composer "rutted together" for a week in a Warsaw hotel after which Liszt wrote a sonata for her.

The mélange of royal or quasi-royal lovers enabled her to invent the title "Marie Elise Rosanna Dolores, Countess of Lansfeld de Heald, Baroness of Rosenthal and Chainquinesse of the Order of St. Therese," a conglomeration of ersatz names and orders which she sometimes reduced to "Marie, Countess de Lansfeld." Some, including the newspapers who followed her career assiduously, had other titles for her, comparing her to Aspasia (Pericles's mistress who is said to have instigated the Peloponnesian War), Madame Pompadour, and "a modern Cyprian."

She reached New York on the *Humboldt* in December 1851, with bookings at the Broadway Theater where with a troupe of twenty dancers she performed a routine called "Diana and Her Nymphs," she and the nymphs in diaphanous costumes, and an extravaganza of Spanish dances titled "Un Jour de Carneval a Seville."

In San Francisco, where her arrival went largely unnoticed, she took a new lover, one Patrick Purdy Hull, who had sailed to California to supervise the 1850 federal census, decided to stay, and launched a newspaper to compete with the city's other ten dailies.

The announcement that Lola Montez would open at Yankee Robinson's American Theater on May 26, 1853, as Lady Teazle in Sheridan's *School for Scandal*, caused the press to catch up with her as she played to capacity houses for three weeks. The *San Francisco Herald* called her "a lioness"; the *Alta California* wrote of her as "a gallant spirit."

Montez's finest performance, for which she earned $16,000 a week, was her titillating "La Tarantelle," or "Spider Dance." In this lively, music-accompanied act she scuttled around the stage, shedding spiders from her whirling, multicolored petticoats (under which she wore the ever-popular flesh-colored tights), and stomped on them to the orchestra's crescendo. According to Joseph Jackson, "The spiders were merely contraptions of rubber and whalebone, and Lola's dancing, spiders aside, was no better than that of a hundred less advertised coryphées. But there was the aura of delicious scandal about Lola."

Her doting husband Pat Hull wrote with partisan enthusiasm in his newspaper that "Lola apparently represents a country girl in some flowery mead" who "unwittingly gets on top one of those huge nests of spiders found during the Spring time in the meadows . . . she commences to dance and the cobwebs entangle her ankles." He said the result was "a fascinating amalgamation of polka, waltz, march, mazurka and jig."

She performed in Sacramento City with mixed success. Volunteer firemen there serenaded her, but she stalked off the stage one night when some drunken miners laughed at one of her routines—perhaps the spider dance, which some of her critics thought more laughable than fascinating. She told a reporter the incident was the work of some enemies who had followed her from Europe.

Her engagement at Marysville met with dwindling audiences but her appearance in the town was enlivened by the story that she had evicted Hull from their hotel room by throwing his belongings into the street—and then Hull, at the end of her dainty toe, as well.

In July 1853, Lola bought a cottage in Grass Valley, a mining town of 3,000 inhabitants west across the Sierra from Lake Tahoe. The settlement was famed for the quartz-gold discovery there, and the particular riches of the Gold Hill outcropping. She rusticated there among the manzanitas, jasmines, and wild roses, planted a garden, bought shares in the Eureka Gold Mining Company, and entertained miners, visiting dignitaries, and other performers making tours of the mine settlements.

Among those who fell under Lola's spell was Alonzo Delano, the big-hearted "Cyrano of California" who crossed the plains in '49 and moved to Grass Valley in 1850 after trying his hand at mining and banking. Now a newspaper writer whose humorous sketches were published under the name "Old Block," Delano wrote of her, "She is taking the hearts of our people by her affability and good nature."

She remained in Grass Valley two years, occasionally working on stage, more often seen tending her garden or riding horseback while puffing a *cigarillo*.

During her stay in the Grass Valley she made trips down to San Francisco to divorce Pat Hull. She had once stood trial in England for bigamy and had learned her lesson about legally shedding husbands before dancing another marriage tarantella. In her petition she claimed Hull suffered from "a distressing constitutional affliction." (The affliction was unnamed, but was probably syphilis, which he may have contracted from Montez. After suffering a stroke and paralysis, Hull died in Marysville in May 1858, at the age of thirty-four.)

In 1855, Lola took up with another lover, a young drifter named Noel Follin, and took him with her when she sailed to Australia, where gold deposits had opened in New South Wales and Victoria. Once again, the tour was unsuccessful. She suffered from headaches so severe she confined herself to her hotel room in Sydney for days on end.

She and Follin took passage on the bark *Jane A. Falkinburg* from Newcastle, New South Wales, bound for San Francisco via Tahiti and Honolulu. Their relationship abruptly ended on July 8, 1856, when, a day out of Honolulu, Follin was lost at sea under mysterious circumstances, perhaps a suicide, as some papers reported.

After she returned to California, Montez became interested in spiritualism. She sold her Grass Valley cottage, gave five farewell performances in San Francisco, and in November 1856, sailed to New York on the steamer *Orizaba*.

She never performed again, lived alone the rest of her life, read Scripture, became a member of an Episcopal church, and died, probably of stroke caused by syphilis, on January 17, 1861.

She was buried in Greenwood Cemetery, Brooklyn, the plain marble slab over her grave bearing the stark inscription "Mrs. Eliza Gilbert."

ON DECEMBER 17, 1849, Bayard Taylor of the *New York Tribune* headed home. His gold rush experience had lasted almost six months from his departure from New York Harbor and he had stayed in California longer than he or his employer, Horace Greeley, had intended.

Now the rainy season was delaying outbound passenger vessels and rather than wait for a steamer he decided to take a sailing packet bound for Mazatlán. He found space on a small, rakish Peruvian brig, a onetime opium smuggler named *Iquiqueña*. There were only eight berths available and he felt lucky to get one of them—until the hours passed, then the days, awaiting departure.

"The captain and crew did nothing to falsify the national reputation for tardiness and delay," he wrote. "In our case the *poco tiempo* of the Chagres boatmen was outdone. Seven days were we doomed to spend in the bay before the almost hopeless conjunction of wind, tide, crew, passengers, and vessel started us from our anchorage."

On Christmas Eve, Taylor's eighth day aboard, the little brig was warped through the multitude of vessels and took advantage of the ebb tide and a light breeze to make a run out of the harbor.

As he stood on the main deck in the foggy daybreak to take a parting look at the town and its "amphitheatric hills" he saw a spark through the fog, then a spiraling flame, heard bells and trumpets sounding ashore—and realized San Francisco was on fire.

For more than an hour, as the brig tacked in the channel between Yerba Buena Island and its anchorage, "the roar and tumult swelled, and above the clang of gongs and cries of the populace I could hear the crackling of blazing timbers, and the smothered sound of falling roofs."

He climbed the rigging to get a view: "As the flames leaped upon a new dwelling, there was a sudden whirl [of flame] . . . an embracing of the frail walls in their relentless clasp—and, a second afterwards, from roof and rafter and foundation beam shot upward a jet of fire, steady and intense at first, but surging off into spiral folds and streamers as the timbers were parted and fell."

He heard explosions as the *Iquiqueña* passed Alcatraz Island, and now the brig's skipper determined to return to the bay to offer assistance, tacking back and forth, running out toward the Farallones, sometimes under the lee of Punta de Los Reyes north of the Golden Gate. Ill winds and tidal surges thwarted every maneuver for three days until a flood tide caught the vessel and allowed it to drift back to anchorage.

Taylor hastened to Portsmouth Square, and saw all its eastern perimeter, with the exception of Delmonico's Restaurant at the corner of Clay and Kearny streets, reduced to a smoking rubble. The entire side of the block on Washington Street—the El Dorado, Parker House, Dennison's Exchange, all the great rendezvous of the city—had been destroyed.

THE FLAMES BAYARD Taylor saw from offshore on December 24, 1849, were from the first of six catastrophic fires, all of them ignited by wood-burning stoves, kerosene or whale oil lamps, or criminal activity—setting fires to loot business places. Bancroft wrote that these calamities were the product of "the improvident haste of the city-builders" and "stamped San Francisco as one of the most combustible of cities, the houses being as inflammable as the temper of the inhabitants."

The Christmas Eve fire began at Dennison's Exchange, the immensely popular saloon and gambling palace on the east side of Portsmouth Square. Bucket brigades slogged through foot-deep mud to fight it, but it burned to the ground as did the adjoining Parker House, while the nearby Haley House and Bella Union were severely damaged. E. A. Upton, the gadfly preacher who witnessed so much misery in the city, reported in his diary that "Merchants were flying from all parts of the city with their safes and large sacks of gold dust to the Custom House, which is fire proof, and has a large number of excellent safes. . . . Oh the suffering, the horrid suffering in all its various phases that exist in this city! None but God knows or ever will."

The city had only two hand-drawn fire engines. One of them, imported from the Sandwich Islands, was worn out; the other, a small machine once used by President Van Buren to water his gardens in New York, had been shipped to California to pump water from flooded mineshafts. Neither made a difference.

The second fire, on May 4, 1850, also broke out in a gambling house. For seven hours it raced up and down the hills, destroying three hundred wooden houses and buildings and most of three square blocks north and east of Portsmouth Square. City Hall and the *Alta California* offices were burned out and the damage was estimated at $4 million, about half the value of the gold dug out of California in '49.

This disaster resulted in the establishment of a fine of up to $100 for refusing to help fight a fire and the founding of a volunteer fire department, organized out of donated funds, $600 each, from Sam Brannan and other wealthy city fathers.

Forty days later, on June 14, 1850, a blaze that began in a chimney in the Merchants Hotel jumped along the business district from Kearny Street to the waterfront. Losses were estimated to be $3 million, maybe as high as $5 million.

Frank Marryat arrived in San Francisco Bay on a small vessel with 165 other passengers in the immediate aftermath of this fire and walked around the city, seeing "gun-barrels twisted like snakes . . . tons of nails welded together by the head, standing in the shape of the keg which had contained them; small lakes of molten glass of all colors of the rainbow."

The fourth fire (San Francisco newspapers had by now chosen "conflagration" as the more dramatic word) in ten months occurred on September 17, 1850, and consumed $500,000 in property in the four blocks between Washington, Pacific, Montgomery, and Dupont Streets.

Eight months later, another blaze nearly consumed the city. This fire of May 3–4, 1851, was believed to have been started in a paintshop on Portsmouth Square as incendiary work committed by the infamous "Sidney Ducks," the elite of the outlaw gangs contaminating San Franciso, former convicts and ticket-of-leave men from the penal colonies of New South Wales and Van Dieman's Land who congregated south of Telegraph Hill in a slum called Sydney Town.*

As the Ducks swarmed out of their stronghold to loot the burning stores, firemen did their best with primitive equipment to quell the blaze and prevent its spreading. Ships unloading cargo at the waterfront were endangered until the fire gangs demolished the wooden wharves to create a gap between the vessels and the fires. A warehouse on Commercial Street, owned by the firm of DeWitt & Harrison, was saved by the use of 80,000 gallons of vinegar splashed against the board walls or poured down from the roof.

By the time this fifth calamity ended, eighteen blocks of the heart of San Francisco were lost, 2,000 houses and buildings, with several human casualties and property damages amounting to $12 million.

---

*This vile warren of rickety lodging houses and grog shops, with such names as the Magpie, Bobby Burns, Tam O'Shanter, Noggin of Ale, Hilo Johnny, Boar's Head, and the Fierce Grizzly (with a live female bear chained inside the door), a district where harlots sold their services for a pinch or two of dust, became known in the 1860s as San Francisco's "Barbary Coast."

The sixth and final citywide fire (until the greatest of them all, in April 1906, set off by the aftermath of the Great Earthquake) took place on June 22, 1851. It covered ten blocks of the business district and parts of six others and resulted in a $2.5 million property loss.

"Thus purified by misfortune, and by the weeding out of rookeries and much filth," Bancroft wrote, "the city rose more beautiful than ever from its ashes. Hereafter it was admirably guarded by a fire department (with a phoenix on its shield) which from a feeble beginning in 1850 became one of the most efficient organizations of the kind in the world."

STREET PREACHERS OF the city saw these fiery "misfortunes" in a different light: as punishment for the godlessness and lawlessness of Sodom-by-the-Sea.

The lawlessness, at least, was demonstrable. Gangs of cutthroats had been roaming the city, breaking into shops and homes, terrorizing and sometimes murdering hapless citizens, from the beginning of the gold rush. The criminal element ruled the city from early 1849 until the rise of vigilance committees, followed by sanctioned law enforcement, the weeding out of corruption in city governance, and the creation of municipal courts.

In 1849, San Francisco was already home to criminal "associations," among the first called the "Hounds," a nest of idlers, drunks, and brawlers, most of them dregs from Stevenson's New York Volunteers, recruited for service in the Mexican War. Led by one Sam Roberts, a member of Company E of the regiment who called himself a lieutenant and wore a uniform, the Hounds routinely gathered in their favorite hangout, a rancid saloon called The Shades on Kearny Street. Their headquarters, which they called "Tammany Hall," consisted of a huge tent at Kearny and Commercial. There they drilled with muskets and issued forth periodically to hold swaggering fife-and-drum parades with flags and banners waving, or to terrorize the citizenry, with particular malice toward Mexicans, Chileans, or any people they identified as "greasers" or "foreigners." They were also adept at making forays against helpless prostitutes quartered at Clark's Point and the slopes of Telegraph Hill, and at bullying merchants under the guise of watching over "public security."

The activities of the Hounds and later their even more reckless inheritors, the Sydney Ducks, became so unbearable that the *Alta California* editorialized in 1851 that the threat of lynch law might be the only remedy. The paper suggested a committee of vigilance hunt out the criminals and give them five days to leave the city or face a "war of extermination."

Such a committee was formed in June 1851 in a building at Battery and Pine streets, south of the main business district and owned by the fiery, coarse-grained, and erratic Sam Brannan who served as its "president of the executive committee." The membership numbered 180 men and its bylaws called for the members to arrest, try, and punish men for robbery, murder, and arson, and decreed that every person known to be a criminal "leave this port within five days of this date [June 9, 1851]."

A broadside, probably written by Brannan, and posted throughout the city, was addressed to "the Citizens of San Francisco" and stated, "Law, it appears, is but a nonentity to be scoffed at; redress can be had for aggression but through the never failing remedy so admirably laid down in the code of Judge Lynch." The writer asked, "Are we to be robbed and assassinated in our domiciles, and the law to let our aggressors perambulate the streets because they have furnished straw bail? If so, 'let each man be his own executioner.'"

Headquarters of the committee was established on Sacramento Street in a firehouse protected by a breastwork of sandbags. Two taps on a firehouse bell at "Fort Gunnybags" called the committee into action.

One of the first "cases" handled by the vigilantes was that of Sydney Duck John Jenkins who stepped into the George W. Virgin shipping office on Long Wharf at the end of Commercial Street, and while the clerk was absent, walked out in broad daylight with a strongbox on his shoulder, pushed through the bystanders, and rowed away in a waiting boat.

Brannan's volunteers were rung up and took to boats to follow the culprit. Jenkins saw his pursuers and threw the box overboard. When he was captured and taken to the fire station, he boasted that his compatriots would soon be descending on Fort Gunnybags to set him free.

Brannan, who served as judge in the three-hour trial, had other ideas. He found Jenkins guilty and sentenced him to hang. The condemned man remained certain his fellow Ducks would rescue him, but these cohorts apparently disavowed any association with him and

Jenkins was trussed up and taken to an old adobe close on Portsmouth Square. There the noose was tightened, the free end tossed over a rafter, and Jenkins was hoisted off the ground to strangle to death, to the end chewing vigorously on a plug of tobacco.

City officials—corrupt and often in league with the criminals they piously censured—and a coroner's jury charged Brannan and eight others of the vigilance committee as responsible for the illegal execution of Jenkins. However, since so many others in the committee had signed a document that they were equally responsible, the case was dropped.

On June 22, 1851, the Sydney Ducks made their final show of defiance, starting a fire in a vacant house at Powell and Pacific Streets which, for the sixth time in two years, destroyed several city business blocks and caused millions in rebuilding costs. In the space of ten weeks in the summer of 1851, the vigilance committee tried, convicted, and hanged four men, forced scores of criminals to flee the city, and broke the power of the Ducks.

William T. Coleman, a Kentuckian who became a San Francisco merchant in 1849, succeeded Brannan in leading the Committee and in an essay the *Century Magazine* in 1891 described the atmosphere of lawlessness that gave rise to the vigilantes. He said that when he visited the "new city of Sacramento" in August 1849, "The doors of the houses had no locks, or they were unused; the tents had no fastenings, yet there were no losses of property, as every trespasser knew that in theft he would hazard his life." The miner, he said, was without fear or hesitation in leaving his bag of gold dust under his pillow and go to his camp for a day's work.

This atmosphere of trust, he said, continued through the winter of 1849 and the spring and early summer of 1850 until the tide of argonauts "was met by a flow of the worst element in the world, chiefly from Sydney and other Pacific Ocean ports, and, as a little foul matter will taint a large stream, so this matter seriously changed and endangered current affairs in California. . . . The halcyon days had departed. This was no longer Arcadia."

The vigilance committee remained active two years and disbanded in 1853, deciding its work, and the gold rush, was over.

◀ Schliemann's Gold ▶

ONE WHO WITNESSED the fifth and most destructive of San Francisco's fires, that of the first week of May 1851, was Heinrich Schliemann, a thirty-year-old German-born wanderer. He had arrived in San Francisco on the steamer *Oregon* in April to settle the affairs of a brother who had died of cholera in Sacramento City, and "to inspect the diggings and the different ways gold is won."

Schliemann was residing temporarily in the Union Hotel on Portsmouth Square on the night of May 3 and had been asleep a bare quarter-hour when he was roused by alarm bells and cries in the street, and from his window saw fires spreading. He gathered up his belongings, ran out, and, as he recorded in his multilingual diary, "scarcely reached the end of Clay street when I saw already the [Union] Hotel on fire. . . . Pushed on by a complete gale, the fire spread with an appalling rapidity."

From Telegraph Hill he watched "a frightful but sublime view, in fact the grandest spectacle I ever enjoyed."

He was the son of an impoverished Protestant minister of Mecklenburgh-Schwerin, had been a grocer's apprentice in Germany, a clerk in Holland, a vagabond in Venezuela, and an indigo merchant in Russia, and had demonstrated a linguistic genius wherever he traveled. Before his journey to California, he spoke, read, and wrote English, French, Dutch, Spanish, Portuguese, Italian, and Russian in addition to his native German. He would eventually master thirteen languages, including classical Latin and Greek.

After placing a marble stone on his brother's grave, Schliemann toured the northern mines, visiting Marysville, Nevada City, Grass Valley, and Rough and Ready, before returning to Sacramento. There, in July 1851, he "established a banking house for the purchase of gold dust," purchased an immense safe which took twenty men and twelve yoke of oxen to convey to his office, and began buying as much as 160 pounds of gold dust a day. The gold, he said, he bought at a profit and sold for a greater return to the San Francisco branch of Rothschilds.

By September 1, he entered in his journal, "My business is now on an enormous scale and my profits are large," but he admitted he longed for the "whirlwind of amusements" and "the bustle of business in my beloved Russia, my charming St. Petersburg. . . . Whilst here in Sacramento I can every moment expect to be murdered or robbed, I can in Russia sleep tranquilly in my bed without any fear for my life or property. . . ."

In January 1852, after contracting a fever he believed to be cholera, and convalescing for weeks in a San José hospital, Schliemann was ready to leave California. The state, he said, "seemed destined to become my grave," and he had little good to say about it despite the wealth he had taken from it. He sold his bank and on April 8, 1852, sailed away on the *Golden Gate*, bound for Panama, in a $600 stateroom.

In August he had reached St. Petersburg and in the decade that followed he married, fathered three children, and made another fortune dealing in war materiél during the Crimean War. In his leisure time he traveled to the Holy Land and devoted two years to learning classical Greek in order to read and memorize *The Iliad* and *The Odyssey*, ascribed to the poet Homer and composed in about 850 B.C.

A millionaire and retired from business by 1863, Schliemann devoted the rest of his life to archaeology. He believed fanatically that Homer's great works were genuine history and that the truth of the story of the siege of Troy (in about 1250 B.C.), described in the *Iliad*, could be proven by finding Troy's ruins.

"I loved money indeed," he wrote, "but solely as a means of realizing this real idea of my life."

After a world cruise in which he revisited California, he settled in Paris and in 1868 set foot for the first time in the land of Homer, his life's hero, and began his search for Troy near the mouth of the Dardanelles. With a permit from the sultan of Turkey, his workers began digging in a lofty hill called Hissarlik.

In 1873, he uncovered fortifications and a majestic cache of 8,700 pieces of gold jewelry ("Priam's Treasure," he called it) in an ancient burned-out city he proclaimed to be Troy. By 1890, his diggings had produced traces of nine cities, the oldest dating from the early Bronze Age (2500 B.C.).

In Greece, he also excavated the royal tombs of Mycenae, home of King Agamemnon, leader of the Greeks at Troy; and the buried city of Tiryns, legendary birthplace of Hercules.

All his archeological work, some of the greatest ever performed (and most ruinous, for the haphazard digging techniques of his day), and the treasures he unearthed, were financed, at least in part by the fortune he amassed, without digging, in California.

In December 1890, Heinrich Schliemann collapsed and died, probably from a massive stroke, in a piazza in Naples, Italy.

EIGHTEEN

DEPARTURES

WHILE OVER $81 million in gold was recovered from California mines in the peak year of 1852, geologists and other authorities were predicting that since the great surface placers were mined out, massive, expensive new techniques would be required to retrieve what gold remained. In fact, production slippages began the following year, but the free miner did not have to consult experts to learn that his day in California had passed. Tramping the Sierra foothills, making a test pan in a likely stream, building a cradle or Long Tom, digging a coyote hole—these were relics of an ended five-year-old adventure. Now, big-monied mine corporations were moving in, and hydraulic monitors had begun to obliterate hillsides and old mining camps and poison everything in their path. There was talk of lode mines, and mining the big rivers with dredges.

It was time to move on.

In the 1850s many new prospects cropped up, most of them will-o'-the-wisps, some genuine, that drew thousands from the California mines. In mid-1851, news arrived of gold fields—uncovered along the Macquarie River in New South Wales by an Australian, Edward Hammond Hargraves, who had spent two goldless years in the California mines. Afterward, lucrative diggings were found in Victoria state. Three years later, extravagant stories appeared in Panama newspapers of a gold discovery in Peru, at the headwaters of the Amazon, and similar gossip spread of rich diggings in Patagonia, then Alaska. In 1858, itinerant miners were heading north to the Fraser River and Cariboo Mountains of British Columbia where a genuine gold strike was underway, and late in 1859, a silver discovery in the Washoe country of Nevada drew 20,000 California miners across the Sierra to the Comstock Lode.

Thousands who had labored in the California placers were simply sick of it and sick from it. They had searched for gold, maybe even found a few ounces, but anything they had learned of the miner's craft was accidental, certainly not a career education. And so, those who had other lives gladly headed home to resume them.

Some took ships out of Monterey or San Diego, but the majority drifted into San Francisco to book passage. Here was a fitting place to end the adventure. The city had become the great Pacific entrepôt for people, goods, and gold; indeed, everything there seemed born of and dependent upon gold—banks, business enterprises, warehouses, hotels, saloons, and gambling houses, were created to reap the benefits of the gold mines and people who found and worked them. Further, nearly all the gold seekers who came to California by the Cape Horn and Panama routes had landed there, and the overland pilgrims who crossed the Sierra, and the sand walkers who came across Texas and Mexico, had eventually drifted there.

San Francisco, risen only six years past on the foundations of the unmapped *jacal*-and-tent hamlet of Yerba Buena, had practically defined the word "boomtown," and by 1852 had an assured future as a great metropolis of the newest American state.

San Francisco, so bound up with and identified with the gold rush, was the ideal place to salute off the port quarter of a steamer headed home.

THE FORTY-NINERS actually began leaving in '49 (the year 65,000 of them *arrived*), but the great exodus lay between 1850 and 1852 when 90,000 departed on shipboard, whether they came to the gold fields by the overland routes or not. The returnees had in common, besides a lack of gold, keeping notably fewer diaries and journals of their return trip. Disillusionment and illness had displaced the excitement and optimism of the beginning of the venture, and few wanted to write about failure.

John M. Letts saw the situation differently. A New Yorker who arrived in San Francisco in the summer of 1849, he headed home in the spring of 1850 broke, full of melancholy, his health precarious, taking passage with eighty others on the 700-ton *Edward Everett*. This was the vessel named for Harvard's president which had departed Boston in January 1849, carrying the "Boston & California Joint Mining & Trading Company."

"How different the feelings now! what a change!" Letts said. Writing in the third person but autobiographically, he told of the Forty-niners who, but a year ago, "with a brother or a friend, and with high hopes and vigorous constitutions," had reached California. But now, he said, "brother and friend are sleeping quietly at the base of yonder snow-capped mountain," and the survivors "are bearing the sad intelligence to the bereaved parents, brothers, and sisters." Even the messengers "are obliged to cling to the rigging for support, while they gaze for the last time upon the scene." Many had not only sacrificed health, he said, but were also destitute of means, "and are now reeling about the ship, endeavoring to earn their passage by their labor."

Letts said the *Edward Everett* "seemed a hospital . . . three-fourths of all the passengers were invalids, some of them helpless." Five passengers were "deranged" and confined to their berths "and seemed waiting to be relieved by death."

After nine days at sea, miner G. W. Ray of Maine died and Letts described his burial: "A gang-plank was placed, one end over the rail, the other supported by a cask. A canvas was thrown over the plank and the corpse was laid [on it], rope around the body, tied at the ankles with a canvas bag of sand. Body sewn in the canvas, ensign of California placed over the canvas and the passengers summoned, prayer read by the captain, ensign removed, end of the plank raised and the body dropped into the sea."

Three others, a man, woman, and child, were being conveyed to the states for burial, their bodies preserved in casks of spirits in the cargo hold. Letts did not say, probably did not know, what killed this family, but left the impression they had died, like G.W. Ray of Maine, among the casualties of the mines.

WALTER COLTON OF Vermont, the Yale graduate who won his naval commission from Andrew Jackson, sailed home in the summer of 1849. He had spent his time in California well, launching the state's first newspaper, serving as *alcalde* at Monterey, and writing voluminously of the gold rush for eastern newspapers. "After many sermons preached against money as the root of all evil," Bancroft gruffly said, Colton even tried his hand in the diggings, working on the Stanislaus River for two months before giving up. His *Three Years in California*, published in New York in 1850, passed through several editions and was read assiduously by latecomers to the mines. In Bancroft's opinion, the book "inclined toward the exuberant, and was less exact in the use of words than we should expect from a professed dealer in unadulterated truth, natural and supernatural."

Colton died in Philadelphia in January 1851, at the age of fifty-four.

THOMAS O. LARKIN, the New Englander who had sailed to California via the Sandwich Islands in 1832 and became the United States consul there during the war with Mexico, died in October 1858, in San Francisco at age fifty-six. His dispatches to the *New York Herald* and *Sun* during the gold rush were as influential as those of his Monterey contemporary, Walter Colton.

BAYARD TAYLOR SET out for home for the second time on January 1, 1850. His aborted attempt to depart aboard the Peruvian brig, *Iquiqueña*, had been interrupted by the great Christmas Eve 1849 fire in San Francisco, but now he had passage on the Pacific Mail steamer *Oregon* to Mazatlán and had good company aboard. Among the passengers were Senators-elect John Charles Frémont and William McKendree Gwin, formerly of Tennessee, together with a score of prominent merchants and moneyed men of San Francisco, and several officers of the army and navy.

The *Oregon* touched briefly at Santa Bárbara on the third morning out, then at San Diego, before sliding down the length of Baja California, around Cabo San Lucas, and across the Gulf of California into Mazatlán harbor.

Perhaps influenced by his great friend Ned Beale, who had crossed Mexico in the summer of 1848 carrying the first news of the gold discovery, Taylor decided to travel overland from Mazatlán the 1,200 miles to Vera Cruz. His friends had warned him that a ride alone across Mexico was foolhardy, that the country was still boiling with Yankee hatred and teeming with highwaymen who would waylay him, steal his animals and everything he carried, and cut his throat for good measure.

He bought mules and a horse and had traveled but a day on the trail to Guadalajara when his friends' scenario seemed to unfold as if on cue. A gang of bandits appeared out of nowhere, he said, and accosted him. They took his money (about $25), hunting knife, thermometer, compass, card case, drawing pencils, and some soap ("a thing the Mexicans never use," he said), and bound his wrists together. They spared his letters, books, and papers, and unaccountably left him his horse, an orange, and some tortillas.

"I cannot say that I felt alarmed," he wrote of the experience. "It had always been a part of my belief that the shadow of Death falls before him—that the man doomed to die by violence feels the chill before the blow has been struck. As I never felt more positively alive than at that moment, I judged my time had not yet come."

Some miles down the trail he came upon a place where, in a "desperate assault" eighteen months past, bandits had attacked a camp of soldiers and traders, presumably Americans, killing eleven men. There were shallow graves in the area, and a makeshift gibbet on which three of the bandits had been executed, their corpses now skeletons with some mummified flesh attached. A large sign fastened to the gallows read, *Así castiga la ley el ladrón y el asesino* ("Thus the law punishes the robber and assassin").

He continued his journey without incident: from Guadalajara by *diligencia* to Guanajuato, Querétaro, Mexico City, and Vera Cruz; to Mobile aboard the steamer *Thames*, "Stage to Montgomery, Central Railroad to Atlanta, Charleston, Virginia, a day in Washington to deliver dispatches from Mexico, a day at home in Pennsylvania." Finally, he said, "I reached my old working-desk in the *Tribune* office on the night of March 10 [1850]—just eight months and eight days from the time of my departure."

His "cheerful story" of his experiences in the gold rush, *Eldorado*, dedicated to Lieutenant Edward F. Beale, was published in two volumes in 1850 by Putnam's of New York and George Bentley of London. It contained color lithographs based on Taylor's own sketches. Charles Dickens wrote favorably of it, a circumstance that delighted the author more than the fact that the book enjoyed a fine sale through several editions and foreign translations.

While he was able to savor the celebration of his book, and dine in New York with such eminent men of letters as James Fenimore Cooper and Herman Melville, the great tragedy of his life also awaited him. Mary Agnew, his fiancée, was stricken with tuberculosis. The two were married on October 24, 1850, in Kennett Square, but she died on December 22 and was buried the following afternoon in a blinding snowstorm.

Taylor spent the rest of his life wandering and writing, following the paths of his English contemporaries, Alexander Kinglake and Richard Burton. He traveled to Palestine, Syria, and Arabia; followed the Nubian Nile to Ethiopia and the White Nile to Khartoum; visited Constantinople, Delhi, and Calcutta, and climbed passes in the Himalayas.

In 1854 he accompanied Commodore Matthew Calbraith Perry's historic diplomatic expedition to Japan, and before returning home visited Macao, Hong Kong, Canton, Singapore, and Shanghai.

In 1862, Taylor served a year as secretary to the legation at Saint Petersburg, following which, in Rome and Athens, he "relived the glories of the ancient world," then wandered through Scandinavia and Lapland. In Denmark he met and married Marie Hansen, daughter of a distinguished astronomer, and with her made frequent visits to England where he enjoyed the company of Browning, Tennyson, Carlyle, the Rossettis, and other great figures of Victorian literature.

In February 1878, President Rutherford B. Hayes appointed Taylor United States minister to Germany, a thrilling event for one who had translated *Faust* and had fallen in love with Goethe and all Germanic literature.

The great diplomatic honor was to last eight months. Taylor and Marie reached Berlin in May, and although he was suffering from stomach pains a physician brushed aside his concerns and prescribed some simple exercises and tonics. For a time he lost himself in such diversions as beginning a biography of Goethe, and chatting with Prince Otto von Bismarck, chancellor of the German Empire; Prince Aleksandr Gorchakov, chancellor of the Russian Empire; Benjamin Disraeli, now Lord Beaconsfield, prime minister of Great Britain; and former president Ulysses S. Grant, who came to Berlin on his world tour accompanied by a large entourage of family, army officers, and staff members.

Throughout the summer and fall Taylor suffered from fevers, agonizing muscular cramps, stomach pains, spells of vomiting, and a "persistent feeling of sea-sickness, which made food repulsive." He lost weight at an alarming rate and jokingly remarked that his thinness made him look "almost graceful." His doctors diagnosed him variously, operated on him, apparently to look at his liver, but without result.

He died, surrounded by Goethe's works in the library at the ambassador's mansion in Berlin, on December 19, 1878, at the age of fifty-three.

His literary production was prodigious: letters and articles for the *Tribune*, novels, volumes of poetry, magazine pieces, a staggering personal correspondence, and published lectures. Among his books, delights to the armchair traveler, were *A Journey to Central Africa* (1854), *The Lands of the Saracen* (1855), *A Visit to India, China, and Japan in the year 1853* (1854), *Northern Travel* (1859), *Travels in Greece and Russia* (1859), *By-Ways of Europe* (1869), and *Egypt and Iceland in the Year 1874* (1874).

The editor of Taylor's posthumous *Collected Poems* (1879) said, "To him poetry was a second religion. . . . He held that no achievement of man was comparable to the creation of a living poem."

But his best-known verse, virtually forgotten today, was "Bedouin Song" with an opening stanza once memorized by a generation of school children:

> *From the Desert I come to thee*
> *On a stallion shod with fire;*
> *And the winds are left behind*
> *In the speed of my desire.*
> *Under the window I stand,*
> *And the midnight hears my cry:*
> *I love thee, I love but thee,*
> *With a love that shall not die*
> *Till the sun grows cold,*

And the stars are old,
And the leaves of the Judgment Book unfold!

"Taylor, in my judgment, did not write a single work which was not influenced in one way or another by his age. This was his fate, his dark compulsion," states the poet's biographer Richard C. Beatty. The darkness of this compulsion seems to rest in Taylor's ambition to be greater than a writer of the passing scene. His religion was poetry, he said, but it was his fate to be remembered as a reporter, a profession he practiced brilliantly all his life. Ultimately, his journalism, as epitomized by his travel books, and especially in his gold rush memoir, *Eldorado*, became his enduring achievement.

John Woodhouse Audubon sailed home in July 1850, taking the Isthmus of Panama route. His nine months in California had not been successful and he had sacrificed his health in the terrible march of the "Colonel H. L. Webb California Company" across Texas and northern Mexico between March and October 1849.

His daughter Maria wrote, "My father's homecoming showed him many sad changes, for *his* father was now an old and broken man, and the spirit of the home was no longer joyous." When John James Audubon, the great naturalist-artist, died in January 1851, Maria said, "the break was most keenly and deeply felt" by the family.

Audubon the son succumbed to pneumonia on February 21, 1862, at age forty-nine. At the end, Maria said, he was "overworked and careworn," and to the last, "the California journey was on his mind."

During his nine months in California Audubon completed nearly two hundred watercolors and sketches, those of Mexico done from memory, and left them in storage in Sacramento when he returned to New York. They were later retrieved and taken to San Francisco by John Stevens, an original member of the Webb company, described by Audubon's daughter Maria as "a noble man and true friend," who had accompanied her father to California. Inexplicably, Audubon did not ask for the artworks to be shipped on to New York, but in 1857, when Stevens decided to return there, he bundled up the materials and took them along on the Pacific Mail steamship *Sonora* bound from San Francisco's Vallejo Wharf for Panama.

On the Pacific side of the isthmus, all passengers bound for New York were transferred with their baggage to the Panama Railway (completed in 1855) for the 47-mile ride to Aspinwall on the Atlantic, there to take passage on the luxury sidewheel passenger steamer *Central America* for the final 2,000-mile Panama to New York leg of the voyage.

Aboard the 2,141-ton, three-hundred-foot-long, three-masted, twin-engined, gaudy red, black, and gold-painted steamer were 476 passengers, 102 crew members, 38,000 letters from Californians to their relatives and friends in the east, three *tons* of California gold in ingots and coins, and John Woodhouse Audubon's two hundred watercolors and sketches.

On September 12, 1857, the *Central America* foundered in a hurricane 160 miles off the South Carolina coast and sank, taking all the gold, letters, baggage, and bundled artworks with it, and 425 people to their deaths, among them John Stevens, noble friend of the Audubon family.

EDWARD FITZGERALD BEALE left California in October 1850, and in Washington at last received a promotion to lieutenant. But in 1851 he resigned from the navy after being named general superintendent for Indian affairs for California and Nevada.

In 1857, he accepted a commission to survey a wagon road across New Mexico and Arizona, and for this work experimented with camels as pack animals. He reached Fort Tejon, north of Los Angeles, and the next year returned to the Colorado River and New Mexico, the camel test proving successful. He retraced the route almost in its entirety from Fort Smith, Arkansas, late in 1858, and when the surviving camels were put up for sale by the War Department, Beale bought them and sent them to his 276,000-acre Tejon Ranch, near Bakersfield.

During the Civil War Beale served as surveyor general of California and Nevada. He purchased a home, "Decatur House," in Washington, D.C., in 1870, and divided his time between Washington and his California ranch.

In 1876 he was awarded the diplomatic post of minister to Austria-Hungary, and after returning to Washington from Vienna devoted the rest of his life to business interests, political involvements with the Republican "Stalwarts" of the capital, serving with his wife Mary as host of parties and banquets at his renowned Decatur House, and shuttling between the capital and the ranch. He remained a lifelong friend of Frémont, Kit Carson, and other frontiersmen with whom he had been associated in his youth, and with Bayard Taylor and other friends from gold rush days.

He died on April 22, 1893, at his Washington home, age seventy-one. A newspaper obituary quoted a family friend as saying Ned Beale was "one of the most variously gifted of Americans," and that "to have enjoyed the privilege of a personal acquaintance with him may fairly be said to have been equal to a liberal education."

UPON RETURNING HOME from California in the spring of 1851, Julius Pratt must have heard many a pious, finger-wagging discourse from his father on wasted time, wasted money, and the follies of feck-less youth. If he listened at all, he did so out of duty only. He had but a single regret, that his cherished sister Harriet—whom he called "Sissy"—had died in his absence.

"Her childhood more than mine was sad and serious from the rigid discipline that prevailed in our household," he wrote of her. "Much work and little play was the regime under which her young life was developed. She was always sedate and good, living in an at-mosphere of depression and fear, lest she should transgress uncon-sciously some rule of morals or religion . . . her whole life was one of religious devotion. She indulged in no mirth, but served ever under the banner of duty."

He recalled that just before he sailed on the *Mayflower*, Sissy had given him a needle book containing an assortment of threads with the remark that this "would be her last opportunity for doing any-thing for me, as we should probably never meet again." He said he treated the remark lightly, "supposing she referred to my own proba-ble fatality as the result of the dangers I was about to encounter."

Harriet Pratt married an impecunious minister, gave birth to three boys, "and her constitution failed in the effort to add another to the number," he wrote. She died in childbirth on July 4, 1850.

He had reached Meriden, he said, "laden with the experience of a most romantic chapter of my life, no worse off financially and per-haps a little better than when I left home two years before." Now, he was intent on "enjoying the sweet ministries of wife and home, completely cured of my passion for romantic experience, and ready to take on the harness of hard and steady work for the rest of my life."

Julius Pratt & Company, manufacturer of combs, table cutlery handles, piano keys, and other ivory products, prospered even though his Meriden factory burned down in 1861 at a loss of $130,000.

He rebuilt.

He was also a road-builder, a church-builder, a railroader, a developer of Montclair, New Jersey; a civic leader, a tree planter, and was much revered by family and community.

Pratt's beloved wife Adeline died in November 1907, and on October 14, 1909, he "fell asleep," his daughter said, dying at age eighty-eight at his home in Montclair.

ISRAEL SHIPMAN PELTON Lord, homeopathic physician, cholera authority, gold miner, and choleric chronicler of the gold rush, bought a $125 passage on the mail steamer *Oregon* on February 15, 1851, and departed California, probably never expecting to return.

His sublime cantankerousness had not softened from his experiences in the gold country. The ship stopped over at Acapulco where, he said, "A great deal of liquor was brought on board," but it was tobacco that bothered him the most: "The deck . . . is drenched in spittle, and literally choked with old quids and half smoked segars. How a human being can so degrade himself as to use tobacco. . . . It is only drunkenness in another shape."

He also found the shipboard food execrable. "If the hard bread has been bad, the pork has been worse. Not that it was wormy. No, no, it was too strong for that. Worms know what is palatable and take good care not to get into such pork barrels as ours . . . many and many a savory ten pound morsel of ox carrion has been tossed overboard that must have proved a vomit for a shark." Of the beef served, he said it was Mexican-bred, "tough, sinewy, cock fighting bundles of rattan and rubber done up in calf skin," the bread was "sour and mouldy," the coffee "burnt, black and muddy," the sugar, "uncommon Brown and often buggy."

He composed a poem to memorialize the *Oregon*'s fare:

> *The tea is strong*
> *as a bondsman's wrong*
> *And greasy's the head of a whale*

And the bread as hard
as the teeth of a "pard,"
And tough as the string of a flail.

Dr. Lord reached New Orleans on March 22, 1851, St. Louis on 31st, and on Thursday, April 3, 1851, arrived in Aurora, Illinois, "glad to get home, and with a heap more wit than I had two years before."

To a friend contemplating a journey to the mines, he wrote, "If I should get time, I will give you my reasons why I think ninety-nine out of every hundred who shall hereafter go to California, are either mad-men, fools, or radically unprincipled, and of course, dishonest."

He built a successful medical practice in Chicago, then in Pough-keepsie, and later in Brooklyn. In the 1870s, he returned to California and died in Los Angeles in the early 1890s.

AMONG THE GOLD rush chroniclers who remained in California, Alonzo Delano was the miners' favorite throughout the 1850s. His comic "Old Block" ruminations, often illustrated by his own long-nosed self-caricatures, appeared regularly in *Pacific News*, the *Sacramento Union*, the *Golden Era*, and other San Francisco–area news-papers. His books were also immensely popular in the gold country: *Life on the Plains and Among the Diggings* (1849), *Pen Knife Sketches; or, Chips Off the Old Block* (1853)—which sold 15,000 copies in Califor-nia—and the melodrama, *Live Women in the Mines* (1857).

In Grass Valley, where he met and adored Lola Montez, Delano worked for many years at Wells, Fargo and Company's Banking and Exchange Office. His rollicking life concealed many personal tragedies. The wife he left behind when he took the overland trail to California died in his absence; his only son was an invalid from child-hood; and his daughter was declared insane a short time after she reached her father in California.

On the day Delano died in Grass Valley in 1874, all the town flags were hung at half-mast and all businesses were closed in honor of its distinguished citizen.

DAME SHIRLEY—LOUISE Amelia Knapp Smith Clapp—stayed in California long after the gold rush ended. In 1853, Dr. Clapp sailed for Hawaii without Louise and a year later reached Massachusetts. During his absence, they divorced amicably. Louise remained in San Francisco, where she taught twenty years at the first public school in California and renewed acquaintances with the scholarly Harvard graduate Ferdinand C. Ewer. It was to Ewer she gave the collection of the Rich Bar and Indian Bar letters she had written to her sister Molly. They were subsequently published in his magazine, the *Pioneer*.

She returned east in 1873 and died near Morristown, New Jersey, on February 9, 1906.

The Shirley Letters collection has remained in print since it first appeared in book form in 1922.

SARAH ELEANOR BAYLISS Royce died in 1891 at age seventy-two. Born in England, raised in New York, she became a Forty-niner with her husband Josiah and infant daughter Mary and settled in the Weberville area, where the Royces ran a general store.

In their years in the northern mining towns she recalled the "various periods of convulsion" of the gold country—the San Francisco vigilance committee movement ("which was felt to the very tops of the Sierras"); the Fraser River and Washoe "excitements," which drew miners from their dwindling claims in California to British Columbia and Nevada; "the awful roar of the Civil War" which, she said, "threatened to set every man's hand against his brother, and banish prosperity from our homes"; and the coming of the transcontinental railroad, which carried prosperity into her adopted state.

Thirty years after her arduous journey across the plains, Sarah recalled it all vividly when she wrote of it at her son's request. Josiah Jr., born in a California mining camp in 1855, had become a Harvard professor, philosopher, and historian, and in writing a book on California had the benefit of his mother's firsthand experiences in coming to the state during the gold rush.

Josiah Royce's California history, published in 1886, is little known outside the scholarly world. His mother's slim memoir, her "Pilgrimage Diary," was first published in 1932. It bore the appropriate title, *A Frontier Lady*, and like Dame Shirley's letters, has remained in print.

*   *   *

HUBERT HOWE BANCROFT, after his stint as a laborer in the mines in 1853, moved to San Francisco and with a $5,500 loan from his sister established in 1856 the firm of H. H. Bancroft and Company, the leading publisher, producer, and seller of books on the Pacific coast. By 1869 he had amassed a library of 16,000 volumes (60,000 by 1905, when the Bancroft Library was sold to the University of California), and in 1874 he and his talented staff of researchers and writers began compiling and writing what would become thirty-nine stout historical volumes.

The books were researched and written factory-style, with Bancroft as one of the principal writers, as well as employer, overseer, and editor of the other salaried scribes. The books were all published with Bancroft's name as author, a matter that became the subject of much controversy when some of his employees sought credit for their work.

Sold mostly by subscription, *The History of the Pacific States* cost $4.50 each volume for a common binding, and as much as $10 for "Russian leather." They were immensely successful thanks to the company's aggressive salesmanship.

Bancroft weathered many controversies in his late years, including lawsuits by disgruntled former employees and one instance in which his name was stricken from the roll of significant Californians. This latter case derived from a California pioneer group which in 1893 accused the historian of maligning by a "monstrous perversion of the facts of history" the memories of all members of the Bear Flag rebellion, such figures in the 1846 conquest of California as John Charles Frémont and Robert Field Stockton, and others of the gold rush era—all lumped together as "old Argonauts." These "vaporings of a mind distorted by prejudice, or envenomed by malice," the antagonists said, appeared in Bancroft's *History of California*. By resolution, the Society of California Pioneers struck his name from "the list of Honorary Members of the Society," for "straying far from the domain of an honest writer" and for publishing statements that "did wantonly and maliciously wrong the old Argonauts."

Bancroft's reaction to this was to state that he had not asked for membership in the society and was unconcerned whether he remained a member or not.

He died at his San Francisco home on March 2, 1918, at age

eighty-six. Both principal dailies of the city ran front-page obituaries, the *Examiner* story's opening line serving as an epitaph the historian would have endorsed: "Hubert Howe Bancroft, the one man who preserved the history and materials of all of old California . . ."

SAM BRANNAN'S RISE of fortune began the moment he landed with his Mormon emigrant party at Yerba Buena on July 31, 1846. Within a year he built two flour mills, began a farm at the juncture of the San Joaquín and Stanislaus Rivers, launched the *California Star* newspaper, and opened a fabulously successful store at Sutter's Fort.

He served as president of San Francisco's vigilance committee, by 1850 owned so much property his rentals were netting him $160,000 a year, and by 1856 was said to own 20 percent of San Francisco and a similar percentage of Sacramento City.

He enjoyed twenty years of prosperity, indulging in his "curious variety of enterprises," as Bancroft put it, supporting the Union in the Civil War, and Benito Juárez in Mexico when France installed the puppet Emperor Maximilian there. Brannan bought 3,000 acres of land in the Napa Valley north of San Francisco, built an estate and the largest wine and brandy distillery west of the Mississippi, and threw $5 million into a scheme to build a resort at Calistoga, including a railroad leading into it. He also dreamed of filibustering, talking endlessly of recruiting Yaqui Indians to seize Mexico's state of Sonora, in which he had a huge land grant, a token of gratitude from Juárez, and raising the American flag there.

He renounced his Mormonism when it became convenient to do so. In the *Sacramento Bee* on January 21, 1888, he declared, "I want to say that all these stories about my being a Mormon, and about my bringing a boatload of Mormons here for colonization purposes are simply poppycock. I chartered the ship and brought them out here only as a business venture and not for religious purposes. After the gold mines had been discovered and the Mormons made themselves rich in them, Brigham Young ordered them all back to Salt Lake and fleeced them. That's all I know of the Mormons."

Brannan's great passion for whiskey and women—he was said to have spent a fortune, as had many others, wooing Lola Montez—

caught up with him in 1870 when his wife, Ann Eliza, who freely spent his money during her thirteen years of residence in Europe, divorced him, declaring him "addicted to open and notorious intemperance." Her settlement of $500,000 sent him reeling into bankruptcy. He sold his Calistoga property and others as well, and by 1876 his fortune had vanished, never to be recovered.

In Guaymas, in April 1885, with yellow fever raging around him, he wrote a friend, "Blessed be nothing! What a pleasure it is to be poor. . . . I am as happy as a Clam in a crow's nest, for I have got the world by the Cahonies and don't care a D—n for nada!"

He moved to San Diego, tried his hand at fruit farming at the settlement of Escondido, looking every bit an old Mexican field hand with his ragged clothing and big sombrero, white hair flying as he walked his fields with a cane.

He periodically took to bed in a boarding house suffering from epileptic seizures and bowel ailments, and died there on May 5, 1889.

In the June *Overland Monthly* Brannan was thus described: "His character as a whole was not lovable. His intellectual fibre was coarse. He had scanty education, no refinement of manner, and little delicacy of feeling. His temper was high; his speech often coarse. He was never a polished gentleman and when under the influence of strong drink, as he frequently was, he could be extremely rude and boisterous." But, the writer conceded, Brannan "had many admirable qualities. He was generous, bold, frank, and prompt. His wealth did not make him vain. He had no affectation or false dignity. While very rich he was cordial to those who had been his associates when poor. He was always ready to help those he liked and who needed his assistance. He was generally considered honest."

His estate consisted of deeds and mortgages for his land in Escondido, a "Cloth House" (a tent), a large number of second-hand books, some garden tools, a silver watch, 2,900 shares in the defunct Sonora City and Improvement Company, and two trunks of personal papers.

His body was stored in a vault while the $95 bill for the embalming went unpaid. In the fall of 1890, a friend bought a lot at Mount Hope Cemetery in San Diego for him and paid the mortuary and burial expenses. The grave was unmarked until an admirer erected a headstone on it in 1926:

SAM BRANNAN
1819–1889
California Pioneer of '46
DREAMER—LEADER
and
EMPIRE-BUILDER

A TRUE SON of old California, Don Mariano Guadalupe Vallejo, born in Monterey in 1818, eighth of thirteen children of a foot soldier who came to Alta California with Father Junípero Serra in 1774, died at "Lachryma Montis" (Tears of the Mountains), his home in Sonoma, on January 18, 1890.

Vallejo's superiors in Monterey had sent the self-educated army officer north in 1841 to investigate Indian unrest and the activities of the Russians at Fort Ross, fifty miles north of the presidio at Yerba Buena. At Sonoma he had barracks built for his small cadre of troops, which, because of Mexico's parsimony and general uninterest in its California province, Vallejo was obliged to raise, clothe, feed, and salary from his own funds. He brought his family to Sonoma and fell in love with the Valley of the Moon, as the Indians called it. It was a fecund, primeval place with dark soil perfect to raise corn and grain, great stands of manzanitas and oaks, acres of golden poppies and wild grapes, all the land crisscrossed by crystal streams. He lived there the rest of his life, raising cattle and growing lucrative grain and vegetable crops, and for the pleasure of them, magnolias, Castilian roses, orange and lemon trees, olives, pomegranates, pomelo trees from China, and camphor and locust trees from the Sandwich Islands. For the most part, his life was one of tranquility, a don's life, with his immense rancho, fine library, devoted wife, and great brood of children.

Even before the war with Mexico, Vallejo felt an American takeover of his beloved California was inevitable, and he favored it, seeing no chance for progress in the province under beleaguered Mexico's erratic control. He was as open and generous as Sutter to American settlers, and was similarly rewarded for his good deeds: During the Bear Flag rebellion of June 1846, he had been imprisoned at Sutter's Fort under Frémont's orders, and the experience came close to killing him.

He prospered during the gold rush, however, opening stores in the towns of Napa, Sonoma, and Benicia, supplying provisions to miners.

A powerfully built man with a broad, handsome, and jovial face, Vallejo was described by Thomas Larkin as "very studious for a Californian . . . formal, stiff, pompous and exacting . . . pleasant and condescending, anxious for popularity and the good will of others."

He was survived by his wife of more than fifty years, María Francisca Felipa Benicia Carrillo, and ten children.

"UPON THE DISCOVERER himself, in whose mind so suddenly arose visions of weath and influence," Bancroft wrote, "it fell like the gold of Nibelungen in the Edda, which brought nothing but ill luck to the possessor."

James Marshall, Sutter's "notional" sawmill employee who had caught a glimpse of something shining in the mill's tailrace on the Sunday afternoon of January 23, 1848, saw little else that glittered the rest of his life. He was an innocent; an unimaginative, lonely eccentric who seemed locked in a fatal lethargy, unable to find success for its failure to fall in his lap. This, and the exaggerated estimate of what he felt was owed him as discoverer, "left its impress on his mind," Bancroft wrote with a striking pitilessness, "subjecting it more and more to his spiritualistic doctrines. In obedience to phantom beckonings, he flitted hither and thither about the foothills, but his supernatural friends failed him in every instance."

Typical of Marshall's supineness in attempting to capitalize on his discovery was a statement he made to a friend: "Should I go to new localities and commence to open a new mine, before I could prospect the ground, numbers flocked in and commenced seeking all around me, and . . . some one would find the lead before me and inform their party, and the ground was claimed. Then I would travel again."

Both Marshall and Sutter mined near the Coloma sawmill, claiming the right to the ground around it, and with the aid of the Indians took out an inconsequential amount of gold. Later on, Sutter twice grubstaked Marshall but the New Jersey carpenter had no success.

Bancroft asserts, with scanty evidence, that in his trips to San Francisco, Marshall may have been associated with the "Hounds," the criminal crew that headquartered in a huge tent at Kearny and Commercial Streets. While Marshall drank heavily, he gave little hint that he would have much in common with the street scum that made up this outlaw gang. Still, Bancroft, who had conversations with Marshall, states, "Of course he denies having been one of them, but his knowledge of their watchword and other secrets looks suspicious."

As the years passed the discoverer became increasingly petulant and querulous, discouraged and soured, and when he grew restive under encroachments on his scanty property, he shouldered his forty-pound pack and tramped the mountains and ravines, seeking employment— sawing wood, cleaning wells, gardening—mostly in Coloma, scene of his life's great moment, or in nearby Kelsey.

Marshall said he wandered for more than four years, "feeling under some fatal influence, a curse, or at least some bad circumstances." He went on, "I see no reason why the government should give to others and not to me. In God's name, can the circumstance of my being the first to find the gold regions of California be a cause to deprive me of every right pertaining to a citizen from under the flag?"

These, Bancroft states, "are not the sentiments of a healthy mind. The government was not giving more to others than to him. One great trouble was, that he early conceived the idea, wholly erroneous, that the government and the world owed him a great debt; that but for him gold in California never would have been found."

In 1870, while he was living at the Kelsey Diggings, the settlement between Coloma and Placerville, a resident there wrote, "He is upward of fifty years of age, and though feeble, is obliged to work for his board and clothes, not being able to earn more."

He spent some time as an itinerant lecturer, telling the story of how he found the first gold, but by 1872, destitute, he petitioned the California legislature for a $200-a-month pension. The lawmakers agreed at first, but later cut the sum in half and in 1878 discontinued it altogether when Marshall, attempting to lobby for reinstatement of his original stipend, showed up drunk at the Sacramento assembly.

"Impelled by the restlessness which had driven him west, and over-come by morbid reflections, he allowed many of his good qualities to drift," Bancroft wrote. "In his dull, unimaginative way he out-Timoned Timon in misanthropy. He fancied himself followed by a merciless fate, and this was equivalent to courting such a destiny."

James Marshall, who never married, died alone in August 1885 at age seventy-three, and was buried on a hill overlooking the Coloma mill site where thirty-seven years earlier he took his daily stroll and saw gold.

The Native Sons of the Golden West fraternal club erected a monument to him, dedicated on May 13, 1890. It is a ten-foot-tall statue of Marshall holding a nugget in one hand and pointing with the other to Sutter's sawmill.

"AT ONCE, AND during the night, the curse of the thing burst upon my mind. I saw from the beginning how the end will be," John Augustus Sutter said, years after the gold rush had quieted.

His spectacular California career lasted a decade, from the time he sailed up the Sacramento River in 1839 and found squatter's land to build his fort and New Helvetia agricultural kingdom, to late in 1849 when indebtedness forced him to sell his holdings for $40,000. Afterward he retreated to his his beloved 1,200-acre grain and cattle spread on the Feather River he called Hock Farm. In January 1850, his wife, three sons, daughter Eliza, two sisters, and a brother, were brought over from Switzerland by his countryman and business associate Heinrich Leinhard. The family he had fled fourteen years before thus joined him in his place of exile.

Leinhard, the chief scandalmonger among Sutter's multitude of fair-weather friends, reminded admirers of "Old Sutter," as he called him, of the ignoble side to the once powerful Potentate of the Sacramento. He told of Sutter "shaking from head to foot" in drunkenness as his sons dragged him from the tent of a French prostitute somewhere out in the mining camps. What portion of this was truthful is unknown, but Sutter's heavy drinking was no secret to any who knew him. His costly week-long binges in San Francisco waned with his fortunes, but he drank, often heavily, as he fought suicidal depression and daily battles with the creditors, debtors, squatters, and thieves that plagued his last decade in California. Also, he loved to entertain at Hock Farm as he had at Sutter's Fort, and welcomed visiting dignitaries with banquet tables sagging with food, brandy, and wine. On these occasions he often appeared in full regalia—the uniform, with braid, epaulets, sash, and sword, of the honorary general of "Sutter's Rifles," a San Francisco militia unit.

He managed to hold on to his Hock Farm retreat, with its spacious redwood and adobe house, until June 7, 1865. That night, a fire believed started by vandals burned his home to its foundation as Sutter, Anna, and a few Indian servants stood helplessly under the oaks and sycamores. They watched his last domain, and all the records and mementos attesting to it and to his quarter-century in California, vanish to ashes.

In October 1866, now sixty-three, he left California with Anna and three grandchildren, to move to the old Moravian settlement of Lititz, in Lancaster County, Pennsylvania, a place recommended by a friend for its curative springs. Sutter sought relief from his rheumatism, but more from the grinding, never-ending obstacles of his California life.

He frequented Washington, lobbying by letter and in person for federal redress for his losses caused by the flood of emigrants to the gold country in 1849 and thereafter. Friends advised him to seek no more than $50,000—less than half the estimate of his losses—but he was frustrated at every turn.

He was never destitute, nor petulant and misanthropic as was the hopeless James Marshall. Sutter lived comfortably, had many friends and admirers in the capital, and was a good-hearted and convivial man to the end.

Bancroft met him in Washington in 1876 and the two had a splendid reunion. The historian paid the old man homage, told Sutter how much California owed him for his encouraging American settlement, for his assistance in the American takeover in '46, for his many good deeds to man and state. A few years later, in writing of the gold rush in his massive California history, the historian wrote, "As a matter of fact, the Swiss had nothing whatever to complain of. He was his own greatest enemy. His representations of the disastrous effect upon him of the gold discovery were greatly exaggerated." He said it would have been "far more manly, not to say respectable," if Sutter had lived "modestly on some small portion of the fruit of his labors, or of good fortune, instead of spending his old age complaining and importuning the government for alms." Everything had been given him, Bancroft said, including fertile lands and golden opportunity. "With these he should have been content. The truth is . . . Sutter was not man enough to grasp and master his good fortune." But, he added at the end of his assessment, "It was wholly proper to hang a portrait of Sutter in the hall of the state capitol beside that of Vallejo and others."

Perhaps fortunately for their friendship, Sutter did not live to read the historian's opinions. The man many called the "Father of California" died in a Washington hotel room, at age seventy-seven, on June 28, 1880.

In his 1886 book, *California*, Josiah Royce offered a succinct appraisal of the Swiss: "In character, Sutter was an affable and hospitable visionary, of hazy ideas, with a great liking for popularity and with a mania for undertaking too much."

⊰ Sacajawea's Son & Others ⊱

BOTH JOHN WOODHOUSE Audubon and William Stephen Hamilton, accomplished sons of famous men, reached California by overland trails in 1849, specifically drawn there by the lure of gold.

Samuel Ward, brother of Julia Ward Howe, came to San Francisco and the mining districts in 1849. He is said to have accumulated a $40,000 profit in real estate dealings but lost this fortune and others before departing California in 1854.

One father of notorious sons who reached the gold fields in 1849 was Robert Sallee James, a Baptist preacher with a master's degree in religion from Georgetown College in Kentucky. He and his wife Zerelda Cole James moved to Missouri in 1842, where he began work as a pastor-farmer. His sons Alexander Franklin "Frank" James and Jesse Woodson James were born in Clay County in 1843 and 1847 respectively. Early in 1850 Robert left Missouri with an overland party bound for the California diggings where his brother had already located. Reverend James managed to reach Hangtown (subsequently Placerville) in the northern mines but died of a fever there on August 18, 1850. Many years later, Frank and Jesse ventured out to Marysville, where their father was said to be buried, but were unable to find his grave.

A GRANDSON, AND another son of a celebrated parent, were already *in* California when the rush began.

Navy Lieutenant Joseph Warren Revere, Boston-born grandson of Paul Revere, served with the landing party from the sloop-of-war *Portsmouth* at Yerba Buena in July 1846, and hoisted the flag in front of the customs house, signalling the American takeover of the province. He resigned his commission in 1850 to ranch in the Sonoma Valley, apparently did not prosper during the gold rush, and returned east. He became a brigadier general in the army and was senior Union officer at Chancellorsville in May 1863. After the battle he was court-martialed for a rearward march during the action, but President Lincoln allowed him to resign from the army. He died in 1880.

Jean Baptiste Charbonneau was the son of Sacajawea, the Shoshoni girl who served as Indian interpreter and accompanied her husband, the French trader Toussaint Charbonneau, on the Lewis and Clark expedition to the Pacific and back in the years 1804–1806. Sacajawea gave birth to Jean Baptiste on February 11, 1805, in a Mandan village near the juncture of the Missouri and Knife rivers. William Clark called the baby "Pomp" or "Pompey"— said to be a Shoshoni word for "first-born." Sacajawea, about sixteen years old, carried her son on a cradleboard throughout the laborious portages to the Oregon coast and the return to the Missouri River.

For several years Jean Baptiste lived with the Clarks in St. Louis, receiving a religious education and learning English, his father's French, and some Indian tongues. At age eighteen he was taken to Europe by Prince Paul of Württemberg, a world traveler who had come to St. Louis on a scientific expedition. For six years he traveled with his sponsor to France, England, and even on a North African venture in 1829, after which Prince Paul accompanied the young man back to America.

Charbonneau spent the next fifteen years in the western wilderness, trapping the rivers and streams from the northern Rockies to Mexico, part of the time in the employ of John Jacob Astor's American Fur Company, often as a free trapper working with such redoubtable mountain men as Jim Bridger, Joe Meek, Thomas "Broken Hand" Fitzpatrick, and Jim Beckwourth.

He may have explored Alta California before the war with Mexico, searching for virgin beaver streams, and he served as guide for the Mormon Battalion in crossing the Southwestern deserts, reaching San Diego in January 1847. Before year's end he was appointed *alcalde* at the San Luís Rey mission, and a year later was in the Sacramento Valley gold fields with Jim Beckwourth.

His success or failure at gold mining is not known but he remained in northern California until the spring of 1866 when he departed with two companions for Montana Territory, probably heading for the new gold discoveries around Alder Gulch.

At some unidentified place on the Owyhee River of southeastern Oregon he died of "mountain fever"—probably pneumonia—in mid-May 1866, and was buried by the river near the modern-day town of Danner.

STATE HIGHWAY 49, California's greatest monument to the gold rush and the passageway through its old mining camps and towns, snakes through eleven east-central counties of the state from Sierra City in the north to Oakhurst in the south. It is a well-kept, 200-mile-long, two-lane blacktop with many no-passing zones and sudden plunges in the posted speed limit to 25 or even 15 mph. For the north-to-south traveler, the last forty miles of this road, from about Chinese Camp to Mariposa, are especially wicked in tourist season, the serpentine drive blessedly relieved by such scenic wonders as Don Pedro Lake on the Tuolumne River south of Jamestown, and "turn-outs," wide places in the road where travelers can pull over to check their maps—and their tempers, as pesky tailgaters rocket past.

A gold country exploration should begin where the story of the gold rush began: at Sutter's Fort, today a reconstructed quadrangle lying amid park acreage that somewhat shields it from the traffic racket of the commercial district of midtown Sacramento. After a short drive northeast from the fort on Interstate 80, the journey resumes at the shady village of Coloma, lying athwart California 49 between the towns of Auburn and Placerville ("Hangtown" of the old days). Here, in the Indians' "beautiful vale," lies the 275-acre Marshall Discovery State Historical Park, covering the original Sutter sawmill site which was destroyed by floodwaters in 1856. The replica mill, shaded by black locust, catalpa, and persimmon trees, was built in 1967, using some of the original timbers excavated from river silt and following the plans of the original down to its smallest wooden peg. Above a shady picnic area stands the James Marshall Monument and gravesite. The bronzed zinc statue of the discoverer, erected in 1889, is forty feet high and has bas reliefs of carpentry tools on one side of the plinth, miner tools on the other. Marshall is depicted pointing to the spot on the south fork of the American River where he found gold on that pleasant Sunday afternoon of January 23, 1848. (Looking up at this heroic representation of the quite ordinary New Jersey handyman, one thinks of John Sutter, buried among strangers in the Moravian Brotherhood Cemetery in Lititz, Pennsylvania, and wonders how many visitors to this resting place, and the handful to Sutter's, appreciate the irony.)

Many of the old gold camps shouldering the Sierra foothills are buried under reservoirs, man-made lakes, and the seas of mud created by the lethal hydraulic monitors of the 1850s. But the surviving settlements—most now pastoral villages, a few thriving towns—have timeless features that argonauts like James Carson and Daniel Woods would recognize. Framing these persistent placers and quartz-gold camps are old stands of ponderosa and digger pines, groves of oaks and shag-barked madrones, broad-leafed maples, and red-stemmed manzanita shrubs abuzz with bees and shimmering with butterflies. In their vicinities are golden meadows cleft by rivers, streams, and arroyos; dizzying mountain trails; and the granite spires of the Sierra Nevada rising in the east.

All of the old gold country is lovely, much of it breathtaking (the drive into the northern outskirts of Sutter Creek, for example, and the change in the alpine landscape to rolling hills south of the town of Plymouth). And every bit of it—every crossroad, rivulet, copse of trees, and wildflowered hillside—seems animated by the ghosts of those dauntless gold hunters who came here from faraway places a century and a half ago.

FEW OF THE far-reaching and enduring consequences of the gold rush are in evidence along Route 49, which is just as well. Seeing the places where gold was found is infinitely more interesting to the modern traveler than learning that California gold production gave the nation a needed economic boost after the long war with Mexico; that the gold trade made the transcontinental railroad inevitable; that the rush propelled California to statehood; that it transformed San Francisco into a United States commercial entrepôt and the strategic base of a formidable Pacific power. Even the sagest of contemporary commentators could not have foreseen such weighty geopolitical aftereffects to the Eldorado frenzy. Indeed, a conspicuous feature of the vast amount of 1849–1850 writing on the subject is that so few of the authors anticipated *anything* good deriving from it.

From the outset, the California migration was viewed, in Ralph

Waldo Emerson's words, as "a rush and scramble of needy adventures . . . a general jail delivery of all the rowdies of the rivers." And Emerson's fellow transcendentalist, Henry David Thoreau, trumped even that denigration with his own: "The recent rush to California . . . appears to me to reflect the greatest disgrace on mankind. That so many are ready to get their living by the lottery of gold-digging without contributing any value to society . . . matches the infatuation of the Hindoos who have cast themselves under the car of Juggernaut." He added as an afterthought, "Going to California. It is only three thousand miles nearer to hell."

Emerson, of course, got no closer to the western slopes of the Sierra Nevada than the comforts of his home and lecture podium in Massachusetts, and Thoreau's experiences roughing it in his cabin in Walden Woods pales in comparison to the trials of the luckiest of the pilgrims on the California trails.

I FOUND A good place to think about those rowdies and needy adventurers who scrambled for California gold when I came south on Route 49 from Downieville, the camp where in the autumn of 1849 a Kanaka miner called Jim Crow boiled a salmon in a pot and found gold dust in the broth. I spent a couple of hours in Grass Valley, among the richest gold towns of them all and the place where Lola Montez "rusticated" in 1853. (Her shake-roofed cottage still stands, now occupied by the local Chamber of Commerce, and there are flower beds, so beloved by Lola, in front of it.) I then drove ten miles west to one of the most vivid and enduring reminders of the Forty-niner's world, Rough and Ready.

This serenely isolated settlement, lying among pines and oaks and blackberry brambles, was marked off in 1849 by Colonel A. A. Townsend, who had served with Zachary Taylor in the war with Mexico. The camp earned a distinction other than its name between April and July of 1850 when the federal government tried to levy a tax on all mining claims in the formerly Mexican, newly conquered, and suddenly rich land of California. In response to this bald case of taxation without representation, the unrulier of its populace of three thousand declared Rough and Ready a republic and elected another colonel, named E. M. Brundage, president. At the time of this back-country uprising a California statehood bill was pending in Washing-

ton, and when the document was signed by President Millard Fillmore on September 9, 1850, the camp dissolved its one-colonel executive branch and republic status and returned to its business of
prospecting.

Today, the Rough and Ready visitor can readily picture the arche-
typal gold community of Bancroft's description—the one with leafy
arbors, brush huts, and peaked tents, "in bold relief upon a naked bar,
dotting the hillside in picturesque confusion, or nestling beneath the
foliage." Here, tapping the imagination, it is possible to see, smell, and
hear the "free and bracing life" of the Forty-niner: miners stirring
from their bedrolls at daybreak, cooking a breakfast of coffee, bacon,
and beans; pick and spade noises mingling with the chatter of men
digging coyote holes, shoveling dirt from stream banks and hill slopes,
hammering together rockers, Long Toms, and flumes; canvas walls
glowing in orange lantern light, among them a tent saloon—"the
valve for the pent-up spirit of the toilers"—and its gambling tables
where is heard the nightly "boisterous mirth of the revellers, noisy,
oath-breathing, and shaggy," as they place their pinches of precious
dust on the table and call for the turn of a card.

Except for such that the inward eye can evoke, there is not much
to look at in Rough and Ready, but there is a place to think about a
half-mile west of the Fippin General Blacksmith shop where a rutty
road called Stagecoach Way leads to the summit of a sun-bleached
hilltop and the town graveyard. The plots here are untended and
largely unvisited, most of the old headstones homemade, odd-shaped,
and hand-chiseled, overgrown with weeds and so eroded by the elements that many of the legends have vanished as utterly as those lying
beneath them, while the words on others can be made legible only by
rubbing them with a damp cloth.

At this place atop the northern mines, not many miles from the
bed-and-breakfasts, boutiques, galleries, wine-tasting shops, and truf-
fle and coffee bars of the state's "restored" gold towns, stands a
marker commemorating one Benoni Thompson, who "Died on
August 15, 1902, age 75 years." The stone says nothing else of Benoni
Thompson but it makes you think about that first name and what
happened to this person who was born who-knows-where in 1827.
Did he (or she) come to these northern mines in a wagon company
from the Missouri settlements? Across Texas and northern Mexico to
follow the Gila River route to California? From a Mormon settle-

ment in Utah? Via the Isthmus of Panama? Or did he come around Cape Horn on a leaky brig and wash ashore at this once-roaring camp with the tide of argonauts in '49? And what did Benoni Thompson *do* in the fifty-three years between the gold rush and his death?

Another stone, while bearing more information about the occupant below, is almost as puzzling: "John A. Smith, born June 24, 1826, in Fairfax County, Va., emigrated to Missouri in 1839, and in 1849 to California, where he died June 5, 1863. Peace be to his ashes."

At least we know John A. Smith was thirteen when his family removed from Virginia to the Missouri frontier, was twenty-two when he came to California, and a mere thirty-seven when he died. He might have still been working the placers at Rough and Ready when beset by whatever killed him—illness, accident, homicide?—or perhaps he commuted on muleback to and from the Empire Mine in Grass Valley which, alone, produced more gold than the entire Klondike rush of 1896–1898.

Was his name truly John A. Smith? Or was he one of the countless John Smiths who came to the gold country in consequence of a failed business or a foreclosed farm or a marriage gone asunder? Was he, as were so many, in flight from a felonious brush with the law as was commemorated by the rhyme of those days:

> *Oh, what was your name in the States?*
> *Was it Thompson or Johnson or Bates?*
> *Did you flee for your life or murder your wife?*
> *Say, what was your name in the States?*

Whatever their station in life before they heard the news, John Smith and Benoni Thompson, and uncounted others, came to California for gold and *stayed*, whether they found it or not.

These isolated stones in this isolated place make the visitor wonder: Were these emigrants to Eldorado as characterized by the venerable Emerson and Thoreau—runaways, fugitives, rascals—caught up in fancies of getting rich quick? Certainly a sizable share of them were just that. But consider: what fault could be found in chasing gold in California when in the thirty states of 1849 a twelve-hour day's wage was rarely better than $1.50? What wonder could there be that the news of gold in the Sacramento Valley galvanized the small farmer, toiling toward ruination in a time when crop and land prices were plummeting? Why *wouldn't* the blacksmith, tradesman, clerk, or teacher, even the young physician or lawyer, struggling to feed a family, head out to Eldorado? What was disgraceful about this immense company of dreamers—not just the Thompsons and Smiths, but all of the Mexicans, the South and Central Americans, the Europeans, the Chinese, the Australians, and the Pacific islanders, dreamers the world wide—leaving their homes to dig for California gold, giving no thought to "contributing any value to society" except, they hoped, by bettering their own lives?

None of the rainbow-enders who followed the argonaut trails, most returning home with nothing but their memories and perhaps a trace of gold dust in a pill bottle to show the children, thought it folly to chase such a dream.

ACKNOWLEDGMENTS

THE CALIFORNIA GOLD rush, H. H. Bancroft wrote forty years after it ended, "cleared a wilderness and transplanted thither the politics and institutions of the most advanced civilizations of the world."

Californians know this and have done heroic work in preserving the traces of that frantic era and celebrating it, particularly in these, its sesquicentennial years. In my travels in the gold country I came to appreciate how much Californians know about their history and how interested they are in helping an outsider answer difficult questions.

I am especially indebted to Alphie Liming of the Sacramento Convention and Visitors Bureau for all manner of assistance in my research trips and during the writing of *Eldorado*, from taking me on a tour of Old Sacramento and Sutter's Fort State Historic Park to searching records on the history of the grave of the son of Alexander Hamilton.

The staffs of the Huntington Library and Bancroft Library were invariably helpful; the Museum of the City of San Francisco's expansive materials on the gold rush, and its Web site, have been invaluable, as has Cornell University's "Making of America" Web site and its reference librarians.

In the research and writing of my "Pacific Trilogy" (*Bear Flag Rising, The Conquest of California, 1846; Pacific Destiny: The Three-Century Journey to the Oregon Country*, and this book), I have developed an ever-mounting appreciation of the work of such publishers as Arthur H. Clarke of Spokane and the university presses of Nebraska and Oklahoma—they are in the forefront of the many splendid academic publishers devoted to preserving the documents and history of America's Westering movement.

I greatly appreciate the assistance of such friends as George Skanse, owner of the Book Gallery of El Paso, Texas, for locating rare books and maps; such eminent historical writers as Leon C. Metz, James Crutchfield, Candy Moulton, Don Hellbusch, and Richard C. House, for valuable information and advice; and to Richard S. Wheeler, Win

Blevins, and James Carlos Blake, who took time from their own books in progress to read the early draft of the manuscript of *Eldorado*.

Special thanks to:

McFarland & Company, Inc., Jefferson, N.C., for permission to quote from *"At the Extremity of Civilization": An Illinois Physician's Journey to California in 1849*, copyright © 1995 by Necia Dixon Liles, and Yale University Press, New Haven, Conn., for permission to quote from *A Frontier Lady* by Sarah Royce, copyright © 1932 by Yale University Press.

Finally, my greatest indebtedness is to that cadre of Forty-niners whose writings I have quoted but whose post–gold rush lives I was unable to trace fully, if at all: Henry Bigler, James S. Brown, Victor Forgeaud, Daniel Knower, Daniel Woods, John M. Letts, E. A. Upton, Rev. William Taylor, and Hugo Reid.

SOURCES

American Guide Series. *California: A Guide to the Golden State.* New York: Hastings House, 1939.

Andrist, Ralph K. *The California Gold Rush.* New York: American Heritage Publishing Co., 1961.

Asbury, Herbert. *The Barbary Coast: An Informal History of the San Francisco Underworld.* New York: Alfred Knopf, 1953.

Audubon, John Woodhouse. *Audubon's Western Journal, 1849–1850.* Glorieta, N.M.: The Rio Grande Press, 1969.

Bagley, Will, ed. *Scoundrel's Tale: The Sam Brannan Papers.* Spokane, Wash.: The Arthur H. Clark Co., 1999.

Bancroft, Hubert H. *California Inter Pocula.* San Francisco: The History Company, 1888.

———. *History of the Pacific States of North America: California.* San Francisco: The History Company, 1883–1888; seven vols.

———. *Literary Industries.* New York: Harper & Brothers, 1891.

Batman, Richard. *The Outer Coast.* New York: Harcourt Brace Jovanovich, 1985.

Bauer, K. Jack. *The Mexican War, 1846–1848.* Lincoln: University of Nebraska Press, 1992. (Originally published in 1974.)

Beach, Rex. *The World in His Arms.* New York: G. P. Putnam's Sons, 1945.

Bean, Walton, and James J. Rawls. *California: An Interpretive History.* New York: McGraw-Hill, 1983.

Beatty, Richmond Croom. *Bayard Taylor: Laureate of the Gilded Age.* Norman: University of Oklahoma Press, 1936.

Beck, Warren A., and Ynez D. Haase. *Historical Atlas of California.* Norman: University of Oklahoma Press, 1974.

Beilharz, Edwin A., and Carlos U. López. *We Were 49ers!: Chilean Accounts of the California Gold Rush.* Pasadena, Calif.: Ward Ritchie Press, 1976.

Benemann, William, ed. *A Year of Mud and Gold: San Francisco in Letters and Diaries, 1849–1850.* Lincoln: University of Nebraska Press, 1999.

Bernstein, Peter L. *The Power of Gold: The History of an Obsession.* New York: John Wiley & Sons, 2000.

Bidwell, Gen. John. *Echoes of the Past.* New York: Citadel Press, 1962. (Originally published in 1900.)

———. "Life in California Before the Gold Discovery." *The Century Magazine,* December, 1890.

Bieber, Ralph P., ed. *Southern Trails to California in 1849.* Glendale, Calif.: The Arthur H. Clark Co., 1937.

Billington, Ray Allen. *Westward Expansion: A History of the American Frontier.* New York: The Macmillan Co., 1967.

Bonner, T. D., ed. *The Life and Adventures of James P. Beckwourth.* New York: Harper & Brothers, 1856.

Borthwick, J. David. *Three Years in California.* Edinburgh: Blackwood & Sons, 1857.

Breault, William J., S.J. *John A. Sutter in Hawaii and California, 1838–1839.* Rancho Cordova, Calif.: Landmark Enterprises, 1998.

Brown, Dee. *The Gentle Tamers: Women of the Old Wild West.* Lincoln: University of Nebraska Press, 1968. (First published in 1958.)

Brown, James S. *California Gold: An Authentic History of the First Find; With the Names of Those Interested in the Discovery.* Oakland, Calif.: Pacific Press Publishing Co., 1894.

Browning, Peter, ed. *To the Golden Shore: America Goes to California—1849.* Lafayette, Calif.: Great West Books, 1995.

Bryant, Arthur. *What I Saw in California.* New York: D. Appleton & Sons, 1848.

Buck, Franklin A. *A Yankee Trader in the Gold Rush.* Boston: Houghton Mifflin Co., 1930.

Butruille, Susan G. *Women's Voices from the Mother Lode.* Boise, Idaho: Tamarack Books, 1998.

Carson, James H. *Early Recollections of the California Mines.* Stockton, Calif.: San Joaquin Republican, 1852.

Castro, Doris Shaw, ed. *James H. Carson's California, 1847–1853.* New York: Vantage Press, 1997.

Caughey, John Walton. *California: A Remarkable State's Life History.* Englewood Cliffs, N.J.: Prentice-Hall, 1970.

———. *Hubert Howe Bancroft.* Berkley: University of California Press, 1946.

Cendrars, Blaise. *Sutter's Gold.* New York: Harper & Brothers, 1926.

Chidsey, Donald Barr. *The California Gold Rush.* New York: Crown, 1968.

Clappe, Louise Amelia Knapp Smith. *The Shirley Letters: Being Letters Written in 1851–1852 from the California Mines.* Santa Barbara, Calif.: Peregrine Smith, 1970.

Clark, Arthur H. *The Clipper Ship Era.* New York: Putnam's, 1910.

Clark, William B. *Gold Districts of California.* Sacramento: Division of Mines and Geology (Bulletin 193), 1992.

Cleland, Robert G. *California Pageant: The Story of Four Centuries.* New York: Alfred A. Knopf, 1946.

———. *From Wilderness to Empire: A History of California, 1524–1900.* New York: Alfred A. Knopf, 1944.

Coleman, William T. "San Francisco Vigilance Committees," *The Century Monthly Illustrated Magazine,* November, 1891.

Collins, Carvel, ed. *Sam Ward in the Gold Rush.* Stanford: Stanford University Press, 1949.

Colton, Rev. Walter. *Three Years in California.* New York: A. S. Barnes & Co., 1850.

Dana, Julian. *Sutter of California.* New York: The Press of the Pioneers, Inc., 1934.

DeArment, Robert K. *Knights of the Green Cloth: The Saga of Frontier Gamblers.* Norman: University of Oklahoma Press, 1982.

Delano, Alonzo. *Life on the Plains and Among the Diggings.* Auburn and Buffalo: Miller, Orton & Mulligan, 1854.

Dempsey, David and Raymond P. Baldwin. *The Triumphs and Trials of Lotta Crabtree.* New York: William Morrow, 1968.

Devens, R. M. *American Progress, or The Greatest Events of the Greatest Century.* Springfield, Mass.: C. A. Nichols & Co., 1892.

Dickson, Samuel. *Tales of San Francisco.* Stanford, Calif.: Stanford University Press, 1957.

Dillon, Richard. *Captain John Sutter: Sacramento Valley's Sainted Sinner.* Santa Cruz, Calif.: Western Tanager Press, 1981. (Reprint of 1967 edition.)

———. *Humbugs and Heroes: A Gallery of California Pioneers.* Garden City, N.Y.: Doubleday, 1970.

Driesbach, Janice T., Harvey L. Jones, and Katherine Church Holland. *Art of the Gold Rush.* Oakland, Calif.: Oakland Museum of California, 1998.

Egan, Ferrol. *The El Dorado Trail.* New York: McGraw-Hill, 1970.

———. *Frémont: Explorer for a Restless Nation.* New York: Doubleday, 1977.

Evans, George W. B. *Mexican Gold Trail: The Journal of a Forty-Niner.* San Marino, Calif.: The Huntington Library, 1945.

Fagan, Brian M. *Quest for the Past.* Reading, Mass.: Addison-Wesley Publishing Co., 1978.

Farnham, Eliza. *California In-Doors and Out; or, How We Farm, Mine, and Live.* New York: Dix, Edwards Co., 1856.

Farragher, John Mack. *Women and Men on the Overland Trail.* New Haven: Yale University Press, 1979.

Fehrenbach, T. R. *Fire and Blood: A History of Mexico.* New York: Macmillan Co., 1973.

Ferlinghetti, Lawrence, and Nancy J. Peters. *Literary San Francisco.* San Francisco: City Lights Books and Harper & Row, 1980.

Ferris, A. C. "Hardships of the Isthmus in '49." *The Century Monthly Illustrated Magazine,* April, 1891.

————. "Arrival of Overland Trains in California in '49." *The Century Monthy Illustrated Magazine,* July, 1891.

————. "To California in 1849 Through Mexico." *The Century Monthly Illustrated Magazine,* September, 1891.

Fisher, Vardis, and Opal L. Holmes. *Gold Rushes and Mining Camps of the Early American West.* Caldwell, Idaho: The Caxton Printers, 1968.

Foreman, Grant. *Marcy & the Gold-Seekers: The Journal of Capt. R. B. Marcy with an Account of the Gold Rush Over the Southern Route.* Norman: University of Oklahoma Press, 1939.

Franzwa, Gregory. *Maps of the California Trail.* Tucson: Patrice Press, 2000.

Gardiner, Howard C. *In Pursuit of the Golden Dream: Reminiscences of San Francisco and the Northern and Southern Mines, 1849–1857.* (Edited by Dale L. Morgan). Stoughton, Mass.: Western Hemisphere, Inc., 1970.

Glasscock, C. B. *The Golden Highway.* New York: A. L. Burt Co., 1934.

Gudde, Erwin G. *California Place Names.* Berkley: University of California Press, 1962.

————. *Sutter's Own Story.* New York: G. P. Putnam's Sons, 1936.

Hafen, LeRoy R. *The Mountain Men and the Fur Trade of the Far West,* Volume I. Spokane, Washington: The Arthur H. Clarke Co., 2000. (Originally published in 1965.)

Hafen, LeRoy R., and Ann W. Hafen, eds. *Journals of Forty-Niners: Salt Lake to Los Angeles.* Lincoln: University of Nebraska Press, 1998.

Hafen, LeRoy R., and Carl Coke Rister. *Western America.* Englewood Cliffs, N.J.: Prentice-Hall, 1950.

Hammond, George P., ed. *The Larkin Papers: Personal, Business, and Official Correspondence of Thomas Oliver Larkin, Merchant and United States Consul in California.* Berkeley: University of California Press, 1962; vols. 7–8.

Harris, Benjamin B. *The Gila Trail: The Texas Argonauts and the California Gold Rush.* (Edited by Richard H. Dillon.) Norman: University of Oklahoma Press, 1960.

Harte, Bret. *Tales of the Gold Rush*. Norwalk, Conn.: The Heritage Press, 1972.

Hastings, Lansford W. *Emigrant's Guide to Oregon and California*. Cincinnati: George Conklin, 1845.

Holliday, J. S. *The World Rushed In: The California Gold Rush Experience*. New York: Simon & Schuster, 1981.

Holmes, Kenneth L. *Covered Wagon Women: Diaries & Letters from the Western Trails, 1840–1890*. Glendale, Calif.: The Arthur H. Clarke Co., 1983–1993; 11 volumes.

Howard, Thomas Frederick. *Sierra Crossing: First Roads to California*. Berkeley: University of California Press, 1998.

Howe, Octavius T. *Argonauts of '49*. Cambridge: Harvard University Press, 1923.

Jackson, Donald Dale. *Gold Dust*. New York: Alfred Knopf, 1980.

Jackson, Joseph Henry. *Anybody's Gold: The Story of California's Mining Towns*. New York: D. Appleton-Century Co., 1941.

———. "The Creation of Joaquin Murieta," *Pacific Spectator*, Spring, 1948.

———, ed. *Gold Rush Album*. New York: Bonanza Books, 1949.

Johnson, Susan Lee. *Roaring Camp: The Social World of the California Gold Rush*. New York: W. W. Norton, 1999.

Johnson, William Weber. *The Forty-Niners*. New York: Time-Life Books, 1974.

Kelly, Leslie A. *California's Gold Rush Country*. Huntington Beach, Calif.: Les Kelly Publications, 1887.

Kemble, Edward C. *A History of California Newspapers, 1846–1858*. Los Gatos, Calif.: The Talisman Press, 1962.

King, Clarence. *Mountaineering in the Sierra*. Boston: Osgood & Co., 1872.

Knower, Daniel. *The Adventures of a Forty-Niner*. Albany, N.Y.: Weed-Parsons Printing Co., 1894.

Koenig, George. *Beyond This Place There Be Dragons: The Routes of the Tragic Trek of the Death Valley 1849ers*. Glendale, Calif.: Arthur H. Clark, 1984.

Kowalewski, Michael, ed. *Gold Rush: A Literary Exploration*. Berkeley, Calif.: Heyday Books, 1997.

Lapp, Rudolph M. *Blacks in Gold Rush California*. New Haven: Yale University Press, 1977.

Levy, JoAnn. *They Saw the Elephant: Women in the California Gold Rush*. Hamden, Conn.: Shoe String Press, 1990.

Lewis, Marvin, ed. *The Mining Frontier: Contemporary Accounts From the Amer-*

ican West in the Nineteenth Century. Norman: University of Oklahoma Press, 1967.

Lewis, Oscar. *The Big Four.* New York: Alfred Knopf, 1938.

———. *Lola Montez: The Mid-Victorian Bad Girl.* San Francisco: Colt Press, 1938.

———. *Sea Routes to the Gold Fields.* New York: Alfred Knopf, 1949.

———. *Sutter's Fort.* New York: Prentice-Hall, 1966.

Lord, Israel Shipman Pelton. *"At the Extremity of Civilization": A Meticulously Descriptive Diary of an Illinois Physician's Journey in 1849 Along the Oregon Trail to the Goldmines and Cholera of California, Thence in Two Years to Return by Boat Via Panama.* (Edited by Necia Dixon Liles.) Jefferson, N.C.: McFarland and Co, 1995.

McKittrick, Myrtle M. *Vallejo, Son of California.* Portland: Binfords & Mort, 1944.

Mace, O. Henry. *Between the Rivers: A History of Early Calaveras County, California.* Jackson, Calif.: Cenotto Publications, 1993.

Marks, Paula M. *Precious Dust: The American Gold Rush Era, 1848–1900.* New York: William Morrow, 1994.

Marryat, Frank. *Mountains and Molehills.* Stanford University Press, 1952, Reprint edition.

Marshall, James W. "Marshall's Own Account of the Gold Discovery," *Century Magazine,* February, 1891.

Martin, Don and Betty. *The Best of the Gold Country.* Columbia, Calif.: Pine Cone Press, 1987.

Mather, R. E., and F. E. Boswell. *John David Borthwick, Artist of the Gold Rush.* Salt Lake City: University of Utah Press, 1989.

Miller, Joaquin. *'49: The Gold-Seeker of the Sierras.* New York: Funk & Wagnalls Co., 1884.

Morrison, Lorrin L. *Warner: The Man and the Ranch.* Los Angeles: Privately published, 1962.

Moulton, Candy. *The Writer's Guide to Everyday Life in the Wild West, From 1840–1900.* Cincinnati, Ohio: Writer's Digest Books, 1999.

Muir, John. *The Mountains of California.* New York: The Century Co., 1894.

Muldoon, Sylvan J. *Alexander Hamilton's Pioneer Son: The Life and Times of Col. William S. Hamilton.* Harrisburg, Pa.: The Aurand Press, 1930.

Myres, Sandra. *Westering Women and the Frontier Experience, 1800–1915.* Albuquerque: University of New Mexico Press, 1982.

Navarro, Ramón Gil. *The Gold Rush Diary of Ramón Gil Navarro.* Lincoln: University of Nebraska Press, 2000.

Nevins, David. *Frémont: Pathmarker of the West*. New York: Longmans, Green, 1939.

Norton, Henry K. *The Story of California from the Earliest Days to the Present*. Chicago: A. C. McClurg & Co., 1924.

O'Connor, Richard. *Bret Harte: A Biography*. Boston: Little, Brown, 1966.

Owens, Kenneth N., ed. *John Sutter and a Wider West*. Lincoln: University of Nebraska Press, 1994.

Paul, Rodman W. *California Gold*. Lincoln: University of Nebraska Press, 1969.

———. "In Search of Dame Shirley," *Pacific Historical Review*, May 1964.

Pittman, Ruth. *A Roadside History of California*. Missoula, Mont.: Mountain Press, 1995.

Pratt, Julius H. *Reminiscences, Personal and Otherwise*. N.p.: Privately printed, 1910.

———. "To California by Panama in '49." *The Century Monthly Illustrated Magazine*, April 1891.

Read, Georgia W. "Women and Children on the California-Oregon Trail in the Gold-Rush Years," *Missouri Historical Review*, October, 1944.

Revere, Joseph W. *A Tour of Duty in California*. New York: C. S. Francis, 1849.

Ridge, John Rollin. *The Life and Adventures of Joaquín Murieta*. San Francisco: W. B. Cooke, 1854.

Rohrbough, Malcolm J. *Days of Gold: The California Gold Rush and the American Nation*. Berkeley: University of California Press, 1997.

Rourke, Constance. *Troupers of the Gold Coast*. New York: Harcourt, Brace, 1928.

Royce, Josiah. *California: From the Conquest in 1846 to the Second Vigilance Committee in San Francisco: A Study of American Character*. Santa Barbara: Peregrine Publishers, 1970. (Reprint of original 1886 edition.)

Royce, Sarah. *A Frontier Lady: Recollections of the Gold Rush and Early California*. (Ralph Henry Gabriel, ed.) Lincoln: University of Nebraska Press, 1997. (Originally published 1932.)

Russell, Amy Requa, Marcia Russell Good, and Mary Good Lindgren, eds. *Voyage to California Written at Sea, 1852: The Journal of Lucy Kendall Herrick*. San Marino, Calif.: Huntington Library, 1998.

Scharnhorst, Gary. *Bret Harte: Opening the American Literary West*. Norman: University of Oklahoma Press, 2000.

Seidman, Lawrence I. *The Fools of '49: The California Gold Rush, 1848–1856*. New York: Alfred A. Knopf, 1976.

Sherman, Gen. William T. *Memoirs of My Life*. New York: D. Appleton & Co., 1875.

Shinn, Charles Howard. *Mining Camps: A Study in American Frontier Government*. (Rodman W. Paul, ed.) New York: Harper & Row, 1965. (Originally published in 1884.)

Schlissel, Lillian. *Women's Diaries of the Westward Journey*. New York: Schocken Books, 1982.

Smith, Duane A., and Ronald C. Brown. *No One Ailing Except a Physician: Medicine in the Mining West, 1848–1919*. Boulder: University Press of Colorado, 2001.

Smith, Gene A. *Thomas ap Catesby Jones: Commodore of Manifest Destiny*. Annapolis, Md.: Naval Institute Press, 2000.

Sonnichsen, C. L. *Pass of the North*. El Paso: Texas Western Press, 1968.

Soulé, Frank, John H. Gihon, and James Nesbet. *The Annals of San Francisco; Containing a Summary of the History of the First Discovery, Settlement, Progress, and Present Condition of California*. New York: D. Appleton & Co., 1854.

Starr, Kevin, and Richard J. Orsi. *Rooted in Barbarous Soil: People, Culture and Community in Gold Rush California*. Berkeley, Calif.: University of California Press, 2000.

Steele, Rev. John. *Camp and Cabin: Mining Life and Adventures in California During 1850 and Later*. New York: The Citadel Press, 1962. (Originally published in 1901.)

Stellman, Louis J. *Mother Lode: The Story of Gold Rush Days*. San Francisco: Harr Wagner Publishing Co., 1934.

Stewart, George. *The California Trail*. New York: McGraw-Hill, 1962.

———. *Committee of Vigilance: Revolution in San Francisco, 1851*. Boston: Houghton Mifflin, 1964.

Stone, Irving. *Men to Match My Mountains*. New York: Doubleday, 1956.

Stuart, Granville. *Prospecting for Gold From Dogtown to Virginia City, 1852–1864*. (Paul C. Phillips, ed.) Lincoln: University of Nebraska Press, 1977. (Originally published in 1925.)

Taylor, Bayard. *Eldorado, or, Adventures in the Path of Empire*. Lincoln: University of Nebraska Press, 1988. (Originally published 1850.)

———. *The Poetical Works of Bayard Taylor*. Boston: Houghton Mifflin & Co., 1883.

Thompson, Gerald. *Edward F. Beale and the American West*. Albuquerque: University of New Mexico Press, 1983.

Thompson, Tommy. *America's Lost Treasure*. New York: Atlantic Monthly Press, 1998.

Thrapp, Dan L. *Encyclopedia of Frontier Biography*. Glendale, California: Arthur H. Clark Co., 1988. Three volumes.

———. *Encyclopedia of Frontier Biography: Supplemental Volume*. Spokane, Washington: Arthur H. Clark Co., 1994.

Twain, Mark. *Roughing It*. Hartford, Conn.: American Publishing Co., 1872.

Underhill, Reuben L. *From Cowhides to Golden Fleece: A Narrative of California, 1832–1858, Based Upon Unpublished Correspondence of Thomas Oliver Larkin of Monterey*. Stanford, Calif.: Stanford University Press, 1939.

Unruh, John D., Jr. *The Plains Across: The Overland Emigrants and the Trans-Mississippi West, 1840–1860*. Urbana: University of Illinois Press, 1979.

Varley, James F. *Lola Montez: The California Adventures of Europe's Notorious Courtesan*. Spokane, Wash.: The Arthur H. Clark Co., 1996.

Waite, E. G. "Pioneer Mining in California," *The Century Illustrated Monthly Magazine*, May 1891.

Walker, Franklin. *San Francisco's Literary Frontier*. New York: Alfred A. Knopf, 1939.

Ware, Joseph E. *The Emigrant's Guide to California*. Princeton: Princeton University Press, 1932. (Originally published in 1849.)

Weber, Shirley H., ed. *Schliemann's First Visit to America, 1850–1851*. Cambridge: Harvard University Press, 1942.

Wellman, Paul. *Gold in California*. New York: Houghton Mifflin, 1958.

Wienpahl, Robert W. *A Gold Rush Voyage on the Bark* Orion *from Boston Around Cape Horn to San Francisco, 1849–50*. Glendale, Calif.: The Arthur H. Clark Co., 1978.

Wilbur, Marguerite E. *John Sutter: Rascal and Adventurer*. New York: Liveright Co., 1949.

Benjamin Davis Wilson (1811–1878). Pasadena, Calif.: Privately published, A. C. Vroman, Inc., n.d.

Wood, Raymond F. "New Light on Joaquin Murrieta," *Pacific Historian*, Winter 1970.

Woods, Daniel. *Sixteen Months at the Gold Diggings*. New York: Harper & Brothers, 1851.

Young, Otis E., Jr. *Black Powder and Hand Steel: Miners and Machines on the Old Western Frontier*. Norman: University of Oklahoma Press, 1976.

———. *Western Mining*. Norman: University of Oklahoma Press, 1970.

Zollinger, James Peter. *Sutter: The Man and His Empire*. New York: Oxford University Press, 1939.

INDEX

ABOUT THE AUTHOR

Dale L. Walker is the author of such Forge histories as *Legends and Lies: Great Mysteries of the American West; The Boys of '98: Theodore Roosevelt and the Rough Riders; Bear Flag Rising: The Conquest of California, 1846;* and *Pacific Destiny: The Three-Century Journey to the Oregon Country.* The latter book earned the Spur Award from Western Writers of America as the Best Historical Nonfiction Book of 2000. He lives in El Paso, Texas.